I0085862

Years of Conflict

STUDIES IN FORCED MIGRATION
General Editors: Roger Zetter and Eva Lotta Hedman

Years of Conflict

ADOLESCENCE, POLITICAL VIOLENCE
AND DISPLACEMENT

Edited by
Jason Hart

Berghahn Books
NEW YORK • OXFORD

First published in 2008 by

Berghahn Books
www.BerghahnBooks.com

© 2008, 2010 Jason Hart
First paperback edition published in 2010.

All rights reserved. Except for the quotation of short passages
for the purposes of criticism and review, no part of this book
may be reproduced in any form or by any means, electronic or
mechanical, including photocopying, recording, or any information
storage and retrieval system now known or to be invented,
without written permission of the publisher.

Library of Congress Cataloging-in-Publication Data

Years of conflict : adolescence, political violence and displacement / edited by
Jason Hart.
    p. cm. -- (Forced migration ; v. 25)
Includes bibliographical references and index.
ISBN 978-1-84545-528-6
1. Youth and violence--Psychological aspects. 2. Political violence--
    Psychological aspects. 3. Teenage immigrants--Social conditions. 4.
    Emigration and immigration--Social aspects. I. Hart, Jason, 1963-

HQ799.2.V56Y43 2008
303.60835--dc22
                            2008026630

British Library Cataloguing in Publication Data

A catalogue record for this book is available from the British Library

Printed in the United States on acid-free paper

ISBN 978-1-84545-528-6 (hardback)
ISBN 978-1-84545-529-3 (paperback)

Contents

Acknowledgements

This book is the product of a process that began in 2003. With generous support from the Andrew W. Mellon Foundation I was able to organise a two-term series of weekly seminars at the University of Oxford in the Trinity (summer) and Michaelmas (autumn) terms. My thanks go to the thirteen speakers who kindly took time out of their schedule and travelled to Oxford in order to deliver papers in this series. The work of twelve of these (plus myself) is contained in this volume, joined by contributions from three further scholars. I am indebted to all of these authors for their diligence and patience.

In setting up the seminar series and identifying additional authors I was fortunate to benefit from the advice of my colleagues Dawn Chatty, Jo Boyden and Maryanne Loughry. Various other people at the Refugee Studies Centre have assisted with the production of this book. I am especially grateful to Jesse Newman, Joy Johnston, Bex Tyrer, Ah-Jung Lee, Jamie Chosak, Paul Ryder, Musab Hayatli, and Laurence Medley.

That this volume has reached the light of day is due in no small part to the support and encouragement of three people: my great friend and guide Jo Boyden, my partner Brendan Lynch and my mentor Daisaku Ikeda. I am deeply indebted to all three of them.

I should like to dedicate this book to my mother, Antoinette Hart.

Preface

Jo Boyden

With the emergence of a sociology of childhood in the 1980s and the widespread ratification of the United Nations Convention on the Rights of the Child at the end of that decade, enquiry into the lives and social conditions of children around the world grew immeasurably. While a tradition of research on adolescence and youth has also evolved it has been largely confined to the Global North. Moreover, such work has been sporadic at best and has failed to generate a significant body of theory or data. In the absence of credible evidence and theoretical elaboration, normative assumptions about adolescents have become common currency. Critics of this trend have noted the tendency to frame young people in pejorative terms, as deficient, (and hence in need of education), delinquent (and thus requiring control), or dysfunctional (so necessitating therapy) (Griffin, 1993). Some disparage the common practice of gender stereotyping that identifies female adolescents as 'troubled' and males as 'troublesome' (Stainton-Rogers & Stainton-Rogers, 1992). Others still highlight problems with the frequent practice of exporting conceptualisations of youth generated within Euro-American academe and life-worlds to regions where very different political, social and cultural conditions apply (Bradford Brown and Larson, 2002).

The lack of a significant corpus of reliable research on adolescents and youth is both surprising and disturbing when you consider current world demographics. The World Bank's *2007 World Development Report* (2006) draws attention to the fact that, at 1.5 billion people aged 12 to 24, the current youth cohort is the largest the world will ever see. With the decline in fertility in all regions except sub-Saharan Africa, future cohorts of youth will undoubtedly be smaller; even so, the power of present demographics and their potential to impact dramatically on societies in years to come is evident.

The shortage of detailed research does not deter major global institutions like the Bank from using these demographic data to model potential economic and societal outcomes. The *World Development Report* takes a particular view on adolescence and youth, making much of the demographic dividend that such a large cohort of young people might entail. In emphasising their economic promise, the report highlights the human capital implications of choices made by the young in relation to five key life transitions: continuing to learn; starting to work; developing a healthful lifestyle; beginning a family; and exercising citizenship. In the Bank's view, getting such decisions right will make a major difference to the kind of adults these young people will become, as well as bringing significant societal dividends through their contributions as citizens, household heads, workers, entrepreneurs and leaders. Investment is called for to develop the human capital by expanding opportunity and choice, enhancing capability to make appropriate life decisions and giving young people a second chance when they make 'wrong' choices. This vision seems to be predicated on the idea that the current youth cohort is growing up in conditions of stability and continuity in which society is able to offer active citizenship and meaningful opportunities for work; indeed, in this model stability and continuity would seem to be an essential prerequisite for healthy development in the young.

A far more pessimistic outlook on global demographics and governance is provided by several security analysts and scholars in the United States and Europe who have made a connection between youth and civil conflict. They have come to perceive large youth bulges as dramatically increasing the risk of armed conflict. This apprehension focuses on the fact that an astonishing 80 per cent or so of today's youth is concentrated in developing countries, with significant numbers living in weak or failing states. The contention is that a demographic surge on this scale will inevitably outpace employment, school access and parental authority in the home, this in turn fuelling frustration and resentment among male youth, leading them to delinquency, street crime and military recruitment. The line of reasoning is something like this: 'While not the overt cause of armed conflict, these demographic factors can facilitate recruitment into insurgent organizations and extremist networks or into militias and political gangs– now among the major employers of young men and the main avenues of political mobility in weaker countries' (Cincotta, 2005: 1). According to this view, the prognosis for sub-Saharan Africa is particularly bleak.

Although the demographic dividend and youth bulge arguments convey divergent images of the young, they clearly share an assumption that the fate of whole nations is vested in this cohort – with a particular burden of responsibility on males. Traces of earlier ideas about 'troublesome' young men with little or no sense of moral and social responsibility making the wrong life choices are also very evident. These dominant discursive representations are extremely compelling and so it is hardly surprising to find that they have become increasingly influential globally in policy and research circles. Yet the projections based on macro-level statistics do little to capture the lived reality as experienced by many of the young people who are growing up today in conditions of political violence and displacement. At the same time, in representing the young as inherently 'troublesome' and conjuring up alarm about their apparent penchant for violence it becomes all too easy to overlook the true generative processes in armed conflict as they apply in specific contexts.

Years of Conflict responds to a pressing need for empirical evidence and theory in relation to adolescents and youth living in societies at war. In keeping with the World Bank conceptualisation it makes the case for understanding these phases in terms of life-course transitions and social and institutional transformation from childhood to adulthood. But in highlighting the striking variations in how adolescence and youth are understood and experienced in different settings, it departs radically from the World Bank view. In so doing, it eschews the notion of human development and transition as a linear path in which there are 'right' and 'wrong' options and choices. Furthermore, it shows that young people can embrace discontinuity and instability.

In reflecting directly on young people's experiences and perspectives of political violence and displacement the volume also brings into question many of the assumptions underlying the youth bulge hypothesis. Whilst acknowledging the profound challenges associated with growing up in an environment of violence and uncertainty, it sheds light on young people's often constructive engagement with adverse societal conditions, the responsibilities they commonly assume, the complex dilemmas they confront and frequently overcome. In doing this, the analysis raises fundamental questions about the nature and outcomes of transitional processes during adolescence and youth, suggesting that risk and uncertainty do not necessarily cause the young to become damaged or a threat to wider society.

This volume thus offers an important counter to the calamitous projections of youth bulge theorists. Indeed, discussions about troublesome youth and dangerous demographics detract from far more important considerations regarding the precise social, economic and political conditions under which young people experience frustration and may turn to violence in specific contexts and historical periods. This kind of analysis requires due regard to the political economy of conflict and displacement and to the conditions under which actual cohorts of young people and the generational category of youth are incorporated into society.

Years of Conflict should also encourage reflection amongst policy-makers and those responsible for the design and delivery of services and assistance to young people in conflict and post-conflict settings. Humanitarian policy and practice draw heavily upon the ideas of mental health professionals and human rights advocates whose work is generally based upon an individualistic perspective. Consequently, responses to youth are often couched in terms of repairing emotional and psychological damage caused to specific persons by exposure to violence and displacement, or preventing and mitigating the violations encountered either by individuals or categories of agglomerated individuals ('women', 'children', 'the disabled', etc.). Obscured by this approach are the collective dimensions of young people's experience, motivations and aspirations. This volume offers a timely corrective to this individualistic focus. Authors of the twelve chapters contained herein reveal the diverse ways in which the response of adolescents to political violence and displacement is mediated by social relations within the family or more broadly. Thus, for example, we are encouraged to consider the involvement of adolescents in armed conflict as motivated by factors such as a strong sense of social responsibility or, conversely, alienation from the wider society or polity.

At a time when debates around issues such as child recruitment, post-conflict reintegration or peacebuilding risk becoming bogged down in normative assumptions and rhetoric *Years of Conflict* offers fresh stimulation to researchers and practitioners alike. It is an essential read for anyone interested in hard evidence and grounded theory, whether in the name of sound scholarship or effective policy and practice, and anyone who is prepared to question received wisdom.

References

Bradford Brown, B. and Larson, R.W. 2002 'The Kaleidoscope of Adolescence: Experiences of the World's Youth at the Beginning of the 21st Century', in B. Bradford Brown, R.W. Larson and T.S. Saraswathi (eds) *The World's Youth: Adolescence in Eight Regions of the World*. Cambridge: Cambridge University Press, pp. 1–20.

Cincotta, R. 2005 *State of the World 2005 Global Security Brief #2: Youth Bulge, Underemployment Raise Risks of Civil Conflict Worldwatch Institute*, http://www.worldwatch.org/node/76

Griffin, C. 1993 *Representations of Youth: the Study of Youth and Adolescence in Britain and America*. Cambridge: Polity Press.

Stainton-Rogers, R. and Stainton-Rogers, W. 1992 *Stories of Childhood: Shifting Agendas of Child Concern*. Hemel Hempstead: Harvester Wheatsheaf.

World Bank 2006 *World Development Report: Development and the Next Generation*. Washington, DC: The World Bank.

Introduction

Jason Hart

Over the past decade and a half increasing attention has been paid to the consequences of armed conflict for the young. Even prior to the publication of Graca Machel's landmark report to the United Nations in 1996, scholars were seeking to understand the impact of conflict, particularly upon the psychological well-being of children (Machel, 1996). Much of this work was informed by the emerging discourse of trauma and tended to focus on the damage done to the young by exposure to violence and displacement (e.g. Garbarino et al., 1991; Quota et al., 1995; Macksoud and Aber, 1996).

The post-Machel literature may be distinguished from this earlier body of writing in three main ways. First, there has been an increasing insistence on children's agency. The belief that the young are capable of acting upon their circumstances and influencing the direction of their own lives and those of others has led to critique of assumptions about victimhood that had previously underwritten many studies and the majority of organisational interventions. Researchers and practitioners increasingly insist on approaching the young as potentially resourceful and capable, even amidst the most adverse of circumstances. 'Resilience' is steadily replacing 'trauma' as the focus of psychologically oriented enquiry (Ungar, 2005), while for practitioners the young are to be 'enabled' and 'empowered' rather than simply 'assisted' (Ackermann et al., 2003). In terms of the modalities of research and practice there seems a greater willingness to engage with the young as subjects of knowledge rather than simply as the objects of adult expertise.

Secondly, the most recent writing pays greater attention to the contexts of children's lives. Established traditions of enquiry have been shaped primarily by mental health practitioners and rights activists. Both have relied heavily on instruments and measures that are highly normative and context-blind. Thus, for example, diagnostic tools have been used to identity post-traumatic stress disorder (PTSD) across diverse settings. Similarly, the text of the 1989 United Nations Convention on the Rights of the Child (UNCRC) has been employed as a universal checklist for incidences of rights abuse. As a result a plethora of data on levels of PTSD and on child rights violations in different war zones has been gathered. This is gradually being supplemented by studies of the ways that suffering, survival and well-being are understood and experienced within everyday life in actual settings of political violence and displacement (Das and Reynolds, 2003).

Thirdly, expanding beyond a focus on psychological state alone, studies now embrace a range of conflict-related phenomena employing the perspectives and methods of a range of disciplines. Such phenomena include the particular challenges faced by children separated from primary caregivers (Ressler et al., 1988; Tolfree, 2004), the specific experiences of girls (Mackay and Mazurana, 2004) and, most especially, the causes and consequences of military recruitment (Brett and McCallin, 1998; Brett and Specht, 2004; Rosen, 2005; Wessells, 2006).

The emerging research has the potential to furnish us with a more holistic and contextualised understanding of conflict and its consequences for the young. However, in certain key respects our view lacks important specificity. This is particularly noticeable with respect to age and maturity. Through the almost universal acceptance of the UNCRC by the world's nation states, a dividing line between 'adulthood' and 'childhood' at age eighteen has been resolutely asserted. One consequence of this is the construction of a rigid category of the population – 'children' – amongst whom commonality is assumed and important differences are often ignored or downplayed. Thus, issues that are liable to have particular relevance for specific age groups are often generalised to all under-eighteen-year-olds. Furthermore, these issues are not considered in their relationship to the life stage of those specifically affected. There are important differences between, for example, those in early childhood and others – still within the general category of 'childhood' – who are liable to be engaged in explicit processes of transition towards the role, responsibilities and status associated with adulthood. As will be explained, these processes are considered in this book as definitional of 'adolescence' as a socially constructed phase in the life cycle which occurs, more or less, in the second decade of life.

Many of the phenomena associated with 'children' living in situations of armed conflict and displacement are either specific to or have particular resonance for young people at different stages from early childhood to adolescence. For example, recruitment to military groups, although commonly conveyed as a generic children's issue, principally involves adolescents. However, the authors who have considered this phenomenon in terms of the social and physiological processes commonly experienced in the teenage years are still vastly outnumbered by authors who treat all under-eighteen-year-olds as essentially the same, often infantilising adolescents (Read, 2002; Beirens, this volume: 139–62; Tefferi, this volume: 23–37).

With one exception, all the authors in this volume write about specific locations – East Africa, the U.S.A., Tanzania, Liberia, South Africa, Jordan, Iran, Peru, Western Europe, Afghanistan and Colombia. None suggest global applicability for their observations and yet, read together, they point to important commonalities of experience amongst young people in the second decade of life. These commonalities may be understood as indicative of a general difference between this age group and younger children. An underlying aim of *Years of Conflict* is, therefore, to call attention to such difference and prompt further reflection about its implications for research and practice.

Overview of Approaches

The origins of this book lie in a seminar series held at the Refugee Studies Centre, University of Oxford in 2003. My colleagues and I were keen to invite speakers from a variety of disciplines and locations. A core of anthropologists and psychologists were joined by speakers from other backgrounds both within and outside academia. Bringing insights from such diverse sources together is something of a departure in a field of enquiry that has tended to maintain clear distinctions both between disciplines and between scholars and practitioners. This book benefits from the combination of chapters that convey rich ethnographic detail and those that offer the insight of professionals who have worked extensively – as psychologists and agency personnel – with a wide variety of conflict-affected and displaced populations.

The combining of disciplines and of practice and academic research demonstrated in the book as a whole is also evident in many of the individual chapters. Joanna de Berry, for example, brings to bear both her training as an anthropologist and her experience as a staff member of a large NGO in a discussion of youth programming in post-Taliban Afghanistan. Nearly twenty years of field experience in East Africa provide the material for psychologist Hirut Tefferi's consideration of the ways that conflict interacts with the institutions of adolescence. Cordula Strocka, in a chapter that reflects on the processes of conducting research with youth gangs in Ayacucho, Peru, describes why and how she moved from a research methodology learned during her training in psychology, to a participatory approach more familiar to anthropologists and development practitioners. Kenneth Miller and colleagues writing about refugees in the Bay Area in the U.S.A., Andrew Dawes discussing young people in 'post-conflict' South Africa and Diana Alvis Palma reflecting on her work with adolescents affected by multiple forms of violence in Colombia combine insight derived from extensive experience as mental health workers with a deep commitment to locating individual suffering within socio-political context. The chapter of Hanne Beirens differs from all others in the book in that the location of her enquiry is not geographical but organisational. Here the author utilises her training in sociology to interrogate the ways that the United Nations High Commissioner for Refugees (UNHCR) thinks about and seeks to protect adolescent child soldiers. The chapter by Liesbeth de Block is especially innovative. Here the author – drawing on her background in education and media – shares understanding about the lives of adolescent refugees in various European countries acquired through engagement with young people as consumers and producers of media.

The remaining four chapters are all rooted in the tradition of anthropological fieldwork. Each in its own way uses ethnographic practice to explore issues and groups that have been largely overlooked by scholars and portrayed in simplistic terms by humanitarians. The chapter by Gillian Mann illustrates the value of investing in slow, painstaking research in order to gain insight into the lives of undocumented adolescent refugees whose lives are, of necessity, largely invisible from public view. Similarly Mats Utas demonstrates the centrality of trust to ethnography in a chapter about the involvement of young men in Liberia's civil war, young men whose engagement in brutal violence few have sought to understand in such depth. Finally, the chapters by Homa Hoodfar and Jason Hart hint at the ways that the researcher's own gendered identity may be germane to exploration of the complex relationship of adolescent refugees to the conditions of exile and the project of return.

Adolescence

It may seem curious that a book which endeavours to move beyond normative assumptions should take 'adolescence' as its focus. While 'childhood' has come to be seen as a universally valid notion that is given substance in culturally specific ways, 'adolescence' is often considered as peculiarly Western: an artifact of modernity. Commentators have noted, for example, that 'adolescence was invented with the steam engine' (Musgrove, 1964: 33) and that it was 'on the whole an American discovery' (Demos and Demos, 1969: 263) However, this view is partly due to the influence of developmental psychology in shaping popular understanding.

G. Stanley Hall was the first to speak of 'adolescence' within the field of developmental psychology in the late nineteenth century (Hall, 1904).

Heavily influenced by Darwin's ideas, Hall believed that human development followed similar lines to human evolution, with the adolescent phase similar to the turmoil believed to precede the emergence of civilisation. He thought that physical development occurred in leaps rather than gradual transitions and that these changes were accompanied by psychological upheaval, known as 'storm and stress' (Petersen, 1988). As Durkin has explained: 'He regarded the instability, anguish, and intensity of adolescence as a necessary precursor to the establishment of adult equilibrium' (1995: 515). This branch of thought posited three key characteristics of adolescence: conflict with parents, mood disruptions and risk behaviour (Arnett, 1998). Although Hall's ideas were not based on empirical research and were challenged by others at the time (Thorndyke, 1904, cited in Petersen, 1988), they influenced academic research and long dominated popular understandings of adolescence (Durkin, 1995; Rogoff, 2003).

It seems that, despite the number of biological, social and organisational changes that young people experience during the second decade of life, only 5–15 per cent report psychological disturbances (Durkin, 1995). Petersen (1988) cites research by Offer and Offer (1975) demonstrating that a minority of adolescent boys experience 'tumultuous' growth during adolescence, while the majority experience continuous growth. Anthropologist Margaret Mead on the basis of fieldwork with young people in Samoa concurred with this view, suggesting that the turmoil and rebellion associated at that time in Europe and North America with 'adolescence' was not a necessary universal (Mead, 1943). More recently, Bame Nsamenang dismissed the consideration of adolescence by psychology as 'a Eurocentric enterprise', arguing that 'the field would have been different had adolescence been 'discovered' within the cultural conditions and life circumstances different than those of Europe and North America, say, in Africa' (2002: 61). In fact, historical and ethnographic evidence encourage a broader conceptualisation of adolescence not limited to psychological development and views of 'storm and stress' alone. As a period in the life course its length, the terms by which it is labelled and the practices that it involves may vary.

Anthropologist Alice Schlegel draws our attention to the existence of 'adolescence' both in language and social practice across diverse societies and cultures as 'a period between childhood and adulthood during which its participants behave and are treated differently than either their seniors or their juniors' (1995: 16). However, in her view it is incorrect to assume, as many have done, that this stage necessarily relates to the development of a person's productive role in an industrial society (Durkin, 1995: 507). A period of preparation that may be understood as 'adolescence' is also evident across rural and pre-industrial societies where occupational roles are assumed gradually within a family-based economy. Schlegel goes further to point out that even amongst primates a social stage between 'childhood' and 'adulthood' – that can be understood as 'adolescence' – is noticeable. Her suggestion, that we see adolescence as 'a response to the growth of reproductive capacity' (ibid.), draws attention to the construction of 'adulthood' in terms of the ability to procreate. However, in any given context such ability will, of course, be a matter not only of biology but also of social possibility: involving negotiation of various regulations and obligations that are themselves shaped through the interplay of ideational and material factors. From that perspective we must wonder about the inevitability of adolescence as an institution.

The evidence commonly suggests that the length, even the existence, of a discrete period of life that may be labelled 'adolescence' relates largely to factors such as gender and socio-economic standing. Giving the lie to claims that adolescence is a modern invention, Shulamith Shahar notes that medieval authors of medical, didactic and moral works commonly distinguished three periods of early life – infantia from birth to age seven; puerita from 7–12 (for girls) and 7–14 (for boys); and adolescentia from 12 or 14 to adulthood (Shahar, 1990: 22). Nevertheless, as this author then proceeds to explain, in the case of girls 'the transition from childhood to married life with all the responsibility and duties it entailed was very rapid, without the transitional stage undergone by young men from the nobility and urban class before they married and settled down' (p. 30).

If the existence of adolescence – as a clearly demarcated period of life – depends on factors of culture and political-economy we cannot assume its universality. On the other hand, we should be attentive to the possibility of its emergence in response to wider changes. For example, the expansion of educational provision, urbanisation, changes to marriage laws and evolving cultural norms have all contributed to a marked increase in the marriage age of girls around the globe over the past three decades (UNFPA, 2003: 16) Where once marriage and entry into (gendered) adulthood may have followed soon after menarche (Boyden, 2001: 187) the possibility of young women experiencing a more extended period of transition to adult roles and responsibilities has grown.[1]

Conditions arising from political violence and displacement may exert their own influence on the extent of an adolescent, transitional life stage: in some cases causing a drastic shortening. For example, it has been commonly noted that in refugee camps where there is fear of sexual violence parents may marry their daughters off at an early age as a protection strategy (Boyden et al., 2002: 35). Furthermore, the death, disappearance or disablement of parents or other caregivers can compel young people to take on fully the roles, if not the status, of adults (ibid.: 39ff). Alternatively, as Tefferi (this volume: 23–37) describes, the inability to perform conventional rites of passage as a consequence of displacement, can create obstacles for boys in their efforts to achieve adult status.

An understanding of adolescence as a life stage that is malleable in its boundaries and content, but which, at the very least, may be distinguished from childhood by the deliberateness with which preparation for and transition into adulthood are pursued, is central to this volume. Running through the various chapters is a concern for the ways in which political violence and displacement as sociological phenomena affect both the construction of adolescence and the experience of those engaged directly as participants in this life stage, however briefly it lasts. While some authors focus largely on describing the situation of actual groups of adolescents, others pay particular attention to the ideas and practices that shape adolescence and the ways that these are, in turn, affected by political violence and displacement. In some cases the authors employ the terms 'adolescents'/ 'adolescence' extensively, in others 'youth'/'youthhood', and 'older children'/ 'childhood' are used. For some the focus of their discussion is a population group defined by chronological age (at least ten years old), for others age is only one marker, possibly less important than other factors such as marital or occupational status, parenthood or economic independence which denote entry into full adulthood. In general, however, it is likely that this social stage primarily occurs within the second decade of life.

A central theme in the evolving discussion – led by sociologists and anthropologists – of childhood as a social construction concerns power relations between those construed as 'children' and 'adults' respectively. Spanning the clearly defined generational categories of 'adult' and 'child' the position of adolescents is often surrounded by ambiguity. In any society it is likely that adolescence, as a transitional period, will involve responsibilities and opportunities that may be associated with adulthood even when the individuals concerned remain labelled as 'children'. The relations of power between 'adolescents' and 'adults' are thus especially complex since the justifications for maintaining adult authority – greater competency, responsibility, protective function, etc. – are demonstrably questionable.

In settings of political violence and displacement the responsibilities and opportunities of teenagers can multiply literally overnight. School pupils can suddenly become soldiers, political leaders, heads of household and primary caregivers. In countries of asylum they may become translators and cultural brokers for parents and other elders. Yet, we cannot assume that relations of power automatically shift in consequence. Instead, we must remain attentive to the ongoing negotiations of power and status built upon age/generation in any given setting. What are the justifications used – not just by local adults but even by international agencies – for withholding recognition as 'adults' from young people who assume a full adult measure of responsibility? How do gerontocracies maintain themselves, if indeed they do, amidst flux and rapid societal change? And what profile does 'adolescence'/'youth' acquire when political violence assumes an inter-generational dimension? These are questions being explored with particular vigour in sub-Saharan Africa where, as discussed further below, the youthful population of many countries is especially large (Sommers, 2003; Abbink and van Kessel, 2004; Honwana and de Boeck, 2005; Christiansen, Utas and Vigh, 2006).

Adolescence, Political Violence and Displacement

In light of the shift in recent decades from warfare between opposing states to conflict within national borders amidst the heart of civilian life (Kaldor, 2001), questions have emerged about the local-level dynamics that lead to and mediate conflict. Given the large proportion of adolescents and young adults within many countries of the global South, a particular focus has fallen upon this demographic – commonly referred to as 'youth' – and the likelihood of their engagement in political violence. Interest in this subject first emerged in the 1970s (Choucri, 1974). However, it has only been since the mid-1990s that it became a point of significant debate. Prompted by the writings of Kaplan (1994) and Huntington (1996), concerns have been expressed that a so-called 'youth bulge' within a nation's population may increase the chances of socio-political instability. Particularly in the United States policymakers and politicians have been exercised by this notion. In an important addition to the so-called 'youth bulge' debate Henrik Urdal has argued that the relationship between demographics and conflict is more complex than can be assumed on the basis of numbers alone (2004). Factors of economy and governance, together with opportunities for migration, interact with population make-up to influence the potential of youth to utilise their energy in a constructive or destructive manner (Fussell and Greene, 2002; Sommers, 2006).

The demographics are certainly striking and urge greater attention to the relationship of adolescents to political violence. As Table I.1 demonstrates, in contrast to Western Europe and North America, countries in sub-Saharan Africa, South America and Asia tend to have a large proportion of the population in the age range 10–19. Since the latter decades of the twentieth century sub-Saharan Africa and many parts of Asia and South America have also experienced intra-state conflicts and forced population movements ranging from short-lived, devastating genocidal violence in Rwanda to long-term civil war in places such as Sri Lanka and Colombia. In each of the worst-affected countries we can assume a relatively high proportion of young people that might be considered 'adolescents'.

While this book is partly prompted by the realisation that many of the countries affected by political violence are also home to large youthful populations, it does not assume a simplistic causal relationship. Rather, in keeping with authors such as Urdal and Sommers, we consider the complex

Table I.1: Demographic Breakdown by Age Group and Region, 2004

	0–9	10–19	20–29	30–39	40–49	50–59
Western Europe	10.6%	11.6%	12.8%	15.7%	15.8%	12.6%
North America	13.4%	14.2%	13.7%	14.1%	15.5%	12.3%
Asia	17.9%	18.8%	16.9%	15.7%	12.3%	9.0%
South America	18.1%	18.6%	17.7%	15.3%	12.3%	8.6%
Sub-Saharan Africa	30.6%	23.5%	17.5%	11.8%	7.8%	5.0%

Source: U.S. Census Bureau.

interaction of factors that mediate or exacerbate the involvement of adolescents in political violence. Furthermore, each of the chapters considers in detail the impacts of conflict upon this section of the population. Collectively, their discussions cohere into a complex picture of the changes wrought by political violence and displacement upon the lives of adolescents. This picture inevitably depicts immense suffering – physical, emotional and psychological. It also shows the processes by which transition to social adulthood may be transformed and how, due to changing conditions, the possibility of achieving transition may be reconfigured, threatened or enhanced. Indeed, some authors suggest that the vision of adulthood to which adolescents orient themselves may become altered in significant ways.

Structure of the Book

Part I: Adolescence in Context

The first three chapters offer perspectives on adolescence itself and the specific factors that influence its constitution. Embracing between them situations of camp settlement, self-settlement and resettlement, the authors each show how the transition towards adulthood involves the negotiation of others' fears as manifest in efforts to control their actions and movements. Taken together these opening chapters encourage appreciation for the complexities and contradictions of adolescents' lives in settings of conflict-induced displacement. The actions of adults (whether family members or humanitarian agencies) to protect them as children are often confounded by circumstances that require adolescents to bear responsibilities – emotional and social, as well as practical – that are conventionally the provenance of adulthood. Thus, particular risks and vulnerability emerge alongside new opportunities.

In seeking to discern the nature of the challenges and opportunities faced by adolescents as a result of conflict and displacement we need to locate consideration of change not in relation to some assumed universal norm of childhood or adolescence, but with regard to conventional ideas and practices within a given setting. One basic step is to look at how adolescence itself – as a socially constructed stage of life – is restructured in light of conflict and forced migration. This issue lies at the heart of Hirut Tefferi's chapter, in which the author draws upon her experience of nearly twenty years' working with children-focused agencies in eastern Africa to describe the practices and ideas around adolescence in displacement camps. As Tefferi observes, a process of restructuring occurs through the interaction of local ideas and practice with those of humanitarian organisations:

> Furthermore, while young people are, under normal circumstances, expected to perform a considerable amount of productive work and take decisions on certain matters, they are expected by humanitarian agencies to sit in classrooms, usually with children much younger than themselves. Their roles in defending their communities and properties are consistently delegitimised, and adolescents are discouraged from taking part in training or from exhibiting skills that relate to the defence of themselves and their communities. Agencies usually offer services to them only if they are seen as vulnerable, according to such labels as 'unaccompanied children' and 'demobilized child soldiers'. To be sure, I am not intending to endorse the involvement of children as soldiers here, many of whom are forcibly recruited by organizations such as the LRA. Nevertheless, I believe it is important to remember that many young people engage in these activities not only because they are forced by circumstances, but also because they feel that such involvement offers them a sense of independence that they desire in becoming an adult. Unfortunately, many humanitarian agencies have only worked according to their own values and outlook on 'children' and have not acknowledged such complexity in the roles and desires of adolescents.

Tefferi's chapter encourages attention to the responsibilities that may be vested in and welcomed by young people. The successful discharge of such responsibilities enables entry into full social adulthood – a feat potentially made much harder by the conditions of displacement.

For many adolescents, however, political violence and displacement creates an opposite challenge. Rather than concern over maintaining socially significant roles and responsibilities, there is often a sudden and heavy burden of responsibility far beyond that which would normally be vested in a person at this point in the life cycle. In sub-Saharan Africa, where an estimated 30.6 per cent of the population is under ten and where the challenges of conflict are often compounded by those resulting from the HIV/AIDS pandemic, many war-affected communities undoubtedly include teenagers engaged full-time in domestic and paid labour as well as providing emotional support for relatives. Gillian Mann, in her discussion of Congolese adolescents living as unregistered refugees in Dar es Salaam, considers the consequences of bearing such responsibility at an early age. The children with whom she conducted research – including a fifteen-year-old head of household, and the various children compelled to 'carry their parents' worries' – lead tremendously isolated lives with little social or educational opportunity. According to Mann, the burden of responsibility placed upon these young refugees should raise serious concerns about their possibility of achieving 'healthy adolescent development'. It should also lead us to wonder about the longer-term, societal consequences of conflict-induced situations in which children's transition to full adult responsibility is truncated and occurs with little or no adult guidance.

The interviewees upon whose accounts the chapter by Kenneth Miller and colleagues is based are all young adults reflecting on adolescent experience. These are the sons and daughters of refugees now living in the San Francisco Bay Area. While some were born in the U.S.A., others experienced directly the violence that led to their families' displacement at a young age. For many, adolescence was a period of immense challenge due, amongst other reasons, to discrimination and anti-migrant violence, and the need to balance parental expectations of loyalty to ethnic community with the desire to fit in with peers. From several accounts we also learn that the difficulties of establishing a sound sense of self have been compounded by poor communication within the home, in particular parental silence about life in the family's country of origin and the circumstances that led to displacement. While parental discussion of devastating past experiences may be limited, the resulting fears and anxiety find expression in overprotective behaviour. Thus, we learn about young people struggling to find their place in a society radically different from that of the home country, whilst dealing with their parents' evident but unspoken pain and their need for control. This contribution by Miller and colleagues provokes awareness of the undoubtedly huge numbers of young people who, though separated from the direct dangers of war by time and distance, continue to experience the effects of political violence at a profound level within everyday life.

Part II: Adolescents Engaging in Political Violence

A major concern of humanitarians and politicians is with the long-term effects upon young people of growing up amidst political violence. Numerous commentators within academia and the mass media have popularised the notion that young people who grow up in a setting of political violence are corrupted by their experience with the result that they have 'an undeveloped sense of the complexity of moral problems' (Cairns, 1996: 106). This 'lost generation' hypothesis has been particularly applied to adolescents who experience combat directly and in consequence, it is assumed, will be unable to play a constructive role in the building of a stable society once the conflict has ended. Such views commonly rely on a simplistic understanding of socialisation processes, according to which children passively adopt the ideas and behaviour taught to them by adult figures.

That the young are active in the constitution of meaning is a view that has gained currency in the last two decades (see Prout and James, 1997). Sociologists, anthropologists and social psychologists have explored the processes through which knowledge is constructed out of particular experiences, and the wide range of factors – personal and environmental – that serve to mediate (Cairns, 1996). The chapter by Andrew Dawes applies this understanding to the situation of former young fighters in the anti-apartheid struggle in South Africa. He describes four key conditions that may have served to encourage the involvement of these former combatants in criminal violence. A psychologist by training, Dawes moves beyond the intra-psychic in order to provide us with an account that locates the behaviour of former fighters in economic, political and cultural context. In particular his chapter draws our attention to the poverty and low standard of educational provision that continue to marginalise young black South Africans even after the end of apartheid. His contribution moves us beyond simplistic dichotomies between 'victim' and 'perpetrator' to locate the actions of young people in a setting where many of the challenges faced by young people during the apartheid era still remain.

Economic opportunity and marginalisation are also important themes in the chapter by Mats Utas. The focus here is on the motivations of adolescent males who engaged in Liberia's civil war. Again we see the complex interplay of factors, which militates against any monocausal or primordialist account of the war in terms, for example, of an inter-ethnic conflict. Utas situates these young men's often brutal activities in relation to an aspiration for 'modernity' with all that this implies for social, economic and cultural advancement in the setting of Liberia as a 'failed modern state'. This chapter also alerts us to issues around relations of power predicated on age/generation. As Utas explains, the frustration of young males is the product of an interplay between socio-economic conditions and the constraints created by gerontocracy.

Taken together, the chapters by Dawes and Utas bring into question assumed distinctions between 'conflict' and 'post-conflict' and between forms of violence labelled as 'political' and those which appear 'criminal' in intent. In suggesting that poverty (relative or absolute), socio-economic marginalisa-tion, and poor services may contribute to the engagement of adolescents in conflict both chapters provide an important corrective to the core assump-tions of the recent outpouring of literature on the subject of 'child soldiers'.[2] Unlike the authors of much of this literature Utas and Dawes take seriously the capacity of adolescents to fashion a conscious (if discomfiting) response to poverty, marginalisation and oppression through engagement in violence. One implication of their contributions is that the effort to ensure former adolescent combatants forgo the use of violence to achieve personal ends should involve more than an individualistic focus on the young people themselves. Rather, there is likely to be a need for considerable and sustained investment in economic, social and political development over the medium to long term in order to address the conditions that encouraged engagement in political violence in the first place. We may also wonder at the need for transformation of hierarchies built upon age/generation that seem to constrain the young as a matter of course.

The evidence from different war zones suggests that most young people who pursue engagement in political violence are likely to be at least ten years old and probably teenagers. This basic point underlies the chapter by Hanne Beirens. Her work differs from that of Dawes and Utas in that she adopts a primarily institutional focus, exploring how efforts to prevent underage recruitment have been pursued in a large humanitarian organisation – the UNHCR. On the basis of research in UNHCR headquarters and fieldwork in South Africa, Beirens posits that such efforts may be significantly hindered by the insistence on a conceptual framework that addresses recruitment as a generic 'childhood' issue. She alludes to the same complex interplay between conditions, experience and motivations that both Dawes and Utas suggest are central to the process by which adolescents come to engage in armed conflict. Furthermore, she locates this process in relation to the specific challenges of adolescence. However, since 'adolescence' may be constructed and experienced differently across contexts, her argument explicitly counters the normative approach that currently guides most agency programming around child recruitment. Instead, Beirens encourages humanitarians to pay greater attention to context and to work on the basis of evidence.

Part III: Gendered Adolescence in Exile

The challenges and opportunities that emerge in the context of political violence and displacement are never encountered uniformly. While the experience of adolescents is likely to be distinct from that of younger children, relative age, social class/caste, ethnicity and numerous other factors will invariably have a mediating effect. In many conflict-affected settings gender may play an especially important role, influencing the level and nature of risk, responsibility and opportunity. For example, in settings of displacement adolescent girls may be particular targets for would-be traffickers looking to supply a local or more distant sex trade (de Berry, 2004). This threat or concern over sexual violence in general may encourage parents to marry their daughters off early. As a protection strategy this entails other challenges and forms of risk for young women. Conversely, conventional gendered ideas may put adolescent girls at an advantage over their male peers. The domestic roles and responsibilities often considered the sole domain of females may be easier to continue in a displacement camp than the activities expected of adolescent males – for example in providing for the family budget or cooking pot. Thus, young males may suffer particularly from frustration, loss of status and anxiety about the possibility of achieving respected adult status.

Both authors in this section touch upon the gendering of challenge and opportunity. We also learn from them how gendered visions of adulthood may be bound up with the destiny of a community-in-exile. The chapter by Homa Hoodfar conveys the concerns of adolescent Afghan refugees residing in Iran. Faced with the prospect of enforced return to Afghanistan – a country that many of Hoodfar's young informants have never seen – some stark differences emerge between the experiences and fears of males and females. While for all these young people life in Iran involves negotiating disrespect and discrimination, girls in particular are anxious about the looming prospect of departure for Afghanistan. For many, it seems, the gains made in raising their status are threatened by return to a country imagined as less enlightened about the place of women in society. In addition, the economic, social and political difficulties of life in Afghanistan are seen as liable to produce a situation of crisis in which families might respond by marrying off their daughters as a desperate strategy for survival.

Jason Hart's chapter also focuses on adolescents and gender in a setting of prolonged displacement – in this case amongst Palestinians in a refugee camp in Jordan. However, unlike the Afghans in Iran, these young people have little prospect of return. Instead, they seem likely to live out their lives within the camp as at least two generations have done before them. In such a setting Hart considers the ways that adolescent males serve to maintain the distinctiveness of the camp as a community-in-exile – potentially eroded by time and political neglect – through their performance of an idealised masculinity. In this process boys lay the groundwork for their claim on full membership of the community of the camp as respected adult males. Like Hoodfar in her discussion of Afghan young women, Hart describes the negotiation of gendered identities by adolescents – in this case male. In both examples we witness the effort of young refugees to empower themselves in the face of powerful forces of marginalisation.

Part IV: Responding to Adolescents

In November 2005 representatives of various UN agencies and international NGOs (INGOs) came together in Geneva, through the facilitation of the UN Children's Fund (UNICEF), for a 'Global Consultation on Adolescent Programming in Emergency and Transition'. While natural disaster was also considered, the main focus was upon adolescents in situations of political violence. This meeting built on a number of recent agency-initiated studies documenting the experience of programming in various settings (for example, Hart, 2004; UNICEF, 2004; UNDP, 2006). One notable feature of the literature and discussions to date has been the enthusiasm to develop participatory approaches in programming with adolescents. The motivation for this extends beyond concern to uphold children's participation rights as articulated in the UNCRC. Indeed, there is an increasingly common conviction that involvement in the development and implementation of projects may yield important benefits for adolescents, enhancing their sense of well-being and even helping to increase protection (Newman, 2005).

In the midst of this widespread enthusiasm about participatory adolescent programming the chapter by Joanna de Berry sounds a helpful warning note. Here the author offers observations drawn from her experience as a humanitarian worker in Afghanistan in the period following the fall of the Taliban in 2001. Not only are programmatic aims and methods revealed as inappropriate but the underlying assumptions about adolescence itself – for example as a period characterised by egalitarian relationships amongst peers (Schlegel, 1995: 19) – are challenged in the implementation of programming with young Afghans. The dissonance between agency thinking and the reality of adolescents' lives is exemplified by the account of a local youth group (supported by an international agency) in which the leader responded to internal struggles and accusations of corruption by bringing in members of his warlord father's militia. Armed men thus besieged the premises of this group, using armed force to make his opponents back down. As de Berry explains, Afghan youth do not exist outside the wider political and social environment in which survival involves alliance with powerful forces. International aid agencies in Afghanistan have learned this lesson through experience and, it seems, are now making changes accordingly.

Diana Alvis Palma has spent many years working as a psychiatrist and therapist with young people in her native Colombia. In her contribution to this book she moves from a general overview of the situation to accounts of some of the adolescents she has encountered: young people struggling to move their lives beyond the violence that has engulfed them and their families. This author describes how she and colleagues have sought to respond to the immense suffering experienced. The essence of this response is characterised as the promotion of 'resilience': an approach that acknowledges pain while seeking to involve young people in a dialogue about how they may move their lives forward. In contrast to much of the current psychological work with young people in settings of political violence that sidesteps issues of justice, this author keeps in clear view the need for the restitution of rights as part of the scenario of healing. As Alvis Palma argues, a socially engaged and future-oriented approach is particularly important when working with young people, given their common concern to build a decent life for themselves.

Part V: Researching with Adolescents

The accumulation of insight derived from field-based research is vital for the development of programming relevant to the conditions, capacities, aspirations and experiences of adolescents in diverse settings. While the need for rigorously acquired findings is often voiced by practitioners, the manner in which research should be conducted in the often challenging conditions of political violence and displacement is less often a topic of discussion. This is not a question simply of methods or techniques but also of the attitudes and sensitivities that researchers bring with them to their endeavours. The final section of the book offers discussion of research in two very different settings. In both cases the authors offer honest reflection upon their own learning that will undoubtedly have a broad resonance.

The increasingly influential discourse of participation within humanitarian initiatives noted above has also become an important element within field-based research. The chapter by Cordula Strocka reflects on the author's use of this approach in her fieldwork with youth gangs in a province of Peru that experienced some of the worst fighting in the war between Sendero Luminoso ('Shining Path') rebels and the government. In Strocka's view 'the purpose of participatory research is to increase participants' understanding of their situation and their ability to act upon that knowledge in order to create positive change for themselves'. However, as she learns through experience, positive change in the lives of the young male members of these gangs is hard to achieve in an environment of suspicion where socially active young people are linked in popular memory with the young members of Sendero Luminoso from Peru's recent and violent past. This is a troubling observation that points to a lingering impact of political violence with which adolescents are compelled to contend. It also encourages us to think further about the challenges of pursuing participatory methods in a fragile setting with a history of political violence.

The chapter by Liesbeth de Block similarly focuses on the actual conduct of research with adolescents. Like Strocka, de Block is concerned to approach young people less as objects of research and more as participants in a process that may yield them direct benefit. In this case, the author engaged young refugees in London's East End in a video production project intended to impart skills and provide the opportunity for participants to explore and express diverse aspects of their lives. This project was connected to parallel projects in five other European countries with communication between the adolescents in each location conducted via the Internet and the exchange of self-produced videos. One intriguing theme to emerge concerns the complexity of identity as evidenced in the videos and through the exchange between participants across the different countries. Far from a narrow focus on 'refugeedom', the videos created by these young people suggest the ongoing fashioning of identities. De Block describes the videos in the following terms: 'They are not portraying images of victims but rather of competent adolescents able to draw on their pasts yet focused more on present processes of settlement and the struggle for social inclusion'. Such content apparently strayed outside the expectations of the organisers and the project design, creating unease but also an important point of learning.

De Block's frank observations illustrate the potential risks of privileging the past. As many of the chapters in this book illustrate clearly, it would be a mistake to assume a priori that adolescents who have undergone profoundly painful experiences need first and foremost to re-explore those experiences and thereby achieve a measure of healing. For some this may be true, but for many it is likely that the urge to address the challenges before them and to realise ambitions for education, personal relationships and economic advancement will be most pressing. Indeed, it may be that securing a decent life as a respected member of adult society is itself a powerful way for adolescents to move beyond the sufferings of the past and present.

As this book hopefully makes clear, part of our challenge as academics and practitioners is to develop flexibility in working with adolescents in settings of political violence and displacement. Not only do we need to avoid assumptions about the importance of the past without closing down possibilities for discussion of experience, we should also remain open to the opportunities as well as the difficulties that may emerge in the worst of circumstances; attentive to both the incredible strengths and the vulnerabilities of young people as they seek to negotiate the transition from 'childhood' to 'adulthood' with all the paradox that this may involve.

Notes

1. While there are trends that would lead us to believe that 'adolescence' – as an acknowledged or de facto period of transition – may have become more commonplace, we should be wary of assuming ubiquity. For example, as contributors to the volume edited by Bradford Brown, Larson and Saraswathi point out, in some locations, including Russia, young people are marrying at earlier ages than before (2002: 2).
2. For a critique of some of this literature see Hart (2006a, 2006b).

References

Abbink, J. and van Kessel, I. (eds) 2004 *Vanguard or Vandals: Youth Politics and Conflict in Africa*. Leiden: Brill.
Ackermann, L., Feeny, T., Hart, J. and Newman, J. 2003 *Understanding and Evaluating*

Children's Participation: A Review of Contemporary Literature. Woking: Plan International.

Arnett, J.J. 1998 'Learning to Stand Alone: The Contemporary American Transition to Adulthood in Cultural and Historical Context', *Human Development* 41: 295–315.

Bame Nsamenang, A. 2002 'Adolescence in Sub-Saharan Africa: An Image Constructed from Africa's Triple Inheritance', in B. Bradford Brown, R.W. Larson and T.S. Saraswathi (eds) *The World's Youth: Adolescence in Eight Regions of the Globe*. Cambridge: Cambridge University Press, pp. 61–104.

Boyden, J. 2001 'Some Reflections on Scientific Conceptualisations of Childhood and Youth', in S. Tremayne (ed) *Managing Reproductive Life: Cross-Cultural Themes in Sexuality and Fertility*. Oxford: Berghahn Books, pp. 175–193.

Boyden, J., de Berry, J., Feeny, T., and Hart, J. 2002 *Children Affected by Armed Conflict in South Asia: A Review of Trends and Issues Identified through Secondary Research*. RSC Working Paper No.7. Oxford: Refugee Studies Centre http://www.rsc.ox.ac.uk/PDFs/workingpaper7.pdf accessed 19/01/08.

Bradford Brown, B., Larson, R.W. and Saraswathi, T.S. (eds) *The World's Youth: Adolescence in Eight Regions of the Globe*. Cambridge: Cambridge University Press.

Brett, R. and McCallin, M. 1998 *Children: The Invisible Soldiers*. Stockholm: Save the Children.

Brett, R. and Specht, I., 2004 *Young Soldiers: Why they Choose to Fight*. Boulder, CO: Lynne Rienner.

Cairns, E. 1996 *Children and Political Violence*. Oxford: Blackwell.

Choucri, N. 1974 *Population Dynamics and International Violence: Propositions, Insights and Evidence*. Lexington, MA: Lexington.

Christiansen, C., Utas, M. and Vigh, H. (eds) 2006 *Navigating Youth, Generating Adulthood: Social Becoming in an African Context*. Uppsala: the Nordic Africa Institute.

Das, V. and Reynolds, P. 2003 'The Child on the Wing: Children Negotiating the Everyday in the Geography of Violence'. Background paper for research programme 'Child on the Wing', Department of Anthropology, Johns Hopkins University. http://anthropology.jhu.edu/child_on_the_wing/documents/CHILD %20WEB%20DRAFT%20ESSAY.pdf

de Berry, J. 2004 'The Sexual Vulnerability of Adolescent Girls during Civil War in Teso, Uganda', in J. Boyden and J. de Berry (eds) *Children and Youth on the Front Line: Ethnography, Armed Conflict and Displacement*. Oxford: Berghahn Books, pp. 45–62.

Demos, J. and Demos, V. 1969 'Adolescence in Historical Perspective', *Journal of Marriage and the Family* 31: 632–38.

Durkin, K. 1995 *Developmental Social Psychology: From Infancy to Old Age*. Oxford: Blackwell Publishing.

Fussell, E. and Greene, M. 2002 'Demographic Trends Affecting Youth Around the World', in B. Bradford Brown, R.W. Larson and T.S. Saraswathi (eds) *The World's Youth: Adolescence in Eight Regions of the Globe*. Cambridge: Cambridge University Press, pp. 21–60.

Garbarino, J., Kostelny, K. and Dubrow, N. 1991 *No Place to be a Child: Growing up in a War Zone*. Lexington, MA: Lexington Books.

Hall, G.S. 1904 *Adolescence: Its Psychology and Its Relations to Physiology, Anthropology,*

Sociology, Sex, Crime, Religion, and Education, 2 vols. New York: Appleton.

Hart, J. 2004 *Children's Participation in Humanitarian Action: Learning from Zones of Armed Conflict.* Report prepared for Canadian International Development Agency and INTRAC, http://www.rsc.ox.ac.uk/PDFs/Childrens%20Participation%20 Synthesis%20Feb%202004.pdf

Hart, J. 2006a 'Saving Children: What Role for Anthropology?' *Anthropology Today* 22 (1): 5–8.

Hart, J. 2006b 'The Politics of 'Child Soldiers', *Brown Journal of World Affairs* XII (2): 217–26.

Honwana, A. and de Boeck, F. (eds) 2005 *Makers and Breakers: Children and Youth in Postcolonial Africa.* Oxford: James Currey.

Huntington, S. 1996 *The Clash of Civilizations and the Remaking of World Order.* New York: Simon and Schuster.

Kaldor, M. 2001 *New and Old Wars: Organized Violence in a Global Era.* Stanford: Stanford University Press.

Kaplan, R. 1994 'The Coming Anarchy', *Atlantic Monthly* 273 (2): 44–76.

Machel, G. 1996 *Impact of Armed Conflict on Children.* New York: United Nations and UNICEF.

Mackay, S. and Mazurana, D. 2004 *Where are the Girls? Girls Fighting Forces Northern Uganda, Sierra Leone and Mozambique, Their Lives After The War.* Montreal: Canada International Center for Human Rights and Democratic Development.

Macksoud, M. and Aber, L. 1996 'The War Experiences and Psychosocial Development of Children in Lebanon', *Child Development* 67 (1): 70–88.

Mead, M. 1943 *Coming of Age in Samoa: A Study of Adolescence and Sex in Primitive Societies.* Harmondsworth: Penguin Books.

Musgrove, F. 1964 *Youth and the Social Order.* London: Routledge and Kegan Paul.

Newman, J. 2005 'Protection Through Participation: Young People Affected by Forced Migration and Political Crisis'. RSC Working Paper Series No. 20. Oxford: Refugee Studies Centre.

Offer, D. and Offer, J. 1975 *From Teenage to Young Manhood: A Psychological Study.* New York: Basic Books.

Oldman, D. 1994 'Adult-Child Relations as Class Relations', in J. Qvortup, M. Bardy, G. Sgritta and H. Wintersberger (eds) *Childhood Matters: Social Theory, Practice and Politics.* Aldershot: Avebury.

Petersen, A. 1988 'Adolescent Development', *Annual Review of Psychology* 39: 583–607.

Prout, A. and James, A. 1997 'A New Paradigm for the Sociology of Childhood? Provenance, Promise and Problems', in James, A. and Prout, A. (eds) *Constructing and Reconstructing Childhood: Contemporary Issues in the Sociological Study of Childhood.* London: The Falmer Press, pp. 7–33.

Quota, S., Punamaki, R-L., El-Sarraj, E. 1995 'The Relation Between Traumatic Experiences, Activity and Cognitive and Emotional Responses among Palestinian Children', *International Journal of Psychology* 30 (3): 289–304.

Read, K. 2002 'When is a Kid a Kid? Negotiating Children's Rights in El Salvador's Civil War', *History of Religions* 41(4): 391–409.

Ressler, E., Boothby, N. and Steinbock, D. 1988 *Unaccompanied Children: Care and Protection in Wars, Natural Disasters and Refugee Movements.* Oxford: Oxford University Press.

Rogoff, B. 2003 *The Cultural Nature of Human Development.* Oxford: Oxford University Press.

Rosen, D. 2005 *Armies of the Young: Child Soldiers in War and Terrorism.* New Brunswick: Rutgers University Press.

Schlegel, A. 1995 'A Cross-Cultural Approach to Adolescence', *Ethos* 23 (1): 15–32.

Shahar, S. 1990 *Childhood in the Middle Ages.* London: Routledge.

Sommers, M. 2003 *Urbanization, War and Africa's Youth at Risk: Towards Understanding and Addressing Future Challenges.* Washington DC: Basic Education and Policy Support and Creative Associates.

Sommers, M. 2006 *Youth and Conflict: A Brief Review of Available Literature.* Washington DC: USAID/EQUIP3.

Thorndike, E.L. 1904 'The Newest Psychology', *Educational Review* 28: 217–27.

Tolfree, D. 2004 *Whose Children? Separated Children's Protection and Participation in Emergencies.* Stockholm: Save the Children.

UNDP 2006 *Youth and Violent Conflict: Society and Development in Crisis?* New York: United Nations Development Programme.

UNFPA 2003 *State of World Population 2003: Investing in Adolescents' Health and Rights.* New York: United Nations Population Fund.

Ungar, M. (ed.) 2005 *Handbook for Working with Children and Youth: Pathways to Resilience across Cultures and Contexts.* Thousand Oaks, CA: Sage Publications.

UNICEF, 2004 *Adolescent Programming in Conflict and Post-conflict Situations.* New York: United Nations Children's Fund.

Urdal, H. 2004 *The Devil in the Demographics: The Effect of Youth Bulges on Domestic Armed Conflict 1950–2000.* Social Development Papers: Conflict Prevention and Reconstruction Paper No.14. Washington DC: The World Bank.

Wessells, M. 2006 *Child Soldiers: From Violence to Protection.* Cambridge, MA: Harvard University Press.

PART I
ADOLESCENCE IN CONTEXT

1

Reconstructing Adolescence after Displacement: Experience from Eastern Africa*

Hirut Tefferi

Introduction

This chapter explores the impact of armed conflict and displacement on adolescents in eastern Africa. It asks how dramatic changes brought about by war and forced migration affect the traditional ideas and practices surrounding adolescence and thereby influence the actual lives of young people. It is based on my extensive experience as a female psychologist from Ethiopia working with war-affected children since the late 1980s. My work has taken me to Somaliland, Somalia, Ethiopia, Kenya, southern Sudan and northern Uganda. By writing about eastern Africa, I am aware of the fact that I am dealing with a large geographical area with a good deal of cultural diversity. Nonetheless, through my work I have come to recognise the ideas, issues and practices relating to adolescence that, if not existent in all locations, are certainly familiar in many locations. While I do not wish to downplay the importance of distinctive cultures and particular communities, I believe it is still useful to reflect on the general trends and offer observations that may support detailed enquiry in any given location.

Much of the conventional discussion of conflict and its impact on young people has tended to focus on a single issue – such as military recruitment or

* Reprinted from *Children & Society* 21 (4): 297–308 with permission of Blackwell Publishing.

gender-based violence. To address the limitations to this approach, this chapter instead seeks to consider a less obvious but potentially more fundamental challenge to those young people in later childhood. As I shall explain, adolescents in conflict-induced displacement experience much difficulty in achieving their adult status and full membership in society. In this context, many adolescents have chosen to migrate or join a military force as an alternative means to attaining prized adult status. However, these alternatives also present many contradictions and challenges. Not only is their immediate well-being put under threat, but both returning migrants and former combatants may encounter a challenge to their claims on full adult membership of home communities as a result of their actions. As I shall suggest, this kind of social impact – while less immediate and obvious perhaps than other dimensions of young people's experience of conflict and displacement– nevertheless has important and potentially very long-term consequences for them and their communities. In order to understand how exactly such consequences come about it is first important to know a little about the conventions surrounding adolescence in eastern Africa.

Conventional Notions and Practices of Adolescence in Eastern Africa

Throughout eastern Africa, adolescence is commonly defined as a period from the end of childhood towards the full entry into adult responsibilities. Certainly, adolescence is not a moment or a sudden switch from childhood but rather a gradual process within which particular rites and practices may serve to mark the changing status of the individual. If adulthood is considered as a period of full membership in the community, adolescence is a transition to and a trial period of adulthood. Of course, there are important differences in the ways in which adolescence is understood within the region. For example, in rural areas it relates strongly to the assumption of growing degrees of responsibility by individuals. During this period, adolescents are expected to increasingly share the responsibility of their parents and villagers, especially in terms of productive activities and defending property such as cattle and land and upholding the name of the family or the tribe. In contrast, for their peers living in urban and more privileged areas, adolescence is a time when they continue to attend schools and are largely considered as 'children'. Nevertheless, commonalities exist in that adolescence is conceptualised as an important period of transition from childhood to adulthood.

In terms of the practices surrounding adolescence, transition is achieved and marked in various ways within different communities. However, in most rural communities, initiation ceremonies are commonly employed to mark the end of childhood and entry into formal adulthood. The preparation for and conduct of initiation ceremonies involve elders in the community in guiding the physical, social, political, psychological and spiritual development of young people. During initiation ceremonies, adolescents are taught to take on adult roles and responsibilities within their families and communities. Afterwards, they are expected to show signs of independence, responsibility and ability to care for parents, extended family and community members.

In general, social responsibilities are defined according to gender, and success in performing their designated roles is related to the attainment of ideal masculine and feminine status. Girls, for example, are generally taught to be good wives and mothers. They are advised on appropriate social behaviour, duties and responsibilities (particularly towards husbands and in-laws) and on their sexual and domestic roles. They learn to groom themselves, and to contain anger and frustrations caused by the behaviour of spouses. Many are expected to marry even before they experience their first menstrual cycle (menarche). Girls who show signs of possessing supernatural powers may be encouraged to develop these skills through association with traditional healers or spiritual leaders in their communities.

On the other hand, males are expected to imitate their fathers, spending more and more time away from home, performing adult tasks in farming, participating in traditional courts, and so on. In this way, they are gradually introduced into the political life of their communities. Those who seem particularly suited for leadership may be invited to participate with elders and community leaders during political functions. Initiation ceremonies particularly emphasise the role of males in defending their community's economic and social interests and understanding the relationship of their community to others. Initiates learn to identify other groups as friend or foe, judge the necessity of inter-group conflict, and display acceptable behaviour during different phases of conflict. In addition, in many communities courage and the capacity for aggression are strongly associated with the attainment of adult masculine status. As part of the transition to adulthood, boys are therefore required to display physical strength and tolerance for pain and hardship. They are also expected to exhibit skills necessary for protecting themselves, those around them and the interests of their communities. During initiation ceremonies, activities focus on building physical prowess and bravery, and boys are coached in survival skills by male relatives such as elder brothers and uncles. Failure of a boy to perform the expected tasks is a humiliation not only for the individual but also for the whole family or clan.

All in all, initiation ceremonies are highly significant not only for the adolescents themselves but also for their community at large. The successful conduct of initiation ceremonies is indicative of the well-being and moral standing of a community. Conversely, interruptions in initiation ceremonies are thought to signify the failure of a community and its political leadership, as well as a collective decline in morale and values. It is often believed that the community will pay for such failure for several generations.

The Impact of Conflict and Displacement on the Transition to Adulthood

In the countries in eastern Africa that this chapter focuses on (namely, Ethiopia, Eritrea, Somalia, Sudan and northern Uganda), violent social upheaval and political turmoil have undermined the basic structures and functioning of many communities as well as the practices and values of the population. In particular, conflict and displacement have led to the disruption of institutions and practices that would conventionally serve as a framework for the transition to adulthood. The following examples are illustrative of such disruption.

Breakdown of the Family and Community Structures

Throughout eastern Africa, social roles and responsibilities are distributed to a large extent in relation to age and generation. Older community members have traditionally been expected to provide leadership and guidance for younger generations to assist them in their successful achievement of transition to adulthood. However, large-scale displacement during protracted conflicts in this region have brought about radical changes to the traditional hierarchies and social systems characteristic of many communities in eastern Africa and particularly undermined the role of elders. In some cases, the negation of conventional, age-related social hierarchies and the role of older generations has been a deliberate aim of parties to the conflict. For example, the socialist revolution in Ethiopia during the mid-1970s attacked the feudalistic social structure and, in doing so, intentionally undermined established family, communal and religious values. Thus, social hierarchy built upon age and generation, according to which respect for elders was strongly upheld, was replaced by a common belief that the elders as well as the values and powers associated with them were backward. This went hand in hand with the assumption of far greater power by younger generations.

In addition, military engagement by adolescents has led to the reversal of the roles of parents/adults and their children as those adolescents with weapons came to hold a significant amount of power over civilian adults. In southern Sudan, for example, where community elders had previously played the most prominent role in overseeing the administration of community affairs, adolescent boys and young adults who bore modern weapons usurped the role of the elders. The consequent demise in the status of elders has, in turn, had a significant impact on the adolescents' development and disrupted the conventional framework for their transition to adulthood.

Finally, conflict-induced displacement has also made the transition to adulthood practically impossible to attain for many adolescent boys. Within displacement camps, younger adult males often experience an increase in power in relation to their male elders. Since they are more likely to be educated and to possess the means to communicate with aid providers, at least some will be given significant power and responsibility. They may be asked to oversee efforts such as the distribution of rations, registration of refugees, provision of support for soldiers and recruitment of fighters for armed groups. Such increased power, however, has had a negative impact not only upon the authority of elders but also upon the opportunities of adolescents. Due to such changes in the social hierarchies of displaced communities, many adolescent boys have found that the social mobility which had existed in peacetime now largely disappeared, as young adult males are often reluctant to graduate into the now-devalued social space of the elders. Furthermore, they are equally hesitant to relinquish their new-found power within the camps to inexperienced adolescents. As a result, many adolescents come to remain in a state of social suspension and are unable to assume the expected roles and responsibilities of 'adults'. Such decreased social mobility and the resulting inability to make the effective transition to adulthood have been a source of great frustration for many adolescent males in displaced situations.

Suspension of the Practices around Transition

As previously discussed, initiation ceremonies are essential to the process of moving from the status of a 'child' to that of an 'adult' in eastern Africa. In many communities, an individual's transition out of childhood is not considered complete without the performance of such ceremonies. As initiation rites are conducted in agreement between different groups of people, they require a certain level of political and social cohesiveness. In situations of conflict-induced displacement, however, such cohesion is hard to achieve.

In the absence of the ceremonies, the position of young people clearly no longer 'children' but not yet initiated often becomes highly ambiguous and problematic. Even when they are in their thirties or forties, those uninitiated may still not be recognised as full adults. Due to the resulting stigmatisation, disruption of initiation ceremonies is thus loathed by adolescents seeking to obtain respected adult status. In many communities, completed initiation is represented by physical markings on adolescents' faces or bodies in the form of scarification, tooth removal or tattoos. These markings are of such symbolic importance that in southern Sudan, for example, adolescents who were unable to undergo initiation ceremonies due to conflict began forcibly removing the teeth of their related peers, so as not to be seen as cowards or outsiders despite their uninitiated status. Such actions are indicative of adolescents' fierce desire to attain the respect associated with adulthood despite the impossibility of using traditional methods for doing so.

Introduction of New Discourses and Practices of 'Childhood'

For the adolescents in displacement situations in eastern Africa, the ambiguities of adolescence and the challenge to attain adult status are further complicated by the introduction of new discourses about childhood by international humanitarian organisations. In light of different international and regional standards, adolescents under the age of eighteen are categorised as 'children' in need of protection. They are seen as possessing a certain set of rights that international humanitarian organisations strive to realise on their behalf. Such notions are often in contradiction to local ideas about young people in their second decade of life. This has led to much confusion and frustration for many young people who are frequently confronted with contradictory expectations regarding their competencies, roles and responsibilities.

For instance, following initiation ceremonies young males are commonly expected to contribute to and defend their communities through gainful employment or soldiering. Indeed, adolescents often fill the ranks of both rebel groups and state armies, composing a significant proportion of eastern Africa's fighting forces. As soldiers they take on a variety of roles, engaging in direct combat, guarding checkpoints, assisting commanders and conducting military intelligence work. However, in relation to humanitarian interventions, adolescents in displacement situations must regularly recast themselves as vulnerable, dependent children in order to escape legal punishment or gain priority for relief assistance. Furthermore, while young people are, under normal circumstances, expected to perform a considerable amount of productive work and take decisions on certain matters, they are expected by humanitarian agencies to sit in classrooms, usually with children much younger than themselves. Their roles in defending their communities and properties are consistently delegitimised, and adolescents are discouraged from taking part in training or from exhibiting skills that relate to the defence of themselves and their communities. Agencies usually offer services to them only if they are seen as vulnerable, according to such labels as 'unaccompanied children' and 'demobilised child soldiers'. To be sure, I am not intending to endorse the involvement of children as soldiers here, many of whom are forcibly recruited by organisations such as the Lord's Resistance Army (LRA). Nevertheless, I believe it is important to remember that many young people engage in these activities not only because they are forced by circumstances, but also because they feel that such involvement offers them a sense of independence that they desire in becoming an adult. Unfortunately, many humanitarian agencies have only worked according to their own values and outlook on 'children' and have not acknowledged such complexity in the roles and desires of adolescents.

For those categorised as 'child soldiers', demobilisation processes can be particularly challenging as disarmament during war often works against a boy's claim on the ideal masculine status of an adult. As a southern Sudanese man explained:

> It is unthinkable for me to pick up a weapon and fight when my young grandson is around. It is his duty to contribute what he can to the struggle ... I cannot see what he shall do staying in the village. That [staying in the village] is for girls and for boys younger than four years (Interview conducted by author in Akot, southern Sudan, 1999).

That many adolescents must deny or repent their involvement in activities considered honourable and respectable by their communities in order to access relief assistance is a source of much confusion and frustration for the young people. I have witnessed this situation in refugee camps in Ethiopia, Kenya, Sudan and Uganda.

A similar conflict in expectations of adolescents' roles and responsibilities occurs with the introduction of modern education systems among displaced populations. While education through traditional initiation ceremonies is lost or curtailed, formal 'Western-style' education has become an important component of humanitarian assistance and an integral aspect of life for young people in many refugee and internally displaced person (IDP) camps. Emergency education programmes emphasise the importance of young people's attendance at school, and suggest radically different standards for successful personal development. Along with the proliferation of primary and secondary schools has come a great stress upon the value of formal academic achievements among populations with no prior exposure to educational services. As a result, educational achievement has gradually become a measure of young people's maturity. This, of course, stands in stark contrast to more traditional indicators of maturity, including successful passage through initiation ceremonies, marriage and mothering for girls and work in the fields or other gainful employment for boys. Increasingly, adolescents are finding it necessary to redefine their future goals and aspirations, and postpone traditional social roles and responsibilities to fit those dictated by modern education systems. In many cases, this poses a direct threat to adolescents' identity and self-esteem, since school is often perceived to be only for young children, thus making a return to the classroom a step backwards from initiation and adolescents' pursuit of adult status.

Destruction of Family and Community Ties

Conflict and displacement not only affect the ways in which 'adolescence' as a life phase is imagined and structured but also undermine the ties that bind young people to family and community. In ideal circumstances, attachment to community is developed through processes of socialisation and initiation that involve the inculcation of established values. In many conflict situations, however, the destruction of families, communities and traditional rituals often means that adolescents miss out on engagement with the established processes through which a sense of group belonging is developed. Moreover, due to severe economic problems some parents may push their children to take responsibility for supporting their families even through behaviour that would previously have been considered unacceptable. Military forces can take this further, exploiting the poverty and the breakdown in social relations experienced by young people to draw them systematically into extreme acts of violence unacceptable to the norms of society. The most obvious recent example in eastern Africa is Rwanda, where early recruits to the Interahamwe particularly included young men displaced by war and rural poverty living near the capital Kigali. As Alison Des Foges has reported:

> Authorities first incited attacks on the most obvious targets – men who had acknowledged or could be easily supposed to have ties with the RPF – and only later insisted on the slaughter of women, children, the elderly, and others generally regarded as apolitical. ... the 'moral authority' of the state swayed them to commit crimes that would otherwise have been unthinkable (Des Foges, 1999: 14).

Given the weakened social fabric, armed groups often assume a central role in socialising displaced adolescents, raising them to contribute to their cause. During the conflict in southern Sudan, for example, some 15,000 adolescent boys were sent by their families to the Pignudo refugee camp in western Ethiopia. Many of these families were convinced that their children would have a better future if they were reared and educated by the SPLM (Sudanese People's Liberation Movement). These boys learned to follow routines and instructions given to them by the SPLM and indeed learned such valuable skills as building their own huts and schools while receiving military training. In another example, many war-affected adolescents in Ethiopia and Eritrea[1] were gathered in institutions by the government or liberation fighters, where they were accommodated and provided with education and some kind of vocational skills training. In general, they were given relatively higher standards of upbringing than those outside such institutions. At the same time, they are often taught to define themselves as either the children of the government or of the liberation fighters and are consistently exposed to war propaganda as part of the encouragement to replace their fallen 'relatives' in the armed struggle.

Practical Challenges to Subsistence and Survival

Although boys and girls face different challenges, they both struggle for survival and subsistence in ways specific to their life phase and different from young children or adults. Satisfaction of nutritional needs during adolescence is very important, and the consumption or lack of certain food items is believed to seriously impact both the physical and the psychosocial development of adolescents. However, conflict-induced displacement has often made it difficult for adolescents to meet their most basic subsistence needs. For example, milk, fish and butter occupy a central place in celebrations among the Oromo people in Ethiopia, and are considered among the most important food items for southern Sudanese adolescents. However, the conditions created by displacement in this region have made it particularly difficult to obtain such items.

Also, boys in displacement situations face enormous challenges to show their bravery by hunting and fishing, as they are expected to do by convention. Hunting and fishing are often impossible for refugees due to restrictions set by host governments. Even when such activities are allowed, competition for meat and fish is fierce, and local populations often have better access to the sources of such items.[2] Furthermore, customs surrounding food preparation have also undermined adolescent boys' ability to satisfy their subsistence needs. For instance, southern Sudanese boys are traditionally taught to express their needs for food only to close female family members, specifically mothers and aunts, and are restricted from engaging in food preparation. As a result, unaccompanied adolescent boys living in refugee camps in Kenya and Ethiopia lack the necessary skills for preparing their own food. In addition, since food preparation is strictly reserved for females, boys are usually embarrassed to perform such tasks, and often wait until after dark to cook to avoid being seen. In general, many refugee boys do not know how to ration their food or eat at appropriate times and may sell their food in order to buy cigarettes, sweets or alcohol, only to go hungry later.

For adolescent girls in eastern Africa myriad practical challenges exist during war and displacement. Under normal circumstances, they are expected to provide support for their communities, particularly men, elderly people and boys. During situations of conflict-induced displacement, the burdens they are expected to bear usually increase immeasurably. Often, girls take responsibility for keeping their families together, caring for younger children and incapacitated adults, and supporting them financially through income-generating activities. In particular, those girls who arrive in refugee camps as unaccompanied minors face enormous difficulties.[3] Due to their perceived vulnerability, most unaccompanied girls were quickly placed by their communities with families so that they could be cared for. In reality, however, many girls are required to spend most of the day preparing food and doing other household chores for large families upon whom they depend for subsistence. Many girls have reported leading difficult, unhappy lives, especially since they could not access the support of their own extended families. This emerged, for example, in a survey on foster care and alternative arrangements conducted in Kakuma refugee camp in Kenya, in 1994/95.

Coping with the Challenges of Transition to Social Adulthood

As I have described, adolescents in many locations across eastern Africa face numerous problems and challenges arising from conflict and displacement. Some of these are of an immediate, practical nature but many others relate to existential issues: questions of social status, group belonging, values and aspirations. I now turn to describing some of the key coping strategies that young people have employed in order to address these challenges to their physical, socio-economic and psychological well-being. As I shall explain, none of these are without problems of their own.

Joining a Religious Community

Displaced adolescents – particularly those living without immediate kin – have become involved with the religious groups active in many of the camps in eastern Africa. For example, in Kakuma camp in Kenya young Sudanese refugees have dropped out of school to spend time in church. Their devotion to church activities is frequently very strong, in some cases bordering on fanaticism. In the midst of an uncertain social landscape, these new converts to Christianity can certainly benefit from gaining an avenue to community belonging through the church groups. However, in many of such groups the adolescents are required to adopt values or behaviour different from those upheld by older generations within their original communities, often explicitly rejecting familiar beliefs and practices. For example, traditionally they may have gods such as birds or clouds. Membership of such church groups often involves the conscious rejection of the gods that they used to believe in. In almost all cases, the young participants change their names to biblical names, such as John, Mary, Luke, and so on. This poses challenges in many ways, particularly for reuniting the children with their families.

International Migration

Many adolescents have been sent away from war-torn areas of eastern Africa for safety or to get an education and a lucrative job with which to support their families and clan members back home. This has been particularly noticeable in Somalia and Somaliland from where large numbers of adolescents were sent to Europe. However, there is often a significant contradiction in the expectations placed upon these young people. For example, while they are often expected by their families and communities to uphold tradition in terms of adhering to dress codes, religion and conventions governing social interaction, they are also expected to adjust to life and achieve success in the cities of Europe and North America, where secularism, autonomy and an individualistic orientation are prized.

Likewise, while they are seen by their communities as adults upon whom the future of their family and clan depends, these same adolescents on arrival in the host countries find themselves labelled as 'unaccompanied minors'. As such, they are often swept up into complex national systems of protection and rehabilitation, according to which they are often treated as vulnerable and in need of adult support and supervision. These conflicting demands and expectations – to act as mature adults and work to satisfy the economic demands of their communities and to be vulnerable children in need of assistance – has proved to be difficult for many adolescents abroad to reconcile.

In addition, many of the adolescents who leave their country in search of safety and protection abroad and reach their destinations through involvement with smugglers and traffickers face a serious identity crisis as they are often given new identities in the smuggling process, including new names, addresses and areas of origin. Throughout eastern Africa individual names are of great importance. They are expressions of the wishes of parents and are commonly used to define individual personality and recall significant ancestral or communal events that took place around the birth of the child. Most adolescents strictly adhere to their new identities for fear that exposure of the truth will jeopardise their status in the host country. However, when everything in their new environment is already so unfamiliar, adjustment to these new identities may be particularly difficult for these young people, as they suggest a complete break from all that is known and familiar to them.

The contradictions and challenges not only pertain in the countries of asylum but also exist in their 'home' for those adolescents who return and seek to reintegrate in their original communities. For example, research that I conducted in Somaliland in 2003 revealed that many of the returning youth experienced rejection and discrimination by local people. In the view of locals they were guilty on two counts. First, they had not delivered the expected material benefits. Secondly, they had lost their culture and identity. As one young man reported: 'This morning, when we arrived to attend a meeting, a group of young girls told us to go back to where we have come and take our bad ways with us. They said that they have no use for us here, and that we have become Christians' (Tefferi, 2003: 14).

According to some studies, the problems of rejection by the home community may be particularly acute for adolescent females, as they often carry especially heavy burdens of meeting the social expectations regarding acceptable attitudes and behaviour (Ayotte, 2002: 8). Furthermore, the differences between the norms of the home and host communities for young women are often far greater than those for young men, and this makes their reorientation and reintegration process all the more challenging.

Military Recruitment

In certain well-known cases – notably the LRA in northern Uganda – children and adolescents have been forcibly and cruelly recruited by different factions in the armed conflict. Nevertheless, it would be misleading to assume that all recruitment of adolescents has occurred in this way: there are still many situations in eastern Africa where young people have engaged with military groups in the absence of such coercion. It is, therefore, important for efforts at prevention to understand the reasons for recruitment.

First of all, in the midst of weakening family and community structures, adolescents tend to perceive that joining a fighting force may offer them better opportunities to fulfil their social and psychological needs – such as the need to be seen as worthy and capable individuals with access to resources and power. For males, engagement with fighting forces tends to provide opportunities to attain the 'masculine' status that is much prized amongst peers. For others, social and economic stagnation and the loss of educational opportunities lure them to military recruitment. In such a situation, peer pressure usually plays a significant role in stimulating the desire to enlist. Adolescents who are separated from their families and have moved out of their communities tend to succumb to peer pressure more easily. For their part, those who recruit adolescents often do so by promising them social power and economic opportunities that are lacking in their communities.

As increasing numbers engage with military groups for extended periods of time, military involvement may become a normalised aspect of growing up – one further potential dimension of the reconstructing of 'adolescence'. At the same time, it is important not to assume that military recruitment is necessarily and always at odds with existing values and practices in young people's home communities. Boys in particular are often raised to perceive the passage to manhood as involving the achievement of independence on one hand and the fulfilment of a duty to defend their kin and community on the other. In striving to meet these expectations, it is acceptable and sometimes encouraged for boys to go to places outside their communities. Thus the act of joining fighting forces has a merit at both the individual and social level. In addition, involvement with military groups may offer them a sense of continuity with pre-conflict life that is otherwise not possible in displacement situations. For example, under normal circumstances, Dinka adolescents in southern Sudan name their bulls to express their personal identities. They also compose poetry for them and decorate their horns and body to express their personal wishes, frustrations, likes and dislikes. In a survey of southern Sudanese refugee children in Ethiopia, carried out by Save the Children Sweden in 1998, adolescents reported that they missed their cattle more than anything else.[4] Conflict-induced displacement, however, has denied them this meaningful access to cattle and thereby generated a sense of terrible loss in these young people. In this situation, military groups have been known to compensate for this loss by providing their recruits with proto-weapons – in the form of sticks – to care for. They train their adolescent recruits to treat the sticks as they would their weapons in the future – decorating them, and even sleeping with them at night. In this way, military groups are able to create some form of continuity with the past, or 'home', for their recruits even as they push them away from their peacetime identities and towards a new identification with the armed struggle.

While the reasons to join a fighting force are complex and, in many respects, logical, direct involvement with military groups inevitably carries enormous risks and challenges not only in physical but also in social, psychological and emotional terms. Even with the termination of involvement, problems do not necessarily cease but instead take new forms. Return of former young combatants to life within their families and communities may be fraught with obstacles. Some young soldiers are rejected by their families or co-villagers due to their previous actions. This has been a notable problem for adolescents who were part of the LRA in northern Uganda, even for those who were abducted. Given their acts of extreme brutality – far outside the bounds of acceptability – integration back into the community has often been hard to achieve.

Furthermore, even when former combatants are allowed to return home, their experiences may hinder a successful re-engagement with community life and the regular activities associated with the individual's age and social status. The story of China Keitetsi from western Uganda illustrates these difficulties. Having escaped from Museveni's National Resistance Army, China returned to her mother's home and a new set of challenges:

> I could not really feel at home there, it seemed as if everybody in the village was sloppy, never knowing what to do, and always talking before thinking. Despite that, I wanted to stay, but people failed to recognize me as the one I wanted them to see. I believed that I was above any civilian, making me to have the final say, but no one seemed willing to let me … I was looked upon as a mad kid, I was marked, which somehow 'closed the case' for me. No one seemed able to help me, but of course, I never asked for any (Keitetsi, 2004: 146–47).

Ultimately, the contradictions between a civilian life and the life that she had experienced as a soldier proved to be too great to reconcile:

> Suddenly I realized that I would have to start all over with my life, if I wanted to make it. But there was no turning back, because I saw my childhood long

gone. I realized that I simply didn't fit into this community, being a small girl with a vast military experience. I hardly knew anything but the ways of a soldier, so I decided to restart, as a recruit (Ibid.).

For adolescent girls, the process of reintegration can be additionally fraught with specific challenges. For instance, some live as 'bush wives' – a practice particularly associated with the LRA. They are often treated as the property of army commanders, and are required to perform household chores while contributing to the armed struggle. Despite the crucial role they play during conflict, girls are generally not recognised as part of the armed forces and are thus overlooked in reintegration and rehabilitation pro-grammes. Many bush wives also bear the children of their captors and are exposed to HIV/AIDS and other sexually transmitted diseases (STDs). Though for some mothers their children are a source of emotional support, for many others they are the reminders of their terrible experiences. Adolescent girls in this situation and their young offspring are thus often extremely vulnerable psychologically and socially.

Final Thoughts

Clearly, there are numerous reasons why the processes involved in moving into adulthood are subject to change in many parts of the global South, including eastern Africa. Urbanisation, the growth of globalised mass media and the HIV/AIDS pandemic are some of the contemporary phenomena that are shaping the ideas and practices associated with 'adolescence' as a distinct life phase. My aim has been to show how, in many settings in eastern Africa, conflict and displacement have also impacted negatively upon the traditional processes through which young people reach towards adulthood. Nevertheless, while conventional sources of support and guidance may cease to function, and established initiation practices are suspended, the concern of young people to achieve adulthood will inevitably endure. From this perspective, migration, membership of religious groups and military recruit-ment may promise alternative means for young people to attain respected adult status. However, as I have suggested, young people who migrate, join religious groups or enlist face further challenges. Not only is their immediate well-being put under threat, but they may still encounter direct opposition to their claims on full adult membership of home communities as a result of their experience.

Rather than recognising these challenges, humanitarian agencies have often, unwittingly, created additional problems for adolescents. Lack of attention to the specific situation of those in late childhood – their roles, responsibilities, aspirations and competencies – has often given rise to interventions that are experienced as belittling and disempowering for the very young people they wish to help. Given the findings I have discussed in this chapter, I believe agencies need to engage more deeply with conventional ideas and practices, thereby helping to create support for processes that enable young people to achieve effective transition into adulthood. To be sure, a complete 'return' to the pre-conflict/displacement way of life is likely an unrealistic goal. Nevertheless, with due sensitivity and a flexible attitude, outside actors could enable the development of new processes that ensure that the current generation of young people is equipped to construct lives as the adults they wish themselves to be.

Notes

1. In Ethiopia, many displaced adolescents were taken into the Children's Amba, a large-scale orphanage for children of fallen heroes. Something similar occurred in Eritrea, where refugee children and the sons and daughters of freedom fighters were placed in the Zero School – a revolutionary 'boarding school behind the lines'.
2. Indeed, in a study conducted among displaced Ethiopian adolescents, they identified the lack of sufficient food and clothing as a major factor influencing their well-being.
3. Generally, there are far fewer unaccompanied girls in refugee camps than boys. For example, in 1989, the Pignudo camp in Ethiopia was home to roughly 15,000 unaccompanied southern Sudanese boys, and fewer than 100 unaccompanied girls.
4. It is common practice to name a child after a particular bull that is given as a dowry to a wife's family.

References

Ayotte, W. 2002 *Separated Children, Exile and Home-country Links: the Example of Somali Children in the Nordic Countries.* Copenhagen: Save the Children Denmark.

Des Foges, A. 1999 *Leave None to Tell the Story: Genocide in Rwanda.* New York: Human Rights Watch.

Keitetsi, C. 2004 *Child Soldier.* London: Souvenir Press.

Tefferi, H. 2003 *Review of Model Integration and Voluntary Return, Vocational Skills Training and Alternative Basic Education Projects in Somaliland.* Copenhagen: Save the Children Denmark.

2

Doing Nothing and Being Good: Social Relationships and Networks of Support among Adolescent Congolese Refugees in Dar es Salaam

Gillian Mann

In 2003, it was estimated that almost one million refugees were living in Tanzania, most of whom had fled the ongoing civil conflicts in Burundi and eastern Democratic Republic of Congo (DRC).[1] The large majority of these displaced people live in the western part of the country, where Tanzanian government policy requires all refugees to live in camps or settlements. A very small number of refugees are given permission to live in Dar es Salaam, a city of approximately three million on the Indian Ocean coast. Permits to live in the city are usually granted on a short-term basis, for educational, medical or security reasons. In an effort to discourage refugees from settling in urban areas, the Tanzanian Ministry of Home Affairs does not grant refugees the right to work, except in very exceptional circumstances. While some individuals and families with permits are given financial assistance from UNHCR, nearly all refugees in Dar es Salaam are left to fend for themselves in an environment where tolerance and generosity towards 'foreigners' has diminished in recent years. Once world-renowned for its compassionate acceptance of refugees (and still impressive by most standards), the people of Tanzania have grown weary as a result of the nearly continuous influx of people from the Great Lakes region over the past thirty years.

These settlement policies have helped Tanzania to confine its refugee population to the western border regions. However, given the sheer magnitude of their numbers and the diversity of ways to enter the country, it is difficult for the government to monitor the movements of refugees once they enter Tanzania. Because the city is seen to offer improved opportunities for security, employment, education and personal freedom, many refugees choose to travel to Dar es Salaam to live illegally. Some come directly from their home country, without passing through the official registration procedures. Others leave the refugee camps and make their way to the city, where they may hope to connect with family or friends, or to continue on a longer journey to other destinations, such as South Africa. Still others come with permission to remain for a specified period, but choose to stay after their permit has expired and to live clandestinely. The majority of these urban refugees appear to be men between the ages of twenty-five and forty years of age. However, there are also women who migrate to the city on their own, as well as significant numbers of single- and two-parent families who come with biological, related and unrelated children. Some boys and girls also journey to Dar es Salaam without adults, sometimes in the company of siblings or peers and at other times entirely on their own. It is the situation of these children and families that has not been examined, and has rarely been acknowledged, by academics, practitioners and agency officials.

Given that most refugees live without the documentation required for legal residence, it is extremely difficult to establish how many actually live in Dar es Salaam.[2] There are no specific urban areas, no 'little Bukavu' or 'little Goma', where refugees have settled alongside one another. On the contrary, people are dispersed across the city's numerous neighbourhoods.[3] Many conceal their national identity, preferring instead to live as 'Tanzanians'. These 'strategies of invisibility' (Malkki, 1995) are employed by adults and children in a deliberate effort to live as unobtrusively as possible. Fear of imprisonment, deportation or being forcibly sent to the refugee camps causes most to mistrust Tanzanians, Tanzanian authorities, international agencies and, often, other refugees.[4] The complex and multifaceted nature of the conflict in DRC has meant that those who have fled the war are not always fleeing the same source of persecution. As a result, some of the refugees in Dar es Salaam are seen to be allied with particular political factions, and tensions and mistrust between these individuals and others is not unusual. Furthermore, competition between refugees is common in Dar es Salaam, perhaps because of the scarcity of resources available to them. The result for many is a clandestine existence characterised by a lack of social, emotional and material support. Most have few people to help them with the considerable challenges associated with a life in which poverty, illness, fear and isolation are common. Since many families feel that they have nowhere to turn for assistance, household members come to rely on one another in new and unfamiliar ways. Relationships change and intensify, often in ways that are uncomfortable and challenging for both parents and children. This intensification of relationships happens in adolescent-headed households as well, where fear of exposure is often so great that children are compelled to undertake responsibilities that they feel are beyond their capacities.

The purpose of this chapter is to explore these household relationships and networks of support among Congolese refugees in Dar es Salaam. Its particular focus is on younger adolescents (boys and girls between the ages of ten and fifteen years) and the significant role they play in the provision of emotional support and advice for their parents, especially their mothers. The majority of boys and girls are not comfortable with this role and believe that it is a responsibility that they should not have to shoulder. Most do not want to 'carry [their] parents' worries'. They want to feel protected from their parents' problems. But, in the absence of a reliable social network, adults often feel that they have no one to turn to for emotional support besides their children. This chapter explores how the specific circumstances of exile for Congolese refugees in Dar es Salaam have transformed relationships between parents and children and between children, adults and peers. It also examines the potential implications such a life may have for the emotional, social and cognitive development of boys and girls in this context.

Methodology

The research discussed in this chapter was conducted in Dar es Salaam in 2001 and 2002. Given the illegal and clandestine existence of most urban refugees in Tanzania, issues of trust were paramount. Relationships with children and families were formed slowly, over a period of approximately one year. 'Snowball' and opportunistic sampling methods were employed, in which refugee adults and children were continually introducing me to others.[5] During this period, I came into contact with more than seventy-five adults and one hundred children. Of the approximately forty children whom I came to know on an individual basis, twenty were children who live apart from their parents or customary caregivers.[6] The often extremely difficult situation in which these children live meant that it took a great deal of time to gain their trust and that of their guardians and other adults and children in their lives.

The research methodology was designed to accommodate the sensitive and time-intensive nature of the study. The aim of the research was to collect in-depth qualitative data from a small number of boys and girls, guardians and others in order to better understand the experiences of children in this context. Research was conducted in both French and Kiswahili. Participant observation, interviews, group discussions and child-focused participatory methods were used, both with individual children and with groups. Tools included games, drawing, role play, photography, mapping, ranking, storytelling, singing, radio workshops, and other exercises. Most often, research activities took place at people's homes, and sometimes they involved individual children and at other times I worked with groups of children in a household. At all times, efforts were made to learn about relationships between children and between children and adults, either in the domestic setting or in Saturday workshops held in different parts of the city. Interviews and informal discussions were also held with parents, guardians and other non-parental adults in a variety of circumstances. Staff of refugee- and child-serving agencies were also interviewed. Few verbatim quotes are used in this chapter, as it was often inappropriate to take notes in the course of interviews, conversations and exercises. Instead, it was necessary to write these immediately following informal and formal research activities.

At the beginning of the research process, an advisory group of five children was established in order to guide the design and implementation of the study. Three boys and two girls between the ages of thirteen and sixteen, with representation from Congo, Burundi and Rwanda, came together once every two weeks to explore research questions, to discuss and modify research tools, to verify information already collected and to plan their own research activities. The team worked together to design their own methods for working with children between the ages of six and nine years; after piloting, they conducted research with other refugee children who had recently arrived in Dar es Salaam. The insights provided by these young people has been instrumental to the research and in helping to develop the ideas explored in this chapter.

Daily Life in Dar es Salaam

When refugee children and adolescents are asked what life is like in the city, typical answers include: 'We are always hungry'; 'We are very poor, poorer than before'; 'We don't go to school'; 'We are always sick'; 'We have no mat to sleep on'; 'Our clothes are shabby'; 'We cannot get help for our problems'. These difficult conditions are a reality for nearly all refugee families in Dar es Salaam, who struggle on a daily basis to meet their requirements for food and shelter. Many families eat only once, or sometimes twice, a day. Several of the children who participated in this research suffer from intestinal parasites and varying levels of malnutrition. Health care is prohibitively expensive and many refugees say that they cannot access care without bribing service providers (many Tanzanians make the same claim). Rarely do families have the resources required to pay for transport to a clinic, consultation fees and the costs of prescription drugs or hospital care. Most families live in cramped conditions, and it is common for up to eight or more people to share one small living space. Boys and girls and men and women of different ages may be required to sleep in the same small room, a practice that most Congolese adults would frown upon in almost any other context.

The right of access to education is also denied to many Congolese refugee children living in Dar es Salaam. Even when families are able to hide their national identity in order to enrol their children in school, inability to pay fees, fluctuating family finances and the opportunity costs associated with school enrolment mean that many children and adolescents spend their days at home or doing small jobs in the neighbourhoods where they live. Some refugee children do not attend school because of the perceived social costs associated with participation in the Tanzanian education system. Parents and guardians sometimes fear that a child will betray the family's refugee identity to teachers or principals, who in turn may report them to the authorities or use the knowledge for blackmail. Even those refugees who have permission to live in the city share these concerns because they fear that their legal status can be revoked at any time and therefore any interactions with the Tanzanian authorities or UNHCR are seen as potentially dangerous. The perceived need to avoid any bureaucratic entanglement whatsoever[7] overrides the strong belief held by many that education is essential to changing their predicament.

Those refugee children who do not attend school tend to spend their days engaged in a variety of domestic and income-generating activities. There appears to be a marked division in the activities of boys and girls in these circumstances, although the allocation of responsibilities depends to a large extent on the birth order of the child, the number of children in the household and whether or not a child is being fostered. In general, from the age of six or seven years, girls take on increasing levels of responsibility for childcare, cooking, cleaning, collecting water and other household chores, such as caring for an elderly grandparent or a sick adult in the household. By the age of eleven or twelve, a girl may be almost exclusively responsible for these tasks, especially if she is the eldest female child and her parent(s) or guardian(s) are out of the house for long periods in search of employment or assistance. She may also contribute money to the household through braiding hair, sewing or engaging in transactional sex with older men, among other activities. School-going girls are also involved in these domestic and income-generating tasks, although the duration of their participation and the amount of their responsibility are not usually as great. Boys, too, contribute to the household economy by running errands, collecting water and contributing to childcare tasks when required. However, most boys' responsibilities start in earnest around the age of eleven or twelve, when they begin to assist their parents or guardians in petty trading, such as through selling peanuts and other roadside items, used clothing and Congolese *vitenge*.[8] Others work on their own, providing laundry service for neighbours, hauling sand for local contractors or selling sweets outside school playgrounds.

Despite spending days filled with chores, many non-school-going boys and girls between the ages of seven and thirteen often speak of doing 'nothing' all day long. Days spent with children such as Véronique, thirteen, and Mélanie, eleven, enabled me to catalogue an extensive list of their activities. In the first two hours of the day alone, activities included washing cooking pots and plates from the last evening's meal; waking, bathing and dressing their three younger siblings; building a small cooking fire in the compound; preparing porridge and feeding siblings; collecting water and heating it for use in washing clothes; cleaning and hanging laundry; sweeping the compound; preparing the iron with hot coals and ironing yesterday's laundry; carrying, rocking and soothing baby sister Alice, and entertaining younger siblings Yannick and Gloria through song, dance and games. The entire day was spent in near-constant activity, requiring varying levels of energy. The only breaks Véronique and Mélanie had were when they ate and bathed themselves and when they interacted with me. Their drawings, daily activity charts and journal entries substantiated these observations. Over time, I have come to understand the complex of factors that led these and other children to describe themselves having done 'nothing' all day long. First, many adults and children in this context (and elsewhere) conceive of out-of-school time in terms of idleness, especially time that is spent within the household setting (see Reynolds, 1991). Secondly, when Véronique and Mélanie and others say that they have done 'nothing' all day long, they also mean that, for financial or security reasons, they were unable to leave home, to see friends or to visit family members elsewhere in the city. These are the activities that give them pleasure and that they describe as interesting and fun. Days spent solely in the domestic sphere are the norm for many of the Congolese refugee boys and girls who participated in this research.

Fear, Mistrust and Harassment

Congolese refugees of all ages describe their life in urban Tanzania as one of social exclusion, discrimination and harassment. These feelings are common for young children, adolescents and adults in a variety of circumstances. Despite their near-constant efforts to conceal their identity, it is not unusual for the people I know to walk down the street and have a Tanzanian adult or child call out to them, '*Wakimbizi! Wakimbizi!!*'. This Kiswahili term for refugees is widely considered to be derogatory, because the public conception of a refugee is that of an idle beggar who lives off the generosity of others. In the opinion of a ten-year-old girl, 'Even a poor man or a thief is better than a *Mkimbizi*'.[9] Many endure similar insults and mockery on the bus, in the school playground and in their neighbourhood. Young children describe being reduced to tears on a regular basis and say their lives are 'miserable' because they can 'never feel at ease'. Adolescents are equally hurt by such behaviours, as one thirteen-year-old girl commented, 'I feel very bad when I am told that I am a refugee'.

Humiliating and degrading experiences such as these do little to encourage refugee children to reach out and form friendships with Tanzanians. In fact, many Congolese boys and girls in Dar es Salaam are taught from a young age, or learn from experience, not to trust those beyond their household and/or family. The pervasiveness of this attitude struck me one day when I was with a ten-year-old girl and her eight-year-old sister near the city centre. Together with the girls, I asked a stranger on the street for directions to the place we were looking for. When his instructions turned out to be incorrect, the ten-year-old turned to me and said: 'You must never believe Tanzanians'. This young girl, like many of her peers, had come to feel that Tanzanians could not be relied upon for help, even for something as simple as directions. While parents are often surprised by the comments children make in such circumstances, boys and girls know about and respond to the profound sense of suspicion that underlies the relationships between many refugees and Tanzanians and between many refugees themselves. Most learn early on to keep secrets and not to trust others. Throughout this research, I observed children declining to speak to ostensibly friendly, enquiring adults, and listened as others instructed their siblings in the art of evading strangers' simple questions. In a culture where children speak when spoken to, these small acts of resistance are symptomatic not only of the fierce desire for self-protection, but also of deeply ingrained suspicion and fear.

Most often, boys and girls learn to trust their own instincts and to withdraw quietly in the face of negative interactions with Tanzanians. For example, Hélène, fourteen, told me of an encounter that she had on a minibus on her way to work braiding hair. She described how a friendly man in his forties struck up a conversation with her. Initially, she felt okay about talking with him and said that she enjoyed the chance to be out of the house and to be 'free' to interact with others. Soon the man began to ask her questions about herself, and Hélène became nervous. She said she started to give vague responses to his very direct questioning and this behaviour frustrated the man, who became quite aggressive in his questions. 'You're not from Dar es Salaam, are you? Where is your home?' he asked her. 'Kigoma', she answered. 'Which part of Kigoma?'. 'Kigoma town', she replied. He looked quietly at her for a few moments before he said in a loud voice, 'You're a refugee, aren't you?' Hélène looked away from him and from all of the eyes on the bus that had turned to look at her. As she silently looked out of the window, the man began a long diatribe on the ungrateful, greedy refugees who have taken over Tanzania, destroying all the good land and cutting down all the trees. 'Driver', she called out quietly, 'Next stop please'.

Hélène's efforts to remain quiet in the face of unkind treatment from an adult male are understandable given the power dynamics and the public nature of this interaction. But, when children have been treated badly by other children, they do not always withdraw and turn the other cheek. Sometimes they respond by verbally abusing or physically fighting with those who have insulted them. While retaliation may offer a child the momentary satisfaction that defending oneself can bring, fighting back has its costs. Because of their clandestine, or at least unobtrusive, urban existence, many refugee families try to have minimal interaction with unknown Tanzanians in an effort to reduce their perceived chances of being reported to the authorities. In this respect, refugees recognise the power of Tanzanian citizens to destabilise their already fragile existence. Consequently, when a refugee child has a conflict with a Tanzanian peer, refugee parents and guardians see this occurrence as a grave threat to the safety and security of their family. Despite the adults' view on the legitimacy of the child's actions, the child will often be punished in order to emphasise the potentially disastrous consequences to the family should the Tanzanian child tell his or her parents that they were in a fight with a refugee. The result is that the child is often angry and resentful of the perceived injustice of being punished for defending an identity that they have been raised to be proud of. These sentiments are often coupled with a sense of disillusionment with parents and guardians for failing to support them in doing so. Sophie, thirteen, clearly articulated the frustration she felt after her father heard her yelling at a Tanzanian neighbour who regularly taunted her for being a refugee. He did not offer her the support she wanted. Instead, he angrily insisted that she understand that she is Congolese 'inside the house' and Tanzanian 'outside the house'. 'But I cannot be both. It isn't right', Sophie told me.

This sense of being unfairly treated is further exacerbated by the choice of punishment the child receives: parents and guardians frequently respond to such incidents by restricting the already limited mobility of the children in the household. This action is taken in an effort to minimise future potentially negative interactions with Tanzanian children. Punishment might include not being allowed to leave the house, or only being allowed to leave the house in the company of an adult household member. It might also mean being refused the ability to go to school and being forced to remain at home all day. These measures are often more severe for children who live with extended or unrelated families. For boys and girls in these circumstances, membership of the household may be more tenuous. Guardians may be particularly harsh with them because actions that jeopardise the safety of the family may be seen not only as careless but as an affront to their generosity and an indication of a lack of gratitude on the part of the child.

When parents and guardians feel that the security of the family is particularly at risk, all children in the household may be required to stay at home. Children are clear that such limits on their personal freedoms are excessive and cruel. Adults, on the other hand, do not see any alternative and believe that such actions are necessary protective measures. In the course of this research, I met several children as old as twelve years who had gone several months, and in one case two years, without leaving the small part of the neighbourhood in which they lived. I met one ten-year-old boy who, in a period of twenty-four months, had gone no further from his home than the kiosk that was fifty metres across the road. Congolese refugee boys and girls describe this isolation as one of the worst parts of their lives in Dar es Salaam, because, despite the sometimes cruel treatment of peers and others, it is the activities of playing with friends and going to school that provide children with what they see to be the few pleasant distractions in their life of exile. The absence of these happy events compounds their discontent and dissatis-faction, not only with life in general, but more specifically with what they see to be a lack of good judgement on the part of those who care for them. These negative sentiments are again aggravated by the feeling many children (especially boys) have that education is the only way to escape their current circumstances, and that, by denying them the right to attend school, their parents or guardians are condemning them to a life of misery. While adults view their actions in such situations as the only means of preserving the security and stability of their families, these measures may inadvertently undermine inter-generational relationships, thereby reducing the familial strength and sense of collective unity they had originally sought to maintain.

As a consequence of these and other actions, many Congolese refugee boys and girls in Dar es Salaam have few opportunities for social interaction beyond the household level. Even when opportunities to meet others do present themselves, the feelings of mistrust and fear of exposure are often so ingrained that some children remain withdrawn from others. Nearly all children who participated in this research who were able to remember their lives in DRC commented that they have fewer friends in Dar es Salaam than they did at home, and that their relationships with peers in Tanzania are rarely intimate. Indeed, many of these boys and girls had very little experi-ence of making friends and often lacked confidence in their interactions with other children and adults.

Many authors argue that friendships are among the central ingredients in children's lives from as early as age three through adolescence (Rubin, 1980; Hartup, 1996; Corsaro, 2003). They argue that the developmental signifi-cance of friendships in childhood and adolescence should not be under-estimated, as friendships occupy, both in reality and in the worlds of thought and fantasy, a large proportion of children's waking hours (Rubin, 1980). Children who have friends have been shown to be more sociable and self-confident than those who do not (Garmezy and Rutter, 1983). Close relationships with peers provide cognitive and social support on a daily basis and thus serve a protective function for children, especially those who are living in stressful situations (Sandler et al., 1989). For a lot of refugee children in urban Tanzania, limited mobility and fear of exposure mean that they lack many of the developmental opportunities associated with having friends. They have few chances to interact and play with others, to share experiences, to feel empathy, to agree and disagree, to negotiate with one another and to support one another in the achievement of shared tasks. While children can learn from their parents and siblings how to develop these skills in a specific environment – the hierarchical household – it is from interaction with peers that they can learn to relate to others in a wide range of social situations. Opportunities to practise and therefore develop these crucial life skills may be particularly important for younger adolescents because this develop-mental period is considered to be the time when children begin to reach out to adults and peers and to develop extra-household networks of support (Savin-Williams and Berndt, 1990). The implications for many of the refugee children who participated in this research are serious: without the opportunities to learn these skills, to develop supportive relationships with peers and others, the isolation these boys and girls feel will only magnify and the interpersonal competencies necessary for successful social relations will be even more difficult to acquire.

The additional child development implications of this isolation are considerable. The lack of intellectual stimulation offered through schooling and extra-curricular activities, if not provided elsewhere, can affect a child's developing cognitive capacities. The inability to explore and discover the world around them may delay the development of context-related problem-solving skills. Furthermore, children's lack of opportunities to play and interact with a variety of people of all ages may inhibit their ability to make future relationships. These are skills that require practice; they are competencies that are learned through good and bad experiences, through perseverance and through making mistakes. For refugee children, they are skills that are particularly important because displacement has meant, in some cases, the complete disconnection and loss of long-term relationships and support systems. For children who live without adult care or without the attention of loving adults, and especially for those whose parents have died, the re-establishment of relationships with peers and supportive adults is essential to the dismantling of the isolation and loneliness expressed by many boys and girls in this context.

The child protection implications of the seclusion of many refugee children are equally significant because it is extremely difficult to become aware of the needs and circumstances of those boys and girls who live in such situations. Monitoring and care for children's needs become the sole respon-sibility of those people with whom the child lives. Yet all families, regardless of their circumstances, need the support of friends and others to meet the needs of the children under their care. Furthermore, assistance may be impossible to provide for those children who may be in abusive situations. Moreover, the vulnerability of such children may be augmented by their lack of the skills and confidence necessary to form stable and trusting relationships with those who might be able to assist them. Equally if not more significantly, many of the children who participated in this research are not learning the essential skills of self-protection – skills that in their own country would be considered vital for full maturation into adulthood. Under these circumstances, how can they become 'proper' Congolese adults if they can't learn such life skills?

Changing Inter-generational Relationships

Lacking networks of extra-household support many children come to rely on their parents for assistance that, under different circumstances, they might have sought elsewhere – from friends, teachers, aunts and uncles, neighbours and others. This reality was made clear to me one morning in a discussion with a non-school-going thirteen-year-old girl from Bukavu, eastern DRC, whom I had visited countless times over our ten-month acquaintance. In the midst of washing her younger siblings' clothes, she told me that she and her fifteen-year-old sister were being sent to Kigoma to live with their paternal aunt. When I asked her if she had told anyone else that she was leaving, she said no, that she had no one to tell: 'I am alone here. I have no one to share secrets with'. When I followed up by asking her who she talks with when she feels sad, she said she keeps her feelings to herself most of the time but that she sometimes tells her mother. 'What does she say?' I asked. 'Nothing', she responded. 'What can she do? She has her own problems. She says she can't help me'.

Many children described similar efforts to enlist the emotional support of adults. Most felt strongly that, while their parents loved them, they were simply unable to cope with the additional burden of listening to their child's problems. More importantly, perhaps, was the widespread view of older adolescents that parents were not the most appropriate people to turn to for assistance of this kind. In a workshop with girls and boys between the ages of twelve and eighteen, it was unanimously agreed that friends were the first people to turn to when faced with a problem. If friends were unable to assist, then an uncle or aunt, neighbour or teacher could be approached (whom a child turned to for support depended in part on gender, age, birth order and the structure of their social network). Parents were an absolute last resort because, in the opinion of one fifteen-year-old boy, 'they cannot and do not want to hear our problems. But sometimes we have no choice'. Similar notions of parents as inappropriate providers of emotional support, especially in times of stress, have been found among Yao adolescents in Malawi (Mann, 2003b) and Abaluyia children in Kenya (Weisner, 1989). Because there are no ethnographic data on the lives these Congolese refugee children led before they and their families were displaced to Tanzania, it is difficult to know to what extent displacement itself can be assumed to have changed children's and parents' support-seeking behaviours. Further enquiry with adults and children is needed to explore notions of what it means to be a child and a parent in Dar es Salaam and how these ideas and their daily reality are different from people's experiences, both real and imagined, of life in Congo before they fled to Tanzania.

Congolese boys and girls who live in Dar es Salaam without adults are also conflicted about the need to seek advice and support for their problems. This is especially the case if the children have recently arrived in the city and are receiving assistance from UNHCR or from a family member abroad. In both of these situations, children may be approached by concerned adult refugees who want to help them to adjust to their new environment. While these individuals may be guided by the best of intentions, the children who participated in this research said that they feared such people were trying to take their money from them. Teenaged boys with younger, adolescent sisters commented that offers of assistance from adult males were particularly suspect, in part because the girls may be wanted for sex. Most children were torn between wanting to reach out to have the advice and emotional support of an adult, while at the same time fearing that they would be taken advantage of if they did so.

This struggle is particularly problematic for such children because they have even greater levels of responsibility than their peers who live with adults, and yet they have no one to share them with, regardless of how minimal this support may be. Most boys and girls in this position do not even have the potential for assistance with things such as school fees or medical bills. Their monetary and labour contribution to the household is all that there is – when they are sick, for example, they often do not eat because they cannot earn the money required to purchase food. For those children who care for their younger siblings in such situations, their inability to work and perform household tasks such as cooking and cleaning means that others suffer as well. The pressure on boys and girls in this context is extreme.

One family of children who participated in this research includes a fifteen-year-old boy, his twelve-year-old sister and their four-year-old niece. These three children live together in a small room in a high-density area of the city. Each day, the boy tries to find money to feed his sister and niece and pay the rent. He sometimes manages to get piecework on a construction site or to earn a small amount by guarding the car of a local taxi driver. While he is out, his sister looks after their young niece. Because he is very frightened that the Tanzanian government or UNHCR is going to find them and force them to go to a refugee camp, he does not allow his younger sister and niece to leave the courtyard around the house unless it is absolutely necessary. As a result, both girls are entirely dependent on their brother for social, emotional and financial support. This situation is nearly unbearable in the eyes of the boy: 'What choice do I have? I am fifteen years old. I do not know how to raise these girls. I do not know how to look after them. I can take care of myself but I cannot take care of them. Sometimes I do not know what to do. Without me, they would have no food to eat, no place to sleep. But what can I do?'

Such despair at not knowing who to turn to for support is also felt by those children who live as 'guests' with related and unrelated carers. For boys and girls who are experiencing high levels of discrimination and harsh treatment within their guardians' household, it is often very difficult to know what to do. Some children fear that by 'complaining' to others about their living situation, this information will make its way back to their guardian, who will either treat them more cruelly or expel them from the household. Most children in such circumstances have nowhere else to go and the considerable risks associated with confiding in others are usually outweighed by the fear of being left entirely on their own. Most would never consider approaching UNHCR because of their illegal status and the profound fear that they will be forced to go to the refugee camps, which, despite their lack of first-hand knowledge of these places, are widely seen as horrible, unsafe and unsanitary backwaters where individuals have no personal freedom and no control over their own lives. Camps are described as 'prisons' and many children (and adults) believe that ending up there is the worst thing that could ever happen to them. They think that going to the camps means that they will die before ever seeing their family members again. Coupled with this unimaginable outcome is the extreme fear that they will be made to live with a foster family, whose treatment, the children believe, may be even worse than the status quo. Stories circulate about the mistreatment and exploitation of children who have been formally fostered in camps (as opposed to having been spontaneously 'taken in' by relatives or others with whom a previous relationship has been established). Paradoxically, this all-pervasive fear effectively results in depriving them of the right to services such as family tracing and other child protection interventions that are not made available to undocumented refugees.

'Carrying Our Parents' Worries'

Refugee life has affected the social support networks of adults as well as children in Dar es Salaam. Because they feel they have nowhere else to turn, many adults have come to rely on their children for new and different levels of support. The extremely difficult financial situation in which many urban refugees find themselves has led some adults to do things that they would never before have imagined, such as begging for food, selling sex and sending their children out 'to find money', whatever way they can (and without asking questions later about how this money was actually acquired). One fifteen-year-old girl in Dar es Salaam expressed her anger at her mother, who regularly sent her out at night to make money for the family but who never took ownership of the fact that this meant her daughter had to sell sex to feed the mother and siblings. The girl described the hurt and shame she felt when she returned from an evening out and handed her earnings to her mother, who sometimes said nothing and sometimes commented on the small amount of money her daughter had earned.

These difficult interactions between parents and children reflect in part the fear and loss of confidence many adults feel in relation to their ability to care for their families in this context. The ramifications of retaliation against harassment and abuse are perceived to be so severe that many adults suppress their anger and remain quiet in the face of insulting treatment from neighbours, strangers or people in positions of authority. One eleven-year-old girl recounted an incident in which an angry neighbour began shouting at her mother because she had partially obstructed the entrance to the neighbour's home. In a very loud voice, the man repeatedly accused the girl's mother of being a 'useless *Mkimbizi*' who should 'go back to where she came from'. Throughout his tirade, the mother stood nearby, while silently crying and burying her head in her hands. After listening to this attack for several minutes from inside the house, the girl poked her head out the door and reminded her mother of the potential danger of such a public conversation by saying several times, 'Mama – immigration! ... Mama – immigration!' Finally, in the midst of the man's attack, she went outside and led her mother back into the house, where the daughter continued to console her mother.

Such incidents and others like them are not unusual for many refugees in Dar es Salaam and their impact on parent–child relationships is significant. From the perspective of the Congolese refugee boys and girls who participated in this research, protecting and advising their parents is a major consequence of being a refugee child in urban Tanzania. Some of the adolescents involved in this study were resentful of their parents or guardians for imposing their problems on them. Furthermore, several spoke of feeling frustrated and angry when they witnessed or heard about incidents in which their parents had not defended themselves in the face of insulting and degrading treatment. In some cases, including that of the woman who was being insulted by her neighbour, children argued that they had lost respect for their parents because life in Dar es Salaam had made them 'weak', 'unmotivated' and 'unable to stand up for themselves and their family'. These views were strongly articulated by a fifteen-year-old boy whose parents, since arriving in Dar es Salaam, have tended to stay at home all day while their four oldest children move about the city in search of piecework or money or both. The lack of motivation on the part of his parents is particularly difficult for this boy to accept because in DRC his mother and father had both been employed in high-status positions. At home, he said, they would never have allowed him to work instead of going to school, let alone have forced him to drop out entirely. He told me that recently he had grown very tired of his parents' inaction and that most of the time he is so infuriated with them that he contemplates running away and setting up a home of his own. But he tempered these comments with an assertion that he would never leave his family, 'because that is all I have'.

Many parents and guardians are aware of these changes in the nature and content of their relationships with their children. Some spoke of feeling uncomfortable with their reliance on their children, including the mother of the girl mentioned above, who said she often feels incompetent in the face of the challenges of life in Dar es Salaam. Such feelings of inadequacy on the part of parents and guardians are not unusual and can often lead to great frustration and stress on their part. As parents and guardians struggle to assert their power and influence over those they feel reliant upon – their children – household tensions tend to increase. One sixteen-year-old girl, whose family has a permit to live in the city, spoke of the dread she feels whenever she hears that her father is going to visit UNHCR to find out the status of his family's refugee claim. She said that these visits are so frustrating for her father that when he returns home he is inevitably extremely angry, and that this anger is usually taken out on his children: 'Anything we say or do makes him furious and he will yell at us and tell us that we are always behaving badly and that we are making the family's situation worse and causing our parents to suffer. He might beat us for a small thing that he would usually not care about'.

The rage directed towards separated boys and girls in this context can be particularly acute. Children living in related and unrelated households often bear the brunt of their guardians' frustration. Accusations that such children are 'more trouble than they are worth' and that they are aggravating the family's poverty are not uncommon. One thirteen-year-old boy said that, when angry and discouraged, the wife of his older brother would often tell him that it was because of him that the family is in such a terrible situation: if he did not live with them, she would angrily comment, then their documentation would be much more straightforward and they would have no problem getting assistance from the government and refugee-serving NGOs. She would tell him, 'It is all your fault, you do nothing to fix the problem! You just stay at home and eat our food and ask for school fees and money for sweets'. This boy reported that beatings were common under these circumstances and said that he would try to stay as far away as possible from his sister-in-law whenever he sensed that she was in a dark mood. Many children in Dar es Salaam reported this need to tiptoe around their guardians in order to avoid such confrontations. Similar efforts have been described by separated children in Liberia and Rwanda (Tolfree, 2004).

Managing Relations with Parents and Guardians

The refugee boys and girls who participated in this research were very aware of the significant pressures and anxieties under which their parents and guardians were living in Dar es Salaam. Many tried to reduce these stresses in the best way they knew how – through not only 'carrying their parents worries' and protecting them from negative exchanges with others, but also through their behaviour and direct interactions with them.

One of the ways that children try to minimise the impact of their parent's or guardian's stress is by causing as little trouble as possible. This strategy of trying to be the 'good child' is regularly employed by nearly all of the refugee children whom I came to know. While many boys and girls use this approach, it is employed especially by separated children, who describe the need to be as 'good' as they can be in order to avoid being verbally attacked or beaten by their guardians. 'Being good', they say, means trying never to complain, never to misbehave, never to ask for anything, never to do things without permission and trying to be as unobtrusive as possible. It also means being cheerful and helpful and doing household tasks without having to be asked. When children do not follow these guidelines, parents and guardians may become enraged because they perceive the child's misbehaviour as an additional burden that they do not have the energy to deal with. In those instances where the child's misconduct involved or was apparent to those outside the household, adults may also feel that the child has threatened the safety and security of the family. Most separated children living with related and unrelated guardians and some refugee children living with their parents described the discipline they receive under such circumstances to be very harsh and 'too much'.

Some children learn to be 'good' when their parents or guardians are nearby and to take their frustrations and anger out when adult household members are not present. Such strategies were described to me by a young Congolese woman who provided me with her insights and experiences throughout the research process. As the eldest of seven siblings, including one young cousin, she commented that she had come to believe that children are very 'wise': when they are in the presence of their parents, they behave well and do not react to the insults or degrading treatment of others, especially neighbours. But, in the case of her family, when her parents are away from home, sometimes her siblings are very aggressive with those who have insulted them. They may yell or spit at the perpetrators, or they may hit them or threaten them with physical violence. Some of the other children I know also behaved in similar ways. For example, one thirteen-year-old girl frequently told me of the physical fights she had to break up between her ten-year-old sister and other children in the neighbourhood. Another ten-year-old separated girl would often have brawls with her eleven-year-old cousin with whom she lived. In all of these cases, the children involved would keep these activities entirely secret from their parents and guardians because of the known consequences of their actions. While it is particularly important for separated children to be 'good', biological children are also expected to cause as little trouble as possible. It was rarely in the interests of the biological child, therefore, to report such incidents to his or her parents because of the perceived importance of never adding to their stress.

Conclusion

Recent research in human development stresses the links between adolescent well-being and the availability of meaningful opportunities for young people to contribute and feel connected to the community in which they live (Pittman, 1996; Resnick et al., 1997). Access to systems of support, the importance of close, positive and lasting relationships and a sense of being valued are all considered factors essential to healthy adolescent development (Feldman and Elliott, 1990; Leadbeater and Way, 1996). For young Congolese refugee adolescents living in Dar es Salaam, their illegal status means that such opportunities are rarely available to them. Most have to exercise extreme caution in their interactions with others. They learn from a very young age to be suspicious of others and this lack of trust impacts on their abilities to form and sustain relationships with peers and adults. They have few opportunities for social interaction beyond the household level, and are effectively denied the right to leisure, recreation and cultural activities. Many girls and boys spend long periods 'doing nothing', by which they mean being confined to the household and not interacting with their peers. This reality is especially common for separated children, who are more likely to spend their days within the domestic sphere and less likely to go to school, and whose significant workload tends to limit opportunities for play. Some live without the protection of any family and have to fend for themselves and care for younger siblings or relatives. Most serious of all, many boys and girls have no access to support outside of the family, and sometimes receive none within it. The child development implications of this isolation are considerable.

The importance of context in understandings of childhood and adolescence must not be underestimated. The circumstances in which the majority of urban Congolese refugee families live have changed the nature of the relationships between many children and parents. Tensions have arisen as a result of the new roles that each has had to take on. Because they feel they have nowhere else to turn, parents come to rely on their children for emotional support, a situation that most dislike and yet feel helpless to change. Young adolescents feel conflicted because they want to assist their parents but often feel overwhelmed by, or resentful of, the need to 'carry the worries' of the older generation. The result of these changing relationship dynamics is an increase in household pressures and the feeling of many young adolescents that they are caught in the middle: they are expected to be mature enough to provide their parents with advice and significant emotional support but are not granted the freedoms that usually accompany these responsibilities, such as the ability to leave the house without permission. The situation of refugee children in Dar es Salaam is but one example of how the social, cultural, economic and political environment in which young people live affects not only where, with whom and how they spend their time but also who they are and who they will become.

Acknowledgements

This research was conducted with the generous support of the Refugee Studies Centre at the University of Oxford, the Andrew W. Mellon Foundation and Save the Children Sweden under the Tanzania Commission for Science and Technology Research Permit Number 2001-283.
Parts of this chapter are drawn from Mann (2002, 2003a).

Notes

1. http://www.unhcr.ch/cgi-bin/texis/vtx/home/opendoc.pdf?tbl=MEDIA&id=40c6d7730&page=home.
2. The official statistics of the number of urban refugees in Dar es Salaam provided by UNHCR and the Government of Tanzania are inaccurate. Throughout the course of this research, I asked representatives of the Tanzanian government, NGOs, multilateral agencies and refugees themselves to estimate the numbers of refugees living in the city. Estimates varied from 100 (interview 4DAR01) to 10,000 (interviews 11DAR02, 12DAR02) to 40,000 (interview 5DAR01) to 100,000 (interview 7DAR01); estimates given by authorities tended to be at the low end and those given by refugees at the higher end. Those who study African refugees have long argued that official statistics of refugee populations should be regarded with caution and some have argued that as many as half of African refugees have never been counted or registered, preferring instead to settle unofficially in the rural and urban areas of their host country (Sommers, 2001: x). No matter which estimates are considered accurate, it is clear that there are

significant numbers of urban refugees in Dar es Salaam whose circumstances are not yet acknowledged or understood. It is my hope that the debate around numbers will not become yet another stumbling block to addressing the very real problems faced by this population.

3. During the first year of this research (2001/02), I encountered refugees in twenty-six different neighbourhoods of Dar es Salaam.
4. Careful attention has to be paid to the real and perceived threats to security of refugees in this context. In carrying out my research and in writing this chapter, I have deliberately chosen to withhold information that might jeopardise the situation of the families and children whom I know in Dar es Salaam. The irony is that people's consent to their involvement in the research is principally a result of their desire to inform the rest of the world of their situation.
5. This method of meeting people through the introductions of others has also been used with illegal refugee populations in other contexts: for example, MacGaffey and Bazenguissa-Ganga (2000) employed snowball sampling in their research with Congolese in Paris, as did Sommers (2001) in his research with Burundi Hutu living illegally in Dar es Salaam in the early 1990s. In fact, MacGaffey and Bazenguissa-Ganga (2000) argue that this is the only way to do research with people living outside the law.
6. Such children are often deemed 'separated children'.
7. Malkki (1995) and Sommers (2001) describe similar efforts on the part of Burundi Hutu refugees in Kigoma and Dar es Salaam. MacGaffey and Bazenguissa-Ganga (2000) also noted these strategies among undocumented Congolese living in Paris.
8. *Vitenge* are stacks of brightly coloured cloth. The *vitenge* made in DRC are much admired among Tanzanians.
9. *Mkimbizi* is the Kiswahili word for refugee (singular). *Wakimbizi* is the word for refugees (plural).

References

Corsaro, W.A. 2003 *We're Friends, Right? Inside Kids' Culture.* Washington, DC: Joseph Henry Press.
Feldman, S. and Elliott, G. (eds) 1990 *At the Threshold: the Developing Adolescent.* Cambridge, MA: Harvard University Press.
Hartup, W.W. 1996 'The Company They Keep: Friendships and Their Developmental Significance', *Child Development* 67: 1–13.
Garmezy, N. and Rutter, M. (eds) 1983 *Stress, Coping and Development in Children.* New York: McGraw-Hill.
Leadbeater, B.J.R. and Way, N. 1996 'Introduction', in B.J. Leadbeater and N. Way (eds) *Urban Girls: Resisting Stereotypes, Creating Identities.* New York: New York University Press, pp. 1–12.
MacGaffey, J. and Bazenguissa-Ganga, R. 2000 *Congo–Paris: Transnational Traders on the Margins of the Law.* Indianapolis: Indiana University Press.
Malkki, L.H. 1995 *Purity and Exile: Violence, Memory, and National Cosmology Among Hutu Refugees in Tanzania.* Chicago: University of Chicago Press.

Mann, G. 2002 '"Wakimbizi, Wakimbizi": Congolese Boys' And Girls' Perspectives on Life in Dar Es Salaam, Tanzania', *Environment And Urbanization* 14(2): 116–22.
—— 2003a *Not Seen or Heard: The Lives of Separated Children in Dar es Salaam.* Stockholm: Save the Children Sweden.
—— 2003b *Family Matters: The Care and Protection of Children Affected by HIV/AIDS in Malawi.* Stockholm: Save the Children.
Pittman, K.J. 1996 *Preventing Problems or Promoting Development: Competing Priorities or Inseparable Goals?* Baltimore: International Youth Foundation.
Resnick, M., Bearman, P., Blum, R.W., Harris, K., Jones, J., Beuhring, T., Sieving, R., Shew, M., Irelnad, M., Bearinger, L. and Udry, J. 1997 'Protecting Adolescents from Harm: Findings from the National Longitudinal Study on Adolescent Health', *Journal of the American Medical Association* 278: 823–32.
Reynolds, P. 1991 *Dance Civet Cat: Child Labour in the Zambezi Valley.* London: Zed Books.
Rubin, Z. 1980 *Children's Friendships.* Cambridge, MA: Harvard University Press.
Sandler, I., Miller, P., Short, J. and Wolchik, S. 1989 'Social Support as a Protective Factor for Children in Stress', in D. Belle (ed) *Children's Social Networks and Social Supports.* New York: John Wiley and Sons, pp. 277–305.
Savin-Williams, R. and Berndt, T. 1990 'Friendship and Peer Relations', in S. Feldman and G. Elliott (eds) *At the Threshold: the Developing Adolescent.* Cambridge, MA: Harvard University Press, 277–307.
Sommers, M. 2001 *Fear in Bongoland: Burundi Refugees in Urban Tanzania.* Refugee and Forced Migration Studies, Volume 8. Oxford: Berghahn Books.
Tolfree, D. 2004 *Whose Children? Separated Children's Protection and Participation in Emergencies.* Stockholm: Save the Children Sweden.
Weisner, T. 1989 'Cultural and Universal Aspects of Social Support for Children: Evidence from the Abaluyia of Kenya', in D. Belle (ed) *Children's Social Networks and Social Supports.* New York: John Wiley and Sons, pp. 70–90.

3

Growing Up in Exile: Psychosocial Challenges Facing Refugee Youth in the United States

Kenneth E. Miller, Hallie Kushner, Jill McCall,
Zoë Martell and Madhur Kulkarni

Introduction[1]

Much of what is known about the mental health effects of political violence and forced migration on children and adolescents comes from cross-sectional studies assessing symptoms of psychological distress (Arroyo and Eth, 1986; Kinzie et al., 1986, 1989; Ajdukovic and Ajdukovic, 1993; Hubbard et al., 1995; Mghir and Raskin, 1999; Thabet and Vostanis, 2000; Smith et al., 2002). This approach has contributed significantly to our understanding of the patterns of mental health difficulties that are seen, to varying degrees, among refugee youth. We know, for example, that trauma symptoms such as nightmares, intrusive memories of traumatic events and insomnia, often develop among youth exposed to political violence, although there is considerable variability in the severity and persistence of such trauma reactions. Roughly speaking, there seems to be a 'dose-dependent' relationship between exposure to violence and the development of trauma symptoms: that is, greater exposure to violence generally predicts trauma that is both more severe and more enduring. It is noteworthy, however, that elevated levels of psychiatric symptomatology do not necessarily equate with impaired functioning among refugee youth. Despite experiencing numerous symptoms of trauma and depression, young refugees may nonetheless function quite effectively in various domains (Kinzie et al., 1989).

Importantly, recent studies have moved beyond the rather narrow focus on assessing the direct effects of violence by examining factors that either mediate or moderate the effects of violence and displacement on children's mental health. Such studies have advanced our understanding of the pathways by which violence and displacement affect young refugees' mental health, and of the factors that either protect refugee youth or increase their psychological vulnerability. We know, for example, that adolescents who have lived through extreme violence in their homeland may be at least somewhat protected from developing clinically significant levels of distress if they are able to remain together with family members during the resettlement process. In contrast, unaccompanied minors who end up living alone or with foster families appear to be significantly more vulnerable to developing enduring symptoms of depression and psychological trauma (Kinzie et al., 1986, 1989).

Despite the contributions made by psychiatric assessments of refugee youth, a reliance on cross-sectional, symptom-focused methodologies is not without its limitations. An exclusive focus on assessing symptoms of psychological distress implicitly reduces children's mental health to nothing more than their relative degree of psychiatric symptomatology. Such a narrow definition ignores other domains of young people's psychosocial well-being, such as the nature of their social functioning with family members and peers, the quality of their self-esteem, the development of a coherent sense of identity and their capacity for academic achievement. Data regarding the prevalence of psychiatric symptoms, though certainly important, tell us little about how refugee youth are functioning in other psychosocial domains such as these, domains that are essential to a more holistic view of child and adolescent mental health than those implicit in most assessments of psychiatric symptomatology. A holistic approach can provide a richer, more comprehensive – and thus more accurate – depiction of the myriad ways in which young people respond to, and are affected by, their experiences of violence and displacement.

The study on which this chapter is based was designed to address this empirical gap, by using semi-structured interviews examining the psychosocial challenges facing children and adolescents from four refugee communities in the United States – Vietnamese, Cambodian, Afghan and Iranian.[2] This exploratory study was designed to examine a set of interrelated questions, including:

- How do refugee families talk (or not talk) about their experiences of political violence and flight?
- How are children and adolescents affected by these narratives, or patterns of communication, regarding their family's history of violence and forced migration?

- How are youth affected by, and how do they cope with, parental distress related to experiences of war and exile?
- What are the most important challenges that refugee families, and refugee youth in particular, face in adapting to life in the United States?
- What coping strategies and resources do refugee families, and refugee youth in particular, utilise to cope with these challenges?

We opted to use a retrospective design, in which we interviewed young adult participants about their experiences growing up, because we believed that young adults would be ideally situated to reflect on the period of time in which we were interested, namely, late childhood and adolescence. Having recently emerged from adolescence, they would be able to identify changes over time in family dynamics, the kinds of challenges they had faced as children and later as adolescents, and the range of coping strategies and resources they had utilised over time to cope with those challenges.

Given our interest in the psychosocial challenges faced by young people growing up in refugee families, coupled with the dearth of empirical literature in this area, we felt it more appropriate to use a methodology that would permit participants to identify for us the most salient aspects of their experience – that is, the stressors that had most affected them, as well as the coping strategies and resources they and their families had used to manage those stressors. In addition, we wished to explore the ways in which refugee families communicate about their experiences of political violence and forced migration: the narratives that families develop as a way of making sense of and coping with their experiences of violence and displacement. Consequently, semi-structured interviews, which are specifically designed to elicit narratives, seemed an ideal choice both for learning about family narratives and, more broadly, for examining psychosocial challenges and the ways in which participants and their families had coped with them. This chapter examines the salient challenges faced by youth growing up in refugee families; a subsequent manuscript will examine the coping strategies and resources used to overcome those challenges.

Method

Participants

Participants in the study were recruited through flyers posted at several universities in the San Francisco Bay Area, as well as through the snowball method, in which individuals who have been interviewed are asked to identify other individuals who might be interested in the project. We used the following inclusion criteria: (1) participants had to be between the ages of eighteen and thirty-five; (2) they had to have been born in the U.S.A. or come to the U.S.A. with their families by the age of twelve; and (3) their families must have fled their homeland because political violence had made it unsafe to remain there. The findings reported in this chapter come from interviews conducted with forty individuals, including ten participants from each refugee community. Mean ages for the four groups were: Vietnamese, 23.6 years (SD = 2.67); Cambodians, 21.2 years (SD = 2.3); Afghans, 26.1 years (SD = 3.4); and Iranians, 29.5 (SD = 4.0). There were an equal number of females and males in each group, with the exception of the Cambodian sample, which had six men and four women. These four refugee communities each have a significant presence in the Bay Area (and throughout California).[3]

The Interview

The interview, available on request from the authors, covered several domains including: demographics; knowledge and sources of knowledge regarding the family's reasons for going into exile; memories of violence and the journey of exile; family communication during childhood and adolescence regarding the violence of the past and its impact on family members; perceptions of how parents had been affected by their experience of violence and displacement; the quality of family communication generally when participants were growing up; participants' sense of ethnic identity; significant challenges faced by participants' families and by participants themselves in adapting to life in the U.S.A.; and coping strategies and resources used by participants' families and by participants themselves to overcome those challenges.

Procedure

Participants were interviewed by the first author or by graduate students trained in qualitative interviewing. The interviews took place either in participants' homes or in the research office of the first author. Interviews were conducted in English and typically lasted one to two hours. No a priori decisions were made regarding matching interviewers' and participants' gender; however, participants were asked whether they preferred to be interviewed by a male or female. All interviews were tape-recorded and transcribed, and consensus coding was used to ensure agreement regarding assigned codes. This entailed two team members using a code-book to code each interview independently, and then meeting together with a senior team member to compare their coded interviews and reach consensus on any discrepant codes.

Brief Background of Each Refugee Group

Vietnamese

In the wake of the United States' military withdrawal from South Vietnam in 1975, Vietnamese fled their homeland by the hundreds of thousands, hoping to avoid persecution and possible execution, religious discrimination and the loss of previously held status and freedom. By 1995, nearly half of the two million Vietnamese refugees had resettled in the United States, forming large ethnic communities in several metropolitan areas of the United States. These communities have played an essential role in maintaining Vietnamese culture, as well as providing a setting for the sharing of both material and emotional social support (Manh Hung and Haines, 1997).

Although specific subgroups of Vietnamese refugees remain psychologically vulnerable, there is evidence that many, perhaps most, are doing well psychologically, with initially elevated levels of depression and trauma having diminished over time. In fact, one study of Vietnamese boat people in Canada found that, ten years after their arrival, study participants had evidenced better mental health than non-immigrant, non-refugee Canadians (Beiser, 1999).

Compared with other refugee and immigrant groups in the U.S.A., the Vietnamese have fared well in educational and economic terms. Vietnamese culture emphasises the importance of education, and young people are expected to take their studies very seriously. Interestingly, Portes and Rumbaut (2001) found that, although Vietnamese adolescents were doing well academically relative to other refugee and immigrant groups, their self-esteem was actually lower than that of other groups. Portes and Rumbaut, as well as our own data, suggest that this may reflect an especially strong emphasis on academic success among Vietnamese refugee families, which may come at the expense of young people feeling valued simply for who they are. With regard to social expectations, Vietnamese youth are expected to show deference to their parents and older relatives, to minimise conflict in their interpersonal relationships, and in general to maintain their family's honour.

Cambodians

Cambodia was pulled into the Vietnam war by the massive U.S. bombing of the Cambodian border regions where Vietcong soldiers were believed to be hiding. Several hundred thousand Cambodian civilians were killed, and the massive displacement and chaos created by the devastation helped lay the groundwork for the eventual overthrow of the Cambodian government in 1975 by the Khmer Rouge. By 1979, when the genocidal regime was overthrown by Vietnam, more than one million Cambodians had been killed or had died of illness and starvation during the government's programme of radical social transformation and cultural 're-education'. Cambodians fled en masse during and especially after the fall of the Khmer Rouge, mostly to the massive refugee camps and settlements on the Thai–Cambodian border (Mayotte, 1992; Mortland, 1997).

Approximately 150,000 Cambodians were eventually resettled in the U.S.A. Like the Vietnamese, Cambodians were initially scattered across the country, but soon resettled themselves into larger, more concentrated communities in which resources could be shared and traditions maintained. Many Cambodians have had a difficult time adjusting to life in the U.S.A., however. This is partly due to their more rural, less educated background, as well as to the strikingly high levels of psychological trauma and depression in the community. Like other refugee groups, Cambodians are highly reluctant to utilise Western mental health services, opting instead to rely on traditional healers and Buddhist rituals or simply enduring their distress. Similarly to Vietnamese youth, Portes and Rumbaut (2001) found higher levels of academic achievement combined with lower levels of self-esteem relative to other refugee and immigrant youth.[4] Within traditional Khmer culture, youth are strongly expected to show respect for their elders, minimise overt expressions of conflict, conform to family values and norms, and behave in ways that maintain their family's honour.

Afghans

The exodus of Afghans into neighbouring Pakistan and Iran began immediately after the Soviet invasion in 1979; within a few years, approximately six million Afghans, or a third of the pre-war population of Afghanistan, were living in exile. Although three million of these refugees returned to Afghanistan following the Soviet withdrawal in 1989, the civil war (1992–96) and the destruction wrought by the years of war with the Soviets led many Afghans to remain in exile. The violently oppressive rule of the Taliban (1996–2002) on top of natural disasters have continued to push people into exile (Goodson, 2001; USCR, 2002).

Afghans settled primarily in Washington, DC, Virginia and northern California, where they formed tightly knit communities for whom Sunni Islamic religious beliefs and traditional Afghan values continue to be important sources of guidance for daily life.[5] Although precise numbers are not available, the Virginia and northern California Afghan communities are each estimated at between 30,000 and 40,000 individuals (Omidian, 1996).

Compared with other refugee groups, little research has been done with Afghan refugees in the U.S.A. or elsewhere. Afghans in the U.S.A. often struggle financially, though family members pool their resources, and young adults – who generally remain in their parents' home until they marry – are expected to contribute to the family's income. Many Afghans rely on some form of government assistance, as work has been difficult to find for those individuals with limited formal education, limited English language proficiency, or job skills that do not translate readily into their new setting (Omidian, 1996). Community surveys of middle-aged and older Afghans suggest high levels of war-related trauma in the community, as well as depression related to the loss of social networks, social and occupational roles and other stressors (Lipson et al., 1995).

Nevertheless, anecdotal evidence suggests that many Afghan youth are doing well in schools and young adult Afghans are increasinly pursuing university and graduate-level education. Similarly to Iranian youth, whom we discuss below, young Afghans tend to be rather insular, associating primarily with co-nationals. Afghan adolescents are expected to behave in ways that protect their families' honour. This includes behaving respectfully towards their parents and other adults, working hard in school, dressing appropriately, not cursing, avoiding alcohol, and not dating or engaging in premarital sexual behaviour.

Iranians

Iranians are a somewhat unique refugee community in the U.S.A. Whereas most refugee communities are comprised of individuals who have fled their homeland because of violence, many of today's Iranian refugees originally came to the U.S.A. as students and were living here at the time of the Shah's overthrow in 1979 (Bozorgmehr, 1997). When the Islamic revolution made a return to Iran unsafe or undesirable, many Iranians stayed in the U.S.A. and brought their families over to join them. Officially, many of these Iranians are considered immigrants rather than refugees. The creation of a strict Islamic society in Iran following the overthrow of the Shah led those secular or less religious Muslims who had the financial resources to go into exile. Members of Iran's religious minorities, however, such as Jews and Baha'i, were systematically persecuted under the new regime and were therefore able to come to the US with official refugee status and its corresponding resettlement assistance (Bozorgmehr, 1997). By the early 1990s, over 300,000 Iranians were living in the U.S.A., a sizeable minority of whom had personally experienced oppression. The Iranians interviewed as part of the present study reflect the diversity of the Iranian diaspora: our sample includes Iranian Jews and Baha'i, as well as Iranian Muslims, some of whose families were targeted for violence, and others whose families left to escape the fundamentalism of the new regime.

Relative to other refugee and immigrant groups, Iranians are doing very well economically and professionally. This reflects the highly educated background of many Iranians, especially those who were in the U.S.A. prior to the 1979 revolution. It also reflects the financial resources that some Iranians were able to bring with them when they left their homeland. There is a strong emphasis on academic success, including the pursuit of university education. The community remains fairly insular: Iranians, including Iranian youth, socialise primarily within the community, and marriage outside the community is still uncommon. Beyond these few observations, it is difficult to speak in general terms about the experience of adolescence among Iranians in the U.S.A., because of the significant ethnic variation within the community.

A particular feature of the Iranian experience in the U.S.A. is the degree of discrimination that Iranians have experienced since the American hostage crisis in 1979. American sentiment turned harshly against Iran in the wake of the crisis, accompanied by a significant rise in discrimination against resident Iranians, who were demonised in the popular media. This led, not surprisingly, to acts of physical and psychological intimidation. As we discuss below, although not all Iranians in the U.S.A. have been victims of discrimination, for those who have, the experience has been deeply distressing.

Findings

In this section, we examine five types of psychosocial challenges that participants had experienced as adolescents. These include: (1) dealing with the lingering effects of their own war-related experiences of violence and loss; (2) coping with parental distress related to experiences of violence and loss and to the experience of displacement; (3) managing problematic patterns of family communication regarding the past and its impact on family members; (4) negotiating two worlds: managing the process of acculturation and the development of an ethnic identity; and (5) dealing with discrimination by the host society.

Not surprisingly, there was considerable variation among participants in the salience of each of these challenges. For example, family communication was open and supportive in some families and painfully complicated or stifled in others; discrimination was a distressing reality for several Iranian participants, but was rarely mentioned by members of the other groups; and war-related memories of violence and loss were obviously restricted to those participants who had actually spent time living in their countries of origin prior to coming to the U.S.A.

The data also revealed a variety of resources used by participants to negotiate these challenges. Most common among these were: (1) a supportive parent or other relative with whom the participant could communicate openly about present-day concerns and about the family's experience of violence and displacement; (2) a strong ethnic community, which facilitated the development of a bicultural ethnic identity and decreased the likelihood of exposure to discrimination by American peers (adolescents with a strong ethnic community tended to have less contact with potentially hostile American peers, and stood out to a much lesser extent than participants who lived outside their ethnic community); (3) supportive peers, especially – though not exclusively – from within participants' own ethnic group; (4) school, which provided refugee youth with a stable environment, opportunities to develop competencies (academic, social and/or athletic) and, for some youth, access to gifted teachers who became important sources of support and inspiration; and (5) a 'secret life' outside the awareness of parents, in which adolescents could date and engage in other behaviours such as smoking or drinking while avoiding conflict with parents or other adult relatives.

Dealing with Memories of War-related Violence and Loss

Memories of war-related violence were common and generally very clear among the Iranian and Afghan participants, who had lived through at least some of the violence that had forced their families to become refugees. Memories of violence were much less common among Cambodian and Vietnamese respondents, and those memories that South-East Asians did share with us seemed to be a blend of their own recollections and the stories they had heard from parents and other relatives. This difference among participants in the availability of personal memories of war-related violence reflects the nature of our sample. Participants from Cambodia and Vietnam were either born in the U.S.A. or arrived in the U.S.A. by the age of five. Afghan and Iranian participants, on the other hand, spent a considerable part of their childhood in their homeland, and were thus witness to varying degrees of violence. For Afghans, it was the Soviet invasion and subsequent jihad against the Soviets and their oppressive puppet regime in Kabul; for Iranians, there was the violence of the Islamic revolution itself, followed by the terrible destruction of the Iran–Iraq war. Despite these memories, however, there was little evidence of psychological distress or impaired psychosocial functioning related specifically to the violence that participants and their families had survived.

For many participants, the violence of war was described as a kind of normalised insanity. A Vietnamese woman, one of the few Vietnamese respondents with clear memories of her own of the war, described her experience of violence as 'normal':

> I do remember, I can still smell, because we lived by a mortuary or cemetery.
> So every day, not every day, pretty much every week, someone would die and

then you can smell the hair being burned and we'd walk by all the time and stories of kids being drowned in the stream and you'd see … I still see little kids like young … I think Thai kids who are pretty much isolated from … they're not even part of the refugee camps, with big bulky stomachs. And once in a while you'll hear, 'Oh yeah, he drowned here or he drowned there' and that was a part of growing up for me and it was natural. I mean you get shocked, but this is just everyday life.

Of course, the apparent ordinariness of the war as a backdrop to childhood became profoundly unordinary and painful when it hit closer to home. For one young Afghan man whose father was imprisoned for five years by the communist government, the war meant separation from a beloved attachment figure. It also involved anxious visits to a notoriously brutal prison, with books meant for his father, a university professor, hidden in his clothing. For an Afghan woman, the war meant the loss of her father, killed by the Soviet-installed communist regime. Though she was very young when her father was killed, she remembers waiting in vain for him to come home again:

Once you go through something that devastating, when you're 4 years old – I mean I literally stood in front of my house by the door, for those ten months, waiting for my father to get back home, because I wanted to see him, you know … When you go through those ten months as a 4-year-old, and you don't get what you want, you never see that person again, you just … have to just move on, there's nothing in this world that scares you and intimidates you at all … I had a couple of nightmares about my father in prison … I keep having the same recurring nightmare that he's sitting in an attic and it's really dark and there's a chimney in the attic and I'm sitting on top of the house and I'm reaching my hand in and I can't reach him. He's just sitting in this dark corner, and he's really, really skinny. I still have those dreams of him.

Although this woman continues to experience sadness and occasional nightmares related to her father's death, she is by no means traumatised in any clinical sense; on the contrary, she is a highly functioning, resilient individual who has managed to integrate her experience of loss into her life without either minimising or being overwhelmed by it. Although the death of her father was among the most devastating war-related experiences reported in the study, her resilience in the face of that experience was typical. For example, another respondent, a twenty-seven-year-old Iranian male, lived through the violence of the Iran–Iraq war; although he experienced the war as very frightening, he made clear that the experience did not lead to the development of enduring symptoms of psychological trauma:

I remember in 1985, it was getting so bad they were attacking cities. We were hitting them, they were hitting us. This one night it was the loudest sound I've ever heard. It was kind of close and the sound was so loud you can't imagine. The sky was just orange and everybody was trying to get out. I went and saw the ruins and the building got flattened and a lot of people died, so... Yeah, that's a lot to go through ... I just remember we were at my cousin's house and we just got out so fast that I didn't even put pants on. I just had shorts and we jumped in a car and tried to get out of the city. My aunt and cousins had a summer home so we left to go there because the Iraqis were going to continue their attacks and kill us all [laughs]. It was terrible. That was like the scariest thing that ever happened to me ... I guess it makes you grow up kind of fast. I was probably ten years old. War was going on and it's one thing when you're shooting at each other at the border or where it's not affecting you but, when it comes to the city where you live in, that's a whole different story. It wasn't like a psychological thing that dragged on for a long time. It wasn't like post-traumatic stress. But it was pretty scary. There's no doubt about that.

It may have been the passing of time, the availability of supportive family members, the fact of having got away from the violence by going into exile, or the combination of these and other factors; based on our data we cannot say with certainty why the young people in this study did not experience the kind of psychological distress described in some other studies of refugee youth. It is, of course, important to bear in mind that this is a retrospective study, and it is difficult to know what sort of emotional reactions our participants may have evidenced in the immediate aftermath of their wartime experiences. It is nonetheless noteworthy that, despite their exposure to the violence of war and political repression, the participants in this study no longer found their memories overly distressing. They were able to speak readily of what they had lived through, albeit with moments of sadness when those memories involved the loss of loved ones.

We do not mean to imply that we found no evidence of emotional distress in our sample; on the contrary, several participants were in fact struggling with considerable emotional pain in certain domains of their lives, and many had experienced significant distress as adolescents. However, their distress had far more to do with painful family dynamics that had been altered by the experience of war and exile, than by participants' own direct exposure to the violence of war. This is an important point, since few studies of refugee youth have examined the complex pathways by which violence may exert its impact on young people's well-being. The small number of studies that have assessed the indirect effects of political violence on child and adolescent wellbeing have generally found results consistent with our own – namely, that violence exerts its effects most powerfully by altering essential aspects of social environment, especially the structure and functioning of children's families (Ressler et. al., 1988; de Berry et al., 2003).

Dealing with Parental Distress

Parental distress related to experiences of violence and loss, and to the experience of displacement, was quite common among the families of participants across the four groups, particularly among Cambodians. This is not surprising, given the genocidal nature of the violence from which Cambodians had escaped.

Nearly half the sample reported having felt upset while they were growing up by their parents' psychological distress. For some participants, parental distress took the form of psychological trauma (e.g. recurrent nightmares and other sleep disturbances, agitation, avoidance of any reminders of their traumatic wartime experiences). For example, a twenty-seven-year-old Vietnamese woman recalled having been repeatedly frightened by her father's recurrent war-related nightmares after the family had come to the U.S.A.:

> My father would have nightmares … and all he would say is he was just dreaming about Vietnam. We'd all go back to bed because you could hear him screaming. He just woke up wailing and screaming. My mom just woke him up. He just said that he was dreaming about home and Vietnam and we went to bed after that. That's when I hopped off the bed and went into the other room and slept because that's when I was pretty scared.

Other participants focused on their parents' experience of depression related to the loss of social networks and valued social roles. A thirty-year-old Afghan woman, now a graduate student and community activist, spoke with sadness of her parents' distress, and especially of her father's persistent depression, which she felt helpless to ameliorate:

> My mom cried, she was sad and everything, but my dad, it seemed like the pain was so deep that it came straight from the heart. You could see it in his face. He would just, it was just very deep. It was very hard on him … He has lost a lot of his good friends. Either they were killed by the communists or … he was a very social person. So, right now I see that he doesn't have connection with the people that he loved to hang out with … He gets up in the morning and he doesn't have a job … he gets up in the morning and he's just in his room and he exercises and is writing until he goes to bed.

A twenty-eight-year-old Cambodian man described, with visible sadness and anger, how his mother had fallen into what appeared to be a deep depression coupled with severe trauma, while the family was living in France before being granted asylum in the U.S.A. Her severe impairment, which led to a prolonged hospitalisation, resulted in his being placed in a French foster home for two years.

> I think as a refugee my mother suffered from chills, post-traumatic stress. The French made her work for this company and I think their mentality was, the more she worked, the more she'll forget about what happened. The more she'll be able to put aside the past. She was able to … I guess she worked herself into oblivion at that point and I remember she was committed to a, I don't want to call it a mental hospital, but … I had to live with a French family for two years because she could not take care of myself and my sister.

After sharing this story, he reflected that he struggles with a fear of intimacy in his relationships, and wondered whether he had 'abandonment issues' as a result of being separated from his mother in France.

Parental distress occasionally led to a pattern of overprotectiveness, particularly within South-East Asian families. This phenomenon, which has also been documented in studies of Holocaust families (Danieli, 1998; Felsen, 1998), reflected a parental perception of the world as dangerous, and a desire to keep children safe from that danger. Not surprisingly, however, parental overprotectiveness often had the unintended effect of generating anger and rebelliousness in teenagers, who wanted the increased freedom that adolescence in the U.S.A. normally brings.

Respondents who, as adolescents, had experienced their parents as overprotective, now spoke with a mature understanding of their parents' overprotective behaviour. Nevertheless, it was evident from their comments that parental overprotectiveness had often been the source of considerable conflict and distress. Their understanding and compassion had come later on, when as adults they were better able to appreciate the psychological factors underlying their parents' distressing behaviour. We recognise that parental overprotectiveness is not unique to refugee communities, and has in fact been documented in numerous studies of other youth populations, including both immigrant and non-immigrant children and adolescents. In the case of refugee youth, however, parental overprotectiveness has its roots in the unique interaction of familial experiences of intense violence and persecution (which may lead to a view of the world as a dangerous place) and a fear of children losing their cultural identity (a fear common among immigrant families as well), as well as cultural factors that may lead to highly protective behaviour, particularly towards girls. In addition, it is important to note that some of what may be perceived as overprotective behaviour may reflect realistic parental concerns regarding the level of danger in their neighbour-hood, since some refugee families live in impoverished communities where gang violence, substance abuse and other forms of delinquent behaviour are very common.

In sum, the majority of the participants in this study had been keenly aware as adolescents of their parents' experiences of depression and/or trauma. However, parental distress, though upsetting to witness, was not necessarily perceived as having been harmful to participants' own well-being;

rather, it became problematic only when it disrupted the family's functioning, for example by adversely impacting a parent's ability to function as a caregiver, or by generating fear and confusion among children who witnessed but could not understand their parents' evident anguish.

Family Communication Regarding the Past

There is a rich literature on the mental health of children of Holocaust survivors, which suggests that how survivors communicated about their Holocaust experiences affected children's emotional well-being and ongoing psychosocial development (Danieli, 1998; Felsen, 1998). Three patterns of family communication regarding parents' Holocaust experiences have been identified. The first is what Danieli has referred to as a 'conspiracy of silence', in which parents refused to discuss their experience of the Holocaust with their children, perhaps out of a desire to spare the children from their traumatic experience, and perhaps also to spare themselves the retelling and consequent re-experiencing. For children, this pattern could be very frustrating. Their parents' war-related distress remained hard for them to comprehend, and they often felt cut off from their own sense of identity and family history. The second pattern involves parents over-disclosing their Holocaust experience, without adequate attention to their children's interest in, or capacity to understand and tolerate, the distressing material. For children, this sometimes led to an inversion of roles, in which children became carers of their distressed parents. It also led to children feeling overwhelmed and wanting to gain distance from their parents' (and, by extension, their own) history. Finally, there is a third category, perhaps the most common: this involved parents who were able and willing to share their Holocaust experience, and who do so in a responsive manner. This meant providing information in response to children's evolving interest and, most importantly, their developmental capacity to understand and tolerate distressing stories. For children, this kind of open, responsive communication allowed for a greater understanding of, and thus compassion for, their parents, and a more complete comprehension of their own identity and cultural heritage.

When examining patterns of communication about families' wartime experiences in the present study, a critical task was to understand participants' comments against the backdrop of the normal or expected patterns that exist within each of the ethnic communities. We also felt it was important to consider how perceptions of family communication – both in general and specifically regarding experiences of violence and displacement – had been shaped by the study's participants having grown up partly or wholly in the United States, where they were exposed to diverse patterns of family communication in the families of their American peers and in the media. Towards this end, we paid particular attention to examining the ways in which respondents framed their experiences of family communication in terms of the various cultural influences to which they had been exposed.

A consistent finding across ethnic groups was that participants, female and male, had more open, less conflictual relationships with their mothers than with their fathers. Even within the relatively more open relationships with their mothers, however, most participants noted that communication was considerably less open than they had observed among the families of their American peers. An indication of the extent to which participants' values and expectations regarding family communication had been shaped by their exposure to American culture was the degree of frustration and pain several individuals expressed at the lack of more open and supportive communication within their families, despite recognising the culturally normative nature of their families' patterns of communication. This was particularly evident among participants whose families had come from South-East Asia. For example, a twenty-three-year-old Vietnamese woman spoke with visible sadness at the emotional distance in her relationship with her father, which she initially attributed to linguistic difficulties, but subsequently to an underlying lack of open communication:

> I can speak Vietnamese, but like kitchen Vietnamese. Just stuff that you need around the house. You don't talk about feelings or stuff like that. We don't talk about things. In Asian culture, we don't talk about things. It's like Asians and mental health. You don't talk about it. You don't talk about feelings or stuff like that ... [crying now] ... I don't relate to my father.

Another Vietnamese woman, age twenty-six, described a similarly distant and painful relationship with her father:

> I never – I don't really speak to my dad, even since I was a kid ... He was just like, 'Number 5, go get me that thing ...' I'm like, Okay ... they call you by the number of where you were born. I don't know, I kind of make fun of it. It's kind of traditional, I guess. And also convenient, they don't have to remember your name ... And it undermines you a lot.

A young Vietnamese man talked with sadness about the lack of open communication in his family, and its impact on the quality of relationships among family members: 'There is no real, no I can't say there is real conflict, we're kind of at a very like ... How do I describe it? We're very like, emotionally dead to each other in a way ... Just the whole dynamic of the family' (Vietnamese male, twenty-three).

For a twenty-one-year-old Cambodian participant, it was not so much a lack of open communication that distressed her, but rather what she perceived as the critical and unsupportive nature of her parents' interactions with her, which she compared to what she had observed in the families of her American peers:

> They'll say things that hurt your feelings, but deep in their heart they don't mean it because after they say it they feel really bad. That's the Cambodian way of disciplining your kids. Putting them down, constantly putting them down, and the American way is to encourage, you know, like, 'You're really good at this, go for it. I know you can do it!'

On the other hand, several participants either were comfortable with the less open pattern of communication in their families compared with the families of their American peers or described their families as being very communicative. The following quote, from a twenty-three-year-old Afghan male, underscores the variability within any ethnic community, not only in actual patterns of communication but also in perceptions by members of the same ethnic group regarding what is culturally normative. Other Afghan participants did not necessarily share his belief that 'great communication' is typical of most Afghan families: 'Afghan families traditionally are families in which the parents are very careful about their children and family ties, thanks to Islam. Therefore Afghan families almost always have great communication within the families. Our family is no exception'.

Against this backdrop of cultural norms (and within-culture variation) regarding family communication, we now examine the three patterns that emerged regarding communication within families about violence experienced in the homeland and their subsequent experiences of forced migration. Perhaps most striking was the emotional pain that participants felt who had grown up in families where parents refused to talk about their wartime experiences, despite their children's desire to know and understand. This pattern of restricted communication was experienced as painful and frustrating because it made it difficult for children to understand their parents' distress, and because it impeded the development of their own sense of familial continuity and cultural identity. Interestingly, silence about war and the journey of exile did not necessarily mean poor communication generally; rather, in several families there were well-recognised emotional landmines to be avoided, and those generally involved questions about the past.

A thirty-year-old Iranian woman, asked whether experiences of oppression in Iran were ever spoken about in her family, described with considerable pain her father's difficulty in talking or writing about the past, and its impact on her own sense of identity:

> Not at all ... [crying] ... I'm sorry ... I can't talk ... He said he wanted to, my dad wanted to write his memoirs and he was writing it down for the children because he was going to forget so the grandchildren would have this thing, and he hasn't done it yet ... It makes it really hard to know who you are or where

you came from, when somebody doesn't want to talk about anything that has to do with that or something that's kind of like a big part of you.

In the following quote, a twenty-one-year-old Cambodian woman similarly describes her father's silence regarding the Cambodian genocide as well as her sadness at seeing his pain and her frustration at not being able to learn more about her own history:

> My dad would rather not talk about things. He'd just say, 'Okay, they died. That's it'. You know he'll just say, that's what happens in a war-torn society and he just don't wanna look back. And when I discuss the Khmer Rouge conflict with him or anything about genocide, he just goes, 'Yeah'. And he just turns … it just turns really bad and … he gets very solemn. He takes deep breaths and has to sit down. He doesn't want to go further into the conversation. He'll just change the subject or just walk away or something … It sort of hurts me in the sense that he's my dad and I don't want to see him that way because he's been through a lot; and also makes me appreciate him more because he struggled so hard to get me to America, to bring me here and my sister here. But it hurts me in a way, too, because I really wanna know my history.

The desire to know about their own history, and their frustrated attempts to learn more about it at home, led several participants to search for information outside their nuclear families – for example, from grandparents and other relatives, or through various media such as historical texts and films.

The second pattern was one of non-communication about the past, in which parents and their adolescent children shared a mutual desire to avoid discussions of familial experiences of violence and displacement. Among the participants who described this pattern in their families, there were two quite different motivations. For some, the prospect of seeing their parents experience the pain of remembering violence and loss was itself intolerable. There was a visible pain in their parents' eyes, a reflexive shutting down when the topic of the war was raised, that led participants – as children and later as adolescents – to perceive their parents' psychological vulnerability and their need to avoid distressing memories. For example, when asked whether she had ever spoken with her parents about their wartime experiences, one respondent answered: 'No, because I can't handle the response. If my parents show their true, true self, I think that … I have only seen them strong and they have always been my social support and to see them in that much pain … I know it would just really break my heart' (twenty-six-year-old Afghan woman).

In contrast, other respondents professed a lack of interest in knowing about the war-related violence or persecution their parents may have endured. For these individuals, there seemed little to be gained by reopening old wounds their parents had sought to close; moreover, life in the homeland did not seem relevant to the more immediate challenge of creating a meaningful life in the United States. In the words of a twenty-two-year-old Vietnamese woman:

> I figure, if they want to tell me, they can ... But ... if it's as bad as other stories I've heard, I don't know if they'll want to talk about it. So it's kind of like that ... we don't really press each other for that kind of information ... I'm not that curious. Right now, I guess it's really their own deciding, that all I think about now is what's going to happen, I don't really think about what's happened before ... to me, what's past is past.

Finally, several respondents described a more open pattern of communication, which we call responsive communication. It is responsive because it is tailored to the adolescent's level of interest and developmental capacity to understand. The young Afghan woman mentioned earlier, whose father was killed when she was just four years old, described the enormous value of her mother's responsive communication in helping her make sense of and cope with the loss:

> I think the world of my mom for it. I think if I hadn't been told the truth, if I hadn't been talked to and my mother wasn't open with me, I think I definitely would have ... you know, just would have thought that anybody could just disappear from my life ... But my mom has taken the time to explain to me that 'your father left, your father wasn't with us for a reason bigger than what we are, he was fighting for Afghanistan, he was fighting for all for the right to practise Islam and to be free'. I have friends who, you know, are from Afghanistan, whose parents don't say a thing to them, they just think that they can shelter them for the next eight years. It's just amazing that ... you know, we wanna know, even as little kids we wanna know, of course when you're ten–twelve–fourteen years old you should know what's going on. I consider myself very lucky that my stepfather opens up to me, consider myself very lucky that my grandfather opens up to me.

Consistently, participants whose parents had been responsively communicative with them about the past described having had more harmonious familial relationships and seemed generally more at ease within themselves. We recognise that the term 'responsive' implies a value judgement on our part. Indeed, the data suggest that open or responsive communication was in fact adaptive in this particular context. For these young people, who had spent all or much of their childhood and adolescence in America, and who had been exposed to American cultural norms regarding styles of family communication, there was often a strong desire for open communication with their parents, and a sense of appreciation for those parents who were able to talk with them about their families' experiences of violence and displacement. We cannot say, however, whether such open communication would be either desirable or adaptive for adolescents still living in their families' country of origin, uninfluenced by American cultural values and norms.

Managing the Process of Acculturation and Developing an Ethnic Identity

There are important differences between refugee and immigrant youth. These include the history of exposure to violence among refugee families and its impact on individual and familial functioning. In addition, there are important differences regarding the reasons for, and feelings about, leaving their homeland. Immigrants generally leave in search of a better life, moving towards a dream of a greater income, better health care and education, more personal freedoms, and so on. Refugees, in contrast, generally move away from violence that threatens their physical survival. Their emigration is not the rational pursuit of a better life, but a necessary flight out of harm's way. This difference helps to explain the powerful longing that many refugees harbour to return to their homeland, and their reluctance to accept the possibility of remaining in exile.

Despite these differences, it is evident that in certain respects refugee and immigrant youth face a number of common challenges as they adapt to life in the U.S.A. In this section, we examine two such challenges. The first we have labelled 'Negotiating Two Worlds: Managing the Process of Acculturation' and the second we have entitled 'Between Two Worlds: the Challenge of Developing an Ethnic Identity'.

Negotiating Two Worlds: Managing the Process of Acculturation

A critical challenge for refugee (and immigrant) youth is to find a way of living harmoniously in two very different, and sometimes conflicting, worlds: that of their home and ethnic community, and that of school and the larger world of U.S. society (Tobin and Friedman, 1984; Suárez-Orozco and Suárez-Orozco, 2001). The differences between these two worlds are evident in many domains, including beliefs and rituals regarding dating and sexuality, dress, religion, language, gender roles, respect for parents and other older adults, centrality of the family, the use of alcohol and drugs and career choices.

Refugee and immigrant youth in the U.S.A. universally struggle with these differences. What is critical is not so much the struggle itself, but the ways in which it is handled. Some youth reject their culture of origin and attempt to fit into their host society as thoroughly as possible (e.g. dressing 'American' almost to the point of caricature, speaking only English, and rejecting the values and traditions of their ethnic community). Not surprisingly, this approach – which has been variously labelled as 'assimilation' (Dona and Berry, 1999), 'ethnic flight' (Suárez-Orozco and Suárez-Orozco, 2001) and 'dissonant acculturation' (Portes and Rumbaut, 2001), often leads to family conflict as parents react with hurt, anger and disappointment to their children's rejection of their ethnic heritage, and often to their parents' authority as well. This mode of acculturation is also associated with low self-esteem among refugee and immigrant adolescents (Portes and Rumbaut, 2001), perhaps because it entails the rejection of central aspects of their own identity, and because it generates family discord, thus depriving youth of warm, supportive relationships with their parents.

Alternatively, some refugee and immigrant youth resolve the tension between the competing worlds of home and the larger U.S. society by identifying primarily with the former, sheltering themselves in the familiar world of their family and ethnic community. This approach, which has been called 'separation' (Dona and Berry, 1999), the development of an 'adversarial identity' (Suárez-Orozco and Suárez-Orozco, 2001) and 'consonant acculturation' (because these children acculturate at roughly the same pace as their parents; Portes and Rumbaut, 2001), minimises family conflict but may slow down young people's social mobility and development of cultural competence in their new environment.

Finally, many refugee and immigrant youth opt for a third approach to managing the different, often conflicting, values and behaviours of home and host society: they engage in what has been called 'integration' (Dona and Berry, 1999), the development of a 'transcultural identity' (Suárez-Orozco and Suárez-Orozco, 2001) or 'selective acculturation' (Portes and Rumbaut, 2001). Selective acculturation entails finding ways of embracing and maintaining many of the values of one's ethnic culture, while also becoming proficient in, and comfortable with, the values and behaviours of the host society. Refugee youth who selectively acculturate have, on average, more self-esteem and lower rates of family conflict than their peers who opt for either of the other two modes of acculturation (Portes and Rumbaut, 2001). It is important to bear in mind, however, that these strategies of acculturation are by no means fixed and unvarying; rather, they are often fluid, changing over time as young people move through adolescence and into adulthood.

We also wish to underscore that family conflict within refugee and immigrant families is by no means inevitable, at least no more so than in non-refugee/immigrant families, despite the implication in the clinical literature that such families have elevated levels of conflict due to children acculturating more quickly than their parents. In fact, whether inter-generational differences in rates of acculturation lead to conflict depends on a variety of factors, including the particular mode of acculturation that young people adopt at any given point in their development. To the extent that refugee and immigrant youth adopt either a selectively or consonantly acculturative style, family conflict is likely to be minimal. This is precisely because both modes of acculturation honour traditional ethnic values, something parents are likely to appreciate and support.

The following sections illustrate the experience of participants regarding their struggles with two domains of cultural differences: dating and bilingualism.

Dating

Dating is generally frowned upon in the cultures from which our participants were drawn. This is especially true for girls, who may be expected to retain their virginity until marriage, and whose honour may be perceived as depending on their appropriate (i.e. conservative) behaviour vis-à-vis the opposite sex. For boys, the expectations vary somewhat (e.g. premarital virginity is not an expectation in any of the ethnic groups studied); still, dating is at least overtly discouraged among boys from South-East Asian and Afghan families, and dating outside of one's ethnic group is viewed as taboo across all of the groups. That said, it was quite evident that most of the participants in our study did in fact date, and had done so beginning in late adolescence; moreover, several had dated outside their ethnic group. With few exceptions, participants told us that they had always kept their dating experiences secret from their parents, and often from all but their closest friends. Although Western-trained family therapists generally emphasise the value of open communication in families, this rather secretive approach to dating played a highly adaptive function, in that it allowed youth to minimise family conflict while still enjoying the experience of dating:

> I've had boyfriends and I've dated people, but I just haven't told my parents. That's something that I choose not to share with them because I don't think they're open-minded to that at all (Twenty-year-old Cambodian woman).

> My dad would not, he would never let me have any boyfriends, and he would expect me to be a virgin until I'm married. I'm living with my boyfriend now, so – he doesn't know that (Twenty-one-year-old Cambodian woman).

> Well, no way could you talk about dating anybody! You just, as a girl, me and the other girls were like, 'Oh, no, we don't date', you know. The uncles would tease you, or something, and go, 'Oh, the guys really like you', and you'd be like, 'Oh, I wouldn't know' (Thirty-year-old Iranian woman).

The following quote illustrates an interesting finding among our sample of Afghan males, which is that dating non-Afghan girls is seen as desirable, but for marriage it is deemed preferable to marry an Afghan woman for a variety of cultural reasons:

> I personally don't have any problems you know, like, ethnicity is not an issue in terms of dating. Because the person, if the person is a nice person and you like them, that's what's important. But when you get – that's a dating level, we're talking about. But if you're serious, and you want to get married, then there are so many issues that arise...religion, families, virginity (Thirty-five-year-old Afghan male).

Arranged marriage was quite common in the countries from which our participants' families had come, particularly in rural areas. Among the Afghans and, to a lesser extent, the Iranians we interviewed, parental involvement in the choice of a partner was still important, although participants from these two groups made clear that they, and not their parents, would ultimately decide whom they would marry. Among most of the South-East Asian participants, however, the notion of an arranged marriage seemed downright antiquated and unappealing, as illustrated by the following quotes from a twenty-seven-year-old Vietnamese man:

> The past year [my brother has] turned a whole 180 on the whole family and started doing all the culture stuff. Like trying to learn more about our culture, more about our language, more about our foods, even cooking our foods. And the killer, which I want to rip out his heart, he's agreeing to an arranged marriage ... Never met her before!

Language

Refugee youth in the U.S.A. invariably learn English more quickly than their parents. To what extent they retain their ethnic language varies considerably, however. When young people opt to speak only English (dissonant acculturation), or when their parents discourage the use of their ethnic language, communication difficulties may arise as parents and children eventually no longer share a common language. This can be quite distressing for adolescents, who find themselves frequently misunderstood or simply unable to communicate meaningfully with their parents:

> Yeah, we don't communicate, really, we have come to this middle, it's like a middle ground where [my mother] speaks to me in Chinese and I speak to her in English. And you know, it's really hard to communicate, and she doesn't fully understand me. Like I will say something to her and she will say it back to me, she will repeat it back to me, but it's completely different, like she totally misses the point (Twenty-three-year-old Vietnamese man of Chinese ethnicity).

> We don't really speak the same language because I didn't speak English until I was three, but everything I learned was in English, and he [his father] speaks

Vietnamese and his English is really, really, really, really bad. So communication isn't that good … Kinda sucks. Like you can't talk to your parents [crying]
(Twenty-three-year-old Vietnamese woman).

Between Two Worlds: the Challenge of Developing an Ethnic Identity

The development of an ethnic identity can be quite challenging for refugee
and immigrant youth who spend much of their childhood or adolescence in
the U.S.A. In one sense, neither are they truly Afghan, Vietnamese,
Cambodian or Iranian; nor, however, do they experience themselves as fully
American. Of course, the concept of being 'fully American' is complicated,
not only because the U.S.A. is a country comprised almost wholly of
immigrants, refugees and their descendants, but also because there are racial
and ethnic groups whose historical experiences of discrimination and
marginalisation may leave them feeling less than 'fully American' despite
their families' having lived in the U.S.A. for several generations Nonetheless,
for the participants in this study, there was a palpable sense of an American
identity to which they did not yet have access, a sense of not feeling truly at
home in this country. This perception was both more common and more
pronounced among Iranian and Afghan participants than it was among those
from South-East Asia. Perhaps it is a question of time – the families of our
Vietnamese and Cambodian participants had been in the U.S.A. longer, and
perhaps there is a sense of belonging, despite ethnic or racial difference, that
comes with time and the experience of being born in the country in which
one lives. Regardless, we would suggest that refugee and immigrant youth in
the U.S.A. occupy a kind of middle space in terms of their ethnicity. However
much they might wish to wholly occupy one or the other world, this is an
impossibility. Coming of age in the U.S.A. invariably influences their identity
sufficiently to root them at least partly in American culture; yet American
society, with its emphasis on categorising people based not only on visible
differences but also on the number of generations their families go back in the
U.S.A., will always remind them that they are not truly American, but an
ethnic 'other' whose membership in society is still provisional. And,
independently of this ambivalent reception, young people from refugee and
immigrant families are often pulled in two directions, wanting to fit into the
world outside their home and ethnic community, and yet also wanting to
maintain a connection to, and identification with, their ethnic community.

The data from this study suggest that the ethnic identity of adolescent
refugees is an evolving phenomenon; that is, young people growing up in the
dual worlds of ethnic community and American society are in an ongoing
process of sorting out and putting together a sense of their own ethnic
identity. The value of a retrospective design in this study was evident as it

allowed participants to describe the fluid nature of their evolving ethnic identification. Although ethnic identity is not a common topic of discussion or concern among American youth who are not refugees or immigrants, for the participants in this study it was a topic of great importance, about which they had much to say.

The following quote illustrates a young Afghan woman's shift from a consonant mode of acculturation to a more selective or integrative approach:

> I didn't have a balance. And it was hard for me to know which way – I was rebelling against being an Afghan, I wanted to go out and do stuff that Americans did, I wanted to go out to bars, I wanted to go out to clubs, and my parents had a very difficult time with me, 'cause they were like, 'No, that's too much, drinking is not good for you, the reason why it's written about this in the Koran is because it leads to bad, it's the seed of all evil, you're not in control when you drink, you'll say things you don't mean, your motor skills aren't going to be the same, you may get into a car accident, it's just not a good habit to pick up'. So I went through my battling stage, tried to figure out who I was, and I finally can label myself an Afghan-American. I think finally I've achieved a balance, to where, I know my boundaries, you know? I know that I won't drink alcohol. It's forbidden for us in Islam, and I know I don't want to (Twenty-five-year-old Afghan woman).

The next quote reflects a similar shift in acculturation mode and ethnic identity in a young Vietnamese man:

> I think, when I became a citizen in twelfth grade in high school, up until that point I didn't want to become a citizen to tell you the truth ... because I kind of felt that it was like selling out to a certain degree. And I was losing my central identity, you know. Like now, I feel comfortable in both societies. And so, I would consider myself a Vietnamese-born...person living in America ... who has ties to both cultures ... you still appreciate the long black hair or a woman who speaks the Vietnamese language or understands the traditional side of things. In terms of the American side of things, you also want a woman to be able to speak her mind and who is comforting and self-supporting. So, I think, personally, it is a little bit more difficult to find a blend of that in a person, but it is possible (Twenty-three-year-old Vietnamese male).

The Influence of Discrimination on Ethnic Identity

Comments regarding ethnic identity such as those of the Afghan woman and Vietnamese man quoted above were typical for participants in this study, with one exception: Iranians. Not all of the Iranian youth we interviewed reported experiences of discrimination, but, among those who did, its impact on their self-esteem and ethnic identity was quite powerful. And, even for those Iranian respondents who did not directly experience discrimination, there was an acute awareness of the hostile, almost demonic portrayal of Iranians in the U.S. media and popular imagination following the hostage crisis of 1979. For several participants, it became difficult not to internalise these negative images, and that internalisation led to a rejection of their Persian roots. The discrimination took many forms, from negative portrayals in the media, to hostile remarks, to physical assaults. One woman, who as a teenager was beaten by peers simply for being Iranian, became socially withdrawn as a way of avoiding the intense harassment to which she was subjected:

> I think I just shut down. I really did shut down. I just crawled into a shell and became more isolated. And I still am. Like no matter how good I am or how hard I work or how well I do at work, I feel like I'm not good enough. I feel like they still see me as a terrorist (Thirty-five-year-old Iranian woman).

Another woman's comments illustrate the toxic effect of pervasive discrimination once it gets internalised:

> And you have just a, it's just a certain way of decorating everything [for the Persian New Year] and I can't remember some of the things that we did but I just hated it, it was just, it just was a, you know, cultural thing that I didn't want any, you, you want to do as few things that have to do with Iran as possible (Thirty-year-old Iranian woman).

The power of discrimination to threaten young people's self-esteem underscores the importance of community-based interventions that target discriminatory beliefs and practices that may be directed at particular refugee and other minority groups.

To summarise, the participants in this study adopted a variety of acculturative modes, which in turn influenced (and were influenced by) the dynamics of their family relationships. Family conflict was intensified by inter-generational differences in acculturation when those differences entailed refugee youth rejecting the values and traditions of their parents. Conversely, when adolescents sought to maintain the beliefs and values of their ethnic community, through either consonant or selective acculturation, conflict with parents was minimised and parental support was enhanced. The development of an ethnic identity, an important topic to participants, was found to be highly fluid rather than static, changing over time as adolescents matured into young adults.

Discussion

The results of this exploratory study are generally consistent with the findings of other research examining the mental health and psychosocial development of adolescent refugees. It is evident that refugee youth face a complex set of psychosocial challenges as they and their families adapt to life in the U.S.A. For second generation refugee youth, who were born in the U.S.A. or arrived by the age of five, the same challenges are salient as among more recently arrived youth, with the exception of having to deal with the effects of their own direct exposure to the violence of war or political persecution. Exposure to violence has been a powerful predictor of psychological trauma in some studies of refugee youth; however, unlike participants in those studies, the young adults we interviewed had either never experienced such violence, or, in the case of the Afghans and Iranians, had not experienced directly the kind of brutality and loss to which highly traumatised youth in other studies had been exposed (e.g. Kinzie et al., 1986, 1989).

Our findings regarding the fluid, shifting nature of ethnic identity and of the acculturative modes that adolescents adopt underscore the value of retrospective as well as prospective research designs, both of which allow for an examination of the ways in which variables of interest change over time. Our findings are also consistent with those of Portes and Rumbaut (2001), whose longitudinal study of refugee and immigrant youth in the U.S.A. found that acculturation is a complex phenomenon that cannot be readily captured using a linear model – that is, it is not the case that the young are either more or less acculturated; rather, many adolescents selectively embrace aspects of both cultures in which they live. Importantly, an early adolescent who rejects much of her own ethnic culture may grow up into a young adult who strongly identifies with that same culture; conversely, a self-protective immersion in one's ethnic culture may gradually evolve into a more integrative approach that includes aspects of cultural worlds. Adolescents are in a continual state of growth and change, and it is not surprising that their sense of ethnic identity likewise changes over time.

Our findings also illustrate the extent to which exposure to American popular culture influences the ways in which refugee youth perceive and respond to behavioural norms and values traditional to their ethnic community. From ways of conceptualising their parents' distress, to their views on dating and arranged marriage, to their feelings about patterns of communication within their families, the lens through which our participants viewed their families and ethnic communities was deeply influenced by their exposure to the values and norms of their American peers and the images they had seen in the popular media.

It is also important to note the areas of both similarity and difference when comparing the psychosocial challenges facing refugee versus immigrant youth. Clearly, there is considerable overlap. Both groups may face discrimination, and both must contend with the reality of living in two worlds, that of their ethnic community and that of the larger U.S. society. However, unlike immigrant youth, adolescent refugees (and U.S.-born children of refugee parents) often grow up with parents who are struggling with the psychological aftermath of their experiences of war-related violence and loss. The impact of such experiences on parenting represents an important focus for future research, given the growing evidence that political violence and displacement impair parenting, which in turn affects young people's well-being.

Notes

1. Correspondence should be addressed to Kenneth E. Miller, at the Psychology Department, San Francisco State University, 1600 Holloway Avenue, San Francisco, CA, 94132, USA. This research was supported by a grant from the College of Behavioral and Social Sciences at San Francisco State University. Thanks to Diana Ortega, Karola Brent, Josh Westheimer, Nilofar Sami and Michael Williams for their assistance with this project.
2. Throughout this chapter, we use the terms 'psychosocial' and 'psychological' interchangeably to refer to young people's emotional, intellectual and social well-being (i.e. their mental health). 'Psychosocial stressors' are social factors that affect children's mental health, including their ongoing development of core capacities such as the capacity for healthy interpersonal relationships within and outside of the family, the development of their self-esteem and the gradual internalisation and development of moral and spiritual values.
3. It would be actually more accurate to use the term Vietnamese-American, Cambodian-American, and so forth, since all of the participants had gained American citizenship by the time of the study. As we discuss below, however, there was considerable variation in how participants defined their ethnic identity, with some individuals opting to include the '-American' following their familial ethnicity (e.g. Afghan-American), and others referring to themselves solely as Afghan, Iranian (or Persian), Vietnamese or Cambodian. For the sake of a simpler nomenclature, participants in this study are referred to by their families' country of origin.
4. In the present study, several Cambodian participants provided poignant illustrations of their parents' powerful emphasis on achieving academic success, an emphasis that paid of academically but that also contributed to tension in the parent–adolescent relationship. The following quote illustrates this phenomenon:

> I knew my multiplication tables when I was in second grade, or first grade. Like, [my dad would] seriously write them out on binder paper and stick them on my wall. He'd make me sit there for like half an hour and read them. I don't know, there's a lot of things that he ... like I know that most families, they wouldn't have their, their parents probably wouldn't sit them on their bed and like read these multiplication tables and tell me that ... and drill them, you know? Like, I don't know if most families would do that. He did, though (Twenty-year-old Cambodian woman).

Another Cambodian respondent expressed sadness that her parents' emphasis on academic achievement was not complemented by a nurturing, supportive approach to other aspects of her behaviour. She attributed this to traditional Cambodian culture, which she contrasted somewhat negatively with what she perceived as a more supportive approach to parenting among her American peers:

> My parents are not really ... they're not harsh. I mean they'll say mean things to us, but they think that would encourage us to do better. But, they've never done anything bad to us. I mean they'll say things that they don't mean, like you know ... they'll, you know, curse or whatever. They'll say things that will hurt your feelings, but deep in their heart they don't mean it because after they say it they feel really bad. My Dad would say, 'I don't really mean to say these things to you, but sometimes I'm just really mad and I just don't want you to do bad things so I just say it to make you mad so you can think about them', but that's the Cambodian way of disciplining your kids. Just putting them down, constantly putting them down, and the American way is to encourage, you know, like, 'You're really good at this, go for it. I know you can do it!' (Twenty-one-year-old Cambodian woman).

5. The exception to this is the relatively small population of Hazara Afghans, who are Shi'ite Muslims.

References

Ajdukovic, M. and Ajdukovic, D. 1993 'Psychological Well-being of Refugee Children', *Child Abuse and Neglect* 17(6): 843–54.

Arroyo, W. and Eth, S.I.E. 1986 'Children Traumatized by Central American Warfare', in R.P.S. Eth (ed) *Post-traumatic Stress Disorder in Children*. Washington, DC: American Psychiatric Press, pp. 101–20.

Beiser, M. 1999 *Strangers at the Gate: 'Boat People's' First Ten Years in Canada*. Toronto: University of Toronto Press.

Bozorgmehr, M. 1997 'Iranians', in D. Haines (ed), *Case Studies in Diversity: Refugees in America in the 1990s*. Westport, Conn.: Greenwood Press, pp. 85–103.

Danieli, Y. (ed) 1998 *International Handbook of Multigenerational Legacies of Trauma*. New York: Plenum Press.

de Berry, J., Fazili, A., Farhad, S., Nasiry. F., Hashemi, S. and Hakimi, M. 2003 *Children of Kabul: Discussions with Afghan Families*. Westport, CT: Save the Children and UNICEF, Save the Children Federation.

Dona, G. and Berry, J.W. 1999 'Refugee Acculturation and Re-acculturation', in A. Ager (ed), *Refugees: Perspectives on the Experience of Forced Migration*. London: Pinter Press, pp. 169-95.

Felsen, I. 1998 'Transgenerational Transmission of Effects of the Holocaust: The North American Research Perspective', in Y. Danieli (ed) *The International Handbook of Multigenerational Legacies of Trauma*. New York: Plenum Press, pp. 43–68.

Goodson, L. 2001 *Afghanistan's Endless War*. Seattle: University of Washington Press.

Hubbard, J., Realmuto, G.M., Northwood, A.K. and Masten, A.S. 1995 'Comorbidity of Psychiatric Diagnoses with Posttraumatic Stress Disorder in Survivors of Childhood Trauma', *Journal of the American Academy of Child and Adolescent Psychiatry* 34(9): 1167–73.

Kinzie, J.D., Sack, W., Angell, R., Clarke, G. and Rath, B. 1986 'The Psychiatric Effects of Massive Trauma on Cambodian Children: II. The Family, the Home, and the School', *Journal of the American Academy of Child Psychiatry* 25(3): 377–83.

Kinzie, J.D., Sack, W., Angell, R., Clarke, G. and Rath, B. 1989 'A Three Year Follow-up of Cambodian Young People Traumatized as Children', *Journal of the American Academy of Child and Adolescent Psychiatry* 28(4): 501–04.

Lipson, J.G., Omidian, P.A. and Paul, S.M. 1995 'Afghan Health Education Project: A Community Survey', *Public Health Nursing* 12(3): 143–50.

Manh Hung, N. and Haines, D. 1997 'Vietnamese', in D. Haines (ed) *Case Studies in Diversity: Refugees in America in the 1990s*. Westport, Conn.: Greenwood Press, pp. 44–56.

Mayotte, J.A. 1992 *Disposable People?: The Plight of the World's Refugees*. Maryknoll, NY: Orbis Books.

Mghir, R. and Raskin, A. 1999 'The Psychological Effect of the War in Afghanistan on Young Afghan Refugees from Different Ethnic Backgrounds', *International Journal of Social Psychiatry* 45(2): 148–49.

Mortland, C.A. 1997 'Khmer', in D. Haines (ed) *Case Studies in Diversity: Refugees in the US in the 1990s*. Westport, Conn.: Greenland Press, pp. 167–93.

Omidian, P.A. 1996 *Aging and Family in an Afghan Refugee Community*. New York and London: Garland Publishing, Inc.

Portes, A. and Rumbaut, R. 2001 *Legacies: The Story of the Immigrant Second Generation*. Berkeley, CA: University of California Press.

Ressler, E., Boothby, N. and Steinbock, J. 1988 *Unaccompanied Children: Care and Protection in Wars, Natural Disasters, and Refugee Movements*. New York: Oxford University Press.

Smith, P., Perrin, S., Yule, W., Hacam, B. and Stuvland, R. 2002 'War Exposure among Children from Bosnia-Hercegovina: Psychological Adjustment in a Community Sample', *Journal of Traumatic Stress* 15: 147–56.

Suárez-Orozco, C. and Suárez-Orozco, M. 2001 *Children of Immigration*. Cambridge, MA: Harvard University Press.

Thabet, A. and Vostanis, P. 2000 'Post-traumatic Stress Disorder Reactions in Children of War: A Longitudinal Study', *Child Abuse and Neglect* 24: 291–98.

Tobin, J. and Friedman, J. 1984 'Intercultural and Developmental Stresses Confronting Southeast Asian Refugee Adolescents', *Journal of Operational Psychiatry* 15: 39–45.

USCR 2002 *World Refugee Survey*. New York: US Committee for Refugees.

PART II
ADOLESCENTS ENGAGING IN POLITICAL VIOLENCE

4

Political Transition and Youth Violence in Post-apartheid South Africa: In Search of Understanding

Andrew Dawes

Introduction

It has often been suggested that the violence learnt by youth in a war or political struggle, and the psychological trauma they have experienced are likely to threaten prospects for peace and non-violence in the post-conflict society. In the run-up to the transition from apartheid to democracy, South Africans began to speak of 'lost generations' of young people who would emerge from the conflict as 'unsocialised' and with a propensity for violence that would threaten the social order of the post conflict period (Chikane, 1986; Dawes, 1994b; Reynolds, 1995). Similar concerns have been expressed in other theatres of political struggle, including Northern Ireland, Palestine and Israel (Cairns, 1996).

It was true that generations of young South Africans had made enormous sacrifices in terms of lost years of education. There were appalling acts of violence (and celebrations of violent acts) by the young. Many young people, both white and black were psychologically traumatised by what they had done and what had been done to them, as the Truth and Reconciliation Commission reports and other accounts have recorded (Straker and the Sanctuaries Treatment Team, 1987; Reynolds, 1995; Foster et al., 2005). At

the same time many showed remarkable reslience and political understanding beyond that expected for their years.

During the closing years of the apartheid period, the lost generation
discourse was fuelled by (frequently) racist images of rampaging violent and
uneducated (black) youth in the media. Black as well as white commentators
expressed deep concern that South Africa would reap the whirlwind when
democracy finally arrived (Straker, 1989). The fear was that the new
democracy would be undermined by the violent criminality of the cohort of
young adults who would inherit the peace (Chikane, 1986). Were these
concerns valid? Can one attribute criminal and interpersonal violence in a
'post political conflict' society to the psychological damage caused to the
young during the conflict?

This chapter seeks to address these questions, taking into consideration a
range of complex and interlocking factors. The first, and more substantial,
part of the chapter explores links between political violence in the past and
criminal violence in the post- apartheid period. The second section discusses
possible measures for reducing the threat of continued violence. Before
proceeding, however, it is necessary to locate South Africa in relation to the
supposed trajectory of conflict to post-conflict.

South Africa: A 'Post-conflict' Society?

As is well known, in 1994 a negotiated political settlement led to a democratic
order and the cessation of what was, in effect, a low-intensity civil war. In that
sense, South Africa is at peace. Hostilities have ended, there are no armed
groups contesting power, and three multiparty elections have been held.

However, the fact that South Africa is formally at peace does not mean
that the post-apartheid political and economic order is uncontested. For
example, since the late 1990s, there has been significant tension within the
ruling alliance of the African National Congress (ANC), the Communist
Party and the Congress of South African Trade Unions (COSATU). As I
write, a national one-day strike is under way against the ANC's neoliberal
economic policy. Many youth are on the street.

Notwithstanding the efforts of the Truth and Reconciliation Commission
(TRC) to 'heal the nation' as the slogans of the day put it, racial tension and
racism are not dead. Legislation to restore land to (or provide compensation
for) those dispossessed under apartheid was passed in 1996. This Act,
designed to benefit blacks, has produced new racial conflict as white farmers,
whose land once belonged to blacks, resist redistribution by refusing to sell
their farms to the state.

Despite enormous gains in housing provision since the mid-1990s, millions
live in simple shacks without basic services. Many have been on housing

waiting lists for years. Recently, street demonstrations calling for more housing have turned violent as barricades have burnt in the streets, police have been stoned by protesters (young and old) and protesters have been shot.

These actions feel like a flashback to the bad old days. While popular uprisings were previously focused on the structural violence of apartheid, today they are a response to contemporary structural inequalities that are a function of the prevailing economic order, itself a legacy of the apartheid system. The structure of South African society remains fundamentally stratified on economic lines, with persons of colour – black Africans in particular – constituting the vast majority of the urban and rural poor. As under apartheid, race and class remain largely intertwined (Seekings and Natrass, 2005; Natrass and Seekings, 2001).

According to Galtung (1990), a society is structurally violent when institutionalised economic, cultural or political practices lead to inequality of opportunity and social exclusion. Thus a free market system in a democratic society that has high levels of inequality (as is the case in South Africa), and that contains few protections for the poor and socially excluded, may be considered structurally violent. Such societies create structurally unequal opportunities for survival, development and access to material resources as well as social capital.

Contemporary South Africa, despite its democratic institutions, remains structurally violent and one of the most unequal societies in the world (Seekings and Natrass, 2005). The most commonly used measure of inequality is the Gini Coefficient where values may range from 0.00 to 1.00, with the latter indicating extreme inequality of income distribution. In 1995, the South African Gini was 0.59. By 2002 it had risen to 0.64 (United Nations Development Programme, 2003). Beyond the numbers, an earlier UNDP report on South Africa captured the essence of the experience of the sentiments shared by many of the poor: 'The dull ache of desperation, the acute tensions generated by violence and insecurity, the intricacies of survival and all its emotions – despair, hope, resentment, apathy, futility and fury' (UNDP, 2000).

While there have been enormous advances in all spheres of life, South Africa is not free of conflict. However, it is correctly described as 'post-conflict' in the sense that the political conflict that marked the country for decades and which was associated with ongoing political violence and repression has ended.

Pre- and Post-apartheid Violence and the Role of the Young

Rather like Europe and the United States of America, South African history is written in blood. Oral tradition has it that prior to colonial conquest in the seventeenth century conflict between indigenous groups occurred. Since European settlement, the country has experienced colonial occupation, civil war, slavery, battles for ascendancy within black chieftaincies and the violence of the apartheid system itself.

It is common to mark the onset of political violence in South Africa as commencing with the Soweto uprising led by adolescent schoolchildren and youth in 1976. Of course this is false. Instead, this event marked a dramatic upsurge in the scale and youthfulness of the movement that played such a central role in the demise of the apartheid regime.

The situation of youth in South Africa was arguably most similar to that in Palestine during the first intifada, and to Northern Ireland in the 1970s and 1980s. At the time these were not conventional war situations – they were popular uprisings in which much of the conflict was played out by young people of school-going age on the streets. In the three cases – South Africa, Palestine and Northern Ireland – at least some of the youth were involved in the perpetration of violence, and all of them experienced attacks by security forces on themselves, their homes and their families (Punamaki and Suleiman 1989).

In all these situations even adolescents have been actively involved in paramilitary groups and have played roles in guerrilla activities, sabotage and the like (Straker, 1988; Punamaki and Suleiman, 1989; Cairns, 1996). The young and their elders have been part of disempowered groups that have rejected the legitimacy of the existing political order. In all cases, in one way or another, they have struggled either against the occupation of their country, or for equal rights, reflecting the capacity of the young to act with political, moral and ideological agency.

Writing for the Truth and Reconciliation Commission hearings on the effects of political violence on young blacks in particular, Pamela Reynolds and I noted that there were no statistics on how many of the young were involved in conflict (Reynolds and Dawes, 1999). We observed that no liberation organisation can give accurate lists of the membership of children and youth, and that the numbers of children who were imprisoned cannot be accurately calculated.

Various writings at the time gave numbers of young detainees. The figures vary and the sources are not always given. For the year 1986, for example, published figures on the number of those under eighteen years of age who were detained vary from 300 to 2,677, to 4,000, to 8,800. An often quoted figure exists for the period 1985 to 1989 of 24,000 children and adolescents held in detention. There were an estimated 51,000 detentions without trial between 1984 and 1988; many were children, but many more were parents.

Blacks under eighteen were killed, abducted, raped, tortured, poisoned, imprisoned for long periods without trial, denied rights while imprisoned and harassed mercilessly for their politics and actions. Others were forced to flee the country. Young people experienced the terror tactics of the state, including threats, misinformation, smear campaigns, harassment of kin, intrusion into domestic space and closure of schools.

As the political struggle in South Africa intensified, it became ever more public. Teenagers would often lead the assault against the soldiers and police. They would participate in the murder of officials in public places accompanied by large crowds singing and cheering them on. Often the killers would use the necklace method – a car tyre placed around the neck of a collaborator and set alight. Children would sometimes watch too, chanting the macabre slogan 'Viva necklace' as the victim died before them.

The 'Lost Generation': A Racist Narrative?

I always find it of interest that the concern about violence in the post-apartheid South Africa is a concern about the experience of blacks. I raise this because of the silence about the socialisation of white male youth into violence. From the late 1960s, every white male was conscripted into the South African Defence Force (SADF) on leaving school (at seventeen or eighteen years of age). Hundreds of thousands participated (willingly and otherwise) in the violent repression of blacks inside the country, as well as serving in the Namibian and Angolan theatres of war (Korber, 1992). There is minimal research on these issues in South Africa. However, Korber's study powerfully demonstrates the lasting traumatic impact on a young conscript of his involvement in atrocities. For many, the experience must have been similar to that of American conscripts in the closing chapters of the Vietnam war.

Given the fact that far more young whites than blacks were exposed to military violence through conscription and soldiering in the years subsequent to 1976 (a new cohort was enrolled each year), it is of interest that they were not constructed as part of the 'lost generation'. This was a term reserved for the young who were black, undereducated, poor and supposedly prone to political and other forms of violence. One must also consider a couple of key differences in the discourse that separated young blacks from whites. The political violence of the former was framed as 'illegitimate' – it aimed to undermine the state. Also, perhaps most frightening, the violence seemed to be out of the control of a command structure of elders – it was being orchestrated by youth who had abandoned education to participate in political struggle.

In contrast, the young white men were well educated, defending their country and under the control of a formal military command structure – in essence they were constructed as carrying out the legitimate military business of the (illegitimate) regime. They were supposedly contained by a traditional military structure. How could they be 'lost'? The matter did not arise. The 'lost generation' was therefore, by definition, 'black and dangerous' (Straker, 1988).

There is a strongly psychological undertone to this discourse – one suggestive of damage and victimhood, while also containing a lurking fear of the power of an apparently unsocialised youth. Its origins are not clear. Professional psychology must bear some responsibility in casting the young as damaged victims whose moral compass would have been fatally flawed by disrupted socialisation and participation in violence.

The discourse of damaged generations was used in the psychological literature on the Northern Irish troubles before it appeared in South Africa (Cairns, 1987, 1996). Locally it took root in the popular imagination. For example, on 20 April 1986 during a period of heightened state repression and counter-violence, Percy Qoboza, then editor of a black paper *City Press*, wrote: 'If it is true that a people's wealth is its children (and youth), then South Africa is bitterly, tragically poor. If it is true that a nation's future is its children, we have no future, and deserve none'. Qoboza was one of many black journalists who spoke out against the regime at the time and, wittingly or otherwise, drew on a psychologised discourse of a damaged youth to warn of the consequences for the nation's future.

In spite of the many accounts of suffering, reviews of the limited research literature that existed on the psychological status of young people involved in the political struggle did not support a notion of generations of 'lost youth' or damaged cohorts. Rather a picture of extraordinary resourcefulness and resilience was evident (Straker, 1988; Swartz and Levett, 1989; Dawes, 1994a,b).

Despite its importance, in what follows I want to suggest that the individual psychological level of analysis is not sufficient on its own to account for levels of interpersonal violence in a post-conflict society. A range of structural and other conditions are also at play.

Broadening our Understanding of Causal Factors in Post-conflict Violence

In an essay written some years ago (Dawes, 1994), I argued that socialisation into the acceptability of political violence and participation in non-political violence could not on their own account for criminal and interpersonal violence in the post-conflict society. Certain additional structural and institutional conditions are also necessary. I postulated six conditions that need to be considered to account for criminal interpersonal violence in a post-conflict society. Four of the original six are relevant to present-day South Africa:

- Condition 1: The involvement of youth in political violence as a predictor of post-conflict violence.
- Condition 2: The extent of criminal violence in the society prior to and during the political conflict.
- Condition 3: The extent to which the post-conflict society has an entrenched culture of male violence.
- Condition 4: The capacity of the post-conflict political and economic context to satisfy the basic needs for survival for the majority.

I shall explain, in turn, how these points relate to the South African case.

Condition 1: The Involvement of Youth in Political Violence as a Predictor of Post-conflict Violence

Barbarin and Richter (2001: 66) have suggested that: 'Contemporary experience of violence in South Africa is a compelling demonstration that the genie of political violence is more difficult to put back in the bottle once it has been let out. Instead it reappears in new guises and is energised by new motives such as economic competition, politics, crime and the territorial wars of youth gangs'. There is some validity in this observation. However, it is problematic to argue that contemporary violence is fundamentally the consequence of the political events of the past. The evidence suggests that the 'new motives' are in fact the product of long-standing conditions that pre-date even the violence of the anti-apartheid struggle. I return to this point below. I am interested here in considering the role of exposure to political violence in shaping the proclivities to violence in youth.

It is very difficult to make solid connections between past and contemporary violence. Psychological research can help us with this issue to some extent. Research on inner city violence and developmental pathways into violent conduct suggests that at least a proportion of former young combatants would grow up to use interpersonal violence to deal with conflict and for their own instrumental purposes (Loeber et al., 1993; Kupersmidt et al., 1995; Parker et al., 2004). A proportion – particularly those drawn into gang activity – become habituated to violence in the world around them. They may come to celebrate violence as part of a gang culture that valorises the strong and violent male who has little empathy for those weaker than himself (Loeber et al., 1993; Loeber and Farrington, 1997), and demonstrate moral disengagement from their victims (Bandura et al., 1996; Bandura, 1999). The gang also provides a strong group identity and protection for its members. Members carve our reputations of one kind or the other, including a 'rep' as a killer.

War also provides opportunities for strong hero identification, particularly in young males. The tendency may be particularly noteworthy in societies that have strongly articulated ideals of male potency, that accept the legitimacy of certain forms of male power and even violence, and where the political struggle is underpinned by a strong and widely legitimated ideology. In South Africa, these conditions were met.

Anyone who has dealt with young ideologically committed combatants will see at least some similarities with the members and structures of an inner city gang. In saying this, I do not mean to deny the key differences between young combatant groups and the inner city gang: notably the presence in many of the former of a political ideological commitment that is superordinate to the objectives of the combatant group. On the face of it, many of the children of the Palestinian intifada or the principled 'young lions' of the South African conflict would be good exemplars of ideologically motivated young actors in political violence. Yet there is no doubt that, in some settings, the line between combatants and inner city gangs is probably very thin. In South Africa what were known as the Comtsotsis were a case in point: they were young gangsters who became involved in the political struggle for their own ends (Scharf and Ngcokoto, 1990).

In addition to learning violent styles of being, similar to the young combatant, children who grow up under circumstances of chronic violence at home and in their neighbourhoods are at risk for type 2 trauma (Terr, 1990, cited in Osofsky, 1995), and what South African author Gillian Straker called 'continuous traumatic stress' (Straker and the Sanctuaries Counselling Team, 1987). Youngsters who show type 1 trauma display reactions such as nightmares, poor concentration, intense fear and other post-traumatic symptoms. Type 2 trauma survivors, in contrast, typically display a range of psychological outcomes that are a function of living in chronically stressful conditions. They include: proclivities to violence, reduced empathy for victims of violence, emotional numbing, constricted affect, impulsivity and impaired concentration, and, most importantly, hyper-vigilance to the potential threat of violence (a tendency to misread benign social cues).

There is little doubt that in South Africa a proportion of young people – we have no idea how many – have probably emerged from the conflict with long-term emotional problems. Certainly this is confirmed by certain South African community-based therapeutic programmes deigned to assist former combatants who have participated in criminal violence in the post-conflict society, and who have long-term stress-related problems (Robertson, 2003).

It is essential to note the co-occurrence of age, political violence and poverty in the backgrounds of former combatants. The vast majority of those who fought the township and rural wars of the early 1990s were drawn from very poor communities within which violence was all too common in children's lives, notably gang and domestic violence. There were no systematic studies of children's exposure to criminal violence in the 1980s. However, Pinnock's (1984) work on the youth gangs of the time and other reports, such as that of Marks and Andersson (1990), suggest that criminal violence was prevalent, particularly in communities forcibly disrupted by apartheid.

The line between political involvement and criminal activity was often very blurred (Scotch Madlope interview with the author, Johannesburg, 1997). After the end of the conflict, there was no political role for the majority of young people. As I have noted, the limited evidence available suggests that many felt abandoned by those for whom they fought. They had little education, and they had almost no chance of finding work. In a context of no adult social security provision and potential starvation, an unknown number of these youngsters took up their AK-47 rifles (originally supplied by the liberation movement and smuggled across the border), and joined the ranks of criminal gangs. They became involved in bank robberies, carjacking and other violent crime.

However, Straker's (2003) case studies of young revolutionaries in the late 1980s and early 1990s show very clearly that, even in desperately poor communities, the criminal route was by no means inevitable for former teenage combatants, particularly where alternative moral repertoires and paths of action were available. Not surprisingly, she found that those who did pursue a criminal path were generally low in social competence, had very disrupted care relationships and were less cognitively competent than their non-criminal peers. Clearly, the 1980–early 1990s generation was not all 'lost' by any means.

In any event, psychological research on outcomes of children exposed to violence shows that pathways to adolescent and adult violence are more complex than those suggested by the mechanistic narrative of 'lost generations' exposed to political violence. One needs to look beyond the psychological level of analysis. Instead, we need to understand the effects of youth participation in violence during political conflict as one of several factors in determining the level of violence post-apartheid.

Condition 2: The Extent of Criminal Violence in the Society prior to and during the Political Conflict, and Condition 3: The Extent to which the Post-conflict Society has an Entrenched Culture of Male Violence

Earlier I took issue with my colleagues and friends Oscar Barbarin and Linda Richter about whether the violence we see today is a consequence of the political events of the past. While there are, no doubt, particularities in the form taken by violent crime since 1994, the evidence suggests to me that the new motives and forms to which my colleagues point are in fact better seen as long-standing conditions. It is deep continuity rather than change that marks the pattern of youth violence in South Africa.

These conditions include a long-standing history of criminal violence and male violence in South Africa that operated in parallel with the political situation and deep structural inequality. Violence and machismo were not new to the youth who engaged in the political struggle. Violent criminal and, particularly, gang activity has long been a scourge of poor South African urban communities, preceding political violence. Marks and Andersson comment that male urban youth gangs were in existence early in the twentieth century, and that high levels of urban unemployment have always created pools of youth attracted to gang life as a form of identity and survival. Even by the 1940s, 'ethnically defined and at times ruthless criminal gangs were an important feature of township experience' (Marks and Andersson, 1990: 52). They go on: 'The recession since the early 1980s has also fostered a growth in the illegal activities of gangs – protection rackets, theft, robbery, the sale of alcohol and drugs' (ibid.).

Crime data are well known for their unreliability, sexual crimes being notorious for under-reporting. In addition, 'South Africa' changed in population composition after 1994. Prior to that time crime in areas in which the majority of black citizens lived was not recorded, simply because these had been designated 'independent black states' and defined as outside the nation. Nonetheless, with these caveats in mind, South African crime data are still instructive.

The available information makes it very clear that, while the national rates of violence are appalling, this has been the situation for many years and seems unrelated to the pattern of political violence of the post-1970s. As in most countries, the bulk of criminal activity in South Africa is conducted by the young – between sixteen and thirty-five years old (Marks and Andersson, 1990). Crime data from 1979 and 1984 and a more recent (and probably more accurate) time series provide evidence of long-standing high rates of interpersonal violence (see Table 4.1).

Does the fact that rates are stabilising in some instances suggest that the possible contribution of the generation who engaged in the political struggle

Table 4.1: Reported Violent Crime in South Africa Time Series (per 100,000 population)

	1979	1984	1995	1996	1997	1998	1999	2000
Murder	27	42	21	20	19	18	18	15
Attempted murder			22	22	22	22	21	20
Robbery + weapon			66	54	50	60	70	74
Rape	63	62	38	41	42	39	38	40
Assault + weapon			189	190	186	187	193	208
Common assault			178	176	165	162	171	199

Source: Data supplied by the South African Police Service CIAC, 2001.

is on the wane as they either get locked up or age? We cannot say. Of course, there could be multiple other reasons such as improved policing and changes in reporting. Certainly, the economy has not improved to the extent that jobs have become available to them, and they would, in any event, have been displaced by younger cohorts entering the criminal justice system.

In Tables 4.2 and 4.3, I have used crime data in an attempt to establish whether areas that had low or high rates of political violence in the period before the democratic elections of 1994 show similar patterns in recent years. If that were so, it would suggest a relationship between the contemporary violence and that which preceded it (bearing in mind the concerns noted above about the reliability of data). For illustrative purposes I have selected recent, and according to the South African Police Service, who supplied them, more accurate data than those collected in previous years. The data presented show the same trends across the provinces for previous periods.

What stands out in these numbers is the fact that the Western Cape – an area with virtually no political violence between 1990 and 1994 (the period of most intense political violence prior to the formation of the new order) but a long history of criminal and gang activity – had, in all but one respect, the highest prevalence of violent crime.

Table 4.3 shows that, on average, only robbery is higher today in areas within which political violence was intense between 1990 and 1994. The very high rate of this crime in the Johannesburg area (in Gauteng) is the main contributor to the size of the figure. While this may partly reflect the effects of the earlier conflict, it is also likely to reflect the fact that, as a region,

Table 4.2: Prevalence of Reported Crime January to April 2000 in Provinces with High and Low Levels of Political Violence between 1990 and 1994

Crime Type	Region				
		Low Level of Political Violence 1990–94		High Level of Political Violence 1990–94	
	National	Western Cape Province	Eastern Cape Province	Gauteng Province	Kwazulu-Natal Province
Murder	15	23	15	18	20
Attempted murder	20	31	15	27	25
Robbery + violence	75	73	34	195	79
Rape	41	55	34	54	36
Assault + weapon	208	308	201	247	124
Assault	200	432	164	372	124

Source: Data supplied by the South African Police Service CIAC, 2001; prevalence per 100,000 of population.

Table 4.3: Average Violent Crime Prevalence in High and Low Political Violence regions 1990–94

	Low Political Violence 1990–94	High Political Violence 1990–94
Murder	19	19
Attempted murder	23	26
Robbery	54	137
Rape	45	45
Assault GBH	255	186
Assault	298	248

Source: Data supplied by the South African Police Service CIAC, 2001; prevalence per 100,000 of population.

Gauteng has the highest Gini coefficient in the country. There are plenty of pickings here for well-armed gangs. The resentful ex-combatant youth engaged in treatment by Robertson (2003) and his colleagues at the National Peace Accord Trust (referred to earlier) were participants in such activities.

Finally, inadequate management of violence by the state may be an additional factor accounting for high rates of criminal violence in some areas. An overloaded police force and judiciary lead to few prosecutions and impunity for perpetrators. To take one example, of 1,165 reported rapes of twelve- to seventeen-year-old girls, only 694 (60 per cent) were prosecuted and, of those, 22 per cent (155) resulted in a conviction (South African Police Service CIAC, 2002).

Despite their limitations, the police figures suggest that South Africa has a deeply entrenched pattern of criminal violence that does not simply result from the experience of political violence during the anti-apartheid struggle.

Condition 4: The Capacity of the Post-conflict Political and Economic Context to Satisfy the Basic Needs for Survival for the Majority

In the South African case, it would seem that the contemporary political and economic context and its (in)ability to satisfy basic needs for survival of the majority have functioned, in combination with condition 3 (the extent of pre-existing criminal violence), to be a major driver of violence among youth.

The late 1980s and early 1990s spawned a number of inquiries on the situation of youth. All pointed to the chronic unemployment and educational underpreparedness of black young people as the country moved towards the post-apartheid era (Community Agency for Social Enquiry and Joint Enrichment Project, 1993; Everatt and Sisulu, 1993; Seekings, 1993). The last study noted that in 1989 only one in ten young people could find work in the formal sector, and that 75 per cent of young people, both black and white, were in danger of becoming marginalised from mainstream society. In 1994, The Cooperative Research Programme on South African Youth was undertaken to provide policy guidance on the situation of youth (van Zyl Slabbert et al., 1994). The report concluded that there was not a 'youth crisis' in South Africa. However, it identified a list of serious problems concerning youth that required interventions, particularly in areas of education, unemployment, poverty and exposure to violence. Apart from the decline of political violence and the rise of the HIV/AIDS epidemic, the challenges relating to the situation of youth throughout this time have remained constant.[1] They are outlined below.

- More than two-thirds of South Africans between the ages of eighteen and thirty-five are unemployed; the vast majority are black (see Figure 1).
- The education system loses half those who enter school. While recent years have witnessed some improvement, only a tiny proportion of students emerge with marks that permit them to enter tertiary education (Chisholm, 2004).
- The economy has only recently begun to stabilise and grow (at about 3.5 per cent p.a.); jobs in the industrial sector have been lost due to trade liberalisation; there are few young people with high-level skills; and more young people are coming onto the job market than can be absorbed.

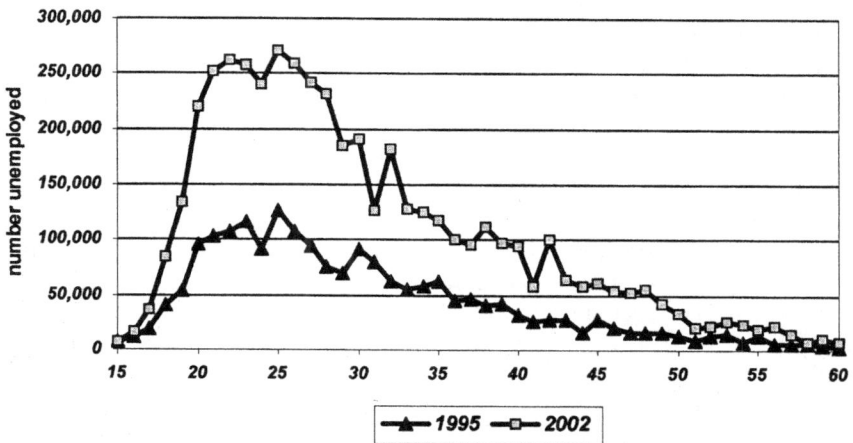

Source: Woolard and Altman (2004), calculated from Statistics South Africa; October Household Survey, 1995; Labour Force Survey, September 2002.

Figure 1: Unemployment by Age: 1995–2002

- Exposure to criminal violence is endemic for many young people. The National Injury Mortality Surveillance System (NIMSS) of the Medical Research Council (2001) shows that contemporary youth are particularly vulnerable to violent assault. In that year, 36 per cent of all non-natural deaths occurred in the fifteen- to twenty-nine-year-old group. Firearms were the major cause of death among children aged ten to fourteen years and accounted for 48.3 per cent of all homicides in this age group. Sharp object homicides (stabbing) accounted for 36.6 per cent of homicides in the fifteen- to nineteen-year age group – a higher percentage than for any other age group. Gun shot wounds constitute 16 per cent of all violent injuries presenting at hospitals. It is young males who account for the overwhelming majority of these victims (Parker et al., 2004).
- The evidence suggests that this high rate of participation in and exposure to violence is related to gang activity. Since 1994, South African borders have opened up. International gangs have not been slow to take up opportunities that this has presented. The high rates of poverty and unemployment among young people make them particularly vulnerable to involvement with gangs and drug peddling.
- Currently fewer than 10 per cent of school leavers are likely to find jobs, and the radical inequality of the society (Gini coefficient = 0.635) is likely to produce marked feelings of relative deprivation (and hostility) in the young who do not have access to the trinkets dangled by the marketing community. In poor Cape Town schools, as in the U.S.A., some adolescents will kill for a pair of running shoes.
- It seems quite clear that an unemployment rate of over 35 per cent on average, significant proportions of the young population living in poverty and many dying of HIV/AIDS all constitute fundamental structural risks that place millions of people on or beyond the edge of survival. Given the population profile, there are significant numbers of desperately poor young people with nothing to do, who could take up violent crime or join gangs just in order to survive.

In sum, I would argue that the evidence, such as it is, suggests that contemporary interpersonal criminal violence in South Africa probably has less to do with direct exposure to political violence during the apartheid years and a lot more to do with a long (and continued) history of structural violence and associated criminal and gender-based violence. The society has long provided opportunities for the young to learn violent approaches to problem solving and survival. These conditions continue in an environment in which most schooling is of poor quality and fails adolescents in their quest for participation in the economy in later years.

Violence Prevention among Children and Youth in Post-conflict South Africa

As noted above, several studies have shown that many young South Africans live in communities in which violence is endemic, frequently permeating multiple settings, including the home, school and neighbourhood. A range of traumatic responses to violence has been reported (Magwaza et al., 1993; Mason, 1994; Ensink et al., 1997; Peltzer, 1999; Seedat et al., 2000; Zissis et al., 2000; Ward et al., 2001).

I have argued that this situation is not in any simple sense the outcome of our political past. The contemporary violence to which children are exposed continues a pattern associated with chronic poverty that has not been addressed since 1994. Yet, despite the high levels of violence, there are certain points we can share on the basis of our post-conflict experience regarding the prevention of youth violence and the protection of children.

First, at the level of the state, the creation of appropriate constitutional and legislative mechanisms for the protection of the most vulnerable in society, in particular the establishment not just of individual rights, but also social rights and protection, is vital. In South Africa, this has been addressed through the constitutional process, which includes key protection for the young. In terms of implementation, we have a long road to travel.

In addition, legislative provisions have to see to it that juveniles are kept out of prisons. South African prisons have very few resources for rehabilitation, and prison is more likely to compound the problems of the young rather than assist them to reform (Dawes and Van der Merwe, 2004). Rehabilitation of young offenders (outside prison as far as possible) is necessary if they are to have a greater chance of returning to society and making a positive contribution. On these counts, once more South Africa has good policy but limited implementation (Sloth-Nielsen and Muntingh, 2001).

Secondly, the state has a role to play in shifting the ideological space from one of intergroup conflict to cooperation – a focus on strengthening links between formerly conflicting groups. This does not mean attempts to dissolve group differences. These will not go away. Rather it means recognising and bridging them.

In the case of the young, a key South African initiative has been the restructuring of aspects of the school curriculum with a focus on national unity, non-racism and non-sexism. While implementation is very uneven, and the effects of these changes on intergroup and gender relations are not known, at least positive ideological elements are being put in place.

Large-scale policy initiatives are not enough. There can be little doubt that exposure to violence on a scale such as is occurring in contemporary South Africa provides many opportunities for the young to learn violent behaviour.

At the same time, repeated traumatisation is also likely to result in psychological states that are associated with aggressive behaviour, particularly in young males. If we are serious about youth violence prevention, children and their developmental contexts require our focused attention. Public health frameworks are of assistance.

Primary-level public health approaches to the problem are typically universal and population-based (for example, training all primary schoolchildren in non-violent conflict resolution skills). Secondary prevention programmes target selected groups at high risk for violent conduct due to the nature of their proximal extra-familial social contexts or to close interpersonal factors (e.g. boys in dysfunctional families in high-crime neighbourhoods). Normally they have not sought help but have been identified by screening or other methods. Particularly during early and middle childhood, growing up in dysfunctional families predicts later delinquency (Loeber et al., 1993). Other risk factors for the development of antisocial pathways derive from internal child states such as social skills deficits and poor impulse control. A South African example of an early preventive intervention is an early school-based child and parent intervention programme for aggressive pre-school children (Jones-Petersen and Carolissen, 2000).

Tertiary prevention is normally high-cost and treatment-based, targeting clinical populations who have already sought help and who have already been diagnosed with conduct or other antisocial disorders. The problem is commonly understood to have a primarily individual-level source and solution. Tertiary-level clinical interventions for children and adolescents who are at risk of conduct disorders and antisocial delinquent behaviour are not a viable option on anything other than a tiny scale. For example, there are only six specialist state child psychiatric facilities in the country (Dawes et al., 1997). Community-based programmes supported by psychiatric facilities do exist, but again the number of children they can serve is minute in proportion to the need (ibid.).

Many families and homes are sites within which children are exposed to violence. Again, resources such as counselling and family support are very limited, and when assistance is offered, for various reasons, the majority of parents cannot or do not avail themselves of the intervention (Bollen et al., 1999).

We know that in South Africa, young people who are diagnosed with conduct disorder or antisocial behaviour, as is the case elsewhere, represent only a part of the population within which a generalised acceptance of aggressive modes of problem solving may be apparent (we have no figures but this is likely). The central challenge is therefore to reduce the numbers who are socialised into aggressive modes of conflict resolution. The trend in South Africa is to focus on the school as the most cost effective and preferred site for primary intervention.

Despite high levels of commitment in school-based violence prevention programmes in South Africa, there is as yet very little evidence of their success in meeting the challenge. There may be successful models, but we lack the evaluation studies, and for that we need staff who are trained in implementation, research and evaluation. The other difficulty these programmes face is that the schools needing most intervention are those that are the most dysfunctional. A recent study showed that it was often the case that implementation was compromised by inadequate infrastructure, very poor school management and overloaded teachers. For example, if there are not pupil attendance registers, we cannot know who received the programme and how often. Forget about randomised controlled trials (Farr et al., 2003). This is not to say that valiant efforts are not being made and that, no doubt, many children may be gaining from these programmes. At least alternatives to violence are being placed before them and anecdotal evidence suggests that many reflect seriously on what they have learnt. Whether the long-term outcomes will fulfil programme expectations we cannot say.

Perhaps the most fundamental change needed, however, is in the structural economic conditions that enable the negative social conditions that, in turn, fuel criminal and interpersonal violence. As indicated above, South Africa is 'post-conflict' in that it is no longer in a state of armed conflict. However, the structural inequalities ensure that it remains a society within which conflict over policy and fair economic distribution exists. In particular, the reduction of structural inequality and poverty and the creation of a society in which hope of a better individual future is possible for the young are essential. In South Africa to date (the time has been short), this has not been possible. I would argue that our failure to advance on this front will remain the primary reason for continued high levels of violence in the future. Indeed, any society emerging from political conflict that starts from a low economic base and a high Gini coefficient, will not achieve a situation of low interpersonal and criminal violence without providing for the economic well-being of its citizens.

In South Africa, child support grants have been instituted for the most vulnerable families (at present R180.00 (about US$28.00) per month per child under fourteen years). This is not enough. Increasing numbers of young impoverished South Africans without hope of a better future, many infected with HIV/AIDS will enter adolescence and young adulthood to face very limited possibilities for a productive future. Some will go on to swell the ranks of the 'desperate, the furious' mentioned earlier. Post-conflict reconstruction is easy to talk about, but a lot more difficult to achieve.

Conclusion

I have argued that it is simplistic to assert links between the exposure of youth to political violence during the resistance period in South Africa's history, and the criminal interpersonal violence that has prevailed since 1994. I have also claimed that the major contemporary drivers of violence in South Africa are both historical and contemporary structural violence manifest in poverty and great inequality, accompanied by a long-standing culture of violence to which generations of young people in high-risk communities have been exposed.

It is obvious that the levels of poverty in South Africa cannot be overturned in the next few generations. This means that future generations will continue to be exposed to violence and, for some, both psychological and situational factors will conspire to set them on a path to antisocial and violent lifestyles.

With the HIV/AIDS pandemic, increasing numbers of children are going to lose sources of emotional nurturance and monitoring as their caregivers die. Their survival needs will be acute. In the absence of other sources of support, it will not be surprising if a proportion turn to crime and criminal gangs as their only survival option.

As family support systems are increasingly compromised by poverty and by the AIDS pandemic, schools have the potential to be places of refuge, support and care. In South Africa, schools will have to be key sites for addressing children's need for health and general well-being. Positive school environments can do much to provide sound developmental settings for children who would otherwise have few resources on which to build their competences (in the fullest sense). This is well established (Luthar et al., 2000). Of course schools have to be functioning well for this to be the case. Many in South Africa are not, and this in itself is a challenge.

Notwithstanding the need to remedy dysfunctional schools, school safety and violence prevention programmes can serve the important function of creating an environment that is safe for children, while at the same time creating opportunities for them to learn alternatives to violence. These are small but essential contributions to reducing the extent to which they are exposed to violence and the trauma that ensues.

Peace education and violence prevention are becoming buzzwords in psychosocial programmes for post-conflict societies. They are important initiatives. However, they are one component of a much wider set of actions that need to accompany the rebuilding of societies emerging from political violence. All the peace education in the world will come to little if not accompanied by improved education and better success rates in school linked to the creation of appropriate employment opportunities.

Acknowledgements

The author is most grateful to Jason Hart for his insightful feedback on drafts of the chapter. Thanks also to Mihloti Mushwana, Zareena Parker, Vanessa Farr and Rene Brandt for their assistance with the preparation of this chapter.

Note

1. South Africa has a population structure in which 36 per cent is constituted by those defined as 'youth' (14–34 years inclusive). The figure has remained stable since 1996. Source: Statistics South Africa.

References

Altman, M. and Woolard, I. 2004 'Employment and Unemployment in South Africa 1995–2002'. Working Paper, April 2004, Pretoria: HSRC.

Bandura, A. 1999 'Moral Disengagement in the Perpetration of Inhumanities', *Personality and Social Psychology Review* 3: 193–209.

Bandura, A., Barbaranelli, C., Caprara, G.V. and Pastorelli, C. 1996 'Mechanisms of Moral Disengagement in the Exercise of Moral Agency', *Journal of Personality and Social Psychology* 71: 364–74.

Barbarin, O.A. and Richter, L. 2001 'Economic Status, Community Danger and Psychological Problems among South African Children', *Childhood: A Global Journal of Child Research* 8 (1): 115–33.

Bollen, S., Artz, L., Vetten, L. and Louw, A. 1999 *Violence against Women in Metropolitan South Africa: A Study on Impact and Service Delivery.* Pretoria: Institute of Security Studies.

Cairns, E. 1987 *Caught in Crossfire. Children and the Northern Ireland Conflict.* Belfast: Appletree Press.

Cairns, E. 1996 *Children and Political Violence.* Oxford: Blackwell.

Chikane, F. 1986 'Children in Turmoil: The Effects of Township Unrest on Children', in S. Burman and P. Reynolds (eds) *Growing Up in a Divided Society. The Contexts of Childhood in South Africa.* Johannesburg: Ravan Press, pp. 333–44.

Chisholm, L. 2004 *Changing Class. Education and Social Change in Post-apartheid South Africa.* Cape Town: HSRC Press.

Community Agency for Social Enquiry and Joint Enrichment Project 1993 *Growing Up Tough: a National Survey of South African Youth.* Johannesburg: CASE/JEP.

Dawes, A. 1994a 'Political Violence and Moral Conduct', in A. Dawes and D. Donald (eds) *Childhood and Adversity: Psychological Perspectives from South African Research.* Cape Town: David Philip, pp. 200–19.

Dawes, A. 1994b 'The Emotional Impact of Political Violence', in A. Dawes and D. Donald (eds) *Childhood and Adversity: Psychological Perspectives from South African Research.* Cape Town: David Philip, pp. 177–99.

Dawes, A. and Van der Merwe, A. 2004 The Development of Minimum Standards for Diversion Programmes in the Child Justice System. Final report for NICRO. Cape Town: Child Youth and Family Development, Human Sciences Research Council.

Dawes, A., Robertson, B., Duncan, N., Ensink, K., Jackson, A., Reynolds, P., Pillay, A. and Richter, L. 1997 'Child and Adolescent Mental Health Policy', in D. Foster, M. Freeman and Y. Pillay (eds) *Mental Health Policy for South Africa*. Cape Town: M.A.S.A., pp. 193–215.

Ensink, K., Robertson, B., Zissis, C. and Leger, P. 1997 'Post-traumatic Stress Disorder in Children Exposed to Violence', *South African Medical Journal* 87 (11): 1526–30.

Everatt, D. and Sisulu, E. 1993 (eds) *Black Youth in Crisis: Facing the Future*. Johannsesburg: Ravan Press.

Farr, V., Dawes, A. and Parker, Z. 2003 Youth Violence Prevention and Peace Education Programmes in South Africa: a Preliminary Investigation of Programme Design and Evaluation Practices. A research report for the Children, Youth and Families Consortium, Pennsylvania State University Philadelphia: Pennsylvania State University.

Foster, D., Haupt, P. and de Beer, M. 2005 *Theatre of Violence. Narratives of Protagonists in the South African Conflct*. Cape Town: HSRC Press.

Galtung, J. 1990 'Violence and Peace', in P. Smoker, R. Davies and B. Munske (eds) *A Reader in Peace Studies*. New York: Pergamon, pp. 9–14.

Jones-Petersen, H. and Carolissen, R. 2000 'Working with Aggressive Preschoolers: a Systemic Community-based Intervention', in D. Donald, A. Dawes and J. Louw (eds) *Addressing Childhood Adversity*. Cape Town: David Philip.

Korber, I. 1992 'Positioned to Kill: a New Approach to the Question of Military Violence', *Psychology in Society* 16: 32–48.

Kupersmidt, J.B., Griesler, P.C., DeRosier, M.E., Patterson, C.J. and Davis, P.W. 1995 'Childhood Aggression and Peer Relations in the Context of Family and Neighborhood Factors', *Child Development* 66: 360–76.

Loeber, R., and Farrington, D.P. 1997 'Strategies and Yields of Longitudinal Studies of Antisocial Behaviour', in J.D. Maser (ed) *Handbook of Anti-social Behaviour*. New York: Wiley, pp. 125–39.

Loeber, R., Wung, P., Keenan, K., Giroux, B., Stouthamer-Loeber, M., Van Kammen, W.B. and Maughan, B. 1993 'Developmental Pathways in Disruptive Child Behaviour', *Development and Psychopathology* 5: 101–31.

Luthar, S.S., Cicchetti, D. and Becker, B. 2000 'The Construct of Resilience: a Critical Evaluation and Guidelines for Future Work', *Child Development* 71 (3): 543–62.

Magwaza, A.S., Killian, B.J., Peterson, I. and Pillay, Y. 1993 'The Effects of Chronic Violence on Preschool Children Living in South African Townships', *Child Abuse and Neglect* 17: 795–803.

Marks, S. and Andersson, N. 1990 'The Epidemiology and Culture of Violence', in N.C. Manganyi and A.B. du Toit (eds) *Political Violence and the Struggle in South Africa*. London: Macmillan, pp. 26–69.

Mason, B.L. 1994 The Psychological Effects of Violence on Children: an Exploratory Study of a Sample of Black School Children from the Natal Midlands. Unpublished Master of Arts thesis, University of Natal, Durban.

Natrass, N. and Seekings, J. 2001 'Democracy and Distribution in Highly Unequal

Economies: the Case of South Africa', *Journal of Modern African Studies* 39: 471–98.

NIMSS 2001 *Profile of Fatal Injuries in South Africa.* Cape Town: South African Medical Research Council.

Osofsky, J.D. 1995 'The Effects of Exposure to Violence on Young Children', *American Psychologist* 50 (9): 782–88.

Parker, Z., Dawes, A. and Farr, V. 2004 'Interpersonal Youth Violence Prevention', in S. Suffla, A. Van Niekerk and N. Duncan (eds) *Crime, Violence and Injury Prevention in South Africa: Developments and Challenges.* Tygerberg, South Africa: Medical Research Council, pp. 22–39.

Peltzer, K. 1999 'Posttraumatic Stress Symptoms in a Population of Rural Children in South Africa', *Psychological Reports* 85: 646–50.

Pinnock, D. 1984 *The Brotherhoods.* Cape Town: David Philip.

Punamaki, R. and Suleiman, R. 1989 'Predictors and Effectiveness of Coping with Political Violence among Palestinian Children', *British Journal of Social Psychology* 29: 67–77.

Reynolds, P. 1995 *The Ground of All Making: State Violence, the Family and Political Activists. Co-operative Research Programme on Marriage and Family Life.* Pretoria: Human Sciences Research Council.

Reynolds, P. and Dawes, A. 1999 'Truth and Youth: Blame and Pain', *ISSSBD Newsletter* 2: 10–11.

Robertson, G. 2003 *Young Lions in the Wilderness – Overview of Wilderness Therapy Intervention with Militarised Youth of Kathorus.* Modderfontein, South Africa: National Peace Accord Trust.

Scharf, W. and Ngcokoto, B. 1990 'Images of Punishment in the People's Courts of Cape Town 1985–7: from Prefigurative Justice to Populist Violence', in N.C. Manganyi and A. du Toit (eds) *Political Violence and the Struggle in South Africa.* Basingstoke, Hampshire: Macmillan, pp. 341–71.

Seedat, S., van Nood, E., Vythilingum, B., Stein, D.J. and Kaminer, D. 2000 'School Survey of Exposure to Violence and Posttraumatic Stress Symptoms in Adolescents', *Southern African Journal of Child and Adolescent Mental Health* 12: 38–44.

Seekings, J. 1993 *Heroes or Villains: Youth Politics in the 1980s.* Johannesburg: Ravan Press.

Seekings J. and Natrass, N. 2005 *Class, Race, and Inequality in South Africa.* New Haven: Yale University Press.

Sloth-Nielsen, J. and Muntingh, L.M. 2001 'Juvenile Justice Review 1999–2000', *South African Journal of Criminal Justice* 3: 384–405.

South African Police Service 2001 *Crime Statistics.* Department of Safety and Security: Crime Information Analysis Centre.

South African Police Service 2002 *Crime Statistics.* Department of Safety and Security: Crime Information Analysis Centre.

Stott, N. 2002 *From the SADF to the SANDF: Safeguarding South Africa for a Better Life for All?* Violence and Transition Series, Vol. 7. Johannesburg: Centre for Violence and Reconciliation (2002). http://www.csvr.org.za/papers/papvtp7.htm accessed 12 June 2003.

Straker, G. 1988 'From Victim to Villain: a "Slight" of Speech? Media Representations of Township Youth', *South African Journal of Psychology* 19: 20–27.

Straker, G. 2003. *Faces in the Revolution. The Psychological Effects of Violence on Township Youth in South Africa.* Cape Town: David Philip.

Straker, G. and The Sanctuaries Counselling Team 1987 'The Continuous Traumatic Stress Syndrome: the Single Therapeutic Interview', *Psychology in Society* 8: 48–78.

Swartz, L. and Levett, A. 1989 'Political Repression and Children in South Africa. The Social Construction of Damaging Effects', *Social Science and Medicine* 28 (7): 741–50.

UNDP 2000 *South Africa: Transformation for Human Development.* Pretoria: UNDP.

UNDP 2003 *South Africa: Human Development Report.* Pretoria: UNDP.

Van der Merwe, A. and Dawes, A. 2000 'Prosocial and Antisocial Tendencies in Children Exposed to Community Violence', *Southern African Journal of Child and Adolescent Mental Health* 12: 19–37.

Van Zyl Slabbert, F., Malan, C., Marais, H., Olivier, J. and Riordan, R. 1994 *Youth in the New South Africa: Towards Policy Formulation: Main Report of the Co-operative Research Programme: South African Youth.* Pretoria: HSRC Publishers.

Ward, C.L., Flisher, A.J., Zissis, C., Muller, M. and Lombard, C.J. 2001 '"Adolescents" Exposure to Violence: Relationships between Exposure and Symptoms', *Injury Prevention* 7: 297–301.

Zissis, C., Ensink, K. and Robertson, B. 2000 'A Community Study of Taxi Violence and Distress Symptoms among Youth', *Southern African Journal of Child and Adolescent Mental Health* 12 (2): 151–61.

5

Abject Heroes: Marginalised Youth, Modernity and Violent Pathways of the Liberian Civil War

Mats Utas

Modern is what some of us think we are, others of us wish desperately to be, yet others despair of being, regret, or oppose, or fear, or, now, desire somehow to transcend. It is our universal adjective. ... But though it is, originally, a Western word and a Western notion ... the idea of modernity has become the common property of all the world, even more prized and puzzled over in Asia, Africa, and Latin America, where it is considered to be just now, perhaps, at last arriving, or, for various sorts of dark reasons, still not doing so, than in Europe and North America, where it is regarded as being, for better or worse, largely in place. Whatever it is, it is pervasive, as either a presence or a lack, an achievement or a failure, a liberation or burden. Whatever it is (Geertz, 1995: 136).

As in numerous other African conflicts, the participation of large numbers of adolescent as combatants was crucial to the emergence and development of the Liberian Civil War (1990–96, 2000–3). In order to understand this war we must therefore give careful consideration to the motivations of these youth and the nature of their involvement. This article discusses why and how young men participated in the war.[1] Drawing on fieldwork conducted in Liberia during 1998[2] it explains how renderings of modernity, traditional myths of violent heroes and masking behaviour were all significant elements in youth participation in that country's civil war. The argument that is forwarded builds on the idea that the constituting and reconstituting of culture and cosmology creates a cultural bricolage in which apparently contradictory phenomena, such as modern weaponry and American action movies relate directly to local ideas of ancestors, witchcraft and mythical heroes. Inside the civil war the main cultural bricoleurs were the rebel youth themselves (Utas, 2003: 86).

I take my point of departure in young people's conceptions of what modernity and a modern state ought to be like. In their minds Liberia, in its different manifestations, has failed to live up to common expectations of modernity – in a similar fashion to what James Ferguson (1999) has argued for the Zambian Copperbelt. Modernity is thus delivered as a meta-narrative and, if the teleological modernity project itself failed, the meta-narrative of modernity is still playing a vital role in contemporary Liberia, as elsewhere in Africa. It is most powerful and socially explosive in spaces where large numbers of individuals are marginalised in socio-economic terms. This is visible in urban settings (Abdullah, 1997, 1998), but also occurs in the rural areas (Richards, 1996), to give two examples from Sierra Leone. In this vein it is important to talk about a meta-narrative of modernity in relation to a meta-narrative of marginalisation and social exclusion where war and social violence of the poor must be seen as manifestations of rage against the politically and economically privileged (Dunn and Böås, 2007).

We should also acknowledge that many combatants saw war as a pursuit of individual power in a situation where everybody fought for themselves. There is nothing novel about this. Rather, the enlistment of young Liberians in rebel armies follows an analogous logic with earlier labour and educational migration inside as well as outside the country. And it also fits well with long-standing configurations of hunters and warriors relating to myths of masculine heroes in the West African subregion. I here try to establish the link between current antisocial youth combatants and long-standing patterns of culture-specific heroes present in local mythology – Sunjata types of morally neutral heroes. In this vein the text looks at the acquisition of various forms of power through ambiguous transgressions of sociocultural frontiers performed by weak, or marginal, subjects.

A Compact History of the Liberian Civil War

The Liberian Civil War started when a small group of men commanded by Prince Johnson entered the eastern town of Butuo, in Nimba County, on Christmas Eve 1989. The Libyan-trained, rather ill-equipped group became known as the National Patriotic Front of Liberia (NPFL) and within weeks it splintered into two factions; one led by Charles Taylor, and the other, the Independent National Patriotic Front of Liberia (INPFL), by Prince Johnson.

The latter, although initially enigmatic and prosperous, abruptly left the scene, in 1993, after first rejoining with Taylor and then moving over to join the West African peacekeeping force (ECOMOG) in October 1992. Eventually, his INPFL soldiers merged with the NPFL or were picked up by other emergent rebel factions. From then on, NPFL became the major player in the war and kept control of much of the Liberian hinterland. Taylor called his territory 'greater Liberia' and selected Gbarnga, in Bong County, first as NPFL HQ and later as the capital of his territory.

Initially NPFL/INPFL warfare was perceived as a 'revolution' in which the peoples in Nimba County (Nimbadians) in particular fought with sticks and cutlasses. But, as time passed and other rebel movements joined in the war, this transformed into acts of terror, whereby largely young rebel soldiers fought each other. Political leaders turned into warlords, with their own private interests fighting over the control of mineral-rich areas and logging concessions (Reno, 1996, 1998, 2000; Ellis, 1998). Within a few years, half a dozen rebel movements had spread terror throughout the country. In that fashion, NPFL, for instance, which originally claimed to be fighting for the Nimbadians, spread fear through the entire Nimba County: NPFL boys looted and molested the very people they were claiming to defend in the war. In seven years of civil war, between 150,000 and 200,000 people were killed,[3] 600,000 to 700,000 refugees fled to neighbouring countries, and the majority of the remnants of a pre-war population of 2.2 to 2.5 million was internally displaced. Subsequent peace talks and elections were held in mid-1997. Ironically, Charles Taylor and his National Patriotic Party (NPP) – formed out of the NPFL apparatus – won a landslide victory and thereby accomplished what NPFL combat failed to do.

Peace under Taylor and NPP remained fragile and from late 1999 an armed faction with support from Guinea turned up in Lofa County. Initially having limited support within Liberia, the new rebel group, which became known as Liberians United for Reconciliation and Democracy (LURD), and its 2003 splinter faction Movement for Democracy in Liberia (MODEL) advanced towards Monrovia and were in early 2003 aided by heavy international diplomatic pressure on Taylor to resign. Their joint effort succeeded in pushing Taylor into exile. An interim government, supported by a large UN peacekeeping force kept a security status quo until elections, won by the veteran politician Ellen Johnson-Sirleaf in November 2005 – giving Africa's oldest republic Africa's first elected female president.[4]

Youth as an Alternative Moral Community

Richard Fanthorpe states that 'conflict itself generates a frantic search for moral community. A frightened and disoriented populace, we are told, tends to seek refuge in ethnicities and/or religious sodalities that offer to take on the burden of their alienation and represent it as a struggle for cultural rights' (Fanthorpe, 2001: 367–68). This is frequently the case. However, other primary identities – such as forming part of a marginalised population, or participation in a fighting faction – might in some cases be of more immediate importance than apparently 'primordial' attachments such as ethnic identity. Although ethnic targeting of civilians was part of the military and political strategies of some of the rebel movements, ethnicity played a limited role in the rank and file soldiers' choice of armed group in the 1989–96 part of the Liberian Civil War. Various militant factions or rebel armies were comprised of soldiers with diverse ethnic backgrounds, and soldiers deserted from one rebel faction just to enter the ranks of former enemy units. Some combinations, such as Krahn personnel in the NPFL line were rare but far from impossible. Thus popular explanations of soldiers running behind ethnic leadership as the foremost root of African wars fall short, at least in explaining the first part of the Liberian civil war.[5] Social factors other than ethnicity traversed the rebel factions and kept rank-and-file soldiers together rather than apart.

To most youth combatants, youth identity – of being excluded from society – appears to have been the core 'touchstone of fraternity' (Scott, 1990: 39), and a common ground for fomenting a 'moral community' irrespective of ethnic background. The focus on youth identity and violence/warfare in this chapter forms part of a larger regional body of literature influenced by the central works of Paul Richards (1995, 1996, 2005), including authors such as Cruise O'Brien (1996), Ibrahim Abdullah (1998, 2004), Peters and Richards (1998), Ellis (1999), Hoffman (2003, 2004, 2005a,b), Böås (2004, 2007), Peters (2004, 2006) and Vigh (2006). More recently the youth/conflict nexus has received a more general pan-African attention (Abbink and van Kessel, 2005).

Liberian Youth and the Meta-narrative of Modernity

I saw *Superfly*, *Shaft*, and other Blaxploitation films in Monrovia (Liberia) in the early Seventies. I remember being particularly struck by the opening sequence in *Superfly* – it seemed an extraordinary cinematic event. I had been living in Monrovia for almost a year, and was fascinated by the lifestyle in that West African city, which identified more with America than with Africa. People spoke English with a black American accent like the one I heard in the movies, on television (in shows like *Good Times* and *Sanford and son*), and in rhythm-and-blues and gospel songs. The cities in Liberia have names like Virginia, Maryland, Greenville, and Harper. I lived on an avenue called Randall Street. All the people in Monrovia liked to trace their family origin to the United States. Most of my friends had already been to America at least once, or were getting ready to join a cousin, a sister, or a friend there. Some referred to

America as 'home.' It was in Liberia that I first learned to speak English, and developed a yearning to go to America myself one day (Diawara, 1998: 247f).

Manthia Diawara's account originates from a time when the modernity paradigm of Africa, in its developmental sense, still remained intact, and opened seemingly unending possibilities for young people. Diawara grew up in Guinea and Mali and spent many summers (and later a full year) of his youth in Monrovia. To him and most Liberians, Liberia had reached far beyond other African states in their efforts to modernise (this image was, however, primarily an urban feature). Liberians often claim that during those times (1960s and 1970s) they had their backs turned to Africa while facing North America. With the Liberian state largely founded by returning slaves (called Americo-Liberians), and with kinship ties continuing across the ocean in North America and the Caribbean, the Liberian elite cultivated an image of being somehow more 'modern' than the rest of Africa. Comparing Diawara's image of Monrovia during the 1970s with the 1998 Monrovia, where I did fieldwork,[6] is in many ways stunning and sad. Monrovia's appearance and appeal have brutally changed. Its once proud modernist buildings rendered in mirror glass lay in ruins, the city's water network was badly damaged and the sewers were constantly overflowing. Electricity had been down for many years. Smoke and noise from private generators had become part of city life.[7] The chaos of hastily installed electricity wires were still intertwined with telephone wires around the city – a throwback to an earlier age. Streets were potholed, and garbage was disposed of everywhere and burned on the spot rather than transported away.

In Monrovia, the food parlour King Burger was an obvious marker of modernity. In pre-war Monrovia there were two such establishments: one on Broad Street and one in the Freeport area. In 1998 King Burger on Broad Street was a seedy place. Being a constituent of the modernity project, food still came in the shape of hamburgers, chicken sandwiches, etc., but its Western menu was becoming rather diluted. Indian ownership added to the globalisation of the menu. In the bathroom, the toilet cistern has been dried out for years and was turned into a hideout for cockroaches, a space contested only by customers' ejected cigarette butts. According to the meta-narrative of modernity, urban space should be taken over by establishments like King Burger. In Monrovia, anno 1998, however, they were standing idle, frozen as peeling monuments to a failed modernity. Ironically, the other King Burger had become host to a money transfer firm. Globalisation was making itself heard there in the form of rapid money transfers provided by Western Union, yet again stressing African post-colonial dependence on the Western world. Huge sums of money are every year transferred into the country from the Liberian diaspora all over Europe and North America. Money from family members working in the Western world sustains a substantial number of Liberians.

The Meta-narrative of Modernity

Modernity has essentially the capacity of a meta-narrative in the African arena, as James Ferguson demonstrates in *Expectations of Modernity* (1999). The concept of modernity, or, as the Liberians like to express it, of 'being developed', 'exposed' or *kwii* (a word used in many Liberian vernaculars), is constructed upon a particular teleological perception of social development. Liberia was seen to develop along the linear expectations of modernity up to the mid-1970s, and yet slowly the picture started to crack as large numbers of young Liberians were permanently displaced into socially and economically marginal situations.

During the formation of the Liberian state, from 1847 and onwards, the desire of young Liberians to urbanise was essential to its success. As the urban centres along the coast grew, young males were hired for employment within trade, shipping, commerce and production. In the process of strengthening and maintaining the Liberian state, young men were also in high demand within the army, police and elsewhere in the civil service. Over time, Liberia developed into a plantation economy (foremost rubber, coffee, sugar cane and cocoa) and yet again young men became the backbone of the labour force. Thus, as expected, the high demands on young men led to new migration patterns where they left rural villages to partake in a national economy based on wage labour. In this process rural economies were transformed and became increasingly dependent on remittances from migrants.[8]

However, along with the economic decline in Liberia, and all of Africa, during the 1970s, the need for wage labourers dwindled. The Liberian state had less money for salaries, and actual wages for plantation workers decreased. Fewer people could subsist on work within the economy of the modern state at a time when a cash-based economy had become an imperative for taking part in the modern world. Young men had earlier been able to rely on the income generation of a few years' work on plantations – or similar forms of employment – in order to establish themselves in their home villages by investing their saved income, as well as their 'modern' social capital, in a farm, a house, wife (or wives) and family. In the context of economic decline it became increasingly difficult to obtain funds and the benefits that followed. They were thus forced, during extended periods of time, to survive on underpaid contracts in towns and plantations. As fewer people could afford to send their children to school, the quality of education was also undermined. Governmental salaries declined in real terms and were paid with increasing irregularity, thus forcing more and more educated teachers to look for alternative, better-paying jobs. Impoverished youth who awaited their chance in towns and cities increased in numbers, creating a context of chronic poverty. For the great majority, political unrest during the

1980s led to increasing tensions.[9] For many, the situation was so hopeless that when the civil war intensified in 1989 the war became an opportunity to obtain what many youth had failed to access through their initial migration from countryside to city or plantation. Economic prosperity and the sensation of power and respect were immediate and most welcome for a newly initiated member of a rebel army, with the AK-47 becoming the equivalent of a credit card (Sesay, 1996) – as it once again connected young men to the dreams of the modern world of goods and money.

The psychosocial side of experiencing disconnection from the rest of the world fits into what Ferguson, borrowing from Kristeva, has called 'abjection'. Abjection connotes being thrown down – to be humiliated and degraded. Studying global disconnects and the consequent abjection in the Zambian Copperbelt, Ferguson observes 'a sense that the promises of modernization had been betrayed, and that they were being thrown out of the circle of full humanity, thrown back into the ranks of the "second class," cast outward and downward into the world of rags and huts where the color bar always told 'Africans' they belonged' (1999: 236).

Among Liberian combatants it is possible to observe the same sentiment; however the notion of abjection would cover not only disconnection from a wider world order, but also from the 'modern' order of things within the national arena of Liberia as well as in local communities.[10] Some events of the Liberian civil war pinpoint a disconnection of modernity. This became real in a very visible way, for example, when sets of electric powerhouses, complete with their wires to connecting towns and the local telephone lines, were dismantled and carried abroad to Guinea or the Ivory Coast by rebel soldiers or sold to Nigeria by elements of the peacekeeping forces.[11] Roads connecting cities and towns were also destroyed, or simply regained by nature.[12] However, it was not the civil war that actually dismantled Liberian 'modernity'. On the contrary, it was the dismantling of modernity in popular imagery that made the war indispensable as failed expectations of modernity led many people to doubt their future, thus providing bedrock for a level of dissatisfaction, which ruthless political oppositions successfully harnessed in the creation of insurgent rebel armies.

Modernity and Afro-pessimism

To many young Liberians, war itself became part and parcel of an African identity – not unlike popular imaginations of Africa in the Western world. Hearing of a war going on in Bosnia, for example, led some Liberians to believe that Bosnia was actually situated on the African continent. War had clearly become a marker of the failure of modernity, and in the minds of the masses it was only Africa that could possibly fail so bitterly. Such a failure is often in public discourse blamed on the immorality and selfishness of the

Liberians themselves, and indeed often the entire African population (see, for example, Diawara, 1998). It was repeatedly explained to me that Africans have not only black skin but also black hearts in opposition to the 'white man'. One of my informants said, jokingly, that when Jesus first arrived on our planet he initially tried to land in Africa, but he bounced! Africa was simply too immoral for a pious being like Jesus to remain. Such ideas echo the messages brought to Liberia by early missionaries and slave traders, as well as the range of colonisers in general, and most probably obtain power from the nowadays vastly popular Pentecostal churches.

Even though Liberia was never formally colonised in the conventional sense, the Americo-Liberian leadership of the country still managed to shape Liberia in the same fashion as other colonising powers (Tonkin, 2002; Utas, forthcoming). In popular thought, the idea of development follows a linear path. So it also holds that the experience of being disconnected from modernity implies exclusion from membership of the larger world (Ferguson, 2002). Such imaginations have provided fuel for many Afro-pessimistic ideas in post-colonial Africa (Diawara, 1998). The rise in Afro-pessimistic ideas has led to the search for alternative paths towards individual status as modern, rather than the abandonment of the meta-narrative itself. The elite of Liberian society still upholds the image of being modern, and global, at least through the possession of the latest technological gadgets, shiny cars and clothes, travel possibilities, and so on. What is different, however, is that it has been limited to an increasingly shrinking elite. Being aware that their fragile positions are becoming ever more contested, these elites are prepared to use whatever means available to retain their position. To young people with a desire for modern pretensions, two pathways appear: either to move to a space where such facilities are imagined readily available for all, that is to say Europe or the U.S.A., or to use brute force to enter the contested space within the national arena. As is clear from the Liberian case, both paths have been used. I am therefore arguing that the war could be seen as individualised competition over a limited modern space.

A Historical Outlook on the Liberian Concept of Modernity

In Liberia, to be 'civilised', or modern, is of long-standing significance for the status of the individual. It is a lucid marker of power for young people especially. To most Liberians, modernity is what comes from distant soils and comes in the appearance of commodities (technology, clothes, etc.), communications, the Western form of education, and world religions such as Christianity and to some extent Islam – but also magic in its various forms. Modernity most obviously appears in the guise of consumption. We might talk about modernity as consumerism, or the seduction of consumption (Baudrillard, 1990; Bauman, 1998). In contrast the popular idea of tradition is what is locally produced, whether it comes in the form of commodities or of the history of ideas. Tradition occupies a space largely dominated by elders. In contesting the power of elders, youth are, therefore, prone to seek status in the modern.[13] If we stick to this emic use of the concepts, there are modern and traditional trajectories (*kwii meni* and *zo meni*, respectively, in Kpelle language) leading to power and respect within Liberian society. Although traditional paths had largely been inaccessible to underprivileged young people, the routes of modernity nevertheless remained within their reach up until the economic crisis of the late 1970s. The increased instability of the 1980s was in part a result of a blockage of paths within the 'modern sphere' as the number of young people taking the *kwii* path continued to grow and simultaneously the pathway was narrowed down, changing the transitory state of youth to a more chronic category of the 'marginalised'.

Kwii and Zo Meni

I intend to go into some detail about the Liberian concept of modernity, *kwii*,[14] and its antithesis, *zo*. I do so by focusing on the terms as pathways to socio-economic power. We shall run into several paradoxes in studying the two paths. *Kwii*, for instance, is linked both to the deceased (carriers of tradition) and to white people (uncontested carriers of modernity).

John Gay's 1973 novel, *Red Dust on the Green Leaves*, describes Kpelle life in the 1930–1940s when the penetration of roads, growing roadside towns, a diversity of traders, missionaries and a civil service started to make an impact on village life in interior Liberia. In this account, we follow twin brothers, Sumo and Koli, on their paths to adulthood. Their life trajectories branch off after bush school (initiation into Poro secret society). At the time, two available routes to adulthood and power were available: those of modernity and tradition (in their emic use). The book makes an effort to view both as being educational: Koli's life goes along the modern trajectory as he follows the dirt roads to 'civilisation' and the missionary school, managed by the 'white man'. Sumo, on the other hand, stays in the village where he eagerly learns traditional wisdom by listening to the old men with medicinal knowledge. Sumo learns to master Kpelle proverbs,[15] and, by way of a wise marriage and the establishment of his own farm, he matures into a position where he can both enter the senior levels of Poro society and become a future candidate for village chief.

Being an allegory on rural Liberia, the book builds up a close tension between Sumo and Koli, in a way representatives of the traditional and the modern, old and new, close and far away, the known and the unknown, respectively – constructing a juxtaposition that appears to be just as valid to contemporary Liberians. The popular idea of a tension between the two different orders of reality, in Kpelle terminology the *kwii meni* and the *zo meni* (Bellman, 1975: 25), remains much the same. Yet, from a rural perspective, 'modern brokers' with knowledge in *kwii* matters have 'eclipsed in political value knowledge of the mystical affairs in the traditional forest' (Murphy, 1981: 674), where urbanites, plantation workers, traditional hunters and warriors (as we shall see) share the same conceptual space. Navigators of the *kwii* paths thus contest *zo* power in the local arena.[16] The seemingly very different paths taken by Sumo and Koli, i.e. the trajectories of tradition and modernity, will ultimately lead to local power, sanctioned within the same cosmology.[17]

Linking Up Kwii Pathways

The young combatants that I have studied yearned for a place within the modernity complex, even if an abstraction, but were socially, politically and not the least economically prevented from knowing that. In this light they had to look for alternative paths. By saying so I am, however, not arguing that they were transcending the ideas of the *kwii* and *zo* paths, but rather that, when they now also found the *kwii* path blocked, in increasing numbers they came to form a category of marginalised youth who in desperation only increased their stakes in the social chessboard by taking up arms. Violence became the augmented means to obtain the symbolic power of modernity. The moral ambivalence of the *kwii* path, trodden by hunters, warriors and migrants and other ambiguous frontier persons (De Boeck, 2000), made these paths particularly suited for the abject heroes of the Liberian civil war. We shall see that their antisocial, 'selfish' – almost like the 'white man' – appearance fits quite well with a cultural concept of the amoral hero, but first we should focus on the dispossessed and disenfranchised youth (the 'dis' people, to borrow from Chernoff, 2003: 31–45), who currently navigate the ambiguous *kwii* pathways.

Encountering the Marginal Subject

Aspiration to become agentive within the public arena, through obtaining a distinct voice in the decision-making processes of the larger society distinguishes 'youth-hood' – as a social space – from both childhood and adulthood. With all its ambiguities, 'youth-hood' is an open-ended project 'everywhere and at all times quite contrasting for different gender, class, or occupational groups' (Durham, 2000: 116). In the Liberian setting, the term 'youth' is most often used to mark certain attributes, such as liminality and marginality, rather than a chronological definition based on age. Liberians who call themselves (or are labelled so by others) youth might be aged up to forty, clearly pointing out that youth in that sense is a social category – in clear conflict with the 'pre-colonial' setting where 'youth-hood' was seen as a demarcated period of time when a person was isolated from larger society, away from family and hometown, in Poro (male secret society) or Sande (female) bush schools in the forest. The person left as a child for bush school and later returned to the town as an adult.[18]

In the wake of urbanisation and the partial withering away of secret societies and 'traditional' offices in contemporary Liberia, 'youth-hood' has become a prolonged period where participation in public will take place without having sufficiently obtained the status of full membership into adult society matters. Thus the length of 'youth-hood' has become highly negotiable: a 'crash course' in Poro or Sande 'business', for example might be sufficient to enter adulthood. Appropriating the right support, both economic and sociocultural and from parents and social networks, would generally implicate a short period of 'youth-hood'. The change between childhood and adulthood could thus be instant. Yet the liminal period of youth varies depending on each personal situation and for a large proportion of the Liberian population, 'youth-hood' actually becomes an extended struggle, played out over many years and met with growing frustration. Chronological ageing is, in itself, not enough to turn into an adult as socio-cultural requirements, like establishing a farm or holding a job, and supporting a family carry enormous social weight. Without advancement in these sectors, 'youth-hood' turns chronic, or at least becomes a period of socially dissipated time.

In discussing the Sierra Leone civil war, Ibrahim Abdullah and other Sierra Leonean scholars have devoted much effort in trying to increase our understanding of 'lumpen youth culture' in Freetown as the root of RUF (Revolutionary United Front of Sierra Leone) and military junta creations – lumpens, being 'largely unemployed and unemployable youths, mostly male, who live by their wits or who have one foot in what is generally referred to as the informal or underground economy' (Abdullah, 1998: 207).

Lumpen youth respond in much the same way to the impact of marginalisation and socio-economic pressures as everywhere in the world, whether it be in urban Africa or in small-town Europe. Youth in this sense can be seen as a social effect of power (Durham, 2000). On the surface, one will find the most striking similarities among young people in similar situations worldwide. Modes of these marginalised youth; including language, bodily postures, dress code, music and film taste, show considerable resemblance across our world due to globalised forms of communication and trade. Yet when the subject of youth is discussed, we often find that rural youth is omitted. The label youth is mostly used, it would seem, in connection with urban style and its modernities. I argue that this is a misconception. The notion of a cosmopolitan mode (Ferguson, 1999)[19] and 'homeboy' cosmopolitanism in particular (Diawara, 1998),[20] resonates not only in urban settings, but in reality carries influences deep into the bush or rainforest. I suggest that rural youth who navigate *kwii* pathways should be seen as the 'urban villagers'. The Liberian Civil War was influenced by homeboy cosmopolitanism, not only as a matter of style, but as a social movement of empowerment. During the course of war, many more young people found access and salvation in cosmopolitan ideals, not only those of urban consumption patterns of commodities and drugs, but also ideas of civic rights and individual value.

Accounting for Violence

In discussions with my core group of informants,[21] in Ganta, Nimba County, we time and again returned to their experience of betrayal in our discussions. This betrayal was experienced on multiple levels – social marginalisation was experienced from several centres – ranging from parents and close relatives moving up to gerontocratic leadership, social servants, politicians on the national level, and equally the international community. The experience of betrayal among marginal youth had not decreased during the war years as social uncertainties had mounted in general and deceit had become a common route to get by. In the post-war[22] scenario, ex-combatants also felt betrayed and let down by the promises of their former warlords. However, such abject sentiments were already an aspect of social marginality prior to the war.

Raised in a climate of abjection, being dispossessed and disenfranchised fuelled what Friedrich Nietsche (1994: 21–37) has called *ressentiment*. This is, in part, an obsession with and aggression directed towards the 'outside' or 'the other' by those who have been 'denied the proper response of action' and 'who compensate for it only with imaginary revenge' (ibid.: 21). To Michael Bernstein, drawing on Nietsche, *ressentiment* is a kind of 'empowered abjection' – the agency of the abject subjects – and he notes: 'in *ressentiment*, for all its shabbiness and self-loathing, there is a potential for extraordinary violence and a rage whose ferocity has been repeatedly mobilized by political movements' (1992: 27). To abject youth, violence became a charter for agency. Abjection and growing *ressentiment* were the main reasons for young Liberians to empower themselves by taking up arms to fight what they saw as social injustice. In this process of self-empowerment, local, social and cultural institutions such as secret societies, warrior guilds, etc. were mimicked in order to gain power. Ambiguous imitation, creating a socio-cultural *bricolage*, is part of navigating social topographies (Vigh, 2006), of moving along modern, *kwii* pathways. Violent manipulation of sociocultural space is one navigational technique in the hands of the abject hero and it will be made clear that a firm mythic base exists for our abject navigators.

Kwii Pathways of the Abject Heroes

In the following section there is an added effort in further understanding perceptions of power in the war. Scrutinising the relationship between mythologised heroes, Liberian leaders and the abject rebel soldiers, it appears that they all, in the emic sense, travel the same pathways of modernity and that they all form part of a *kwii* complementary opposition to local, embedded means of power. As pointed out above, transgressions of the *kwii* and the *zo* are integral to the system and aspects of masking will in the final part of this chapter be highlighted as a technique to attain such transgressions. In Liberia power, according to Stephen Ellis, 'is what it is, inherently neither good nor evil' (1999: 233). This idea of a morally neutral power is especially pronounced in the figure of the hero as defined in culturally specific terms. As pointed out by Donald Cosentino across the region we find a concept of the hero as a morally neutral being (1989: 31). Two examples from the field demonstrate this point:

1. Watching and analysing a Hollywood action movie with some Liberian friends initially made me quite confused, since they did not maintain the binary opposition between the hero and the bad guy in the fashion that I had learned to take for granted. Good and bad remained present in their analysis of the film, but what was striking about their categorisation was that they talked about the 'good hero' and the 'bad hero'.
2. A young woman narrated a story about a Liberian 'war hero' residing in a small town in southern Sierra Leone. The man was a fighter in the ULIMO (United Liberation Movement of Liberia) force, which for some time had fought alongside the Sierra Leone army against the RUF rebels. Rumours reached the rebel soldier that one of his girlfriends – a successful fighter has got many girlfriends – was having an affair with another man. As a response to this, he brought the girl into a public place, laid her on a market table and forced her legs open. He proceeded by forcing a mortar pestle, from the (chilli) pepper mortar deep inside her vagina.[23] The story is not unique: similar things happened to many unfortunate men and women during the civil war. Rather it is something else that catches one's attention: throughout the story, the female narrator attaches the label 'hero' to the perpetrator. It is obvious that she does not imply that the perpetrator is acting in a correct, moral way; rather, as in the case of the movie viewers' responses, the case proposes that the title 'hero' is morally neutral in local terminology.

Sunjata Types of Heroes

To get a better understanding of the cultural specificity of the abject youth hero and indeed social heroism in general, we need to penetrate local mythology. Epics and popular charter myths give us a better understanding of young combatants' functions in the Liberian civil war. The most well-known hero epic in the West African subregion is that of Sunjata. Few Liberians have any direct association to Sunjata, and yet a majority of Liberian charter myths are closely related to this epic as they speak in similar terms of marginal young men and their socio-cultural negotiations of power, their initial powerlessness, and the practices of magic and use of violence to come to alter excluded destinies. Paradoxically, I argue, these heroes are ambiguous frontier characters travelling along the *kwii* pathway in sync with Koli and the 'white man' as the modern and the socially remote are eclipsing the immoral, the violent and the occult.

Sunjata Keita was born the son of a king. However, being the offspring of the king's third wife and being born crippled (at the age of seven he could still not walk), he spent his childhood on the margins of society. Finally learning to walk, he started to develop supernatural strengths, thus contesting the power of the firstborn son of the king, the heir to the throne. When his father died, the ensuing power struggle forced him to go into exile. During these years, he gained further strength, acquired magical skills and became a much renowned and feared warrior/hunter. Sunjata is destined to return, and upon his return, he emerges victorious out of all battles and subsequently rises to power to establish the Mali Empire.[24]

In Sunjata fashion, young West Africans seek to migrate to towns, diamond mines or plantations, or to faraway countries in Europe or the Americas. The incentive is to gain economic and partly magical strength (in a mythologised manner), ultimately returning home to establish themselves in the centre of society. Modern migration myths contain clear allusions to Sunjata-type scenarios, and they may influence the decision of young men and women to leave home.[25] Becoming a warrior, leaving the zo path of village or town for the *kwii* path, is also a form of migration.[26] Breaking with the local community and the social roles one is expected to comply with for bush paths and the skills of warriorhood is clearly a Sunjata response. By taking the *kwii* path one can, like Koli, return to contest the powers of the *zo* path. The conscious breaking with social norms and regulations is another theme present in the Sunjata epic. To reach individual status and power, Sunjata uses antisocial means. Sunjata 'becomes associated with those skilled, secretive, and dangerous practitioners of the occult, the hunters' societies, the epitome of antisocial behavior' (Johnson, 1999: 19). Warriorhood in Liberia is equally breaking with social norms, contesting power through illegitimate violence and practices of the occult, and thus in the emic sense modern. Albeit contesting power, it should be pointed out that it also functions as an alternative model in reaching power.

Some twenty years ago, Bird and Kendall analysed Sunjata as a 'rebel hero' and noted that 'the image of the rebel hero who breaks with, but ultimately returns to his people is not without relevance to the modern Mande child' (1980: 22). In Liberia myths of adventurer–rebel heroes of the Sunjata-epic genre are kept alive to this day. The Sunjata figure appears in various transformed versions. In Gio mythology we find a trickster character called Boya Manjbe, who has a clear affinity with Sunjata. This figure is an *enfant terrible*, a trickster and shape-shifter who frequently behaves immorally to a powerful leadership, not as a Robin Hood or a social bandit, but rather for his own sheer pleasure.[27]

Similar characters can be found among other peoples in Liberia. They are, however, better described in the literature on Sierra Leone. Cosentino has found their presence throughout that country and in his words 'each group had snatched from the manifest Mande myth its own figure of a rebellious youth overturning some sacrosanct ancestral construct in pursuit of some personal sweet latent in the inherited mosaic of images' (Cosentino, 1989: 33). Among the Mende peoples in Sierra Leone, Musa Wo is a similar figure. Like Boya Manjbe, Musa Wo remains amoral to the very end. As Cosentino notes, 'the hallmark of all Musa Wo's actions is volition unrestrained by social considera-tion' (ibid.: 30). While Sunjata-like epic heroes 'are transformed from abused and wilful miscreants into beneficent rulers, Musa Wo begins as an *enfant terrible* and descends to the level of a relentless, obscene, and amoral monster' (ibid.: 22). Having an impressive criminal record Musa Wo, the deposed royal aspirant, descends into an 'entropy of pornographic violence' (ibid.: 28).

In Eric Hobsbawm's typology of social bandits the most extreme category is located in the archetypal 'avenger': 'in romances of the oppressed ... to assert power, any power, is itself a triumph', thus 'killing and torture is the most primitive and personal assertion of ultimate power, and the weaker the rebel feels himself to be at the bottom, the greater, we may suppose, the temptation to assert it' (2000: 71). This is the essence of Musa Wo and I argue that it is this trajectory that has been used by many of the young rebel soldiers in the Liberian civil war – in this case violence is an expression of 'power of the powerless' and empty destruction is the language of abject rejection and *ressentiment*. However, one ought not to forget that a moral ideal is maintained simultaneously, as 'the moral world to which they belong contains the values of the "noble robber" as well as those of the monster' (ibid.: 64) and the abject rebel hero aims at being reborn as a moral and respected citizen. Violence to the marginal being, Michael Jackson writes, 'is the implementation of ... reversal. It is governed by the desperate and magical conviction that by turning back the clock, reversing the sequence of events that comprise one's national history or personal biography, nothingness will yield to being. One will somehow make good what was lost, repair what has been broken, and forget the tragedy that has befallen one' (2002: 5).

Liberian trickster characters have always been modern, i.e. oppositional, beings. Despite drawing upon long-standing ideals of shape-shifting, such images are depicted as perpetual counter-forces to 'traditional' leadership and values. The ease with which they blend with recent encounters of Western rap[28] and reggae icons as well as movie characters points towards that. Paul Richards argues that the Vietnam-war-veteran-outsider character of John Rambo is a classic trickster figure close in spirit to Musa Wo (1996: 59; see also Richards, 1994). Bruce Lee and the often hidden faces of ninja fighters on the screen evoke much the same connotations.[29] Such ubiquitous youth icons 'make their appearance in juxtaposition with images of age and authority, suggesting the persistence of the primal struggle between the overbearing father and the rebellious son that is at the heart of the travails of Musa Wo' (Cosentino, 1989: 34):

> Musa Wo is an archetypal expression of that unresolved conflict: the wild longing for free expression in a tightly constricted society. Neither his per-formers nor his audience knows where he is going. His myth has no ending, and cannot be ended. But his persistence on the road may express what Samuel Beckett has called mankind's pernicious optimism (the dark hope for a happy, if unknowable, end to the adventure) (Ibid.: 36).

Growing Big the Sunjata Way

It should be noted that ideas of empowerment among our abject heroes are closely linked to successful, high-profile political and economic leadership. *Kwii* leaders and patrons are role models, and yet ambiguous ones, for the marginal subjects of the Liberian state, and, after all, national non-localised leadership is fought for and obtained on *Kwii* pathways and in Sunjata ways. If we take a look at the national and thus 'modern' type of leadership in Liberia, we must thus connect the ambivalent and morally neutral concept of a hero with powerful big men. Sunjata types of qualities are prerequisites for rising to power in the current state arena, and yet it is possible to transform one's *kwii* powers to local *zo* authority if one acts skilfully.

In a Sunjata-like fashion, supremacy is obtained through magic powers gathered in distant (social) territories – again viewed as modern. The potency of these magical powers is commonly generated through geographical and social distance. The methods to gain power do not have to fit with a set of moral ideals, as the power of patrons and big men is based on a concept of the morally neutral hero. At a first glance, there is little similarity between the current president Ahmad Tejan Kabbah in Sierra Leone and the now removed Charles McArthur Taylor in Liberia. In fact their paths to state power appear to be quite each other's antithesis. One made a successful career within the UN system, whilst the other, although a U.S. college graduate, was suspected of fraud and was imprisoned in the U.S.A. He later became the main rebel leader of the Liberian civil war. I shall argue nevertheless that part of their success is connected to their appearances as proto-Sunjatas. Their struggle in and then mastery of faraway places herald their successful return. Taylor and Kabbah returned as masterful leaders should do; equipped with their Western university degrees, as mythico-medicinal power. Power in their case, as well as Sunjata's, is established on merits from abroad. 'Individuals who travel to, or learn about, far away lands have privileged access to powerful, mysterious knowledge' (Bledsoe, 1990: 77; see also Ferme, 1994). Kabbah's return is crowned by the fact that a contingent of Western governments offers him support, and the aid money that he scores shows in a symbolic way his mastery of that system. Taylor's return, on the other hand, is even more Sunjata-like. He returns as a warrior, employing magical skills as well as wit.[30] In his effort to gain ultimate power he is fearless and he uses all means of power available to get all the way, thus complying with the ideal of the morally neutral hero. Both Kabbah and Taylor return as mythically 'modern' leaders. But do they transform their leadership into a more morally recognisable authority – thus following Sunjata all the way? Kabbah appears reasonably successful in this task, but Taylor's effort proves futile. In Charles Taylor's case the international community, where he in Sunjata fashion drew some of his symbolic capital from, prevented all attempts of transformation by refusing to wash his rebel manners off. He was inclined to follow the ever-descending path of the trickster heroes of Boya Manjbe and Musa Wo and maybe we could see his continued destabilising efforts in the area (rumours of his involvement in subversive activities in the Ivory Coast and Guinea) as the perpetual effort of an abject Taylor.

Performing Violence behind a Mask

One way of understanding how soldiers can carry out extreme forms of violence is to look at a range of self-masking experiences. The act of masking both physical and psychological selves is a technique for abject heroes of the Liberian Civil War. Masking is influenced both by 'tradition' and by modern, exterior, practices. It is argued that masking during war may, in Sunjata fashion, provide actors with altered social status. Masking, as it is used here, not only is the direct practice of putting on a mask but is used in a wider symbolic sense and appears to be a universal trait of soldiering. Masking of the self implies removing oneself from reality going into a condition of the pseudo-real as proposed by Ben-Ari for Israeli soldiers and Bowden for U.S. soldiers in Somalia.

> Many times it's like a game. A game of learning how to deal with it. There is a certain problem and you have to give a solution. You – I think – cut yourself off

from all sorts of thought about what you're doing, and how and what's happening here. It's a game like a crossword puzzle, of technique, of how you deal with a problem (Israeli soldier in Ben-Ari, 1989: 378).

In my interviews with those who were in the thick of battle, they remarked again and again how much they felt like they were in a movie, and had to remind themselves that this horror, the blood, the deaths, was real (Mark Bowden, *Black Hawk Down: a Story of Modern War*, cited by Fuchs, 2002).

In his attempt to come to grips with Israeli soldiers' action on the battlefield, Eyal Ben-Ari says 'they become other to themselves – real but not really real'.[31] Israeli soldiers comprehend gearing themselves in uniform the first day of duty 'as the donning of disguises' or 'as the bearing of masks' (Ben-Ari, 1989: 378). The sense of masking evokes an alternative behaviour, something that is different from civilian life and in a sense also non-normative. It creates space or 'a legitimate license to behave in ways that they would not normally … associate with themselves' (ibid.: 379). One can suggest that they enter a mode of pseudo-reality where reality appears as 'a game' or 'as a movie' as the citations above suggest. My Liberian informants often made similar references to the feeling of being not 'real' and indeed many descriptions of a specific battle convey the same sense of pseudo-reality. After describing a particular fierce battle, one informant concluded, in a tone of sincere affection, 'being in the battlefield is so sweet. Nothing is as thrilling as fighting when it is going fine'. Ben-Ari (1989, 1998) has proposed that the hyperreality of experiencing 'flow' during 'deep play' (Geertz, 1973), as developed by Csikszentmihalyi (2000), is very important in any effort to understand this type of situation. Flow, in combination with fear and direct danger, shuts off streams of consciousness, making it possible to focus on only a few tasks. In this process, the enemy is dehumanised as the very goal of the mission is to take them out of action. Therefore it is quite conceivable that assaults of extreme violence are taking place. As a 'moral boost',[32] a variety of drugs, taken prior to a battle, further focus the soldier and increase the experience of flow, masking every experience of normality.

During the first years of the Liberian Civil War, rebel fighters wearing wigs, wedding gowns and other female paraphernalia caught international media attention as something truly bizarre (Johnson, 1990; Daniels, 1991). The cross-dressing phenomenon is explained by placing it in its proper context, as in a very interesting article by Mary Moran (1995, 1997). It forms part of a regional preoccupation with masking and masquerading (Cannizzo, 1983; Nunley, 1987; Ottenberg, 1989).[33] In pre-European times and in early Liberian wars, masks, replicating fearless deceased warriors and dangerous animals were carried onto the battlefield to boost warriors' morale and frighten the enemy (Harley, 1950). In Liberia the utilisation of a mask and other regalia is a highly visual way of pointing out that you have entered a morally different role. Christian Kordt Hoejbjerg writing on Loma masking in Guinea and Liberia points out that 'masking serves as a vehicle of transformation and a means of coping with change' and that 'masks consist above all in their transformative role' (2005: 159). Certainly the use of magic power functions in a similar way. When you enter the battlefield and commit atrocities behind a mask and under the influence of magic power, then it is the spirits who are responsible for your actions and not you personally. As Mariane Ferme points out on Sierra Leone:

> The mask confers on the wearer the ability, through assuming a new identity, to carry out such acts of violence legitimately and with impunity, because his or her real identity is concealed. This aspect of masking has always been put to use in war, and particularly in this region's civil wars, where cross-dressing, masks and amulets have played key roles in the material culture of war (2001: 3).

The lack of ordinary personality, not only if masked, but also if one changes one's ordinary behaviour, frightens the other and in the mask-on mode, the self can act with alternate powers, empowered by spirits and other magical capacities. However, once the mask is off, or the magic charms are removed, or the behavioural patterns restored, the powers in the eyes of both the self and the other are gone.[34] At the same time as the power is gone the acts under disguise are left under impunity as carried out by another being. The individual can reconstitute himself as a moral other. Conspicuous violence is a means to get to power for the morally neutral hero. Yet turning the moral upside down, linking to myths of extreme egotistical individualism, can be effective in the short term, but eventually one will have to repent and turn morally virtuous again. Such was the case of my good friend Alex, a diehard fighter in the INPFL, and later the NPFL. In the war, his distinguishing mark had been to cut off the ears of his enemies. This was in stark contrast to his life when I met up with him in 1998. Then he spent most of his time in church, even acting as accountant for a local Pentecostal parish. Upon asking him about this apparent paradox, he shrugged his shoulders and pointed out that 'there are times when you have to do bad, and times you have to do good' – a typical response from an abject morally neutral war hero.

During the war Liberia experienced rapid transformations of warrior traditions and taboos. Masks and other items of symbolic disposition, such as charms, were given new meanings and acquired new guises. Masking procedures modernised as the traditional 'bulletproof' vest were substituted by brutally orange life jackets, and warriors carried masks made out of plastic. From frontier characters we should expect such *bricolage* responses as they after all draw their power from the foreign, and moreover ceremonial objects of power are always ambiguous and alterable. Where 'new' masks are worn we also find people contesting power, aiming at becoming actors on higher socio-political levels. It is the proto-Sunjata response of Taylor and Kabbah, as discussed above, and it is in the act of masking and subsequently de-masking that shapes can be shifted more permanently.

Modernity, Masks and Abject Heroes

> Young men who took up arms could be seen as demonstrators (Young ex-combatant in Ganta, Nimba County, 1998).

In this chapter it has been argued that ideas of a youth revolution, or war as a demonstration, is a partial explanation for participation of a whole generation of disenfranchised and dissatisfied young people, where being socially abject forms part of a meta-narrative of social exclusion. I have suggested that this is the transitional phase that youth have by and large turned into a swelling chronic category of marginalisation and abject economic and social destitution. In a further effort to understand violent acts carried out by young rebel fighters in the Liberian Civil War, this chapter has tried to show how complex emic ideas of modernity correspond with local concepts of abject heroes. In contradictory fashion, ideas of modernity are connected to the abstract whereabouts of ancestors and traditional pathways navigated by warriors. Our abject warriors are understood as modern, or *kwii*, to make use of the emic term. The popularity of Western movie heroes such as Rambo fits well into traditional epics of the Sunjata character, showing the way for predominantly (but far from solely) young men who experience exclusion from the meta-narrative of modernity. In abject rebel hero fashion violence is turned into an instrument to conquer. Fitting into local cosmology, but with clear parallels to soldiering elsewhere in the world, the idea of masking the moral self, as rebel heroes of the Liberian Civil War have been doing, is here discussed under the concept of the morally neutral hero. The mask-on/mask-off idea becomes crucial. One and the same person can appear immoral in one setting just in order to reappear in a moral guise in another social setting and at another time. This makes it possible to leave the warrior identity behind without personal guilt or indeed blame, making it easier for both the person and the setting to re-enter moral society without too many repercussions. The 'modern' shape-shifting qualities of the hero also offer the potential of transforming one's abject social position into that of a big man in society, as rebel soldiers and national politicians are cast in the same frame of *kwii* modernity.

Yet despite his shape-shifting efforts the abject hero of the Liberian Civil War in most cases ultimately fails his goal to permanently shift shape as 'his power to shape-shift ... condemns him to the very marginality he struggles to escape' (Jackson, 1989: 112). Generally shape-shifters are predestined to the path of Boya Manjbe – it is only the few that reach the Sunjata ideal – and shape-shifting is thus a short-term tactical, rather than a long-term strategic response to larger society. And in that vein Liberian combatant youth failed to fully accomplish transformation into possessors of moral power and permanent inclusion in (imagined) modern space at the end of the war and, instead, were thrown back into the marginal space of society from which they had assiduously fought to escape.

Dedication

Without celebrating the horrible acts of human abuse they have committed, this chapter is a tribute to the abject heroes of the Liberian civil war.

Notes

This chapter forms part of a lecture entitled 'Of Masks and Men: Liberian Youth Combatants and the Experience of Marginality', which was given at the Refugee Studies Centre, as part of 'Adolescents, Armed Conflict and Forced Migration: an International Seminar Series', at the University of Oxford on 29 October 2003. The author wishes to thank Jason Hart first for the kind invitation to Oxford and later for profound editorial work. He further wants to thank David Turton and Michael Jackson for enlightening and inspiring discussions concerning themes dealt with in this chapter.

1. In this chapter I take an exclusively male outlook on the Liberian civil war. However, as I have argued elsewhere (Utas, 2005a,b), female discourses on civil war realities and participation do not differ that much from those of the males in this chapter. One particular difference would be that there are fewer mythological characters to hold on to and as such female fighters in the war appear ultra-modern.

2. Fieldwork in Monrovia was conducted among ex-combatant youth between December 1997 and June 1998 and in Ganta, Nimba County between June and December 1998. The fieldwork was mainly based on participant observation and unstructured group interviews. See Utas (2004) for a discussion on field methods in relation to this work.

3. Stephen Ellis (1999) has argued that the death toll was considerably lower. Not surprisingly, statistics from war zones tend, at best, to be skilled guesses rendering quite approximate figures.

4. However, Johnson-Sirleaf is actually only the second female president in Liberia. Ruth Perry was Liberian interim president in 1996–97.

5. For a general critique of popular ethnic explanations of warfare see Allen and Seaton (1999).

6. By coincidence I too, like Diawara, resided on Randall Street in downtown Monrovia.

7. The collapse of state-run electricity is not a necessary outcome of war. In Freetown, Sierra Leone, the electricity system became somewhat more reliable during the war than it had been prior to the war.
8. Compare the current dependence in the global South in general, but Africa in particular, on remittance traffic from Europe/U.S.
9. It is possible to draw many direct parallels with the socio-economic developments in Sierra Leone and I am here influenced by many of the insights of Paul Richards (1996).
10. To talk about a general African disconnect is, however, too one-dimensional, as certain areas of African social life are instead increasingly 'connecting', or what might be labelled globalising (Utas, 2002).
11. The saintliness of Nigerian peacekeepers found in the work of Adebajo (2003) is by and large a falsification.
12. Ferme (2001: 35) has pointed out that in southern Sierra Leone this disconnect was sometimes deliberately actioned by local communities who stopped clearing roads and paths so as to avoid external actors pillaging (both governmental and rebels). This has also been the case in many Liberian settings. For instance, in Nimba County, EU staff complained over the lack of cooperation, among villagers, in the reconstruction of bridges. In some cases they were even met by masked devils of the secret societies, who forced local staff to stop their work. See also Shaw (2000: 33) for a historical comparison.
13. As we know, tradition, even if often contrasted to modernity in popular discourses, is in practice neither constant nor singular and is not to be easily separated from the modern.
14. *Kwii* is the word for modern, developed and/or white in many Liberian vernaculars. Even if there is general agreement concerning the origin of the word, the spelling of the word differs widely from scholar to scholar. I do not suggest that *kwii* is more appropriate than any other spelling of the word, but I have chosen to follow Bellman (1975). The concept has been the focus of much attention in anthropological writing on Liberia from Fraenkel (1964, 1966) onwards (Tonkin, 1981; Brown, 1982; Moran, 1988, 1990, 1992, 2000; David, 1992; Fuest, 1999).
15. Kpelle peoples are renowned for their 'extraordinary use of proverbs and of formulaic ways of dealing with human difficulties. These were their means of putting things into the perspective of the traditional' (Bruner, 1973: xiv).
16. I here use navigation in the sense that Henrik Vigh (2006) proposes in his work on youth as social navigators. See also our jointly edited book *Navigating Youth, Generating Adulthood* (Christiansen et al., 2006).
17. Note that, even if the *kwii* and *zo* order of things are often juxtaposed in popular thought, they can be utilised by the very same person simultaneously (see Tonkin, 1981).
18. This appears as the ideal picture; yet categories of slaves and social pawns could also be seen as structural categories of youth. Compare with 'social cadets' in the work of Bayart (1979) and Argenti (2007).
19. Ferguson describes cosmopolitanism as implying neither travel nor cultural competence: 'it is less about being at home in the world than it is about seeking worldliness at home' (Ferguson, 1999: 212). Undeniably 'cosmopolitanism has special affinity with both privilege and youth but it is reduced to neither' (ibid.: 213).

20. Diawara devotes a chapter in his *In Search of Africa* to the 'homeboy cosmopolitan'. Based on American inner city hip hop culture, the 'homeboy' is 'perpetually on the move, looking to make progress and achieve individual redemption' (Diawara, 1998: 255). In his pursuit, he transgresses borders and categories and shapes individual identities to escape from social bondage. This is highlighted in the 'homeboy's' antisocial behaviour (ibid.: 245). This black American culture of the margin corresponds well to the lives of young Liberians even in the rural areas.

21. The core group of informants consisted of about ten young ex-combatants and at times their girlfriends. Most squatted in the same house, but others hung around the house on a daily basis. The informants' ages ranged from late teens to early thirties.

22. I refer to the period of 1998 as post-war because at that time it was widely believed that the civil war was over. In late 1999, however, as noted above, a new rebel force entered Liberia, again turning the country into a war zone.

23. There is a pronounced symbolism of the mortar being the female sexual organ, and the pestle being the male. The mortar is also subject to taboos for warriors.

24. The Sunjata myth is thoroughly researched (see, for example, Austen, 1999; Conrad and Condâe, 2004; Jansen, 2001).

25. It is, of course, a highly idealised picture, and as we know, many fail – often ending up in circumstances more precarious than those they left.

26. The merging of warrior, hunter and migratory identities is a widely held idea in the subregion and further beyond (see, for example, Cassiman, 2005, on migration in Ghana, and De Boeck, 2000, on the Democratic Republic of Congo).

27. This kind of story should be read as a form of social critique.

28. In Sierra Leone a rebel unit was named after the late American rap musician Tupac Shakur and it is reported that in early October 1998 more than a hundred rebels attacked the northern town of Kukuna sporting T-shirts bearing Tupac's picture (Lansana Fofana – BBC correspondent, *Electronic Mail* and *Guardian*, Johannesburg, 7 October 1998 – http://www.chico.mweb.co.za/mg/news/98oct1/7oc-sierra_rap.html). Furthermore a government militia took the name West Side Boys (or Niggaz) partly because of influences from the same artist (see Utas and Jörgel, n.d.).

29. As is also common in other conflicts, special forces of the various Liberian rebel armies were called ninjas. In the reconstructed (post-1997 election) Armed Forces of Liberia (AFL), a unit of especially hardened soldiers, were also called ninjas.

30. Part of his legitimacy, even after the 1997 election, rests on his warrior, magician and migrant/education identity. This is clear as he is keen to be presented with his honorary titles *Gankay* (strong man in Gola), and less often *Okatakyie* (brave warrior – title given by the Ghanaian business community), *Dahkpanah* (chief medicine man in Kpelle), but also Doctor (an honorary title received from Taiwan) – revealing his educational and migrational status.

31. Lecture Department of Cultural Anthropology and Ethnology, Uppsala University, 4 October 2002.

32. Expression used by the Sierra Leonean army.

33. Yet masking and cross-dressing are a universal trait of rebel heroes (Austen, 1986: 94).

34. A video sequence of the torture of President Doe is instructive. As soon as his captors have removed his magical charms, it is understood that his super-powers have left him (see Utas, 2006).

References

Abbink, J. and van Kessel, I. 2005 *Vanguard or Vandals: Youth, Politics, and Conflict in Africa.* Leiden, Boston: Brill.
Abdullah, I. 1997 'Bush Path to Destruction: the Origin and Character of the Revolutionary United Front (RUF/SL)', *Africa Development* XXII (3/4): 45–76.
—— 1998 'Bush Path to Destruction: the Origin and Character of the Revolutionary United Front/Sierra Leone', *Journal of Modern African Studies* 36 (2): 203–35.
—— 2004 *Between Democracy and Terror: the Sierra Leone Civil War.* Dakar: CODESRIA.
Adebajo, A. 2003 'In Search of Warlords: Hegemonic Peacekeeping in Liberia and Somalia', *International Peacekeeping* 10 (4): 62–81.
Allen, T. and Seaton, J. (eds) 1999 *The Media of Conflict: War Reporting and Representations of Ethnic Violence.* London: Zed.
Argenti, N. 2007 *The Intestines of the State: Youth, Violence and Belated Histories in the Cameroon Grassfields.* Chicago: Chicago University Press.
Austen, R.A. 1986 'Social Bandits and Other Heroic Criminals: Western Models of Resistance and their Relevance for Africa', in D. Crummey (ed) *Banditry, Rebellion and Social Protest in Africa.* London: James Currey, pp. 86–107.
—— 1999 *In Search of Sunjata: the Mande Oral Epic as History, Literature and Performance.* Bloomington: Indiana University Press.
Baudrillard, J. 1990 *Seduction.* New York: St. Martin's Press.
Bauman, Z. 1998 *Work, Consumerism and the New Poor.* Buckingham, Philadelphia: Open University Press.
Bayart, J.F. 1979 *L'Etat au Cameroun.* Paris: Presses de la Fondation nationale des sciences politiques.
Bellman, B. 1975 *Village of Curers and Assassins: on the Production of Fala Kpelle Cosmological Categories.* The Hague: Mouton.
Ben-Ari, E. 1989 'Masks and Soldiering: the Israeli Army and the Palestinian Uprising', *Cultural Anthropology* 4 (4): 372–89.
—— 1998 *Mastering Soldiers: Conflict, Emotions, and the Enemy in an Israeli Military Unit.* New York: Berghahn Books.
Bernstein, M.A. 1992 *Bitter Carnival: Ressentiment and the Abject Hero.* Princeton, N.J.: Princeton University Press.
Bird, C.S. and Kendall, M.B. 1980 'The Mande Hero: Text and Context', in I. Karp and C. S. Bird (eds) *Explorations in African Systems of Thought.* Bloomington: Indiana University Press, pp.13–26.
Bledsoe, C. 1990 '"No Success without Struggle": Social Mobility and Hardship for Foster Children in Sierra Leone', *Man* 25:70–88.
Böås, M. 2004 'Africa's Young Guerrillas: Rebels without Cause?' *Current History* May: 211–14.
– 2007 'Marginalized Youth', in M. Böås and K. Dunn (eds) *African Guerrillas: Raging*

against the Machine. Boulder, CO: Lynne Rienner, pp. 39–53.

Brown, D. 1982 'On the Category "Civilised" in Liberia and Elsewhere', *Journal of Modern African Studies* 20 (2):287– 303.

Cannizzo, J. 1983 'The shit devil', in F. E. Manning (ed) *The Celebration of Society*. Bowling Green: Bowling Green University Popular Press, pp. 125–144.

Cassiman, A. 2005 '"They Have Travelled". Migrants and their Belonging to the Emptied Modernized Parts of the Compound House in Kasenaland (NE-Ghana)'. Conference paper – Aegis 05, London, June 2005.

Chernoff, J.M. 2003 *Hustling is not Stealing: Stories of an African Bar Girl*. Chicago: University of Chicago Press.

Christiansen, C., Utas, M. and Vigh, H. (eds) 2006 *Navigating Youth, Generating Adulthood: Social Becoming in an African Context*. Uppsala: Nordic Africa Institute.

Conrad, D.C. and Condâe, D.T. 2004 *Sunjata: a West African Epic of the Mande Peoples*. Indianapolis: Hackett Publishers.

Cosentino, D.J. 1989 'Midnight Charters: Musa Wo and Mende Myths of Chaos', in W. Arens and I. Karp (eds) *Creativity of Power*. Washington, DC: Smithsonian Institution Press.

Cruise O'Brien, D.B. 1996 'A Lost Generation? Youth Identity and State Decay in West Africa', in R. Werbner and T. Ranger (eds) *Postcolonial Identities in Africa*. London: Zed Books Ltd, pp. 55–74.

Csikszentmihalyi, M. 2000 *Beyond Boredom and Anxiety: the Experience of Play in Work and Games*. San Francisco: Jossey-Bass.

Daniels, A. 1991 'Heart of Darkness', *National Review*, 10 June: 17–18.

David, S.M. 1992 ' "To be *Kwii* is Good": a Personal Account of Research in a Kpelle Village', *Liberian Studies Journal* XVII (2): 203–15.

De Boeck, F. 2000 'Borderland Breccia: the Mutant Hero in the Historical Imagination of a Central African Diamond Frontier', *Journal of Colonialism and Colonial History* 1 (2): 1–43.

Diawara, M. 1998 *In Search of Africa*. Cambridge, MA: Harvard University Press.

Dunn, K. and Böås, M. 2007 *Revisiting African Guerillas: Raging against the Machine*. Boulder, CO: Lynne Rienner.

Durham, D. 2000 'Youth and the Social Imaginary in Africa: Introduction to Parts 1 and 2', *Anthropological Quarterly* 73 (3), 113–20.

Ellis, S. 1999 *The Mask of Anarchy: the Destruction of Liberia and the Religious Dimension of an African Civil War*. New York: New York University Press.

Ferguson, J. 1999 *Expectations of Modernity: Myths and Meanings of Urban Life on the Zambian Copperbelt*. Berkeley, CA: University of California Press.

—— 2002 'Of Mimicry and Membership: Africans and the 'New World Society', *Cultural Anthropology* 17 (4): 551–69.

Ferme, M. 1994 'What "Alhaji Airplane" saw in Mecca, and What Happened When He Came Home: Ritual Performance in a Mende Community (Sierra Leone)', in R. Shaw and C. Stewart (eds) *Syncretism/Anti-syncretism: the Politics of Religious Synthesis*. London and New York: Routledge.

—— 2001 *The Underneath of Things: Violence, History, and the Everyday in Sierra Leone*. Berkeley: University of California Press.

Fraenkel, M. 1964 *Tribe and Class in Monrovia*. London: Oxford University Press.

—— 1966 'Social Change on the Kru Coast of Liberia', *Africa* 36 (2): 154–72.

Fuchs, C. 2002 'Black Hawk Down: Right out the Window', *Critical Voice* – http://www.thecriticalvoice.com:1–3.

Fuest, V. 1999 ' "Modernes" Wissen – "moderne" Macht: zur kulturellen Konstruction formaler Bildung am Beispiel von Geheimbund-Gesellschaften in Liberia und Sierra Leone', *Zeitschrift für Ethnologie* 124 (1): 73–95.

—— 2005a 'The Brookfields Hotel (Freetown, Sierra Leone)', *Public Culture* 17 (1): 55–74.

—— 2005b 'Violent Events as Narrative Blocs: the Disarmament at Bo, Sierra Leone', *Anthropological Quarterly* 78 (2): 353.

Gay, J. 1973 *Red Dust on the Green Leaves; a Kpelle Twins' Childhood*. Thompson, Conn.: InterCulture Associates.

Geertz, C. 1973 'Deep Play: Notes on the Balinese Cockfight', in C. Geertz (ed.) *The Interpretation of Cultures.* New York: Basic Books.

—— 1995 *After the Fact: Two Countries, Four Decades, One Anthropologist.* Cambridge, MA: Harvard University Press.

Harley, G. 1950 *Masks as Agents of Social Control in Northeast Liberia.* Peabody Museum of American Archaeology and Ethnology, Cambridge, MA: Harvard University.

Hobsbawm, E.J. 2000 *Bandits.* New York: New York Press.

Hoejbjerg, C.K. 2005 'Masked Violence: Ritual Action and the Perception of Violence in an Upper Guinea Ethnic Conflict', in N. Kastfelt (ed) *Religion and African Civil Wars.* London: Hurst.

Hoffman, D. 2003 'Like Beasts in the Bush: Synonyms of Childhood and Youth in Sierra Leone', *Post Colonial Studies* 6 (3): 295–308.

—— 2004 'The Civilian Target in Sierra Leone and Liberia: Political Power, Military Strategy, and Humanitarian Intervention', *African Affairs* (103): 211–26.

Jackson, M. 1989 *Paths toward a Clearing: Radical Empiricism and Ethnographic Inquiry.* Bloomington: Indiana University Press.

—— 2002 'The Exterminating Angel: Reflections on Violence and Intersubjective Reason', *Focaal – European Journal of Anthropology* 39: 137–48.

Jansen, J. 2001 'The Sunjata Epic – the Ultimate Version', *Research in African Literatures* 32 (1): 14–46.

Johnson, D. 1990 'The Civil War in Hell', *Esquire*, December: 43–46, 219–21.

Johnson, J.W. 1999 'The Dichotomy of Power and Authority in Mande Society and in the Epic of Sunjata', in R.A. Austen (ed) *In Search of Sunjata: the Mande Oral Epic as History, Literature, and Performance.* Bloomington: Indiana University Press.

Moran, M. 1988 ' "Women and Civilization": the Intersection of Gender and Prestige in Southeastern Liberia', *Canadian Journal of African Studies* XXII (3): 491–501.

—— 1990 *Civilized Women: Gender and Prestige in Southeastern Liberia.* Ithaca, NY: Cornell University Press.

—— 1992 'Civilized Servants: Child Fosterage and Training for Status among Glebo of Liberia', in K. Tranberg Hansen (ed) *African Encounters with Domesticity.* New Brunswick: Rutgers University Press.

—— 1995 'Warriors or Soldiers? Masculinity and Ritual Transvestism in the Liberian Civil War', in C.R. Sutton (ed) *Feminism, Nationalism and Militarism.* Washington DC: Association for Feminist Anthropology/American Anthropological Association, pp. 73–87.

—— 1997 'Warriors or Soldiers? Masculinity and Ritual Transvestism in the Liberian

Civil War', L. Lamphere, H. Ragoné and P. Zavella (eds) *Situated Lives: Gender and Culture in Everyday Life*. New York: Routledge, pp. 440–50.

—— 2000 'Uneasy Images: Contested Representations of Gender, Modernity and Nationalism in Pre-war Liberia', in T. Mayer (ed) *Gender Ironies of Nationalism: Sexing the Nation*. London: Routledge, pp. 113–36.

Murphy, W. 1981 'The Rhetorical Management of Dangerous Knowledge in Kpelle Brokerage', *American Ethnologist* 8 (4): 667–85.

Nietzsche, F. 1994 *On the Genealogy of Morality*. Cambridge: Cambridge University Press.

Nunley, J.W. 1987 *Moving with the Face of the Devil: Art and Politics in Urban West Africa*. Urbana: University of Illinois Press.

Ottenberg, S. 1989 *Boyhood Rituals in an African Society: an Interpretation*. Seattle: University of Washington Press.

Peters, K. 2004 *Re-examining Voluntarism: Youth Combatants in Sierra Leone*. Pretoria, South Africa: Institute for Security Studies.

—— 2006 Footpaths to Reintegration: Armed Conflict, Youth and the Rural Crisis in Sierra Leone. Ph.D., Wageningen University.

Peters, K. and Richards, P. 1998 'Fighting with Open Eyes: Youth Combatants Talking about War in Sierra Leone', in P. Bracken and. C. Petty (eds) *Rethinking the Trauma of War*. London: Save the Children/Free Association Books.

Reno, W. 1996 'The Business of War in Liberia', *Current History*, May: 211–15.

—— 1998 *Warlord Politics and African States*. Boulder CO: Lynne Rienner Publishers.

—— 2000 'Liberia and Sierra Leone: the Competition for Patronage in Resource-rich Economies', in E.W. Nafziger, F. Stewart and R. Väyrynen (eds) *War, Hunger, and Displacement: the Origins of Humanitarian Emergencies*, Vol. 2. Queen Elizabeth House Series in Development and UN/Wider Studies in Development Economy. Oxford: Oxford University Press, pp. 231–59.

Richards, P. 1994 'Videos and Violence on the Periphery: Rambo and the War in the Forests of the Sierra Leone-Liberia Border', *IDS Bulletin* 25 (2): 88–93.

—— 1995 'Rebellion in Liberia and Sierra Leone: A Crisis of Youth?', in O. Furley (ed) *Conflict in Africa*. London: Tauris Academic Studies.

—— 1996 *Fighting for the Rain Forest: War, Youth and Resources in Sierra Leone*. Oxford: James Currey.

—— 2005 'New War: an Ethnographic Approach', in P. Richards (ed) *No Peace, No War: Ethnographic Essays on Contemporary Conflicts*. Oxford: James Currey.

Scott, J.C. 1990 *Domination and the Arts of Resistance: Hidden Transcripts*. New Haven, CT: Yale University Press.

Sesay, M.A. 1996 'Politics and Society in Post-war Liberia', *Journal of Modern African Studies* 34 (3): 395–420.

Shaw, R. 2000 ' "Tok Af, Lef Af": a Political Economy of Temne Techniques of Secrecy and Self', in I. Karp and D.A. Masolo (eds) *African Philosophy as Cultural Inquiry*. Bloomington and Indianapolis: Indiana University Press, pp. 25–49.

Tonkin, E. 1981 'Model and Ideology: Dimensions of Being Civilised in Liberia', in L. Holy and M. Stuchlik (eds) *The Structure of Folk Models*. ASA Monographs, 20. London: Academic Press.

—— 2002 'Settlers and their Elites in Kenya and Liberia', in C. Shore and S. Nugent (eds) *Elite Cultures: Anthropological Perspectives*. London: Routledge, pp. 129–44.

Utas, M. 2002 'Mobile Mania in Dakar – Just a Modernity Mirage?' *LBC Newsletter* (January): 2–3.

—— 2003 *Sweet Battlefields: Youth and the Liberian Civil War*. Uppsala: Uppsala University, Dissertations in Cultural Anthropology:

—— 2004 'Fluid Research Fields: Studying Excombatant Youth in the Aftermath of the Liberian Civil War', in J. Boyden and J. de Berry (eds) *Children and Youth on the Frontline: Ethnography, Armed Conflict and Displacement*. Oxford: Berghahn, pp. 209–36.

—— 2005a 'Agency of Victims: Young Women's Survival Strategies in the Liberian Civil War', in F. de Boeck and A. Honwana (eds) *Makers and Breakers; Made and Broken: Children and Youth as Emerging Categories in Postcolonial Africa*. Oxford: James Currey, pp. 53–80.

—— 2005b 'Victimcy, Girlfriending, Soldiering: Tactic Agency in a Young Woman's Social Navigation of the Liberian War Zone', *Anthropological Quarterly* 78 (2): 403–30.

—— 2006 'War, Violence and Videotapes: Media and Localised Ideoscapes in the Liberian Civil War', in P. Kaarsholm (ed) *Violence, Political Culture and Development in Africa*. Oxford: James Currey.

—— forthcoming. 'Malignant Organisms: Continuities of State Run Violence in Rural Liberia', in B. Kapferer and B. Bertelsen (eds) *Vital Matters*. Oxford: Berghahn Books.

Utas, M. and Jörgel, M. n.d. 'The West Side Boys: Social and Military Navigation in the Sierra Leone Civil War'. Unpublished manuscript.

Vigh, H. 2006 *Navigating Terrains of War: Youth and Soldiering in Guinea-Bissau*. Oxford: Berghahn Books.

6

UNHCR and the Military Recruitment of Adolescents

Hanne Beirens

Introduction

Recent years have witnessed increasing activity by human rights activists and humanitarian agencies to end underage recruitment. In spite of this, our understanding of the reasons why young people enrol and how they make sense of their experiences as combatants remains very limited. Concern about the malign effects of soldiering and certain conceptualisations of childhood and child development have both foreclosed consideration by humanitarian agencies of the processes by which adolescents, in particular, come to take up arms. In this chapter I explore how one such agency – the United Nations High Commissioner for Refugees (henceforth UNHCR) – has conceptualised underage recruitment. As I shall argue, the framework used by UNHCR to guide its work does not adequately engage with the common reality of adolescents themselves: a point that has clear and serious implications for the success of protection efforts.

I begin the chapter by describing the policy framework that UNHCR has developed to guide its activities in relation to underage military recruitment. This framework and the accompanying operational guidelines convey the organisation's moral position and theoretical understanding. As I shall explain, these illustrate that UNHCR has expected its personnel to adopt a primarily legalistic approach to the issue of child recruitment and deployment, requiring them to gather evidence of this violation of child rights and international law.

Drawing upon interviews with UNHCR personnel and consultants as well as a review of UNHCR documents, I shall consider what this approach has meant in practice. I highlight the fact that at field level UNHCR employees have focused their attention primarily on armed groups whose actions in respect of underage recruitment they are obliged to observe, document and report. In comparison, the young people who join the ranks of such groups have received little direct attention. Consequently, there has been a general neglect of the specific situation of adolescents: their experiences, motivations and needs. Although adolescence is used as a term in UNHCR documents, this conceptual distinction from younger children has had little impact upon practice in relation to measures to prevent recruitment.

Accounts by UNHCR staff sometimes revealed a more contextualised understanding of the military engagement of under-eighteens that allowed for consideration of the differences between the situation of adolescents and that of younger children. However, as I explain, it is difficult for these members of staff to act in accordance with their own experiences and observations. Strongly shaped by contemporary global sentiments and underwritten by particular understandings of child development, the framework adopted by UNHCR generally leaves little space for reformulation in light of first-hand knowledge. The conceptual frame within which UNHCR employees operate may in fact echo the experiences in other humanitarian agencies where policies and practices are profoundly shaped by a globally dominant perception on young people's military engagement.

Research Approach

From November 2000 until March 2001, I worked as an intern at the office of the UNHCR in Geneva. I undertook this internship within the framework of my doctorate, which critically engaged with contemporary notions of voluntary child soldiering and comprised two periods of fieldwork. First, this internship was to provide me with a case study for examining the conceptualisations of childhood and adolescence informing international policies and programmes in relation to child soldiers. Secondly, fieldwork in Cape Town with former child soldiers who fought in the South African anti-apartheid struggle presented me with a historical case study to research the context-specific factors and processes that young people identify as informing their decision to participate in armed combat. On a few occasions in this chapter, I shall draw upon that field-based research with young combatants to shed light on the views from within UNHCR vis-à-vis child soldiering and to explore questions prompted by the disparity between the two.

My assignments at two UNHCR departments – the Evaluation and Policy Analysis Unit and the Office of the Senior Coordinator for Refugee Children

– allowed me access to public and internal documents reporting on UNHCR's policies and activities in relation to child soldiering and to discuss these informally with staff members. In addition, my position at UNHCR headquarters facilitated the organisation of interviews with staff members who had been directly or indirectly confronted with the use and recruitment of children in hostilities while stationed in UNHCR field offices. During the first quarter of 2004, I updated and expanded the data I had collected as an intern by conducting telephone interviews with UNHCR staff members and external consultants. Since my departure from UNHCR, several evaluations of that organisation's activities, such as those in relation to the rights and protection needs of refugee children, have concluded and the resulting reports and recommendations have been made public. In my interviews, I sought to gain an understanding of whether and how these evaluation reports and the structural change these provoked had affected the ways in which UNHCR deals with the issue of child soldiering.

UNHCR's Framework

In the 1990s, UNHCR moved the issue of child soldiering to the centre of its international protection and assistance efforts in relation to refugee children and adolescents. *Refugee Children: Guidelines on Protection and Care* (1994) was the first UNHCR document to make explicit reference to the issue of underage recruitment and to outline procedures for staff. However, it was with the *1997 Strategy for Follow-up to the Report on the Impact of Armed Conflict on Children* (UNHCR, 1997) that child soldiering was placed firmly on the conceptual and policy map of UNHCR staff. The 1996 study on the impact of armed conflict on children which the UN General Assembly had commissioned Graca Machel to compile (UNDPCSD, 1996), stated that millions of children were not only caught up in conflicts as bystanders but also as targets. It also suggested that more than 300,000 under-eighteens were fighting in thirty-one conflicts around the world. The release of this global UN study and the subsequent creation of an international Coalition to Stop the Use of Child Soldiers were important events in the development of concern by the international community, prompting further action in terms of advocacy and programming (Goodwin-Gill and Cohn, 1994: 10; Brett, 1997; Bennett, 1998: 30; Becker, 2000). In its follow-up strategy UNHCR moved to identify recruitment as one of five priority issues that personnel working with refugee children and youth have to address. UNHCR stated that, because refugee children and adolescents had been found by the Machel study (UN, 1996) to be particularly at risk of military recruitment (see also Brett and Specht, 2004: 11; Coalition to Stop the Use of Child Soldiers, 2004), it had a strong and mandated interest in ensuring their protection

(Office of the Senior Co-ordinator for Refugee Children, 2001: 3; UNHCR, n.d.a: 1).

The organisation's mandate was drawn upon not only to argue the relevance of the issue to UNHCR, but also to define its role in the global fight against child soldiering: prevention. This humanitarian agency, which was set up in the wake of the Second World War, was granted the authority to protect and respond to the needs of refugees and to devise durable solutions for their plight (UNHCR, 2002: 21). In developing long-lasting solutions for refugee populations, UNHCR was expected to protect them from future uprooting or even becoming the cause of further upheaval and violence. It is within this context of tackling the root causes of forced migration and of working towards enduring peace and durable development that the 1997 follow-up strategy presented the prevention and monitoring of child recruitment as one of UNHCR's five key priorities in relation to refugee children: 'Because the major cause of refugee movements is war, military recruitment of minors is also of concern to UNHCR as a prevention issue. Under-age soldiers are often used to perpetrate atrocities against civilian populations. Recruitment of minors is a highly exploitative practice and is sometimes the precipitating cause of flight' (UNHCR, 1997: 3).

In interviews staff suggested that UNHCR operations had been affected by the military infiltration of refugee and IDP (Internally Displaced Person) camps and subsequent underage recruitment long before the 1994 *Guidelines* made reference to this problem.[1] The increase in intra-state conflicts in the 1980s and early 1990s may have increased the scale of child recruitment (Yu 2002),[2] especially in those camps located close to conflict zones and state borders (UNHCR, 2000; UNHCR and Save the Children Alliance, 2001). However, UNHCR's more recent nomination of underage recruitment as a policy priority has to be primarily understood as reflecting the changing agenda of the international community rather than its own direct experience. Indeed, other humanitarian organisations and NGOs started to take an interest in the plight of child soldiers in the same period.

The impact of wider events on the development – in terms of pace and content – of UNHCR's framework in relation to child soldiering became clear with the adoption by the UN General Assembly of the Optional Protocol to the Convention on the Rights of the Child (CRC) on the Involvement of Children in Armed Conflict in May 2000. This protocol bans the compulsory recruitment of children under the age of eighteen in armed conflicts and raises the age of voluntary participation from fifteen to eighteen.[3] On 29 November 2000, a UNHCR Inter-Office and Field-Office Memorandum (IOM/FOM) was issued to raise awareness of this and the other optional protocol adopted at the same time,[4] explaining the ways in which they modified humanitarian law. In addition to reiterating UNHCR's commitment to the prevention of child soldiering, this internal memorandum constituted a milestone in that it was the first of its kind to stipulate the responsibilities of the organisation's protection officers to monitor, document and report any violations with respect to underage recruitment. (UNHCR, 2000).

My subsequent research at UNHCR headquarters examined how staff have interpreted this task and implemented it. One UNHCR staff member commented that:

> the message sent out by this IOM/FOM is that field officers should monitor. This means that when they are walking in the camps and surrounding areas and are talking to the implementing partners who might have access to areas where UNHCR doesn't have any presence, they should make sure that the issue of under-age recruitment is on the agenda, that reports are made, and that appropriate actions are undertaken. As this data [*sic*] on under-age recruitment is being gathered, Protection officers also need to link in with the system consisting of NGOs [non-governmental organisations] and IGOs [inter-governmental organisations] in the field or outside who have specialist knowledge on the issue, so that the data can be publicised or used for advocacy campaigns.[5]

In the following quote, a former protection officer describes the kinds of activities that field staff would be expected to undertake in fulfilling this particular responsibility:

> As a protection officer, I engaged in activities to raise awareness about underage recruitment and children's rights and cooperated with the Tanzanian police in order to arrest the recruiters. On one occasion, we knew about 170 children who had been recruited and were being transferred to Burundi and Congo to fight for armed forces or groups. We succeeded in capturing the recruiters and reclaiming the children. Those children who were under the age of sixteen were returned to their parents. The others, who according to the Tanzanian Penal Court are responsible for their acts, received corporal punishment – eight lashes.

Constraints and Limitations of UNHCR's Framework

These data suggest how UNHCR positions its staff conceptually, practically and even physically with respect to child soldiering. Conceptualising the military recruitment and deployment of under-eighteens as a violation of children's rights and a breach of international humanitarian law, it directs its staff to adopt a legal approach to address the problem. They are expected to monitor, document and report evidence indicating whether – not why – underage recruitment is occurring in the area where they are stationed. As such, gathering evidence of the presence of this military practice, rather than of its causal factors, requires UNHCR field officers to 'walk through the camps', to pay special attention to interactions between military staff and young people, to record sightings of children in military uniform, to visit hospitals and morgues and talk to staff, etc. Actual engagement with children and their communities regarding the causes of underage recruitment is little required by an approach that focuses primarily on observation rather than analysis.

Given the predominantly legal approach of the agency, it is of little surprise that the single most important obstacle that UNHCR staff mentioned as obstructing the prevention of underage recruitment was the lack of political will. This is illustrated in the following quotes:

> UNHCR being a protection or more legally oriented organisation, what we tend do is that, when we do have a report of children being recruited from the camp, we normally bring that issue up with the relevant authorities in that country. Our focus would be on information supply and hopefully the authorities would take action. UNHCR does not normally directly get involved in taking some actions in preventing the military recruitment ... We sometimes entirely have to depend on the willingness and preparedness of the host country, host government to work on this issue.[6]

> The UNHCR wishes to have a significant impact on the prevention of under-age recruitment, but ... then there is the issue of politics ... For example, in Colombia children serve as combatants in the national army as well as in the armed opposition groups. In Sudan, the SPLA [Sudan People's Liberation Army] guaranteed UNICEF that they would stop recruiting any soldiers under the age of eighteen and would demobilise the underage soldiers currently present in their ranks. They did not live up to that promise. And the United States are determined to recruit anyone above the age of sixteen who voluntarily joins with the consent of their parents.[7]

The 2001/2 evaluation challenged the view expressed previously by UNHCR staff that 'nothing much can be done beyond appealing to local authorities' (Inspection and Evaluation Service, 1997: 10). While recognising this claim as partly legitimate, the 2001/2 evaluation team argued that 'many of the shortcomings' in UNHCR's strategies to protect and assist refugee children and youth:

> arise from too narrow a conception of protection ... the social aspects of protection are inconsistently acknowledged, let alone applied by the Office ... It is important to note that social systems are the frontline of protection of children in both negative and positive terms ... Understanding the social dynamics of a refugee population is therefore vital in regards to risk as well as resources (Valid International, 2002: 67–8).

Instead, UNHCR has relied heavily on the 'vulnerable groups' approach, which identifies 'at risk' or 'vulnerable' groups as targets for interventions.

This approach differs from an approach that screens for risky situations and requires policies and programmes to respond to the factors and dynamics that put the target population 'at risk' or render them 'vulnerable'. The 1997 evaluation report claimed that this often results in glossing 'over the different types of risks faced by groups within a population' and that 'lumping such differences together under a single heading obscures the various kinds of action required' (Inspection and Evaluation Service, 1997: 25).[8]

Child soldiers have been cast by UNHCR as the 'the most vulnerable of the vulnerable' (Ameratunga, 1998; see also McNamara, 1998: 2), reflecting the widely held view of child soldiering as 'one of the most extreme forms of abuse of children and denial of their fundamental rights' (Horemans and Vervliet, 2002: 6, translation by author). Furthermore, the comments that UNHCR submitted to the Working Group on the draft Optional Protocol stated that 'the risks encountered and the fundamental rights denied are similar, whether direct or indirect and whether involving compulsory or voluntary recruitment' (UNHCR, n.d.a: 1). This effectively precludes, first, the need to investigate why the young may enrol and, secondly, how vulnerability might be produced or mitigated in different settings of recruitment.

Piagetian Child Development Theories, the CRC and UNHCR's Approach

The UN Convention on the Rights of the Child (UNCRC), promulgated in 1989, has served to foster the global endorsement and institutionalisation of a rigid dividing line – set at eighteen – that renders as natural the vulnerability of those younger than this age.[9] The claim to universality that this treaty makes and the international policies concerning children and childhood that are deduced from it hinge upon Piagetian ideas about the uniformities of child development (Boyden, 1997; 2000: 2).

Developmental psychology, in which Jean Piaget was a principal figure in the twentieth century, centres around three basic ideas: naturalness, universality and rationality (James et al., 1998: 17). Starting from the premise that all 'humans are part of nature and as such are subject to general laws' (Jahoda, 1992, cited in Woodhead, 1999: 8), developmental psychologists have conventionally set out to study the natural process of maturation and uncover the universal laws of human growth (Woodhead, 1999: 4; Woodhead and Montgomery, 2003: 108). As for cognitive development, Piaget (1972) theorised that this consists of four major stages, in which clearly defined tasks or cognitive abilities are acquired and constitute the basis for the next hierarchical stage. Linking each stage to a particular age range, Piaget's theory also stimulated the use of 'age' as a scientific indicator of child development (Boyden, 2000: 2). Piagetian theories of child development generally treat the cognitively competent and rational adult – the end point of this evolution – as the gold standard by which to judge the level of a child's development (James et al., 1998: 18; Wyness, 1999: 354) and to infer universal prescriptions of what a child needs and how its development is to be structured (Zelizer, 1985: 28; Woodhead, 1997: 66; Woodhead, 1999: 4; Woodhead and Montgomery, 2003: 107).[10]

The CRC has strengthened Piaget's 'authoritative account of what it means to be a child and what is appropriate in terms of quality child care and education' (Woodhead, 1999: 5) by, for example, emphasising the developmental significance of schooling while denigrating that of work (Woodhead, 1997: 74). The majority of textbook childhoods are now portrayed as a period free from social, economic and political responsibilities and as a time when children play, learn and are cared for within the settings of the family and the school. While it may be fair to say that Piagetian child development theories serve as the theoretical backbone or rationale for advocating 'standardised childhoods' (Woodhead, 1997: 78; Woodhead, 1999: 7; Boyden, 2000: 2; Woodhead and Montgomery, 2003), the Convention cannot be considered merely a reflection of Piaget's paradigm. The UNCRC has emphasised the universality of child development at the cost of Piaget's – albeit limited – consideration of the child's environment. Similarly, the UNCRC's definition of the child as anyone under the age of eighteen takes Piaget's use of 'age' to mark transition points a step further. Hence, the CRC goes further towards decontextualised universalism than Piaget's theory of cognitive development.

The Piagetian theoretical framework and its employment within the child rights field profoundly influence interpretations of how children experience and react towards armed conflict (Boyden, 2000: 2). The limited cognitive development of children is said to inhibit them in correctly assessing the dangers of their actions and the operations they are involved in – an argument often rehearsed by other advocates of a universal ban on child soldiering (e.g. the Coalition to Stop the Use of Child Soldiers, 1998: 1; de Silva et al., 2001). UNHCR interviews and documents also claimed that minors do not to have the emotional maturity to cope with the experiences of soldiering, fuelling concerns about trauma.

My UNHCR data suggest that these negative physical and psychological effects are presumed to be of a long-term nature, again echoing claims put forward by other international organisations, such as Amnesty International (1999: 3-4) and the Coalition to Stop the Use of Child Soldiers (1998: 2). Children are perceived as engaging in soldiering in the midst of their maturation processes, which, according to conventional Piagetian ideas of developmental psychology, affect further stages of growth and ultimately the adult personality (Boyden, 2000: 3). In interviews, UNHCR personnel often indicated that they feared for the 'permanent scarring of [the child's] developing personality' (Somasundaram, 2002: 1270). Similarly, an article on child soldiers in Sierra Leone, which was published by UNHCR's Refugees Magazine (2003: 26), claimed that: 'These youngsters became little more than highly dangerous zombies who, even if they survived and escaped the war, were in need of months or years of specialized care'.

Concern about the psychological state of (former) child combatants and the view that psychosocial counselling constitutes an essential part of any strategy towards their demobilisation, rehabilitation and reintegration were conveyed in many UNHCR official documents and guidelines and in my interviews. For example, in reflecting upon their visits to LTTE (Liberation Tigers of Tamil Eelam) girl soldiers who had been captured by the government army, UNHCR field officers in Sri Lanka wrote in their reports that the girls were suffering from post-traumatic stress disorder (PTSD) and were urgently requiring psychotherapeutic counselling.[11] Another UNHCR interviewee stated that: 'In Liberia, the programmes that were suggested by UNICEF to address the needs and rights of the ex-child soldiers were too superficial. UNICEF provided vocational training, but no psychosocial counselling that damaged kids need.'[12]

Overall, the views expressed by UNHCR staff and in agency literature appear to illustrate the predominant belief that uniform patterns, such as PTSD, can be discerned in the reactions of under-eighteens to catastrophic events. Boyden (2000: 4) explains that these patterns are perceived as the result of 'underlying biological and psychological imperatives, social and cultural factors being relegated to a secondary role'. She continues that:

> Such universalistic explanations of childhood and child suffering coexist with, and are to some extent supported by, a medicalised view of children's responses to adversity which stresses individual pathology over and above structural forces ... This explains why throughout the 20th century the individual as victim and patient has in the main been the focal point for intervention, with just a few agencies working at the community level in an effort to restore social structures and a sense of normalcy (Boyden, 2000: 4).

Under-eighteens are also presumed to lack the experience and cognitive skills to foresee and grasp the moral implications of their violent acts (see, for example, Muscroft, 2000: 48). In addition to the belief that children's minds are less formed than those of adults and therefore more malleable, the presumption of children's vulnerability to manipulation is given further weight due to anecdotal evidence from conflict zones (Boyden, 2003: 348). For example, rumour has it that military commanders prefer child soldiers to adults because of their blind loyalty, their susceptibility to indoctrination and their unquestioning obedience of commands, letting no moral dilemmas interfere with the fulfilment of their orders (Gill and Cohn, 1994: 27;

Coalition to Stop the Use of Child Soldiers, 1998: 3; Goodwin-Thompson, 1999: 193). Similarly, one UNHCR interviewee sketched the following picture with regard to child soldiers in Liberia:

> Under the influence of drugs, the pressure of adults and fear, these child combatants had been responsible for committing the most – and also the most cruel – atrocities during the civil war in Liberia. A similar observation was made during the reign of terror under the Khmer Rouge in Cambodia. The type of military training that these children receive robs them from the civilising experiences that are required to become an adult and, as such, diverts them from the normal path of growing up. Instead, the military training and life turns the children into killing machines with no conscience. These children commit atrocities and do things that adults would find very hard to do.[13]

Wessells (1997: 35) claims that internal restrictions towards violence normally develop through 'exposure to positive role models, a healthy family life, the rewards for socially constructive behaviours, and the encouragement of moral reasoning'. Operating within a theoretical framework that allocates an essential role to parents in stimulating and safeguarding children's developmental processes, UNHCR staff often viewed child combatants' separation or isolation from parents, caregivers or family – a common feature of underage recruitment and training[14] – as particularly problematic. They were pessimistic about the ability of young people to achieve healthy development or to respect moral norms and values – that are particularly valued in peacetime in the absence of parents or caregivers (see also Castelo-Branco, 1997: 494; Faulkner, 2001: 495). Furthermore, those who have been exposed to and acted in accordance with an ideology that drastically reduces the value of life and who have sensed the power of a gun were treated as irreversibly damaged in their moral thinking.[15]

The above illustrates the fact that concerns about the malign effects of soldiering seem to obscure the need for analyses of why children and adolescents come to take up arms and how they make sense of their experiences as combatants. Operating within a framework that assumes the vulnerability of all under-eighteens and centres on the physical, psychological and moral damage that soldiering is expected to cause to participants, it is difficult for UNHCR staff to perceive the engagement of children and adolescents as potentially protecting or enhancing their social, economic or political situation – or, at least, as not necessarily constituting the worst option. An external consultant to UNHCR explains it in the following terms:

> A lot of the writing and promotion in the last less than ten years on the topic of child soldiers and [the claim] that more attention needs to be paid to it, has very much been from child rights organisations and the idea that they [children] are especially vulnerable, that there are these particular physical and psychosocial

effects, and that's what should mobilise our sympathy and our actions. And some of that is true, but then, especially I feel for an effective response, without child participation we don't know best what to do, we overlook what their own decisions were in joining, if that was the case, rather than being more forcibly recruited.[16]

Instead, under-eighteens are perceived as not having yet acquired the cognitive competence for hypothetical thought or abstract thinking, which Piaget assigns to the final stage of child development, and therefore as not capable of conceiving alternative survival methods other than soldiering when faced with material and social deprivation or destitution (see, for example, Brett and McCallin, 1996: 114). Likewise, UNHCR argued in its comments to the Working Group:

> The true nature of 'voluntary' recruitment is often open to question, especially in refugee or general displacement situations. Many young people in these situations join groups not through the exercise of free choice but rather are coerced through factors such as the need for physical protection, lack of food and care, destitution, indoctrination and pressure, and the hope of making up for loss of family and community (UNHCR, n.d.a: 1).

The following quote from an external consultant summarises the views of UNHCR about child soldiering: views arising from particular conceptualisations of the child, child development and childhood: 'It's all about psychosocial and physical effects, so very "child as victim, as helpless, mouldable, not an actor in their own right" conceptualisation ... for the most part you will see the conceptualisation of children as something you deal with, rather than work with'.[17]

These discourses rarely indicate an appreciation of or interest in the developmental and social differentiation within the age group of under-eighteens. In particular, there is hardly any consideration of the growth and development that occurs during the second decade of life, which I refer to here as 'adolescence'. The evolving capacities, opportunities and expectations that emerge during adolescence shape experience of and response to armed conflict. On the few occasions that adolescents are mentioned, it is to reaffirm their vulnerability and their need for protection from harmful (adult-instigated) activities. For example, the 1997 evaluation identifies adolescents as the group that suffers the most psychologically during wartime: 'They are old enough to understand the dangers of war but have not developed the maturity to cope with the stress, are less receptive to family support than younger children and experience life in extremes' (Inspection and Evaluation Service, 1997: 17).

Vygotskian Understanding

The writings of Russian psychologist Lev Vygotsky centre around the idea that children's development and experiences of childhood are shaped by local understandings of child development, of 'routes to maturity, as well as maturity itself', which are the product of economic, ecological, social and cultural factors (Woodhead and Montgomery, 2003: 120). Anthropological research has well documented the fact that caregivers in different cultures perceive different risks and opportunities in child development. As a result, they aim to provide tools for and approaches to learning and problem solving that are valued locally and are meaningful to community members (LeVine, 1977; Rogoff, 1990). While the objective of promoting healthy child development may be universal, significant cultural variation exists in understandings of 'appropriate' developmental outcomes for children (Mann, 2003). Drawing upon Vygotsky's critique of Piagetian theories of child development, the importance of embedding 'child development in the social and cultural contexts of their life at a particular point in history' comes to the fore (Woodhead and Montgomery, 2003: 113).

The conceptualisation of childhood as a period of dependency and being free of economic, social and political responsibilities belies the empirical evidence that children in most parts of the world start contributing to the household from an early age and that their household roles rapidly increase as they grow (Zelizer, 1985: 5; Baker, 1998; Levine, 1999; Mann and Ledward, 2000; Mizen et al., 2001; Liebel, 2003). Research into child labour has not only raised awareness about the – sometimes hazardous – conditions in which young people work, but also about their evolving competencies in a particular social arena and the wider contributions they make as members of the community (Gittens, 1998: 67; James et al., 1998; Punch, 2001: 27). Hence, 'by the time that they reach middle childhood, the life phase when military recruitment becomes a possibility and likelihood in areas affected by conflict', children in most parts of the world have taken on major economic and social responsibilities (Boyden, 2003: 348). These responsibilities may have fostered practical skills and the cognitive, emotional and moral development for adolescents to engage with military groups willingly and competently, should the opportunity or necessity arise (Read, 2002).

This underscores the argument that, in order to effectively engage with the problem of child soldiering, researchers, policymakers and practitioners require a more contextualised understanding of childhood and adolescence. The question needs to be posed of how local understandings of childhood and adolescence interact with the cognitive, moral, emotional and physical development of young people. For, once a cultural model of child development is recognised, children's cognition can be conceived as socially and culturally structured (Mann, 2003). Furthermore, working within a

Vygotskian theoretical framework also allows for research into how changes in the social environment affect notions of child development as well as the actual experiences and developmental outcomes. For example, McCauley found that in post-war Liberia adolescents 'are increasingly involved in decision-making in the family, as are women, and there are reported cases where adults are scared to make decisions without consulting children because their income is vital to family survival' (2002: 15).

Alternative Understandings of Child Soldiering

Soldiering might be a constrained choice, but that should not preclude the question of why some young people – living with their families or otherwise – decide that involvement in a particular military group offers the most promising route to protection, survival or social advancement within their circumstances (see, for example, Wessells, 2002: 238). In war-affected areas particular jobs that are 'normally' taken up by child labourers might cease to exist or become less lucrative. This often leads families and young people to redefine their strategies by shifting to the war industry (Richards, 2002: 256). Research has also found that young soldiers sometimes enact a family strategy or dream for social mobility. Given that soldiers still enjoy an elevated position in many societies, becoming a soldier can enhance the social status of the entire family or clan.

While explanations of child soldiering dominant in the international community recognise this (see, for example, Brett and McCallin, 1996), they have generally done so by depicting a social environment in which deprivation and terror have led to a breakdown of societal norms, including those governing parenting and child-rearing (de Berry, 2001; Hart, 2006). Contemporary warfare is perceived as striking at the heart of communities and destroying the protective shields that are normally in place to keep children safe from harm (McNamara, 1998: 2; Office of the Special Representative of the Secretary-General for Children and Armed Conflict, 2000: 12; Amnesty International, 2003). As such, parents are portrayed as pulling children into armed combat through their own presence in an armed group or pushing them to provide for and protect the family (Brett and Specht, 2004). The Nederlandstalige Vrouwenraad, for example, claims that 'hunger and poverty can stimulate parents to sacrifice their children, especially when the armed forces directly give the pay to parents' (2002: 19, translation by author).

The view that children are sometimes recruited with the consent of their parents or caregivers was also expressed by UNHCR staff members whom I interviewed. Rather than presuming neglect on the part of parents or caregivers, however, some interviewees proposed that, in entrusting the care and education of their children to political and military groups, these parents have the well-being of their family at heart. Reflecting on the arrival of sixty child soldiers in a Sudanese refugee camp during the Ethiopia–Eritrea war, one interviewee argued:

> As the parents of these children were often very poor, the recruitment of their children cannot merely be portrayed as kidnapping or abduction. Parents were often convinced that the EPLF [Eritrean People's Liberation Front] would improve the living conditions of their children, such as food or a more nutritious diet. In addition, they believed that it would provide their children with better prospects for the future. For example, the education that the EPLF offered their new recruits was perceived amongst the population as being a model for education.[18]

Access to 'good' education, i.e. education that holds the promise of social mobility, is a recurrent incentive for young people and their families to join armed groups. Another UNHCR interviewee made this claim in relation to child soldiers fighting in Afghanistan subsequent to their receiving education in Pakistani schools funded by religious or political groups.[19] The link between education and soldiering has been identified in previous studies, such as that conducted by Peters and Richards (1998). They found that some underage soldiers fought in Sierra Leone's war to pay for their education. Whenever these young people obtained the necessary funds for another term of schooling, they would leave the military unit, only to return when the term or the money had finished. These adolescents adopted the dual strategy of working as a soldier and undertaking education to improve their social position and status in society.

The argument that soldiering sometimes constitutes a temporary activity or occupation serving a particular purpose that is difficult to achieve through standard channels is also illustrated by de Berry's (2001) case study of Iteso youth in war-torn Uganda. De Berry describes how Karamojong cattle raiding, which the Iteso people had been subjected to for many decades, adopted a new, fiercer form at the end of the 1970s.[20] Not only did the looting endanger the traditional means of subsistence of the Iteso – cattle breeding – it also threatened the rituals marking the social transition from child to adult. 'Cattle are integral to Iteso social reproduction; a man cannot marry a wife and set up a home without the use of cattle in a 'bridewealth' transfer' (de Berry, 2001: 100–1). Although cultural norms prescribed that fathers were responsible for gathering the bride wealth for their sons, they were no longer capable of fulfilling this parental duty. With the traditional path to adulthood obstructed, de Berry observed that young Teso males had to devise alternative ways to obtain their bride wealth. Some chose to join the Uganda People's Army (ibid.: 101–2). This study emphasises again that local understandings of maturity and of routes to maturity framed adolescents' appraisal of their situation. Their subsequent actions, such as becoming a soldier, were also informed by the resources and options that were available to them in a conflict-ridden environment.

Some UNHCR accounts provided evidence that adolescents joined military groups, because they perceived it as a means not only to secure protection and subsistence for the family, but also as a way to transcend social and geographical boundaries (see Richards, 2002; West, 2004). For example, the social status, prestige and masculine image associated with soldiering were portrayed as attracting young people to the profession, just as is the case with adults.[21] In volunteering for military recruitment and deployment youth might also hope to discover new places, pursue a more glamorous and adventurous course in life or travel beyond the reach of their parents. In relation to the young males serving with the Taliban in Afghanistan, a UNHCR staff member recounted:

> Although my organisation makes it a point not to use any military transport, one time during my stay in Afghanistan I was obliged to accept a lift from a military truck [Taliban]. I sat in the back with some Taliban boy soldiers. Observing them during the trip as they sang, laughed and boasted about their adventures and activities, it became very understandable to me that these boys join the Taliban. Not only does soldiering in Afghanistan represent one of the – limited – ways out of poverty and low status in society, these military groups resemble teenage groups in, for example, the States where peer groups get together and are offered the opportunity to see and experience new things.[22]

An article in *Rifugiati* (Refugees) magazine offers a similar argument to explain why the Nicla refugee camp in Ivory Coast, which is located in the vicinity of an ongoing conflict, has become a recruiting ground:

> It is easy to understand what young refugees find attractive about a soldier's life ... The surrounding areas of Nicla have become off limits. Piled together in their camp, they do not have a job, they do not have money, poverty spreads, there are scarce possibilities of education and few other activities are offered to refugees, for whom only boredom, growing frustration and fear remain. In those circumstances many come to the conclusion that they have no other choice but to 'join'. Others are attracted by the prospect of an exciting life and brutal power yielded by whoever holds a gun (2003: 19, translation by author).

Many adolescents participate in political and military groups not only to cope with, but also to alter the deplorable social, economic and political conditions that their communities face (see, for example, Richards, 1996; Peters, 2000). In addition to buffering the negative effects of exposure to violence, ideological commitment has been identified as a basis for children's involvement in armed conflict (Straker et al., 1992; Marks and McKenzie, 1995; Punamäki, 1996; Richards, 1996; Reynolds, 1997; Barber, 1998; West,

2004). Writing about the young people who participated in the first Palestinian intifada, Barber notes their capacity 'to understand political and social history, to make commitments to serving what they perceive to be the legitimate needs of their society, and to engage in specific actions to achieve these needs for prolonged periods characterised by trauma and great personal risk' (1998: 21).

Similarly, those who participated in the South African anti-apartheid struggle often presented their move to violent action as a rational response to a social structure that did not allow them to achieve reforms through standard or culturally approved channels. In the absence of a judicial and political system that respected the basic human rights of the majority of its subjects – including the right to non-violent protest – many adolescents in South Africa could not conceive of any change, and eventually any means of change, within the system. They often felt that there was no other perspective or angle to look from upon the situation other than sheer oppression. This illustrates Hart's claim that 'the experience of oppression and marginalisation may well be understood even by the young and motivate them to risk their lives in combat' (2006: 7). When asked why military commanders insisted on him continuing his training in exile and not participating in military operations in South Africa, a former child soldier told me:

> It was because of my age. I was so young, you see. They wanted me to go to school, to continue my education. Some said to me: 'You are still young, you can become something else [than a soldier]. There are other opportunities for you.' But I told them: 'Let me die for what I believe rather than not doing anything, than sitting aside. For if I do not go and fight for my ideals I will become a coward'.

My interviews with UNHCR staff indicate that such understandings of the reasons why adolescents engaged in military action were present at some level. However, it seems that the framework employed by UNHCR regarding child recruitment prevents such understandings – often born of experience - from informing the development of this organisation's approach.

The Shift to Social Protection: a Change in Agency Thinking?

The 2002 evaluation of activities in relation to refugee children gave impetus to the idea that UNHCR needs to go beyond the legal and physical aspects of protection.[23] My follow-up interviews conducted at the beginning of 2004 reflected this and showed how a move towards the social protection of refugee children and adolescents had also affected UNHCR's strategy towards the prevention of underage recruitment. In addition to monitoring, documenting and reporting any violations of the Optional Protocol, the strategy now included family tracing and reunification, and education. It was too soon to assess the extent to which proposed changes have affected practice at the field level.[24] Nevertheless, I examined any influences these recommendations had on the framework that conceptually and practically positions staff vis-à-vis the phenomenon of child soldiering. My intention in this was to discern likely changes in programming.

UNHCR staff members that I interviewed explained the focus on family tracing and reunification as a response to findings from research that most children who are recruited into armed groups are unaccompanied.[25] Children removed from their parents or caregivers have been commonly understood to suffer a double jeopardy: in addition to the unfavourable conditions of conflict zones, these children are presumed to stand defenceless in the face of aggressive recruitment campaigns, without the protective influence of family (Brett and McCallin, 1996: 113; Ameratunga, 1998: 3; UNHCR, 2000, n.d.b: 5).

With regard to education, UNHCR staff emphasised the significant role of programmes of peace education and child rights campaigns to raise awareness about child rights among the refugee and wider population. The assumption is that if displaced communities, families and children are aware of children's rights, children will refrain from participating voluntarily in armed combat and communities will explore methods to prevent or obstruct forced or coercive recruitment of underage children (Brett, 2001: 19; Verhey, 2002: 2). In relation to the situation in Sri Lanka, for example, a UNHCR interviewee expressed the hope that child rights education for the community would encourage adults to step forward and provide information when LTTE commanders attempted to recruit children.[26] There is still a lack of evidence demonstrating the effectiveness of such advocacy measures when undertaken in isolation from practical assistance to improve the conditions of children's lives.

The value of education and vocational training was seen in terms of providing under-eighteens with structured activities that create a sense of stability and routine, fight boredom and promote personal development. Some interviewees argued that, by keeping them busy, these programmes neutralise one of the most important reasons that young people volunteer for armed combat: 'Education at the same time is a strategy to prevent idleness and boredom and redundancy. Most kids are recruited at the age of adolescence when they are active and when they need something to do. So, regular education programmes and vocational skills training programmes are the main practical prevention strategies'.[27]

Such a normative approach would seem to allow little account to be taken of young people's experience of education. This is a crucial point. While schooling may offer relief from boredom to some, we can also imagine that unless it addresses the social and economic realities experienced by adolescents its efficacy in preventing their military involvement may be limited. My interviews with former child soldiers participating in the anti-apartheid struggle indicated that, while their parents considered education as the ultimate means to progress, their own experiences of Bantu education led them to challenge this claim. On the basis of these experiences and their interactions with politically oriented youth organisations, schooling came to symbolise reform within the apartheid system at best and surrender on the terms imposed by the apartheid regime at worst. The former child soldiers did not believe that education would improve their future prospects, as individuals or as a social group. In the following quote, a former child soldier in South Africa describes the kind of frustration that may propel young people towards military involvement:

> You know, the education is something of a privilege. In fact, each and everyone who is young needs to have education – there is a need – but in South Africa if you don't have money you can't get education, you understand? No education … if you are in Standard 6, maybe you are taking seven subjects, but you find out that these subjects have nothing to do with what you are going to do in the future. You see? So it is just frustrating.

This potential gap between, on one hand, the assumptions about education made by UNHCR and, on the other, the circumstances of adolescents – their experiences, needs and aspirations – points to an underlying problem with the manner in which UNHCR has sought to develop its protection policy. Expanding from a focus solely on legal and physical measures to embrace social dimensions of protection is in keeping with the recommendations of the 2001/2 evaluation team. However, the 2001/2 evaluation team also urged a fuller dialogue at the field level as being essential to understanding the risks and resources that exist in relation to refugee children and adolescents' protection.

Conclusion

> Adolescents are still the, the neglected, overlooked group. So we are trying to do [activities] like HIV/AIDS awareness, but, when it comes down to the hardware of providing secondary education, vocational training and these things where adolescents are getting busy and are engaged, we are mostly lacking funds. So when you look at the numbers of adolescents reached by those programmes it is very limited. And it is mainly a money issue.[28]

The views expressed here come from a staff member at UNHCR. They echo the findings of the 2001/2 evaluation team that considered adolescents to be the most neglected group amongst UNHCR's beneficiaries (Valid International, 2002: 11). While finances may be an important factor accounting for relative neglect of adolescents in terms of quantity of targeted interventions, I have suggested in this chapter that there are also significant shortcomings in terms of the conceptual thinking underpinning those interventions. In my estimation the policy framework of UNHCR has generally failed to grapple with the specificities of adolescents' lives and the particular motivations and social dynamics that lead to their involvement with military groups. The reasons for this failure I have attributed to two main factors: first, a reliance on discourses of childhood and child rights that do little to prompt interest in developmental and social differentiation within the age group of under-eighteens across diverse settings. These discourses have, in themselves, been underwritten by a particular view of child development that assumes universality and downplays the importance of context.

UNCHR's failure to develop strategies for preventing recruitment that address the specific situation of adolescents is also a consequence of the nature of its engagement with the field. From interviews it became apparent that, through their work, individual staff members had gained, sometimes by chance or in passing, valuable insights into the lives, competencies and motivations of adolescents in different conflict-affected settings. At the time of my research, however, such insights seemingly had little bearing on the development of policy. Ensuring that mechanisms are in place for those insights to be channelled and appropriately discussed when relevant policies and activities are developed might constitute a significant step for UNHCR to operate in a more evidence-based manner that responds to the actual settings in which adolescents experience displacement and seek to rebuild their lives.

Notes

1. For example, interview with UNHCR staff member, 6 February 2001, Geneva: UNHCR headquarters.
2. Yu (2002: 1) argues that the shift towards internal warfare is increasingly confronting UNHCR with the problem of 'mixed populations', in which civilians, combatants and criminals seek refuge from violent conflict.
3. 'However, the Optional Protocol allows a slight exception for voluntary recruitment by governments between 16 and 18 years with stringent safeguards regarding proof of age, parental or other legal consent, the truly voluntary nature of the commitment and understanding of the duties involved in the military service' (UNHCR, 2000: 15).
4. The other optional protocol relates to the sale of children, child prostitution and child pornography. For further information see http://www.unicef.org/crc/crc.htm.
5. Telephone interview with former UNHCR staff member, 12 March 2004.

6. Telephone interview with UNHCR staff member, 24 February 2001.
7. Interview with UNHCR staff member, 7 February 2001, Geneva: UNHCR headquarters.
8. The 2001/2 evaluation found that 'vulnerable groups amount to 78 per cent of the population of concern' (Valid International, 2002: 69).
9. It is interesting to note that it was not until the end of the 1980s that refugee children under the age of eighteen, who account for more than half of the persons assisted by UNHCR (McNamara, 1998: 1), came to be perceived by UNHCR as a distinct group whose 'needs, legal status and social status can be significantly different from those of adults, and from each other as well, due to age-related developmental differences' (UNHCR, 1997).
10. The 'universal child, universal child development and the identification of universal conditions required for that development' are needed for the 'save the children' project as described by Hart.
11. Interview with UNHCR staff member, 9 February 2001, Geneva: UNHCR headquarters.
12. Interview with UNHCR staff member, 19 February 2001, Geneva: UNHCR headquarters.
13. Interview with UNHCR staff member, 19 February 2001, Geneva: UNHCR headquarters.
14. For example, reports of UNHCR staff in Sri Lanka referred to cases where parents had searched for children who disappeared from school and had pleaded with commanders at military posts, but who had been denied access to their children. On the part of the children, former LTTE soldiers confirmed that they were not given permission to see their parents unless they had engaged significantly in battle. In relation to the sixty EPLF child soldiers who had arrived in a Sudanese refugee camp, the UNHCR interviewee described EPLF's prohibition of contact with parents as the primary reason for children's departure or escape from the training camps.
15. As such, accounts of UNHCR personnel reflect the anxieties that the international community often entertains about how to exercise control over and integrate child soldiers, that are perceived as socialised in a culture of violence and, hence, as a threat to peace and stability (see, for example, BBC News, 2001).
16. Telephone interview with external consultant to UNHCR, 8 March 2004.
17. Telephone interview with external consultant to UNHCR, 8 March 2004.
18. Interview with UNHCR staff member, 6 February 2001, Geneva: UNHCR headquarters.
19. Interview with UNHCR staff member, 13 February 2001, Geneva: UNHCR headquarters.
20. During the political unrest of the Amin period, the Karamojong saw the opportunity to expand their weapon arsenal.
21. Interview with UNHCR staff member, 20 February 2001, Geneva: UNHCR headquarters.
22. Interview with UNHCR staff member, 13 February 2001, Geneva: UNHCR headquarters.
23. Telephone interview with UNHCR staff member, 24 February 2001.
24. Telephone interview with UNHCR staff member, 24 February 2001.

25. Telephone interview with UNHCR staff member, 30 March 2004.
26. Interview with UNHCR staff member, 9 February 2001, Geneva: UNHCR headquarters.
27. Telephone interview with UNHCR staff member, 30 March 2004.
28. Telephone interview with UNHCR staff member, 30 March 2004.

References

Ameratunga, M. 1998 'Children: The Invisible Generation', *Refugees Magazine* 111 (Spring). Online at http://www.unhcr.org/doclist/publ/3b5696144/skip-180.html accessed 15 January 2008.

Amnesty International 1999 *Child Soldiers: One of the Worst Abuses of Child Labour.* IOR 42/001/1999. London: Amnesty International.

––– 2003 'Children at War in Africa – Rehabilitation of Child Soldiers in Democratic Republic of Congo in Desperate Need of Resources from International Community', *The Wire.* http://web.amnesty.org/web/wire.nsf/September2003print/DRC?OpenDocument, accessed 18 September 2003.

Baker, R. 1998 'Runaway Street Children in Nepal: Social Competence Away from Home', in I. Hutchby and J. Moran-Ellis (eds) *Children and Social Competence: Arenas of Action.* London: Falmer Press, pp. 46–63.

Barber, B.K. 1998 'Deeper Inside a Youth Social Movement: Gaza's "Children of the Stones"'. Paper presented at the Kennedy Centre for International Studies, Brigham Young University, December.

BBC News 2001 'School Trains Suicide Bombers'. BBC News: World: Middle East. http://news.bbc.co.uk/hi/english/world/middle_east/newsid_1446000/1446003.stm accessed 18 July 2001.

Becker, J. 2000 'The New Ban on Child Soldiers', *Monitor* 13 (2): 20–21.

Bennett, T.W. 1998 *Using Children in Armed Conflict: A Legitimate African Tradition? Criminalizing the Recruitment of Child Soldiers,* No. 32, Pretoria: Insitute of Security Studies.

Boyden, J. 1997 'Childhood and the Policy-Makers: A Comparative Perspective on the Globalisation of Childhood', in A. James and A. Prout (eds) *Constructing and Reconstructing Childhood: Contemporary Issues in the Sociological Study of Childhood.* London: RoutledgeFalmer, pp. 190–229.

–––– 2000 *Social Healing in War-Affected and Displaced Children.* Oxford: Refugee Studies Centre, University of Oxford.

–––– 2003 'The Moral Development of Child Soldiers: What Do Adults Have to Fear?' *Peace and Conflict: Journal of Peace Psychology* 9 (4): 343–62.

Brett, R. 1997 'Involvement of Children in Armed Conflicts', *ChildRIGHT* 136: 14–15.

–––– 2001 'Recruiting Child Soldiers: The Link between Displacement and Recruitment', *Refugees* 1 (122): 19.

Brett, R. and McCallin, M. 1996 *Children: The Invisible Soldiers.* Växjo: Rädda Barnen.

Brett, R. and Specht, I. 2004 *Young Soldiers: Why They Choose to Fight.* Boulder, CO: Lynne Rienner.

Castelo-Branco, V. 1997 'Child Soldiers: the Experience of the Mozambican

Association for Public Health (AMOSAPU)', *Development in Practice* 7 (4): 494–96.

Coalition to Stop the Use of Child Soldiers 1998 *Stop Using Child Soldiers!* Geneva: Coalition to Stop the Use of Child Soldiers.

—— 2004. 'Why Do Adolescents Join Armed Groups and Forces? Interview with Rachel Brett', *Child Soldiers Newsletter* 10 (January/February): 8–11.

de Berry, J. 2001 'Child Soldiers and the Convention on the Rights of the Child', *Annals of the American Academy of Political and Social Science* 575 (May): 92–105.

de Silva, H., Hobbs, C. and Hanks, H. 2001 'Conscription of Children in Armed Conflict – a Form of Child Abuse. A Study of 19 Former Child Soldiers', *Child Abuse Review* 10: 125–34.

Faulkner, F. 2001 'Kindergarten Killers: Morality, Murder and the Child Soldier Problem' *Third World Quarterly* 22 (4): 491–504.

Gittens, D. 1998 *The Child in Question*. Basingstoke: Macmillan.

Goodwin-Gill, G.S. and Cohn, I. 1994 *Child Soldiers: The Role of Children in Armed Conflict*. Oxford: Clarendon.

Hart, J. 2006 'Saving Children: What Role for Anthropology?' *Anthropology Today* 22 (1): 5–8.

Horemans, B. and Vervliet, E. 2002 'Inleiding', *NOORDZUID Cahier* 27 (3): 5–8.

Inspection and Evaluation Service 1997 *Evaluation of UNHCR's Efforts on Behalf of Children and Adolescents*. Geneva: UNHCR.

James, A., Jenks, C. and Prout, A. 1998 *Theorizing Childhood*. Cambridge: Polity Press.

Levine, S. 1999 'Bittersweet Harvest: Children, Work and the Global March against Child Labour in the Post-apartheid State', *Critique of Anthropology* 19 (2): 139–55.

Liebel, M. 2003 'Working Children as Social Subjects: The Contribution of Working Children's Organizations to Social Transformations', *Childhood* 10 (3): 265–85.

LeVine, R.A. 1977 'Child Rearing as Cultural Adaptation', in P.H. Leiderman, S.R. Tulkin and A. Rosenfeld (eds) *Culture and Infancy: Variations in Human Experience*. New York: Academic Press.

Mann, G. 2003 'The Cultural Structuring of Child Development: the Case of Sibling Caregiving and the Theory of Mind'. Unpublished M.Sc. dissertation, London School of Economics.

Mann, G. and Ledward, A. 2000 'The Best Interests of "Separated" Children in Rwanda', *Cultural Survival Quarterly*, Summer: 59–61.

Marks, M. and McKenzie, P. 1995 'Political Pawns or Social Agents? A Look at Militarised Youth in South Africa', in Confronting Crime Conference, Cape Town.

McCauley, U 2002 'Now Things are Zig-Zag: Perceptions of the Impact of Armed Conflict on Young People in Liberia'. Stockholm: Save the Children Sweden.

McNamara, D. 1998 *A Human Rights Approach to the Protection of Refugee Children*. London: London School of Economics, UNHCR. http://www.unhcr.ch/issues/children/cm981114.html.

Mizen, P., Pole, C. and Bolton, A. 2001 'Why Be a School Age Worker?' in P. Mizen, C. Pole and A. Bolton (eds) *Hidden Hands: International Perspectives on Children's Work and Labour*. London: Routledge Falmer.

Muscroft, S. 2000 *Children's Rights: Reality or Rhetoric?* London: International Save the Children Alliance.

Nederlandstalige Vrouwenraad 2002 *Kindsoldaten*. Brussels: Nederlandstalige

Vrouwenraad.

Office of the Senior Co-ordinator for Refugee Children 2001 *Short Note on Child Soldiers.* Geneva: UNHCR.

Office of the Special Representative of the Secretary-General for Children and Armed Conflict 2000 'The Impact of Armed Conflict on Children: Filling the Knowledge Gaps'. Draft Research Agenda. New York: Office of the Special Representative of the Secretary-General for Children and Armed Conflict.

Peters, K. 2000 'Policy Making on Children in Conflict: Lessons from Sierra Leone and Liberia', *Cultural Survival Quarterly*, Summer: 56–7.

Peters, K. and Richards, P. 1998 '"Why We Fight": Voices of Youth Combatants in Sierra Leone', *Africa* 68 (2): 183–210.

Piaget, J. 1972 *The Psychology of the Child.* New York: Basic Books

Punamäki, R.-L. 1996 'Can Ideological Commitment Protect Children's Psychological Well-Being in Situations of Political Violence?' *Child Development* 67: 55–69.

Punch, S. 2001 'Negotiating Autonomy: Childhoods in Rural Bolivia', in L. Alanen and B. Mayall (eds) *Conceptualizing Child-Adult Relations*. London: Routledge Falmer, pp. 23–36.

Read, K. 2002 'When Is a Kid a Kid? Negotiating Children's Rights in El Salvador's Civil War', *History of Religions* 41 (1): 391–409.

Refugees Magazine 2003 'Growing Pains', *Refugees Magazine* 1: 23–27.

Reynolds, P. 1997 *Activism, Politics and the Punishment of Children.* Cape Town: University of Cape Town, Department of Anthropology.

Richards, P. 1996 *Fighting for the Rain Forest: War, Youth and Resources in Sierra Leone.* Oxford: International African Institute in association with James Currey.

—— 2002 'Militia Conscription in Sierra Leone: Recruitment of Young Fighters in an African War', *The Comparative Study of Conscription in the Armed Forces* 20: 255–76.

Rifugiati 2003 'Da rifugiati a mercenary…', *Rifugiati* 2: 18–19.

Rogoff, B. 1990 *Apprenticeship in Thinking.* Oxford: Oxford University Press.

Somasundaram, D. 2002 'Child Soldiers: Understanding the Context', *British Medical Journal* 324 (25 May): 1268–71.

Straker, G., Moosa, F., Becker, R. and Nkwale, M. 1992 *Faces in the Revolution: the Psychological Effects of Violence on Township Youth in South Africa.* Cape Town: David Philip.

Thompson, C.B. 1999 'Beyond Civil Society: Child Soldiers as Citizens in Mozambique', *Review of African Political Economy* 80: 191–206.

UN 1996 *Report of the Expert of the Secretary-General, Graça Machel, on the Impact of Armed Conflict on Children.* New York: UNDPCSD.

UNHCR 1994 *Refugee Children: Guidelines on Protection and Care.* Geneva: UNHCR.

—— 1997 *Progress Report on Refugee Children and Adolescents, including UNHCR's Strategy for Follow-up to the Report on the Impact of Armed Conflict on Children.* Geneva: UNHCR.

—— 2000 *Recent Developments in International Human Rights Law Regarding Refugee Women and Children.* Geneva: UNHCR.

—— 2002 *2002 Global Appeal.* UNHCR. http://www.unhcr.ch/cgi-bin/texis/vtx/home?page=publ&id=3b7b87e14, accessed 12 February 2002.

—— n.d.a *UNHCR Comments on the Optional Protocol to the Convention on the Rights of the Child on Involvement of Children in Armed Conflict.* Geneva: UNHCR.

—— n.d.b *UNHCR Review of Achievement of the Plan of Action of the World Summit for Children, and Consideration of Future Action.* Geneva: UNHCR.

UNHCR and Save the Children Alliance 2001 *Action for the Rights of Children (ARC): Critical Issues – Child Soldiers.* Geneva: UNHCR and Save the Children Alliance.

Valid International 2002 *Meeting the Rights and Protection Needs of Refugee Children – an Independent Evaluation of the Impact of UNHCR's Activities.* Geneva: UNHCR (EPAU).

Verhey, B. 2002 'Child Soldiers: Lessons Learned on Prevention, Demobilization and Reintegration', *Newsletter Findings* May. http://www-wds.worldbank.org/servlet/WDSContentServer/WDSP/IB/2002/10/18/000094946_0210030401267 8/Rendered/PDF/multi0page accessed 31 May 2002.

Wessells, M. 1997 'Child Soldiers', *Bulletin of the Atomic Scientists* 53 (6): 32–39.

——— 2002 'Recruitment of Children as Soldiers in Sub-Saharan Africa: an Ecological Analysis', *The Comparative Study of Conscription in the Armed Forces* 20: 237–54.

West, H.G. 2004 'Girls with Guns: Narrating the Experience of War of FRELIMO's "Female Detachment"', in J. Boyden and J. de Berry (eds) *Children and Youth on the Front Line: Ethnography, Armed Conflict and Displacement.* Oxford: Berghahn Books, pp. 105–29.

Woodhead, M. 1997 'Psychology and the Cultural Construction of Children's Needs', in A. James and A. Prout (eds) *Constructing and Reconstructing Childhood: Contemporary Issues in the Sociological Study of Childhood.* London: Falmer Press, pp. 63–84.

——— 1999 'Reconstructing Developmental Psychology – Some First Steps', *Children and Society* 13: 3–19.

Woodhead, M. and Montgomery, H. (eds) 2003 *Understanding Childhood: an Interdisciplinary Approach.* Chichester: Wiley/Open University.

Wyness, M. 1999 *Contesting Childhood.* London: Falmer Press.

Yu, L. 2002 'Separating Ex-Combatants and Refugees in Zongo, DRC: Peacekeepers and UNHCR's "Ladder of Options"', New Issues in Refugee Research, Working Paper 60. Geneva: UNHCR.

Zelizer, V. 1985 *Pricing the Priceless Child: The Changing Social Value of Children.* New York: Basic Books.

PART III

GENDERED ADOLESCENCE
IN EXILE

7

The Long Road Home: Adolescent Afghan Refugees in Iran Contemplate 'Return'

Homa Hoodfar

Often I think I should go and study theology and the Quran, and go and teach men in Afghanistan that what they are doing to women is against Islam, but deep in my heart I know there is very little hope that they are going to change. It is this that worries us about going back to our country. Afghanistan has been haunted by evils for the last thirty years. Do you understand that I am a proud Afghan and love to know all about my country's history and past, but I fear going there? Not because there are no services, or because of economic hardship, because I am a woman. Can you write this in your research so the world will know? I want them to know.[1]

Children and adolescents constitute the majority of the over two million Afghan refugees Iran has hosted since the 1980s. During this period Iran and Pakistan between them received more refugees than any other nations.[2] Neither Iranian authorities nor Afghan community leaders have paid much attention to this particular constituency. For most of the period in exile it was assumed that refugee children and adolescents would attend Iranian schools and be educated by the host country, eventually returning to Afghanistan as the situation there improved. Given the shared linguistic and – to a large degree – cultural/historical framework, this policy appeared non-problematic.[3] However, by 1996, after years of hosting several million refugees with little financial aid from the international community, Iran adopted a policy of 'forced voluntary repatriation' towards its Afghan refugees.[4] Since the fall of the Taliban in 2001, Iran has stepped up its repatriation programme,[5] creating new anxieties in the lives of children and adolescents most of whom have been born and/or brought up in Iran with little or no recollection of life in Afghanistan.

Despite the prolonged stay of Afghan refugees in Iran, no activities to help with the readjustment or integration into their country of origin have ever been directed at young Afghans in Iran. Nor have there been any of the usual international humanitarian interventions, which, in any case, often overlook the ethnic, political and social identities of the young.[6]

This chapter describes the concerns and strategies of adolescents in the face of the forced-repatriation policies of the Iranian authorities. It looks at the diverse ways in which they as young refugees cope with their multiple identities as Afghans, youth, daughters, sons, Muslims, students and workers in a not-so-friendly Iranian society and the extent to which they feel these experiences may have prepared them for a new beginning in Afghanistan. Particular attention is given to gender issues and the experiences, concerns and aspirations of female adolescents. How do they and their male peers assess and reinterpret gender roles and gender relations both within the family and within the wider society? How are ideas about 'return' gendered? Examining some of the more pronounced unintended consequences of the forced-repatriation strategies that Iranian authorities have adopted, the chapter explains the role and value of collective space in which young people can reflect on their experience as refugees as well as deal with their anxieties about repatriation – a space in which they can carve out identities for themselves and seek to build the confidence to face repatriation and life in a new home among new realities.

The Context

Estimated at five million, in the period 1982–2002 Afghans refugees constituted the largest refugee population in the world. As the Soviet military moved into Afghanistan in support of the perceived oppressive and unwanted measures of the government, hundreds of thousands of refugees poured into neighbouring Iran and Pakistan. Some also went to India, while smaller numbers left for Europe and North America. Given the multi-ethnic nature of Afghanistan, it appears that language, religion, available resources and geographical proximity were important factors influencing the choice of destination. Thus, the majority of Afghan refugees to Iran were Dari/Farsi-speaking, ethnic Tajiks, Farsis and in particular Hazara, who, like Iranians, are Shia Muslims. In addition, some Uzbeks, Norestanies and a few smaller ethnic groups came to Iran. The majority of the Pashtu-speaking Afghans, along with a smaller number of Tajiks and a small number of other groups, left for Pashtu-speaking areas in the north-west provinces of Pakistan and Quetta. Beyond some kin interactions there was little formal communication between the refugee communities in the two countries.

The two host countries applied two very distinct refugee policies. The consequences of these policies for international refugee regimes, for the Afghan refugees and for Afghanistan, as well as for the host countries, merit scholarly attention in their own right but are beyond the scope of this chapter. In Pakistan the majority of Afghan refugees were confined to camps in the North-West Frontier provinces, ostensibly to facilitate the delivery of aid and services, but clearly also for purposes of surveillance (UN, 1988, 1990) and for the mobilisation of *mujahidin* ('freedom fighters') to fight the Soviets in Afghanistan. However, in Iran only a very small percentage of Afghans were confined to camps (and only after the early 1990s). These different policies had important consequences for the refugee communities, particularly for adolescents.

Afghans arrived in Iran in the years immediately after the 1979 revolution that established the Islamic Republic of Iran. The new regime welcomed the refugees as fellow Muslims in need of protection. In contrast to Pakistan, which received considerable direct and indirect international financial support and recognition, Iran did not receive any significant international assistance to deal with its refugee population, particularly in the 1980s. Since the Islamic Republic did not have the means to support this large influx of refugees, Afghan families arriving in Iran dispersed and settled throughout rural and urban areas in search of a livelihood. It was understood, however, that Afghans were entitled to all citizenship rights such as access to education and health care, access to subsidised food and, most importantly, access to the labour market. As non-citizens, however, they were barred from participating in national elections.

Most Afghan refugees considered this early period of their time in Iran as a golden age when they were treated with dignity and respect and even those who were not Shia Muslims felt a strong allegiance to Ayatollah Khomeini and his vision of a 'borderless community of Muslims'. This policy changed in 1992. Partly this was a consequence of the Russians' departure from Afghanistan in 1989, which removed the main justification for Afghans remaining in Iran. It was partly due to the fact that Iran had grown impatient with the lack of recognition of its considerable contribution to solution of the world refugee problem. During this period and for many years, Iran was the largest (and still remains one of the top) refugee-receiving countries despite the eight-year-long Iran–Iraq war (1980–88). The post-Khomeini governments were less ideological and more pragmatic and were preoccupied with the post-war reconstruction of Iran as well as with making sure that they would be re-elected to office. Thus the idea of repatriation of Afghans became a fixed component of the regime's policies from 1992. This was despite: (a) the bitter civil war in Afghanistan that lasted until 1994;[7] (b) the ascendance of the Pakistan-backed Taliban regime, whom the Iranian regime bitterly opposed; and (c) the fact that the Hazara Shia minority – who formed the majority of Afghan refugees in Iran – were particularly disadvantaged under the Taliban regime and had already suffered a brutal massacre of several thousand, principally in Mazar-i-Sharif.[8]

A major component of the Iranian policy of repatriation has been the exclusion of undocumented Afghans from the labour market. The absence of financial and material support for these refugees was assumed to constitute an incentive for them to return to Afghanistan. However, given the extent of the informal economy, control of the labour market proved difficult, and thus a companion strategy was instituted entailing the expulsion of children of undocumented Afghans from elementary schools and secondary schools run by the government. Undocumented Afghan refugee children and adolescents make up the largest segment of the Afghan refugees in Iran. Tens of thousands of Afghan children were thus denied access to education. This exclusionary policy has created complex and unintended consequences for the Afghan communities in Iran, particularly for adolescents, some of which are explored in this chapter.

Given the importance that education has acquired in the eyes of Afghan refugees living in Iran,[9] this policy focused the attention of Afghan families and communities on the needs of their children. Collective strategies have been developed to address children's educational needs including, most significantly, the establishment of informal Afghan schools on the outskirts of several towns and cities. Thus, by the late 1990s Afghan children and adolescents in Iran found themselves, for the first time, in an exclusively Afghan educational environment, with students of different ethnic and socio-economic backgrounds studying together. The schools quickly developed a wider role, offering resources not only for their students, but for young people who might have dropped out of school and for the minority of Afghan students still in the Iranian school system. Even in places where there were no Afghan schools, young people formed clubs and groups, produced news-letters and organised small events and study groups to read books or watch documentaries about Afghanistan. Such activities were unheard of during the 1980s and early 1990s, particularly amongst low-income Afghan youths.

The Afghan schools and clubs offered a space where young Afghans could share their worries and plans for the future, and collectively reflect on different aspects of Afghan culture and family structure, many of which they did not agree with or accept, particularly concerning gender and inter-generational relations. They pondered dominant cultural values, shared their dreams and discussed the discrimination they faced as Afghans in Iran. They shared strategies for addressing conflicts with their families, well aware that despite all their frustration with very hierarchical parental attitudes and the gap between their lived experiences and their familial ideals, their families remain the only reliable sources of support. This was particularly the case for female adolescents, who were the most disadvantaged in the family and yet had no other reliable support. The strategies adopted by these young women will be considered later in the chapter.

In the rest of this chapter we examine the different ways that male and female youths were reflecting on their lived experience as refugees and considering the prospect of return to a home never seen in Afghanistan. How did the youth understand and assess their 'Afghan-ness' and other identities in light of their probable repatriation? How did the worries and anxieties of male and female adolescents differ? The chapter illustrates the need to pay closer attention to the innovative, but often neglected, manner in which adolescent Afghan refugees resolve the contradictions of identity in crafting new ones for themselves. Appreciation of and the willingness to engage the creativity of this generation of Afghan refugees could yield significant benefits for Afghanistan and its social policymakers, as the country engages in processes of rebuilding.

The Research and the Context

This chapter is based on data from two different but related studies. The first was carried out in 2001. One hundred Afghan youth aged twelve to eighteen in the cities of Tehran, Mashhad and Qom were interviewed (see Table 7.1). Sixty-four of them were between the ages of twelve and fifteen and twenty-six were between sixteen and eighteen. The study intended to map the experiences, concerns and self-perception of Afghan youths in Iran. The second study focusing on Afghan youth in Iran was part of a larger project – 'Living with the Effect of Prolonged Armed Conflict and Forced Migration' – under the auspices of the Refugee Studies Centre at the University of Oxford. It incorporated in-depth research based on the findings of the first study, and included sixteen months of fieldwork in Tehran and Mashhad. The two sites were chosen for their very different community structure. In addition to investigating the experiences and coping strategies of Afghan

Table 7.1: Location and Sex of Interviewees in the First Study (2001)

	No. of boys	No. of girls	Total interviews
Tehran	22	23	45
Mashhad	15	20	35
Qom	10	10	20
Total	47	53	100

Table 7.2: Location and Sex of Interviewees in the Second Study (2002–3)

	No. of boys	No. of girls	Total interviews
Tehran	13	20	33
Mashhad	8	10	18
Total	21	30	51

youth in Iran, we examined the communal and institutional practices that have influenced their experience as young refugees.

The data were collected through participant observation, focus group discussions, two youth newsletters and photographic and essay competitions (we received 134 essays). In the final stage of the research we carried out fifty-one in-depth interviews with young people and their families (thirty-three in Tehran and eighteen in Mashhad – see Table 7.2). The interviewees included five young people between the ages of eight and eleven, twenty-three between twelve and fifteen and twenty-four between sixteen and eighteen years old. In Mashhad the interviewees were drawn from a neighbourhood adjacent to the largest and oldest Afghan colony in Iran. In Tehran the hub of our research was one informal Afghan school, which provided many of our interviewees and connected us with others through links with youth in surrounding Afghan and Iranian schools and neighbourhoods.

It should be noted that our last set of interviews were carried out during a time of extreme pressure on the Afghan community to repatriate. In both sites the primary preoccupation of the young people was their imminent repatriation and its implications for their future lives. This was a topic on everyone's mind.

Family and Inter-generational Relations

Family remains at the centre of the lives of Afghan adolescents in Iran and is the primary source of their support and protection. It is also the source of frustration and tension arising from parental constraints. Not surprisingly, then, family and family relations were among the topics most commonly discussed by our adolescent informants. Endless discussions focused on the kind of Afghan society and family they dreamed of, and of what they would do to create an Afghanistan different from the one presented to them by their elders – 'forced on them' as one female interviewee, fifteen-year-old Homira, put it:

> we wish to create a different environment for our children, so that they can take for granted some of the basic rights we so worry about. So that they can feel they are in control of their destination [*sic*]. Then they can focus on making a

different Afghanistan so that their children never again have to suffer what we, as their parents did.

Despite their considerable loyalty to parents and family, the adolescents questioned the structure and exceedingly hierarchical, non-democratic nature of family life. Eighteen-year-old Mahmoud described the generic Afghan family structure, irrespective of class or ethnicity, as 'very hierarchical, where the elder men, fathers and sons occupy the most important positions. Where daughters had far less value than sons and where the role of females has been to service men and make them comfortable'. This was typical of the way most our participants described Afghan families.

The issue of gender relations was a prominent topic of discussion; young people of both sexes were in agreement that women and girls are considered lesser beings, subject in various ways to the will of their fathers and brothers, and then their husbands. The girls, and sometimes their male peers, found this unacceptable. While some mothers sympathised with their daughters and lamented the gender ideology that has denied them and their daughters many of their basic 'Islamic rights', in other cases mothers agreed with the conventional outlook. In these situations our young women interviewees were particularly frustrated and felt without *pousht-o-panah* (support and protection). Sixteen-year-old Nelofer, a life-long resident of Mashhad, explained:

> not only my father thinks that girls are useless and that their only value is in their bride price ... even my mother likes her sons more, since she says that they are going to take care of her in the future but the girls are useless and will belong to others. Always when we cook *abgousht* (stew), the meat is for boys and the good fruits are for boys since they will work and will be the breadwinners. But our hours of housework and cleaning pistachio nuts, for which my father collects our wages, does not count. The boys go wherever they want but we are not allowed to go anywhere, unless they permit us. They have the authority over us. They intervene in our marriage. They say no to my suitors without asking me ... in the family there is no justice for women.

It is important to note that it is not only girls who paint this picture of the family dynamic. Most of the boys that we interviewed described similar situations, whether or not they agreed with the dominant gender ideology. Sixteen-year-old Reza said the following:

> In the past like my family I assumed that boys are naturally better. However, now that I am older and observe the society with keen eyes I have changed my view and I think that boys and girls are equal. I have learnt this here in Iran, where you can see that women can achieve as much as men. But most Afghan families cannot accept this. You can't find any single Afghan family who will not discriminate between their daughters and sons. I think the Afghan society thinks that boys are superior to girls and it is the power of boys that makes them

superior to girls. Families give rights to boys and they have the right to choose and to make decisions. Boys are allowed to express their ideas but daughters' ideas are rarely accepted. On the other hand, the Afghans think that only boys are able to earn money and work and that is why they usually pay more attention to boys. A son is a symbol of future support and when a boy is born they are happy. They don't care much for girls because they always think that girls belong to others, it means she will marry and go. Among Afghans, the boy usually stays with the parents till the end and supports them but girls marry and leave ... They don't respect girls. When we wanted to go out for picnic, whatever the boys would say was accepted. Whatever the boys say at home is the rule and they usually don't pay attention if it is right or not. Specially, the oldest son is the little king at home.

It is the inevitability of female oppression and potential mistreatment within the Afghan communities that is of continuous concern to adolescent Afghan women in Iran, particularly in light of the threat of repatriation. Girls we interviewed worried that any unexpected crisis, particularly financial, might result in their being married off without any say in the matter. They were fully aware that this was not due to a lack of parental love but rather to concern over limited resources and the necessity of prioritising the collective good of the family, in which girls hold only transitory status. When times become particularly hard, families may treat adolescent daughters as a resource in various ways: their wage-earning capacity may be exploited, and more disturbingly, they can be used as exchange brides for their brothers (see below) or married off to the suitor willing to pay the highest bride price. Many of our informants highlighted such practices.

Some of the young women expressed the view that their lives were much harder than those of their mothers, since the latter knew no other reality, believed all Muslim women in the world shared this fate, and fully accepted the view that God created them to serve men. As seventeen-year-old Homira explained:

> Our situation is very different. We live in a different world where even the most observant Muslim woman may go to university, get a job, fall in love and choose her husband, travel, and if the husband tries to oppress her she divorces him. When we know all this and yet have to live like our grandmothers, life becomes unbearable.

Her friend continued:

> Sometimes, I so worry about what is going to happen to my life that I cry at night for hours. Sometimes I pray that they give me to a man who is good. Sometimes, I dream about how I would protect my daughters and wish that God gives me only daughters so that I help them to have a good life, but then I worry that maybe my husband would divorce me and take my daughters away from me if I had no sons.

Then she laughed and said: 'Dr Hoodfar, you may laugh at us because the rest of the world has passed these kinds of worries a hundred years ago, but we Afghans had to fight everybody else's war so we did not have time to develop ourselves and our society'.

Education and Work

Our data as a whole revealed a complex picture of family life and the situation of adolescent females. For example, we discovered that in many families at least some daughters were able to study while their brothers had to engage in full-time wage-earning activities to support the family. In part this was due to the unacceptability of young, unmarried Afghan women working outside the home. The exceptions to this are teaching, nursing, medicine and some white-collar jobs, but such positions are rarely accessible to Afghan migrants even if they have the necessary qualifications. In other cases daughters worked cleaning and packaging nuts or doing needlework in the evenings at home, which did not interfere with their few hours of schooling. Because daughters are generally not expected to contribute financially to the household, many of the girls we interviewed told us they worked to pay for their education so as not to burden the family and thus decreased the risk of being taken out of school.

Our observation of several schools in Tehran indicated that there was not a significant difference between the number of boys and girls at the primary level; however, in the three secondary schools where we worked the number of girls was actually higher than that of boys. As far as we could ascertain, this situation is totally unlike other Afghan diaspora communities, and it certainly contradicts the insistence of most of our interviewees that girls are always negatively discriminated against. Moreover, in the whole of our sample there were very few boys in the secondary school who were not engaged in economic activities.

Boys were encouraged to work as soon as they were able. The pattern this followed varied; some worked part-time and studied part-time. However, among most refugee families crises have inevitably arisen; the main breadwinner might fall ill or lose his or her job, or an employer could decide to withhold wages (this happened quite frequently since many refugees work illegally and have no recourse to justice). In such cases boys would have to drop their studies to work full-time. One consequence of this instability is that by the time Afghan boys get to secondary school they tend to be older than their Iranian counterparts and, in most cases, than their female classmates. This has worked as a disincentive. In addition, they have limited study time due to part-time job requirements and often do not do as well as female students.

Expectations around future gender roles also contribute to the smaller number of adolescent male refugees attending secondary school, as they are very aware that the diploma granted by 'informal' Afghan schools is not recognised by the Iranian government, and therefore does not facilitate entry to university. For most of these young men a high school diploma will not make a difference to work opportunities in either Iran or Afghanistan, and they are better off gaining skills in the labour market. Those students in the Iranian schools who, for financial reasons, were forced to drop out had little chance of re-entry even with the necessary papers; and, for those who made it through and passed the dreaded university entrance exam, the high university fees often thwarted further education. The prospect of return to Afghanistan suggested specific additional problems. They worried that they had no knowledge of the market in Afghanistan. How could they find a job or start a business? How would they be treated as workers?

Female students contended with different constraints from males, in part because of more limited options in the job market. However, a diploma, even from an informal Afghan school, allowed them to become teachers, considered amongst the most respectable and acceptable jobs for women.

Families that had supported their daughters' education to the high school level or beyond felt it was important that they graduate in order to qualify for teaching in the Afghan schools, thus bringing respect to the family. In many cases it was mothers who supported their daughters' education, hoping to ensure them a more secure future. As one mother said: 'the history of war in Afghanistan shows one never knows the future. The best defence for any woman is her education because wherever she goes it will be an asset for her, and if she loses her parents and her husband she can honourably work and provide for herself and children'.

Most of the young women and girls viewed education as a means for personal and social transformation, not only in terms of increased job opportunities, but also as a way to enhance their contributions to their families and society, and to gain recognition and respect as role models for future generations of women. Many of them were the first generation of women to achieve formal literacy in their families. Given the importance of Islam as a source of legitimacy in these deeply religious communities, our interviewees frequently referred to Islamic discourse and religion as the framework for their unconventional (by traditional Afghan standards) activities and dreams. They held up the ideal of the educated Muslim woman with a deep understanding of Islam, living according to Quran, in opposition to the Taliban ideology of tradition in the name of Islam. Thus, while parents viewed education, particularly for girls, in pragmatic terms as the most important means to access appropriate jobs and achieve social mobility, the girls themselves hoped that by working in visible and respected jobs they would help restructure the position of women in the family and in Afghan society. They acknowledged that much had changed in their families. It was the possibility that these still fresh changes might be reversed that caused the major worries about repatriation.

It was not only the young women who drew on Islam as a force for social and structural change. Many of the mothers justified their advocacy and support of their daughters' educations in the name of Islam, crediting Ayatollah Khomeini for enlightening them on the true responsibility of parents, particularly mothers. They told us that the early policies of the Iranian government under Ayatollah Khomeini led the Afghan community to understand education and literacy, for both males and females, as being as important as any of the pillars of Islam, and a requisite of being a good Muslim. Their statements referred to a slogan of the Islamic Republic in the 1980s prominent on many billboards around the country, reading 'A good Muslim is an educated Muslim', and signed by the Ayatollah, suggesting their duty as parents was to raise good Muslim sons and daughters.

The frequent references to Islam must be understood within the framework of the acceptance of Afghan refugees by Iran based on their membership in the global community of Muslims – the *umma* – and their need of protection. Similarly, the Afghan refugees' claim to safe harbour and their sense of entitlement derived from their religion rather than notions of rights as citizens or refugees.

Marriage in the Time of Socio-Political Crisis

Marriage proved to be a major source of anxiety for girls particularly in view of imminent repatriation. Marriage is a pivotal life event for Afghans of all ethnic groups and everyone is expected to marry and have many children. In fact, the ultimate marker of adult status is marriage and parenthood. All of our male interviewees hoped to marry and have their own family. They expressed little anxiety over their future marriages and did not articulate any link between repatriation and their marriage prospects. This can be attributed in part to the fact that adolescent boys considered themselves too young for marriage. As one fifteen-year-old told me, his parents did not have the resources and it would be a long time before he had enough money to find a bride. Generally male and female adolescents face very different scenarios when it comes to marriage.

In practice sons would have a say in choosing their future brides, particularly if they are paying part or all of the wedding expenses. However, this is not the case for daughters. Theoretically, once the father or other male relative has decided whom the girl should marry, she is expected to obey. Many young Afghan women we interviewed found this unacceptable. In particular they found the interventions of the extended family frustrating. As seventeen-year-old Zohreh put it, 'marriage for most of us is like the inevitable nightmare, if not a gate to hell. Everyone else, our uncles, our father, our brothers, everyone but ourselves, dictates our future and there is little that we can do about it'.

To remain unmarried was commonly understood as unacceptable and to reject marriage the equivalent of heresy: everyone was quick to point out the Prophet's injunction that all Muslims should marry. Young women were not rejecting marriage or parental involvement outright. However, they envisaged a different kind of marriage institution, one that would give them more space and treat them as people in their own right if not totally equal to their husbands. Realising that this may be too much to expect at this time, they simply wanted to have a say in who they marry and the right of refusal. Many of our female interviewees compared their lot with that of their Iranian peers, as in the following statement by a seventeen-year-old girl engaged to marry someone she had never met: 'I do not want to live or marry like your Canadian students, but I should have the same rights as my Muslim Iranian friends. Iranians give more freedom to their daughters and to women, and they have managed to develop their country better and the country as a whole is more Islamic, not less'.

While the extent to which young Iranian women experience freedom is open to debate, it was assumed that they are given the opportunity to accept or refuse a potential husband. Moreover, although women must observe the dress code of the Islamic Republic, they are able to participate in public life and interact with the opposite sex, albeit within limits. Certainly most young Iranians consider their freedom very curtailed and may not agree with the picture painted of them by Afghan youth. However, by repeatedly pointing out the Islamic nature of Iranian society, Afghan youths were strategically employing an acceptable line of reasoning in negotiating for more space and rights with their parents and the community.

Our young female informants frequently told us that the Iranian government's growing pressure on refugees to return to Afghanistan had made them increasingly anxious about the whole issue of marriage and about their educational opportunities. Researchers have observed for other Muslim refugees that at times of instability and uncertainty parents try to marry off their daughters to safeguard their honour and that of the family.[10] For Afghan refugees the situation is even more complex because of the involvement of a substantial bride price. Many young women told us that with the threat of deportation looming more fathers are marrying off their daughters to whoever offers a decent bride price. With many facing return to Afghanistan after absences of more than two decades, these are socially and economically uncertain times. Fathers are anxious about their daughters' security in the event of repatriation and are agreeing more readily to suitors' requests than they might have done a few years earlier. In fact, some of the parents who adamantly supported their daughters' high school education and hoped to see them through university when I interviewed them in 2001 had taken their daughters out of school and married them off by the time of my return two years later. Many of our female interviewees were very unhappy about this. As one sixteen-year-old girl said, 'This is a kind of discrimination between us and our brothers. We are always viewed as a problem by our parents, even though girls work so hard to help the family in every way they can and even though our parents see that in Iran daughters are viewed the same as boys'.

The custom of bride price has served especially to disadvantage daughters particularly in times of economic crisis.[11] Many of the young girls told us stories of parents giving their daughters in marriage solely because the bride price was needed to pay rent or raise capital to start a small business. Many parents readily acknowledged this was the case. One mother who told us girls should not marry before they reached their twenties and should at least finish high school before marriage regretfully announced that she had to give one of her daughters in marriage at the age of twelve: 'We needed a roof over our heads. We had no one to borrow from and in any case we could not pay a loan back. We could not sleep in the street. So I agreed to her marriage at too young an age to save the rest of us'.

Similarly to the situation of Laotian refugees described by Krefeld, the interests of the collective are often placed above the interest of individuals.[12] Sons are also implicated in such sacrifices, having to leave school early in order to help support their families. However, for sons this does not always mean loss of control over their futures, while for girls, given the legal, cultural and structural limitations placed on women in Afghan society, marriage inevitably means that neither she nor her parents retain much influence over her destiny.

Many families of modest means also look to their daughters as a way of financing their son's marriage, marrying off a daughter to the suitor offering the highest bride price so that they in turn can provide a decent bride price for a daughter-in-law and a wedding for their son. However, some families, in order to avoid the heavy costs associated with a son's marriage, have engaged in the exchange of brides: one family would provide a daughter as a bride for another family's son, receiving that family's daughter as a wife for their son. In this practice only males have a say in the choice of bride, while the girls must simply accept their fate. Our female interviewees perceived this as the worst possible type of marriage: not only were girls pawns in a process where they have absolutely no say but, given the close intertwining of families, if either marriage goes badly there are negative consequences for the other couple as well.

Women who were members of very conservative, traditional families were particularly unhappy, seeing the injustice in the rules regulating their lives and rejecting the assumption that these were Islamic rules. They were aware of how women live in other Muslim societies. Seventeen-year-old Fatemeh put it in these words:

> They tell us this is the way God has created the world and that men are in charge of women, but we know that it is not God but men, and worse, the very father and brother who are supposed to protect you, that treat you like an animal they own. You see this is why we are unhappier than our mothers, who did not know about other Muslim societies.

The majority of Afghan refugees vulnerable to deportation are not from influential ethnic groups or socio-economic classes, and are thus most subject to a downward spiral of unfortunate circumstances. In large part, marrying their daughters off was also seen as a way of protecting girls from being violated or behaving inappropriately in the process of uprooting and resettlement in Afghanistan, where conditions are difficult to predict and security hard to ensure.

Our female interviewees said women often feel powerless to resist, and pointed to reports of an increase in suicides by young Afghan women in Iran as well as Afghanistan, which they believe stem in part from women's despair over the lack of control over their lives and destinies.[13] Several of them noted that many of the young street girls in Iran are Afghan women who fled their families to escape oppression, only to wind up suffering on the streets, still powerless and unable ever to return home. Such cases acted as deterrents to girls pondering how to assert themselves and demand more respect and autonomy within their families. There is no recourse if a girl runs away from her family; in fact, they fear that she could face death at the hands of brothers, uncles or fathers for shaming the family. They noted that their brothers have no understanding of what they suffer every day in worrying about and fearing for the future.

Strategies of Adolescent Girls

In spite of the numerous challenges and difficulties, the girls we came to know were far from passive victims and had adopted strategies to deal with unwanted marriages and discriminatory treatment within the family. The piecework that they took on at home to pay for their education and contribute to the household was also a means of gaining positive attention from their parents. They worked hard at their studies, hoping good grades would further discourage their parents from planning early marriages for them.

Realising the enormous power of religion as a source of legitimacy for social practice, both boys and girls took religious learning very seriously, attending classes and watching TV programmes on religion. While all young Afghans had adopted Iranian clothing styles, adolescent girls dressed much more conservatively than their Iranian peers. This was partly to reduce parental anxiety about family honour and partly to avoid sexual harassment in the streets; as Afghans, teenage girls said they felt they were more vulnerable than their Iranian counterparts. Dressing more conservatively also underscored their adherence to Islamic principles, making it easier to pursue activities that were not traditional by Afghan standards, such as going to school or to Quranic classes. Girls pointed out to their parents the Islamic nature of their pursuits. Some of them spent time teaching their mothers about religion and the Islamic rights of women. In this way, girls attempted to make allies of their mothers. A number of those we came to know had started to teach the Quran to Afghan and Iranian children at the mosque or at school, free of charge, bringing respect and honour to themselves and their families and increasing their standing in the wider Afghan community. Yet they stressed that they just wanted to be good Muslims living according to Islamic values. By implication they could thus also resist those aspects of Afghan culture which, they pointed out to their parents, contradicted Islam. In all these ways girls increasingly overcame traditions that would limit their rights

(Re)Constructing Afghan Identity in Iran

Both males and females were preoccupied with their situation as Afghans in Iran. They said they felt like unwanted guests and that, for the most part, Iranians did not treat them with dignity. While this experience was shared by many of our interviewees, most felt powerless to challenge the situation, bitterly aware that their marginal social and legal status as undocumented refugees afforded them few rights. They feared that raising even the slightest objections could jeopardise their tenuous residency. One common way of addressing discrimination and bolstering their sense of worth was to remind themselves, as well as others, that as members of the global Muslim community (*umma*) they should be entitled to work and live anywhere in the Muslim world. While this was empowering to an extent, it generally did not persuade Iranians. Commonly in discussions or arguments with Iranians they were dismissed as *aghanoftadeh* (backward), attacking not only individual worth but their collective culture and history. Afghan youth continually looked for ways to counter such stereotyping. They concurred that Afghanistan faced major social and economic problems due to twenty-five years of war and destruction. However, they were quick to point out that suffering the effects of foreign-imposed warfare was not an indication of inherent backwardness; they argued that given security and peace and the opportunity to go to school young Afghans would do well. Seventeen-year-old Samir put it this way:

> Iranians think backwardness – *aghanoftadehgi* – and problems of war are some sort of genetic disease that all Afghans carry. I was born here in Iran, went to school here, I played football here, I helped them with their studies, and I worked many nights when they were asleep to clean their streets in order to pay our rent. If they had to live with the hardships that Afghans have lived for these long years, they would be psychologically destroyed if not dead long ago. Yet, when they talk to me and my Afghan friends, they tell us in a thousand different ways that we are backward. It is not the poverty, but this assumption that we are less than them that eats away at the soul of every Afghan youth here.

Sixteen-year-old Ahmad, who, along with several of his friends, had had a long conversation with me about Palestinian refugees in the Middle East on a previous occasion, said:

> I sometimes envy Palestinian youths because, even if they have the same kind of problems, the whole world, or at least the Muslim world, understands their concerns and treats them with respect. It is respect that we need, not food and not even schools, because now we have our own schools, even if they are not as equipped as the Iranian schools.

While sometimes parents complained that their children had become more Iranian than Afghan, picking up Iranian attitudes and values, none of the youths interviewed – including those born and raised entirely in Iran – considered themselves Iranian or even Afghan-Iranian. In various ways they told us repeatedly that they were of Afghan blood, their parents were Afghan, and they would always be Afghan even if they lived in Iran for ever. Many young people, however, acknowledged that their strong sense of Afghan identity was somewhat recent. The Afghan schools had created a safe space for them to speak among themselves and collectively reflect on Afghanistan, the war, their identities and the reasons they were targets of discrimination. Through these discussions, adolescents had come to feel more comfortable identifying themselves as Afghan, and a sense of belonging had emerged that was not evident prior to the establishment of the schools. Some of the boys told us that formerly, as students in Iranian schools, despite their academic accomplishments they were uncomfortable acknowledging their Afghan identity for fear of being treated differently. This also prohibited their involvement in extra-curricular activities. They told us that being in Afghan schools had given them confidence and a pride in their heritage and that they hoped to be able to help their culture to flourish and provide a more thriving atmosphere for the younger generation.

Issues of Return

In spite of this new-found pride many were clear that they had no desire to 'return' to Afghanistan, or certainly not until completing school and other training. They readily acknowledged that Afghanistan has a lot of catching up to do, in terms of rebuilding its economy and government institutions. The young people saw no contradiction in proclaiming their Afghan identity and not wanting to live in Afghanistan. The boys more than girls often justified this by stating that as Muslims they should be able to live anywhere in the Muslim world; and some further emphasised the idea by pointing out that Ayatollah Khomeini had declared 'there is no border in Islam'. Girls, however, stressed their need to finish their education so that they could help Afghan society build and develop. They pointed out that they needed to delay their return until they had attained a university degree, even a high school or nursing degree or something that would allow them to contribute to their society. In short, while boys were worried about accessing the labour market and earning a living to support themselves and their families, girls, who are expected to be provided for by their families, justified their desire to stay and complete their education in terms of service to the wider society.

As far as our interviewees were concerned a return to Afghanistan should be dictated solely by whether individuals and families had skills or other resources to offer in the rebuilding of the country. In Mashhad, fifteen out of the eighteen adolescents interviewed said they did not wish to go to Afghanistan and would delay doing so as long as they could. They worried about the lack of security, jobs and infrastructure, including schools, and some noted that they did not have the guarantee of a roof over their head either. Both genders, however, shared the opinion that they would not yet be of much help to their society: 'My friends and I want to go back to Afghanistan when we are educated and ready and can do something useful. If we go now at most we will be a simple labourer, with no jobs there. That is not helping Afghanistan. That is adding to the problem' (a sixteen-year-old male student and worker in Mashhad).

Among our interviewees in Tehran, many had for the first time been offered lessons on the history and geography of Afghanistan in their Afghan schools and were pleased to tell us about what they had learned. They also spoke of going to Afghanistan to help rebuild and develop. Of the thirty-three interviewees two male students doubted that they would ever live there. Most of the others strongly believed that any hope for the future lay in the hands of young people, and were eloquent about their desire to go to Afghanistan when they were capable and ready to help the country recover. However, more than half of our Tehran youth sample expressed an interest in going first to visit and familiarise themselves before returning in the future for good. This seemed to be a strategy for dealing with their anxieties about the unknown: 'It is not the hardship but not knowing what to expect, which we find unsettling', as one sixteen-year-old female student told us.

Large segments of the refugee population originate from rural Afghanistan and had to learn to live in Iran's large urban centers. Now they worry about fitting in to village life, where basic services and facilities are lacking. Seventeen-year-old Mahmmud, who came with his parents to Iran at the age of seven from their village, expressed this concern as follows:

> Imagine how hard it was coming from a small village in the middle of the mountains with no services to live in Tehran with 12 million people. It took my family a very long time to learn about city life. Now how can we go back to a village when there is nothing, and drought and bombing have destroyed it? Where would we go? Like many other people we would have to go to the cities, where there are no jobs or housing for us. It is not that we do not want to go to our country. It is that the conditions are not ready for us.

The youth's nationalistic language was often in sharp contrast to that of their families, who presented disinterest in returning to Afghanistan in terms of lack of security and basic services, economic factors, issues concerning the health and education of their children and the ethnic discrimination they might face. Some said they did not want to repeat the mistake they had made by returning after the Russian withdrawal in 1989. Others were cynical about the prospects of rebuilding the country, as exemplified in the following statement: 'It has taken twenty-five years of war to ruin Afghanistan, but it will take 125 years to rebuild it – if ever – and only if the outside powers allow it'. The rhetoric of public good and rendering service to Afghanistan was conspicuously absent from the responses of parents.

While all of the adolescents were preoccupied with economic concerns, the job market and their educational prospects, the girls specifically wanted to know about women's rights in Afghanistan, and to what extent these rights were different from those of men. Knowing that I and my research associate, Sarah Kamal, had been in Afghanistan, they bombarded us with questions, wondering how the situation for women in Afghanistan differed from that in Iran. They worried that even with a high school education they might not be able to work in Afghanistan given the constraints faced by women there. They wondered what would happen if another Taliban-type government came to power. Having read an article about women's rights in pre-war Afghanistan, sixteen-year-old Zahra said: 'I think it will be a long time before women in Afghanistan can live like women did before the war, or like the women in Iran. War has taken more than lives.'

An eighteen-year-old told us that, although she thought the Taliban were evil, she also felt like thanking them for forcing the issue of women to the fore. Now that the role of women in Afghan society has become of national and international interest, she wondered if this would help resolve some of the questions around Afghan traditions and customs that in fact have no support in Islam, and she said she hoped that maybe one day the rights of women and daughters would be respected.

While young women worried particularly about gender discrimination, many of their male peers – particularly Hazaras – focused on ethnic prejudice. They feared that in Afghanistan they would be subject to discrimination and there would be no mechanisms in place to protect them. Eighteen-year-old Masoud told me:

> I can put up with discrimination here in Iran: although it makes me upset I can live with it because I say, 'Well, I am not Iranian and they [the government] have to take care of Iranians first.' But, when I am treated badly and disrespectfully in my own country and I am powerless to do any thing about it, how can I live? To be excluded in your own country is more dreadful. I dream of my country and yet I am so frightened of it. Do you understand? We feel that the rest of the world does not want to understand us. They talk about Afghans but they do not know that Afghans think of themselves as Pashtu, Hazara, Tajik … and there is a hierarchy of ethnicities. Would that change one day? Maybe, I like to believe, but I also have to be realistic.

Many adolescent refugees have cultivated a sense of nationalism and a collective identity as Afghans; and simply do not understand why there should be discrimination and hostility between ethnic groups in Afghanistan. Sometimes parents avoided referring to the ethnic hostility directed towards the Hazara and other minority groups in their homeland. However, threatened with repatriation they have felt obliged to prepare their children by telling them stories of suffering at the hands of other Afghans, particularly Pashtuns, who were the ruling elites. They often resort to Islamic idioms, saying that the Prophet Muhammad also suffered at the hands of those who assumed superiority. But none of this has made the issue of inter-ethnic discrimination easier to understand for adolescents raised as part of an Afghan collective in Iran. Many have responded with disbelief, and some said they wanted to experience the situation for themselves: 'I want to go and find out why there is discrimination. For instance we are Qezelbash [one of the smaller Afghan ethnic groups] but when we went to get identity cards we were told to say we are Tajik, and I want to know why this is so' (an eighteen-year-old male student).

Their collective suffering in Iran and their labelling as a group by Iranians has led to the forging of a collective Afghan identity. Many young Afghans living in Iran have come to embrace this pan-Afghan identity regardless of ethnicity or class. As in the past, however, most of their parents today do not refer to themselves as Afghan, but rather as members of their ethnic group.

Conclusion

There is a pressing need for more research on adolescents and children in settings of prolonged displacement where new generations of refugees are born and brought up in contexts that they are not allowed or encouraged to call home. We need to develop a better understanding of the dynamics of social and cultural change amongst adolescents in such settings, because of both the profound impact on individual lives and the implications for any plan for repatriation, reconstruction and resettlement. There is a need to add new dimensions to the study of refugee youth, beyond generational differences and inter-generational relations.

Presenting some of the intimate worries and preoccupations of young Afghan refugees in Iran, this chapter has examined the different ways that young males and females have experienced life as refugees and have constructed ideas about the future. The nuanced strategies that they have developed to cope with their multiple identities as Afghans, youth, daughters, sons, Muslims, students and workers in not-so-friendly Iranian society are an indication of an active agency that is easily overlooked. In the case of adolescent girls we have shown this agency in terms of the negotiation of gender roles and gender relations within the family and wider society.

Our observations and interviews of Afghan adolescents in Iran (both male and female) indicate that they critically analyse the values of family and community, particularly with regard to marriage, education and the labour market. They are also seeking to introduce fundamental changes into their families and communities. Some of the changes have been in response to external factors. Others are a response to their own immediate needs as refugees joining the labour market, taking advantage of education opportunities and actively learning and interpreting the meaning of their religion. Having studied their religion, they question their parents' practices. By using the legitimate force of religion, which their elders have used for generations to disarm and control young people, they introduce new ideas in order to make their family less hierarchical and more receptive to their needs. The female adolescents, who are more disadvantaged then their male counterparts – notably in terms of marriage practices – are particularly insistent on learning more about Islam and distinguishing between 'true' Islam and Afghan cultural practices in order to promote their rights within the family and society. Thus the adolescents have striven to introduce change without alienating the parents and other kin who remain their main source of support in an uncertain world.

While family is the primary site of their intervention for change, the youth are not neglectful of the national culture and inter-ethnic relations. They are preoccupied with national and international affairs that led to war and the destruction of Afghanistan and that led to their exile and displacement. They reject the predominant ethnic hierarchies (to which many of their elders are wedded) that contradict a sense of equality and citizenry. They stressed that they are determined to change that. However, they feel they need new tools to take on such a huge task. 'To struggle against your elders and against history requires more than devotion. We need to have our education and promote our abilities', said seventeen-year-old Sima, while her classmates nodded approvingly. Her informal Afghan school was closed once again by the police. She was thus airing her criticism of Iranian authorities' repatriation polices while declaring her nationalism and her goal of returning, albeit at a later date than Iranian authorities are pressing on them. The young people, particularly the girls, stressed a need to empower themselves through education in order to be able to provide service for fellow Afghans and build a better Afghanistan. They frequently referred to Dr Sima Samar, who has managed to change so much on her own.[14] They are keenly aware that, if they succeed, in the process they will also transform conventional limitations on themselves as women within the family and society. However, their anxiety and doubt stem from their realisation of the enormously challenging tasks they see ahead for themselves. They worry whether they will have the necessary skills and opportunities to reshape their society in the image they see as just and fair for their children.

Notes

I would like to thank Jason Hart for considerable support and his help in improving the focus of the chapter. I also want to thank Marlene Caplan for her enthusiastic support of 'The Afghan project' and her insightful comments and editing. Last but not least I thank Sara Kamal, who spent nine months in Iran with the Afghan youths, generating much trust and friendship as well as creating an intellectually stimulating and empowering atmosphere among our research community.

 1. Sixteen-year-old Afghan refugee woman in Iran interviewed by the author.
 2. Refugee Report, 1992.
 3. Interestingly, Iran followed different educational and settlement policies for the half-million Iraqi refugees who came to Iran during the same period in the 1980s.
 4. Frelick (1999); Rajaee (2000); PRIO (2004).
 5. During this same period the repatriation of Afghans in Pakistan has proceeded at a rate unprecedented in recent decades.
 6. Boyden (1997); Woodhead (1997); Hart (2004).
 7. Rashid (2001).
 8. Ibid.
 9. Hoodfar (2004).
10. Krefeld (1994); Zolfaqar (2000); Swaine with Feeny (2004).
11. Dupree (1984); Tapper (1991).
12. Krefeld (1994).
13. Indeed, while no statistical evidence has been collected on the subject of young

female suicides, the phenomenon has been very widespread and people and national media frequently talk about it. Several missions and women's groups as well as UNIFEM have started to research the phenomenon (see 'The Narrative Report of Women's Self-burning Mission to Herat', prepared by the Gender and Law Working Group: Herat Mission Report, 17–21 February 2004, supported by Gender and Justice UNIFEM [United Nations Development Fund for Women] Afghanistan).

14. Sima Samar, a medical doctor and a Hazah by ethnicity, had established a non-governmental organisation that ran over thirty schools for children and several clinics and hospitals in Afghanistan and in Pakistan. She became the first Minster of Women's Affairs in Karzai's transitional government. But the powerful fundamentalist forces brought a dubious 'blasphemy' charge on a very questionable basis against her and she was forced to leave office. Beside her NGO work, she also serves as director of the Independent Afghan Human Rights Commission.

References

Boyden, J. 1997 'Childhood and the Policy Makers: a Comparative Perspective on the Globalization of Childhood', in A. James and A. Prout (eds) *Constructing and Reconstructing Childhood: Contemporary Issues in the Sociological Study of Childhood.* Basingstoke: The Falmer Press, pp. 190–229.

Dupree, N.H. 1984 'Women and Emancipation before the Saur Revolution', in N. Shahrani and R. Canfield (eds) *Revolution and Rebellions in Afghanistan.* Berkeley: Institute for International Studies.

Frelick, B. 1999 'Refugees in Iran: Who should Go? Who should Stay?' *Refugee Reports* 20 (6) (June). Available at http://www.reliefweb.int.

Hart, J. 2004 'Beyond Struggle and Aid: Children's Identities in a Palestinian Refugee Camp in Jordan', in J. Boyden and J. de Berry (eds) *Children and Youth on the Front Line: Ethnography, Armed Conflict and Displacement.* New York: Berghahn Books, pp. 167–88.

Hoodfar, H. 2004 'Families on the Move: The Changing Role of Afghan Refugee Women in Iran', *Hawwa: Journal of Women of the Middle East and the Islamic World* 2 (2): 141–71.

Krefeld, R. 1994 'Buddhism, Maintenance and Change: Reinterpreting Gender in a Lao Refugee Community', in L.A. Camino and R.M. Krefeld (eds) *Reconstructing Lives, Recapturing Meaning: Refugee Identity Gender and Culture Change.* Australia: Gordon and Breach Publishers.

PRIO 2004 *Afghan Refugees in Iran: from Refugee Emergency to Migration Management.* Oslo: International Peace Research Institute.

Rajaee, B. 2000 'The Politics of Refugee Policy in Post-revolutionary Iran', *Middle East Journal* 54 (1): 44–63.

Rashid, A. 2001 *Taliban: Islam, Oil and the New Great Game in Central Asia.* London: I.B. Tauris Publishers.

Refugee Report 1992 'Afghan Refugees in Iran Short Changed by the World Community: Iran Invites Western Agencies to Assist', *Refugee Report,* 28 August: 13.

Swaine, A. with Feeny, T. 2004 'A Neglected Perspective: Adolescent Girls' Experiences of the Kosovo Conflict 1999', in J. Boyden and J. de Berry (eds) *Children and Youth on the Front Line: Ethnography, Armed Conflict and Displacement.* New York: Berghahn Books, pp. 63–86.

Tapper, N. 1991 *Bartered Brides.* Cambridge: Cambridge University Press.

UN 1988 *First Consolidated Report.* Geneva: UNOCA.

UN 1990 *Third Consolidated Report.* Geneva: UNOCA.

Woodhead, M. 1997 'Psychology and Children's Needs', in A. James and A. Prout (eds) *Constructing and Reconstructing Childhood: Contemporary Issues in Sociological Study of Childhood.* Basingstoke: The Falmer Press, pp. 63–84.

Zolfaqar, F. 2000 *Internally Displaced Muslim Women: Political Valiance in Sri Lanka.* Sri Lanka: Muslim Women Research and Action Forum.

8

Dislocated Masculinity: Adolescence and the Palestinian Nation-in-exile*

Jason Hart

In his seminal study of nationalism, Benedict Anderson observed that 'in the modern world everyone can, should, will "have" a nationality, as he or she "has" a gender' (1991: 5). Over the past two decades numerous authors have brought these two themes together, exploring the relationship between nation and gender across diverse contexts (e.g. Yuval-Davis and Anthias, 1989; Kandiyoti, 1991; Parker et al., 1992; McClintock et al., 1997; Yuval-Davis, 1997). This work has commonly considered the constructedness of dominant accounts of gender within different nationalisms. Thus, the representation of gendered roles and practices as the immutable expression of biologically rooted difference has been revealed for its relationship to historically specific efforts to secure the viability of diverse projects of nationhood.

Much of the early literature focused on femininities and women drawing attention, for example, to the ways that particular visions of womanhood are commonly invoked to mark out the boundary between the nation and a degenerate Other (Kandiyoti, 1991; Martin, 2000; Mayer, 2000a). Comparable enquiry into the relationship between the construction of masculinities and the delineation of national community has emerged more recently (e.g. Mosse, 1996; Nagel, 1998; Lewis, 2000). This work still has many gaps, not least in its geographical reach. In relation to the Islamic

* Reprinted from *Journal of Refugee Studies* 21 (1): 64–81.

Middle East, discussion of masculinity in general terms has been notably sparse (Sinclair-Webb, 2000a: 9; Ouzgane, 2006: 1).

This chapter considers the interplay between nation and masculinities in the Palestinian refugee camp where I conducted doctoral fieldwork in the late 1990s. The 'nation' referred to in this chapter is, therefore, divorced from any state. Instead, I discuss masculinities in relation to Palestinian nationalism in exile. As the late Edward Said noted, 'Each Palestinian community must struggle to maintain its identity on at least two levels: first as Palestinian with regard to the historical encounter with Zionism and the precipitous loss of a homeland; second, as Palestinian in the existential setting of day-to-day life, responding to the pressure in the state of residence' (1992: 121). In the refugee camps in Jordan the struggle to maintain Palestinian identity has been particularly explicit for reasons that I shall explain. My purpose here is to consider this struggle in two specific dimensions. First, I am concerned with the masculinities constructed by and for adolescent males who, like their parents and in some cases grandparents, were born into one of the ten recognised camps in Jordan. I consider the relationship of these masculinities to what will be referred to henceforward as the nation-in-exile. Through the employment of ethnographic material, I intend to demonstrate the ways in which young males – through the performance of a particular, dominant vision of masculinity that I label *mukhayyamji* – serve to reproduce the camp as an authentic location of this exilic national community.

My second aim in this chapter is to consider the implications for individual young men of the interplay between masculinities and the reproduction of the camp as the heartland of the displaced Palestinian nation. We need to ask about the consequences both for those who fail or choose not to uphold the idealised, *mukhayyamji* adolescent masculinity and for those who evince the skills and qualities that this entails. As I shall argue, while the former risk marginalisation from the camp as a moral and socio-political community, the latter face marginalisation from the economic life of wider Jordanian society and, with that, endanger the transition to social adulthood. Thus, a set of paradoxes emerge for young males that reflect the ambiguous position of the Palestinian refugees in Jordan at a specific moment in the history of Jordan and the Palestinian national struggle.

Fieldwork

The ethnographic material employed in this chapter was produced by doctoral fieldwork while resident in Hussein Camp, Amman, between February 1997 and September 1998 (Hart, 2000). At different times I lived inside and on the edge of the camp and involved myself as much as possible in the settings in which the daily lives of the young were principally conducted: UN Relief and Works Agency (UNRWA) schools, the youth clubs, neighbourhood streets, as well as homes. The principal focus of my research lay in the relationship of children – nine years old and above – to 'Palestine' as a notional homeland that they and perhaps even their parents had never seen. Masculinity was not an initial theme of enquiry.

As a foreigner, ignorant of the ways to behave in this new and strange environment, I found that younger children became my best teachers, possibly due to the fact that they were also engaged in an explicit process of learning how to conduct themselves. They were often less inhibited than their parents and older siblings in telling me when and how I was failing to behave appropriately. After six months of this education, a colleague pointed out that I wasn't simply being socialised in some abstract, gender-neutral manner: both boys and girls were instructing me how to become a proper *zalame* – a 'regular guy'. Perhaps my best teacher was ten-year-old neighbour Muhannad,[1] who berated me quite regularly for my failings in this regard. On one early visit to my house, he found me hanging out my washing to dry. Immediately he asked, 'Who did your washing?' He responded sternly to my explanation that I had done it myself with the words, '*Eib. Inte zalame*' ('Shame on you. You're a guy'). I then asked him who else might do my washing since I lived alone. He thought for a moment and then suggested Randa, our twelve-year-old neighbour whose family were my particular friends. As I well knew, together with her older sister, Randa was already doing the washing for her parents and five brothers.

While observation and everyday conversations such as this informed my growing sense of the dynamics of gender within the camp, it was discussion with people outside the camp that made me aware of the significance of adolescent masculinity as a marker of the distinctiveness of Hussein Camp. 'Outsiders' – including Palestinian refugees living in adjoining neighbourhoods and taxi drivers working in the general area of the camp – frequently made reference to the young males in the camp, expressing either admiration or anxiety for their presumed toughness, independence and cunning. Such views echoed sentiments commonly voiced by my neighbours in the camp who spoke in humorous but approving terms of the *mukhayyamji* boys of the camp. As I came to understand, *mukhayyamji* was a term used to describe a particular style of idealised masculinity amongst adolescent males. Although only one defined model, *mukhayyamji* enjoyed dominance in certain settings: the lad who could demonstrate the skills and dispositions associated with this masculinity often attracted the admiration of peers and family members. I shall return to consider the *mukhayyamji* in more detail. However, it is first necessary to explain something of the context in which the *mukhayyamji* and other masculinities were being constructed at the time of my fieldwork.

Political Context

Hussein Camp was established in 1952 and, according to UNRWA figures, in 1998 it housed around 30,000 registered Palestine refugees. It seemed likely, however, that the true figure was closer to 50,000. I never encountered or heard of any Palestinian residents who were not Muslims, although there were a few non-Palestinians renting housing units, most particularly Pakistanis, Egyptians and Iraqis. I contend that in popular imagination Hussein Camp was considered, above all, a 'Palestinian' space.

At the time of my fieldwork the camp was, in many respects, indistinguishable from the surrounding neighbourhoods of east Amman. Visually it displayed the same low-quality housing and poor infrastructure. As refugees from 1948 and their offspring, its inhabitants were seemingly no different from many other residents of a city where, according to the popular view, as many as 80–90 per cent of the population were also of Palestinian origin. On an official level, nevertheless, Hussein remained a 'camp' (and not a 'neighbourhood' or 'suburb' of Amman) due to its registration as such with the United Nations.[2] Within the discourse of Palestinian nationalism, the refugee camps in Jordan and elsewhere in the Middle East have figured as symbols of resistance and of the *sumud* ('steadfastness') of ordinary Palestinians in the face of Israeli intransigence and international indifference. For example, according to the 1988 Palestinian Declaration of Independence 'the unflinching resistance of the refugee camps outside the homeland [has] elevated awareness of the Palestinian truth and right into still higher realms of comprehension and actuality'.[3] The existence of Hussein and the other camps was physical evidence of the consequences of dispossession and the continuation of Palestinian community life in exile. Furthermore, it was from the camps that the Palestinian guerilla groups emerged in the 1950s (Massad, 1995: 469). More particularly, Hussein Camp was a key site during so-called Black September of 1970, when the Palestine Liberation Organisation (PLO) fought and lost against the Jordanian Army and were subsequently expelled from the country (Hirst, 1984).

In early 1998 the Amman municipal authorities began to demolish hundreds of houses in and immediately adjacent to Hussein Camp in order to make way for a new road. The compensation paid to those refugees dispossessed of their homes was generally paltry. UNRWA appeared to avoid involvement in spite of their mandate to promote the welfare of Palestinian refugees, and the PLO remained silent, thereby strengthening the belief of many residents of Hussein Camp that Arafat and the nationalist movement had effectively abandoned them in the wake of the Oslo Peace Process.[4]

In the view of many of my neighbours the events surrounding the building of the road highlighted their impotence and marginalisation within Jordan and the wider world. A common perception existed that the new road was merely an excuse to begin the gradual dispersal of the camp population as a community whose political aspirations were now at odds with the Jordanian regime in its efforts to build closer political and economic ties with Israel: a development thoroughly endorsed by the United States and other Western powers. In addition, the destruction of the homes was seen by residents of the camp as the first step towards the dismantling of the camp.

This brief historical overview is intended to highlight one point of particular relevance for our discussion: the fragility of both the camp itself and the Palestinian national project constructed within and through the camp. If, as the rhetoric of the PLO had earlier asserted, the refugee camps were heartlands of the struggle for national liberation, events in the mid-1990s suggested to many residents that their place in relation to the PLO-led struggle had become marginal or even irrelevant.

The Growing Importance of Islamic Observance and the Islamist Movement

Amongst the various societal processes that may have had significant bearing on the lives and ideas of young males in Hussein Camp at the time of my fieldwork, the growing influence of the Islamist movement was particularly significant. This influence should be seen as both symptomatic of and, to some extent, responsible for the increasing levels of religiosity in the camp witnessed from the mid-1980s onwards. It would be wholly inaccurate to suggest that the many residents of the camp who were becoming more engaged in religious ritual and study were all supporters of Islamist groups such as the Muslim Brotherhood (*al-Ikhwan*). Rather, these groups provided the driving force for a general trend towards the employment of symbols and texts associated with Islam to explain and understand the struggles of life in Hussein Camp. At the time of fieldwork the Islamists – popularly referred to by the generic term *shuyukh* (plural of *sheikh*) regardless of group affiliation – had gained control of various institutions in the camp hitherto the domain of the nationalist factions. Most notable amongst these was the camp youth club, run by an elected committee of mostly middle-aged men. Until that point, the committee had always been composed of members of one or other of the nationalist factions.

At the time of my fieldwork, the Islamists were also engaged in a programme of constructing new facilities, such as small schools of Islamic learning (*qutab*), youth and community centres and mosques. A clear focus of their energies was the engagement of boys and young men in their activities, with particular outreach to 'orphans' – young males who had lost at least their fathers, if not both parents.

The historicity of masculine style can be particularly demonstrated through the influence of the Islamists. During the course of my fieldwork a group of residents mounted an exhibition about the history of the camp youth club over the decades since its founding. Looking through the material I came across photographs from the 1960s and 1970s of young male bodybuilders, dressed in small swimming costumes, proudly exhibiting their oiled, muscular bodies. This was an image that seemed entirely at odds with the activities of young males and ideas about masculinity in the late 1990s. To contemporary eyes, especially those of Islamists, such preening was seen as immodest, even unmanly. The swimming costumes themselves contrasted sharply with the bathing attire that they promoted, consisting of high-waisted baggy shorts extending down to the knee.

Media Consumption

In addition to these developments within the immediate locale, residents of the camp in the late 1990s were also experiencing increasing exposure to globalised media. Satellite television with news and entertainment from around the Arab world and beyond was increasingly commonplace in homes. Many families also appeared to own video players and a growing number were starting to access the Internet. The views and images that adolescents received from these media blended with the stories of relatives and neighbours who had travelled abroad to produce ever more complex understandings of the wider world. The construction of idealised young masculinity in Hussein Camp should be seen as occurring in this setting of local politics and globalised media consumption.

Adolescent Masculinities and Power

In considering the relationship between nation and gender it is vital to acknowledge the plurality of masculinities constructed in relation to different nationalisms (Cornwall and Lindisfarne, 1994: 18; Connell, 1995: 37). These various masculinities are liable to differentiation as they intersect with factors of class, ethnicity and age (relative and chronological). For example, Peter Loizos has called attention to the marked differences between the masculinities of young unmarried males, mature married householders and the elderly in modern-day Greece, highlighting the importance of position in the life course in its intersection with masculinities (1994: 67–68).

Not all masculinities are equal, however. In his book *Gender and Power* (1987), Bob Connell proposed the notion of 'hegemonic masculinity', drawing on the Gramscian understanding of hegemony to suggest ascendancy achieved not merely, or even necessarily, through the use of naked power but by the compelling force of cultural and ideological norms (ibid.: 184). As Connell explained 'hegemonic masculinity' is not totalising and exclusive but 'is always constructed in relation to various subordinated masculinities as well as in relation to women' (ibid.: 183).

In this discussion I am particularly concerned to consider the relationship of a particular, dominant form of masculinity in Hussein Camp – *mukhayyamji* – in relation to other delineated masculinities. While, as I shall show, the *mukhayyamji* was hegemonic in certain contexts, it was not universally valorised even within the camp. For all the rhetorical claims to unity and common history amongst its Palestinian residents, the camp was not a homogeneous social and political space and different adolescent masculinities were called forth in different locations. The schools, mosques, youth clubs, *qutab* and coffee shops each had the potential to endorse a different hierarchical ordering of young masculinities.

In addition, a young man who enjoyed a privileged position within the camp due to his successful claim on *mukhayyamji* masculinity was liable to find that the display of many of these qualities either failed to register within wider Jordanian society or marked him out as an unwelcome outsider or threat. As we shall see, this had particular relevance for young men in the camp at the point when they sought to pursue a livelihood within Amman and thereby move towards full social adulthood.

Institutional Masculinities

Contemplation of the interrelationship between masculinities and institutions is vital to the understanding of how dominance is achieved. As Connell points out, 'hegemony is likely to be established only if there is some correspondence between cultural ideal and institutional power' (1995: 77). Cut adrift from the PLO, which had historically spoken for all Palestinians, and subject to a highly ambiguous relationship to the Jordanian state, the national community-in-exile lacked institutions that might call forth and legitimate specific masculinities. Various authors have shown how, in particular, the army plays a critical role in both representation of the nation and the construction of hegemonic masculinities (e.g. Kanitkar, 1994; Allen, 2000; Kaplan, 2000, 2003; Mayer, 2000b; Sinclair-Webb, 2000b). However, no organised military force equivalent to a state army existed for the residents of the camps in Jordan. Although the fathers and uncles of young men in Hussein Camp had been active as *fedayeen* (freedom fighters) with the PLO, such opportunities had long since ceased by the late 1990s. Meanwhile the Jordanian army was commonly seen as exclusionary – the sole preserve of the 'Bedouin', as my friends in the camp often referred to Jordanian citizens of Jordanian (rather than Palestinian) origin.

In the absence of support from formal institutions such as the military for models of masculinity, the family and local neighbourhood played an especially important valorising role. Here, children from the earliest age were caught up in the processes of gendering, encouraged by older siblings and other household members into particular gendered roles, behaviours and dispositions. The disparity between boys and girls as well as between different masculinities was impossible to ignore. Even a younger brother's position within the home was privileged in comparison with that of his sisters, and yet, since age was also a central index of authority, in relation to his older brothers his position remained lowly (Kandiyoti, 1994: 206). It was his elders who constituted models of powerful male performance. Both they and female relatives would encourage a young boy to copy their example. As he came to prove his toughness amongst his peers in the neighbourhood, his skill in football, his ability to handle conflict, so he would win approval from his male kin. As he enacted the role of the commanding senior male in his father and brothers' absence from the home, so he would provoke delight and amusement for his mother and sisters. 'Look, he's a real *mukhayyamji*', they would laugh approvingly.

The neighbourhood (*haara*) served in many ways as an extension of the family. Neighbours might be a practical resource in numerous ways, helping to meet one another's economic, social and educational needs. Reputation was also gained or lost here and just as the behaviour of one individual within the neighbourhood could tarnish his or her family's reputation, so the actions of a few families might earn a whole neighbourhood a poor reputation within the camp. For a boy the streets of the camp near his home that formed his neighbourhood were usually a crucial site of interaction and activity. It was here that much of his leisure time would be spent from the moment he could walk until his late teens, sometimes beyond. Indeed, it was an important part of the performance of *mukhayyamji* masculinity that a young male was seen regularly and often in the neighbourhood, rather than remaining in the home – commonly conceived of as a 'private' and 'female' space. It was in the local streets that he would meet up with his peers for a game of football, to make kites in the summer, to play marbles in winter. Together they might hatch a plan to earn money by selling small items such as chewing gum or sweets prepared by their mothers.

The intense sociality of the streets of the camp was a remarkable phenomenon. I never encountered it to the same degree in the poor Palestinian neighbourhoods close to the camp, and it seemed virtually absent in the bourgeois areas of Amman. During the period of fieldwork, many of my neighbours were evicted from their homes to make way for the new road. I visited some of the families who relocated to areas away from the camp and, when I asked the adolescent boys of these families what they missed about their old homes, the first thing mentioned was always the life of the *haara*.

Successful demonstration of the *mukhayyamji* masculine style depended upon the acquisition of particular knowledge and skills. The processes by which boys came to acquire these were often indirect and subtle. Lave and

Wenger's notion of learning through 'legitimate peripheral participation' in a 'community of practice' seems to fit well here. This they have explained as follows: 'we mean to draw attention to the point that learners inevitably participate in communities of practitioners and that the mastery of knowledge and skill requires newcomers to move toward full participation in the sociocultural practices of a community' (Lave and Wenger, 1991: 29).

The peer group, which was embedded within the wider community, provided a crucial forum for the development of an adolescent's values, attitudes and behaviour. Full acceptance as a member of adult society in the camp was partly the consequence of successful participation in this group at the level of the *haara*. I discuss later the consequences for a young man who failed to demonstrate the behaviour or attitudes associated with idealised *mukhayyamji* masculinity. But first we should consider the nature of this masculine style in more detail.

Mukhayyamji Style

This term *mukhayyamji* itself comes from the Arabic word for camp – *mukhayyam*, with the Turkish suffix -*ji* used commonly in occupational terms, for example, *kahrabji* ('electrician'), *kundarji* ('shoemaker'/'cobbler'), and also to describe personal habits or predilections, such as *niswanji* ('womaniser') or *sukkarji* ('alcoholic'). Although often uttered with a hint of playful irony, it was generally a source of pride for an adolescent male to be considered by friends, neighbours and family as *mukhayyamji*, which may be translated, inelegantly, as 'genuinely of the camp'. This word is used as both noun and adjective.

The *mukhayyamji* was commonly defined in opposition to the inferior and derided style and person of the *tant* (pl. *tantaat*), which equates with the English slang words 'poofter' or 'nancy boy'. This is in keeping with Connell's suggestion about the relational nature of hegemonic masculinity to other, inferior, masculine styles. To be labelled a *tant* was an extreme insult for which some form of strong response – verbal or physical – was vital if an adolescent boy was to defend his standing.

A range of criteria existed by which someone might be consigned by his peers to this category. Many related to appearance. At the time of fieldwork overtight jeans and highly coloured shirts rendered one suspect, in spite of the fact that these were very popular in many other parts of the city. Hair was also a significant marker: sporting a haircut known as 'marines', especially if this was shaped with a liberal dousing of hair gel, was a further way to gain a reputation as a *tant*.

There was a particularity about the strict attitude to such matters within the camp to the extent that some youth would wear certain clothes only if they were going outside its confines. On several occasions my neighbour, nineteen-year-old Aysam, was visited by a male cousin from the Gulf, who was invariably turned out in full *tant* style, including strategically ripped jeans. Aysam had worked hard to build his standing within the neighbourhood and wider camp, overcoming the disadvantage of being a younger son. Fearing the tarnish to his reputation by association with his cousin, Aysam refused to accompany the visitor through the streets of the camp. Yet, when off for an evening of flirting downtown, he usually slipped away discreetly in very similar attire, thereby suggesting the location-specific primacy of *mukhayyamji* masculinity.

From the perspective of *mukhayyamji* masculinity, full membership of the socio-political and moral community of the camp required physical strength, by definition not possessed by the *tant*. Not only should an adolescent male be willing and able to hold his own in any confrontation, but he should also come to the immediate support of other boys in his neighbourhood in the event of a fight with peers from elsewhere. Such a duty appeared to endure from the early teens to the early twenties. Although a true *mukhayyamji* would not go looking for trouble, should a fight break out, he should be prepared to enter it immediately to save the reputation of himself and his neighbourhood. Describing this responsibility of the young *mukhayyamji*, sixteen-year-old Ahmed told me: 'If people know that the *shabaab* ['lads'] in your neighbourhood are strong, others passing through keep their heads down and don't look at the women. They show respect'. As this quote suggests, a central concern of *mukhayyamji* adolescents was the aggressive protection of women. A neighbourhood unable to fight successfully left its female members open to unwelcome interference, dishonouring all. It was, of course, assumed in this that women were weak and in need of male protection.

From the perspective of *mukhayyamji* masculinity the relationship between brother and sister was especially critical. It was vital for an adolescent boy to secure the modesty of his female siblings through ensuring their physical inaccessibility to unrelated peers (see Joseph, 1994). The importance of this relationship was revealed in common ripostes to jibes of being a *tant*, which often invoked the sexuality of the taunter's sister. These included rhetorical statements such as *'is'al ukhtak iza ana tant'* ('ask your sister if I'm a *tant*') or the teasing rhymes *'ana tant? wa ana barrakib 'ala tiis ukhtak jant'* ('Am I a *tant*? I'll stick my dick up your sister's arse'). Through such ripostes the tables are turned as the taunter is accused of being unable to prevent others gaining sexual access to his sister. At the same time, the *'tant'* also reclaims his status by suggesting that he has the skill and courage to get to another lad's sister and the prowess to engage with her sexually: impossible feats for a 'real' *tant*.

The increasing importance of religiosity in the camp was also evident in the performance of *mukhayyamji* masculinity. On numerous occasions, I encountered groups of boys arguing over the correct approach to some question of personal behaviour or belief in light of Islamic teaching. Different quotations were cited or alluded to, suggesting that the ability to engage forcefully in such debate, armed with a range of appropriate passages from the Koran or Hadith, was an esteemed aspect of masculine performance. Of the different groups of adolescents familiar to me in the camp, most seemed to be led by individuals who were highly skilled in determining the appropriate moral stance in any given situation with reference to memorised quotes. Aysam was one such person, always quick to explain a particular action as '*haraam*' ('forbidden') or *masmuuh* ('permitted') for the guidance of friends and younger boys.

In keeping with this appreciation of religious knowledge was the denigration of those considered not properly observant or respectful of Islam. Boys who were thought to blaspheme, who did not observe the fast (*sawm*) or who were believed to be ignorant of the basic tenets or practices of Islam were often labelled as *zinekh* ('foul'/'disgusting', pl. *zinkhiin*) by their peers. Other activities such as stealing from friends or consistent dishonesty were also criteria by which a boy might be consigned to the category of *zinekh* – distinct, in discursive terms, from that of *tant* but nevertheless a form of masculinity deviant from the ideal of the *mukhayyamji*.

At the same time, it is important to note that the *mukhayyamji* masculinity did not command necessary approbation within settings particularly dominated by supporters of the Islamist movement. Here adherence to Islamic teaching and practice, studiousness, modesty and obedience seemed particularly admired qualities amongst adolescent males. The overt toughness and independence of the *mukhayyamji* were not appreciated. This clash in visions of adolescent masculinity seemed to come to a head in the youth club, where many of the young men who had formally been active ceased their involvement when men sympathetic to the Islamist movement took control. In some cases these young men claimed they had been thrown out or left after being made to feel unwelcome.

Amongst older boys, from about fourteen years of age, explicit reference was also made to sexuality and sexual desire. According to informal discussions and everyday references, it seemed that sexual activity amongst teenage boys, specifically anal intercourse, was fairly commonplace. Arguably this was a consequence, at least in part, of the sexual unavailability of female peers. Amongst groups of lads gathered together in the neighbourhood streets on summer evenings, conversation turned several times to reminiscence of sexual adventures with other males, eliciting gales of conspiratorial laughter. Adolescents around fifteen or sixteen years old spoke unabashedly about their recent encounters while those older, in their late teens and early twenties, related tales of their former activities, implying that they had long since abandoned such practices. In all cases, my informants stressed that they had taken the 'inserter' role. Nobody ever told me about their experiences as 'insertee' but all were quick to name others who were reputed to do so. Given the significance of age in structuring relative status amongst adolescent males, no lasting stigma appeared to attach to younger boys who took the role of insertee. The observation of Roscoe and Murray is germane here: 'the traditional paradigm of status-differentiation, which always places sexual partners in distinct categories depending on who penetrates whom, mitigates any of these patterns from developing into an identity in the modern sense' (1997: 7).

Thus it is misleading to assume that a sexual act involving an adolescent male penetrating someone younger, by say three or four years, would necessarily lead to an enduring label equivalent to 'homosexual' being applied to either. However, an adolescent who took the role of insertee in acts between peers was considered by my neighbours as extremely suspect. Allowing other males to penetrate him was a sure sign that he must actually desire it and, thus, demonstrated inherent deviance and weakness. This was the clearest, most unambiguous expression of '*tant*-hood' – the diametric opposite of *mukhayyamji*. Young men who were believed to enjoy such sexual activity were routinely taunted as they passed through the neighbourhood, often by the same people who claimed to have penetrated them.

Marking Out National Territory

There was a specificity about the idealised, 'hegemonic masculinity' among male youth in the camp, expressed in the character of the *mukhayyamji*, which located in physical space the more general notion of *zalame* ('guy', 'fellow'). Indeed, the boundedness of the camp in its socio-political and moral as well as its physical dimensions was partly reinforced by young men through the modality of this masculinity. Just as the category of *tant* was deployed as the 'other' against which the true *mukhayyamji* was partially constructed, so this term also reinforced a distinction between the adolescents of the camp and those in adjoining areas of the city. The great majority of inhabitants of these areas were also Palestinians with refugee status, many of them with relatives in the camp.

On the frequent occasions that boys and youth discussed with me their contemporaries outside the camp in collective terms, they referred to them as *tantaat*. This included, for example, ten-year-old boys attending the UNRWA school when discussing their classmates. The rationale for consigning boys from outside the camp to this category changed with age. For the younger boys, strength, skill at football, courage and independence were common considerations. For those in their mid- to late teens, the focus was more on attire, diet, sexual activities and the control of women's movements, dress and sexuality. For a young man from his mid-teens on, demonstrating his strong appetite for women and his desirability was also a facet of *mukhayyamji* masculinity. To do this, he would generally go to other parts of the city with his friends to see and be seen by women. The nearest suitable locale was a commercial district close by – Jabal Hussein[5] – where young people would gather most evenings to drink fruit juice and flirt. The only young women from the camp allowed to socialise here were in family groups. The unaccompanied girls at this spot were, therefore, believed to be from Jabal Hussein itself, which contributed to the perception amongst young males from the camp that their peers living in this area were all *tantaat* since they had not prevented their sisters' unshielded appearance in front of so many unrelated young men. Although adolescent boys from outside never accepted the label of *tantaat* when applied to themselves collectively, they echoed many of these sentiments in describing the *mukhayyamji*yyin as streetwise, skilled at sports and tough. In fact, so tough did many younger boys believe the latter to be, that they preferred not to enter the camp for fear of physical harm.

This perception of toughness was commonplace not just amongst other young men but throughout Amman society. The view that the camp was full of streetwise and menacing *mukhayyamji* males was one that I heard often from people of all social classes living outside the camp. This notion kept many of them out, serving to reinforce the separateness of the camp from the rest of the city and its distinctiveness as a socio-political and moral space. On the other hand, I met numerous people living outside the camp, all of them of Palestinian origin, who expressed admiration for the *mukhayyamji* adolescents. In their eyes, these young males had not become softened by the comfortable life in Amman that many Palestinians now enjoyed. They were still tough and would still be able, if required, to fight for the recovery of Palestine. In this sense, the *mukhayyamji* masculinity served to reinforce a view of the camp as the authentic heart of the Palestinian community-in-exile not only in the estimation of its residents but amongst outsiders as well.

Tant-hood and Nationalism

What of the adolescents who failed or chose not to live up to the ideal of *mukhayyamji* masculinity? The experience of Rami illustrates how individual performance intersects directly with the wider politics of the Palestinian nation-in-exile as embodied in the community of the camp. I first met Rami through the chance introduction of a neighbour. At that time he was in his late teens. Within my own frame of reference Rami would certainly have been considered effeminate and it was apparent that his behaviour marked him out as a *tant* amongst his peers in the camp. I was keen to get to know him better since he differed in many ways from most other young men in the camp that I knew. However, my neighbours consistently discouraged me from associating with him and, unaware of his address in a particularly labyrinthine part of the camp, I failed to make contact independently. On a return visit in 2003 I met Rami by chance. By then he was in his early twenties and worked in a shop outside the camp. In response to my question about his memories of adolescence in the camp he told me the following:

> It was very, very hard for me to live in the camp. I couldn't always go out because of the *shabaab* [lads] in the street giving me trouble. Boys asked me to have sex with them for money. I told my older brother, who spoke to them. The *shabaab* were afraid of my family, I have a lot of brothers. But they used to say that I had had sex with them even though I hadn't. In the street people would talk about my clothes and jewellery – 'You're not like a man, you're a girl'. But, if people came from outside, for example for a wedding party, and made trouble for me and called me a *tant*, the *shabaab* would protect me. It was like 'He's our *tant*'.

Rami lived above the shop where he worked and returned to the camp, a short distance away, as infrequently as possible. He was proud to come from there but it was not, in his estimation, a good place for him to be. Like several other young men, Rami characterised his relationship to the camp in the following words '*Ana ibn al-mukhayyam, mish mukhayyamji*' ('I am a son of the camp, not a *mukhayyamji*'), suggesting a measure of distance – whether in physical or attitudinal terms – from the camp. Conversely, Rami's evident failure to demonstrate the qualities associated with the *mukhayyamji* or any other admired form of adolescent masculinity placed him outside – literally and morally – the national community-in-exile as still imagined by and through the camp. In certain senses, he had become the Other marking off a particular adolescent-masculinised imagining of the nation.

Rami's position in relation to the camp as a socio-political and moral space tells us a good deal about the relationship between adolescent masculinity, sexuality and the Palestinian nation-in-exile. In contrast to younger boys unable to prevent themselves from being penetrated by someone older, Rami was seen as a person who enjoyed such acts with peers and was thus liable to be construed as a *maniac*[6] a colloquial and highly perjorative term that most closely approximated to the notion of 'homosexual' in the everyday discourse of young men. From the perspective of the camp he thereby confounded the crucial distinction between homosexuality and homo-sociality. As noted earlier, sexual acts between adolescent males were accepted providing these involved two people between whom a clear imbalance of power already existed – most commonly due to relative age. Since penetration, at least in normative terms, always (re)produced social distance and inequality between the inserter and insertee, it was thus incompatible with the fundamental egalitarianism of homosocial relations. Within the imaginings of nation this has particular relevance for, as Parker et al. have observed: 'Typically represented as a passionate brotherhood, the nation find itself compelled to distinguish its "proper" homosociality from more explicitly sexualised male–male relations, a compulsion that requires the identification, isolation, and containment of male homosexuality' (1992: 6). The Palestinian nation-in-exile, as constituted in Hussein Camp, strongly invoked the 'passionate brotherhood' mentioned by Parker et al. Therefore, it was perhaps inevitable that a young man who was considered to enjoy the role of insertee could have no place within the camp as authentic location of that national community-in-exile.

Masculinities and Social Adulthood

For young men in Hussein Camp the transition to social adulthood was not solely a matter of chronological age. While graduation from school was an important achievement for those who remained within the formal education structure, this was also insufficient in itself. In this setting, as elsewhere in much of the Arab Middle East, marriage and parenthood were important markers of respected adult status. However, in order to marry a young man would have to accrue considerable material resources to cover the costs of a marital home, a wedding party and the *mahr* ('bride price'), which often took the form of items such as a wardrobe of new clothes for the bride and gold jewellery. Since employment opportunities within Hussein Camp were meagre, most young men were obliged to pursue livelihood strategies beyond the camp. Previous generations had generally enjoyed greater degrees of mobility, the Gulf, in particular, offering jobs across a range of technical and professional sectors to young Palestinians with a reasonable level of training. Indeed, the UN-run education system for Palestinian refugees had oriented itself towards preparing the young for work in the Gulf and elsewhere in the Arab Middle East (Schiff, 1995). However, such opportunities decreased steadily during the 1980s and came to an abrupt termination with the first Gulf War when many Palestinians were thrown out of Kuwait and other countries. Several of my neighbours in the camp were amongst these returnees from the Gulf.

The Jordanian economy in the late 1990s was far from vibrant. Across the public and private sectors wages were generally low and the possibilities for young men without tertiary-level education to earn a reasonable living were especially limited. Much of the employment at that time was in services and light industry, where wages would barely cover living expenses, let alone the costs of marriage. Even these low-paid jobs were hard to come by and ability alone was often insufficient to secure employment. A prospective employee also needed *wasta* – or 'Vitamin W' as my friends in the camp sardonically called it – a term that translates as 'connections' or 'influence'. Almost by definition, residence in one of the refugee camps related to a lack of *wasta*. Moreover, young men often expressed a strong sense that the negative attitudes of outsiders towards the camp were manifested in discrimination over employment. Several claimed to have lied about where they lived at interviews – a strategy that often seemed to backfire.

In practice, young men from the camp did succeed in gaining reasonable employment, and thereby acquiring the economic capacity to wed. However, in doing so they had not emphasised the traits of *mukhayyamji* masculinity – toughness, independence and strength. Through studiousness and diligence they managed to overcome the obstacles arising from residence in the camp. In their demeanour these young men generally did not display the kind of aggressiveness that was associated with the *mukhayyamji* in the minds of outsiders and many seemed to build connections beyond the camp that were helpful for employment.

Conclusion: the Paradoxes of *Mukhayyamji* Masculinity and the Nation-in-exile

In the late 1990s the sentiments of secular nationalism were still strongly evident in Hussein Camp, particularly within the domestic sphere of home and immediate neighbourhood. This served as an important source for the reproduction of a particular, dominant model of masculinity, which I have referred to in this chapter as *mukhayyamji*.

Nevertheless, beyond the camp, the difficulties encountered by those who maintained the *mukhayyamji* performance of toughness and independence in securing a livelihood indicate a paradoxical vulnerability created by this style of masculinity. In the late 1990s there were many unmarried young men in Hussein Camp, who occupied a social space between adolescence and the social adulthood conferred by marriage and children. No longer admired symbols of youthful potency, independence and toughness, their position in the socio-political and moral life of the camp was ambiguous and uncomfortable. Moreover, their position mirrored the profoundly ambiguous situation of the refugee camp at that time.

On one hand, through the demonstration of toughness, independence, strength and potency they had served to reinforce the distinctiveness of Hussein Camp as a socio-political and moral space, preventing its submergence into Amman's ever-expanding ribbon of working-class neighbourhoods that circled the city. These young men had been a visible reminder of the refugees' enduring self-identity and of their continuing ability and determination to reclaim their homeland. While other Palestinians accepted the compromises necessary to obtain some measure of comfort in Jordanian society, young *mukhayyamji* males amongst the population of the camps, such as Hussein, exhibited a reassuring loyalty (*ikhlaas*) to the idea of return.

On the other hand, the 'true' *mukhayyamji* risked his own transition to social adulthood. Since the PLO had little interest in the Jordanian refugee camps, let alone a need for young fighters and activists, a validated route to an explicitly 'Palestinian' adulthood was not obvious. Furthermore, following the compromises of the Oslo Peace Process, 'return' was a more distant possibility than ever. Meanwhile, prevented from migration in search of well-paid work, young refugees were unavoidably dependent upon economic opportunities within Amman. This was at a time, following Jordan's peace treaty and growing cooperation with Israel, when overt expressions of toughness and potency identifiable with the refugee camps were little appreciated by the authorities and a potential embarrassment to upwardly mobile Palestinians. Caught between an insecure and fractured project of nation, and the demands of a local economy and polity for conformity, *mukhayyamji* masculinity appeared to offer adolescent boys in Hussein Camp a short-lived moment of empowerment.

Notes

1. All names in this chapter have been changed and identifying details of some informants obscured.
2. UNRWA is the UN agency mandated since 1950 to provide relief for the Palestinian refugees.
3. Full text of the Declaration is available at http://en.wikisource.org/wiki/ Palestinian_Declaration_of_Independence Retrieved 10 August 2006.
4. The Oslo Peace Process, which formally commenced with the signing of a 'Declaration of Principles' by the PLO and the State of Israel, arguably offered the possibility of Palestinian statehood. However, the issue of refugees from outside the West Bank and Gaza was left for discussion at the would-be end point of the process. For many commentators and in the estimation of most of the residents in the camp who discussed this with me, Arafat had effectively agreed to drop the aspiration for return in exchange for the promise of a state.
5. *Jabal* is the Arabic word for 'hill'. Hussein Camp was situated at the foot of this hill, in the valley between Jabal Hussein and Jabal al-Nuzha. The area of Jabal Hussein was built only after the creation of the camp and has become a largely bourgeois neighbourhood, housing families formerly from the camp and wealthier Palestinians, including many 'returnees' from the Persian Gulf states following their expulsion at the end of the 1990 Gulf War.
6. Literally 'one who is fucked'.

References

Allen, H. 2000 'Gender, Sexuality and the Military Model of U.S. National Community', in T. Mayer (ed) *Gender Ironies of Nationalism: Sexing the Nation.* London: Routledge, pp. 309–28.

Anderson, B. 1991 *Imagined Communities: Reflections on the Origin and Spread of Nationalism*, 2nd edn. London: Verso.

Connell, R.W. 1987 *Gender and Power.* Cambridge: Polity Press.

—— (1995) *Masculinities.* Cambridge: Polity Press.

Cornwall, A. and Lindisfarne, N. (eds) 1994 'Dislocating Masculinity: Gender, Power and Anthropology', in A. Cornwall and N. Lindisfarne (eds) *Dislocating Masculinity: Comparative Ethnographies.* London: Routledge, pp. 11–65.

Hart, J. 2000 'Contested Belonging: Children and Childhood in a Palestinian Refugee Camp in Jordan'. Unpublished Ph.D. thesis, University of London.

Hirst, D. 1984 *The Gun and the Olive Branch: The Roots of Conflict in the Middle East.* London: Faber and Faber.

Joseph, S. 1994 'Brother/Sister Relationships: Connectivity, Love, and Power in the Reproduction of Patriarchy in Lebanon', *American Ethnologist* 21 (1): 50–73.

Kandiyoti, D. 1991 (ed) *Women, Islam and the State.* Philadelphia: Temple University Press.

—— 1994 'The Paradoxes of Masculinity', in A. Cornwall and N. Lindisfarne (eds) *Dislocating Masculinity: Comparative Ethnographies.* London: Routledge, pp. 197–213.

Kanitkar, H. 1994 '"Real True Boys": Moulding the Cadets of Imperialism', in A. Cornwall and N. Lindisfarne (eds) *Dislocating Masculinity: Comparative Ethnographies.* London: Routledge, pp. 184–96.

Kaplan, D. 2000 'The Military as a Second Bar Mitzvah: Combat Service as Initiation to Zionist Masculinity', in M. Ghoussoub and E. Sinclair-Webb (eds) *Imagined Masculinities: Male Identity and Culture in the Modern Middle East.* London: Saqi Books, pp. 127–44.

—— 2003 *Brothers and Others in Arms: The Making of Love and War in Israeli Combat Units.* Binghampton, NY: The Haworth Press.

Lave, J. and Wenger, E. 1991 *Situated Learning: Legitimate Peripheral Participation.* Cambridge: Cambridge University Press.

Lewis, L. 2000 'Nationalism and Caribbean Masculinity', in T. Mayer (ed) *Gender Ironies of Nationalism.* London and New York: Routledge, pp. 261–82.

Loizos, P. 1994 'A Broken Mirror: Masculine Sexuality in Greek Ethnography', in A. Cornwall A. and N. Lindisfarne (eds) *Dislocating Masculinity: Comparative Ethnographies.* London: Routledge, pp. 66–81.

Martin, A. 2000 'Death of a Nation: Transnationalism, Bodies and Abortion in Late Twentieth-century Ireland', in T. Mayer (ed) *Gender Ironies of Nationalism: Sexing the Nation.* London: Routledge, pp. 65–88.

Massad, J. 1995 'Conceiving the Masculine: Gender and Palestinian Nationalism', *Middle East Journal* 49 (3): 467–83.

Mayer, T. 2000a 'Gender Ironies of Nationalism: Setting the Stage', in T. Mayer (ed) *Gender Ironies of Nationalism: Sexing the Nation.* London: Routledge, pp. 1–24.

—— 2000b 'From Zero to Hero: Masculinity in Jewish Nationalism', in T. Mayer (ed) *Gender Ironies of Nationalism: Sexing the Nation.* London: Routledge, pp. 283–308.

McClintock, A., Mufti, A. and Shohat, E. (eds) 1997 *Dangerous Liaisons: Gender, Nation and Postcolonial Perspectives.* Minneapolis: University of Minnesota Press.

Mosse, G. 1996 *The Image of Man: Creating Modern Masculinity.* Oxford: Oxford University Press.

Nagel, J. 1998 'Masculinity and Nationalism: Gender and Sexuality in the Making of Nations', *Ethnic and Racial Studies* 21 (2): 242–69.

Ouzgane, L. (ed) 2006 *Islamic Masculinities.* London: Zed Books.

Parker, A., Russo, M., Sommer D. and Yaeger P. 1992 'Introduction', in A. Parker, M. Russo, D. Sommer and P. Yaeger (eds) *Nationalisms and Sexualities.* London: Routledge, pp. 1–20.

Roscoe, W. and Murray, S. 1997 'Introduction', in S. Murray and W. Roscoe (eds) *Islamic Homosexualities.* New York: New York University Press, pp. 3–13.

Said, E. 1992 *The Question of Palestine*, new edn. London: Verso.

Schiff, B. 1995 *Refugees Unto the Third Generation: UN Aid to Palestinians.* Syracuse: Syracuse University Press.

Sinclair-Webb, E. 2000a 'Preface', in M. Ghoussoub and E. Sinclair-Webb (eds) *Imagined Masculinities: Male Identity and Culture in the Modern Middle East.* London: Saqi Books, pp. 7–18.

—— 2000b '"Our Bulent is Now a Commando": Military Service and Manhood in Turkey', in M. Ghoussoub and E. Sinclair-Webb (eds) *Imagined Masculinities: Male Identity and Culture in the Modern Middle East.* London: Saqi Books, pp. 65–92.

Yuval-Davis, N. 1997 *Gender and Nation.* London: Sage.

Yuval-Davis, N. and Anthias, F. (eds) 1989 *Woman–Nation–State.* Basingstoke: Macmillan.

PART IV

RESPONDING TO ADOLESCENTS

9

The Challenges of Programming with Youth in Afghanistan*

Joanna de Berry

Youth in any culture lead complex lives. With the end of childhood come additional choices and responsibilities, priorities and decisions. Conflict, and the political and social upheaval this brings with it, only adds to the challenges they must face, the risks that must be negotiated, and the responsibilities that may be given or taken. Programming that aims to support war-affected youth through times of conflict must take into account the complexity of their lives if it is really to engage with them and create a positive impact. Commonly, however, in designing and implementing projects for war-affected youth there is not enough attention given to the reality of the circumstances in which young people live and develop. As a result programmes may be based on overly simplistic notions of their needs and may fail to offer real assistance. This chapter considers the development of programmes for war-affected youth (primarily male) in Afghanistan. It shows how the programmes that were extended to Afghan youth did not entirely correlate to their needs, expectations and priorities. This disjunction between the assumption of international aid agencies about the needs of young people and the reality of their lives showed in both the design and the implementation of programmes, giving rise to a number of challenges that had to be confronted. This chapter details these challenges and uses the lessons learned from this experience to advocate for better-informed support to war-affected youth.

* The author is writing in a purely personal capacity. The views expressed herein do not necessarily reflect those of the organisations named.

Background

In September 2001 the international aid community rediscovered the humanitarian needs of Afghanistan. The attacks of 11 September blazed a terrorist trail from Al Qaida cells in the mountains of Afghanistan to New York. In denouncing the attack and launching the Coalition war on terror in Afghanistan, America and Britain brought global attention once more to this remote and forgotten country. What the world found there was not only a collapsed state where the Taliban hosted international terrorists, but also a humanitarian crisis so severe and so long ignored that the population were on their knees with hunger and disease. Years of fighting and poverty had been exacerbated by a four-year drought. Swathes of the population were on the move having come down from their infertile and dry lands to live in IDP camps. The health and mortality rates were the worst in the world, women were institutionally discriminated against and infrastructure was non-existent. Although some aid agencies had remained and continued to deliver services and programmes throughout the Taliban period, the lack of funds available for Afghanistan from the international donor community and the sheer difficulty of access and outreach under the Taliban restrictions meant that interventions were minimal. In late 2001, however, everything changed. As the Coalition bombers pounded the Taliban and Al Qaida positions, other armies of journalists and aid workers waited in the wings. And, in November 2001 when the Taliban fell, the borders of Afghanistan opened to an emergency response: new levels of funding, new humanitarian actors, new missions and new responses were initiated.

Many of the responses were focused on meeting immediate survival needs so, for example, large-scale food distributions were put into place. But, alongside these responses for basic survival requirements, the humanitarian community also brought with them the learning and experience of other emergency situations and the acknowledgement that a broad range of emergency and development strategies would be instantly applicable in order to lay the foundations for rebuilding the country. Protection, psychosocial support and human rights work were at the forefront of the new humanitarian commitment to Afghanistan. In a remarkable achievement UNICEF advocated for education to be one of the first priorities to be delivered in the country. UNICEF raised funds and planned for an education response alongside basic emergency interventions. Just as they launched nationwide campaigns to make up for lost years of immunisation campaigns, rapidly reaching out across the country to immunise against polio, so they also launched a national 'Back to School' campaign. In March 2002 after the distribution of 6,000 temporary school tents and the recruitment of 70,000 new teachers, three million Afghan children returned to school. A third of these children were girls, who had not been allowed to study formally under the Taliban. Seeing girls in the long snaking queues that formed outside schools when they reopened in March 2002 as children waited for registration was perhaps the greatest symbol of the potential and hope for Afghanistan in this new era and of the opportunities that lay ahead if the peace could be sustained.

But there was another notable cohort of young people in the queues outside the quickly repainted school buildings and temporary tents. These were the teenagers, who despite their age, were standing in the queues to register for primary schools. Girls were registering for primary schools because for five years under the Taliban only a few of them had managed to continue their education through illegal and informal 'home-based schools'. For the rest their education had been severely disrupted and they had not managed to progress through the school system. Now in order to have any education at all they had to start back at the bottom of the class ladder. Likewise boys had suffered a loss of education: many of the Afghan teachers had been women and, when women were barred from working in all services apart from health, the formal education system had more or less collapsed, with too few male teachers operating on too few resources to begin to cover the educational demands even of boys. Such youth could see the impact of life under the Taliban most clearly in the gaps in their own schooling and class achievement. Boys as well as girls saw the 'Back to School' campaign as a chance to catch up on these missing years. Yet the emphasis of the campaign was on smaller children and, when headmasters and headmistresses, overwhelmed by the numbers of children registering for school places in the 'Back to School' campaign, had to make choices about who had a place in the class and who not, it was invariably the adolescents who were turned away.

There was recognition that the youth of Afghanistan were going to need specially focused interventions. It was not only that they didn't fit neatly into existing provision, as shown so clearly in the case of primary school registration, but it was also recognised that they had special circumstances. A comprehensive situation analysis of young people in Afghanistan published in 2001 highlighted the particular vulnerabilities of teenage boys and girls. The report pointed out that Afghanistan had at that time the highest proportion of married teenagers in the world: 54 per cent of girls and 9 per cent of boys were married by the time they were eighteen. For girls, this was a source of concern since it transpired that most early marriages were made against their will, often to much older men and away from the support of their homes and families. Early marriage also took girls to early pregnancy with all the myriad threats to physical health associated with it. Boys in addition bore the brunt of economic responsibility for their families, working in hazardous and arduous conditions, often moving away from their families in patterns of migratory labour (Global Movement for Children, 2001).

It was therefore clear that adolescents in Afghanistan deserved and demanded special programming approaches. And, in the months after November 2001 and into subsequent years, several international and local development agencies began to initiate youth-focused programming. Yet the process did not run smoothly, and the bulk of this chapter highlights some of the challenges faced in the early stages. In doing so, I draw on direct experience of establishing research and programming for Afghan youth, whilst working as an adviser for the NGO Save the Children. The piece explores some of the complications faced in both defining the content of interventions for and with young people and inadequacies in the process of implementing those interventions. What this chapter illustrates is that the cause of these programmatic challenges stems from aid agencies seeking merely to extend existing projects, designed with other purposes and for other beneficiaries in Afghanistan, to adolescents. Such an approach proved inadequate with respect to the complexity, political engagement and agency of young people themselves. The chapter draws on lessons learned from the experience of programming for Afghan youth and illustrates new directions that were consequently taken to deliver effective broad-based youth-focused support.

Before analysis of the programmes, however, the chapter starts with a fuller exploration of who youth in Afghanistan are and what their lives are like.

Young Afghans

This chapter uses a social rather than an age-based definition of 'adolescence'. Instead of defining adolescents as those who fall into a certain age category, a social exploration of adolescence refers to it as a particular social status, with certain social characteristics Age-based definitions of 'child' and 'adolescent' offer only a limited insight into the experience of a young person in Afghanistan. Nor do age-based definitions capture the multiple experiences of adolescents and the relational stages of change and transition that accompany the process of growing up. Instead it is more revealing to look at social experiences of being a young person and local understandings about what constitutes the relative positions of 'child' 'adolescent' and 'adult'.

Taking this perspective in Afghanistan it is clear that, according to local understandings, young people change from being a child to an adolescent at puberty. But the length of time they live as an adolescent is differentiated by gender and other life changes. A girl will be considered an adult woman as soon as she is married and this position is confirmed with the birth of her first child. A young man, however, may continue to occupy an intermediate status even though he is married and has a child. The reason for this gender-based difference is that for a woman being a wife and a mother is the most important and significant social change of the statuses open to her. For men, in contrast, the defining point of their social career is to be the head of a family, something that only truly occurs on the death of their father when they assume responsibility for relatives and households. There is no contradiction for men to be a husband and father and simultaneously an 'adolescent' or 'youth'; for being truly a 'man' is a status that only comes by being amongst the eldest generation in the family.

In addition to this, for many young Afghan people the concept of adolescence with its overtones of liminality, lack of responsibility, transition and apprenticeship for adulthood is an experience they never have. If an Afghan girl, as is common, is married at puberty she will move straight from being a child to puberty and then to adulthood in the space of a few months. Likewise both girls and boys in Afghanistan often shoulder the same levels of responsibility as adults from an early age. Sometimes children as young as eight bear heavy economic and domestic responsibility. One of the clearest impacts of war and poverty in Afghanistan is that, for the majority of families, their children's economic roles have assumed critical importance for the livelihoods and coping strategies of entire families. With the loss of adult males, the eldest boy of a family has had to quickly assume his father's place and provide for a widowed mother as well as siblings. With poverty, boys in particular have entered the marketplace and assumed the economic roles of adults. In the words of one commentator:

> significant in the childhood of Afghans is the lack of adolescence, with children moving from a period of relative freedom in early childhood to the sudden social changes associated with adulthood in the sub-teens ... adolescence is a function of a literate pluralistic society which can afford to waste half a man's life in socialization or preparing him to live as a productive member of his society ... life in Afghanistan is too short and resources too scarce to allow such a luxury (Dupree, 1973: 31).

The small minority of families in Afghanistan who can afford to allow their children the luxury of an adolescence are wealthy. The young of these families have the benefit of full-time education, some even making it to one of the handful of universities in the country. Thus adolescence in Afghanistan is shaped not only by gender but also by class, and within these parameters there are many different pathways of what it is to be a developing young person.

Responsibility consistently emerges as one of the key themes in the lives of Afghan youth. Indeed, research shows that adolescent boys and girls value in particular the economic contribution they can make to their families and their responsibility for bringing in income and running the household. As some young people interviewed in Kabul responded:

It is good to be our age because we can work and help our family to make money.

Now we are older we can think about money and how to earn it.

I sell my embroidery and I contribute to my family and this makes me glad because my father's salary is not enough (de Berry et al., 2003).

But the benefits of their responsibility are not only economic; Afghans believe that such responsibilities seal relationships between family members and that through them young people exhibit respect for their parents and elders, respect that is a vital part of Afghan understandings of morality and sociality. In addition the responsibilities are seen as good training for unmarried girls and boys, leading to the skills they will bring to their own household on marriage. And, in a culture where leisure or recreational opportunities are infrequent, parents and young people alike said that they value responsibilities and activities to keep young people busy and occupied (de Berry et al., 2003).

Yet, as discussed above, the economic responsibilities of young people have assumed exaggerated importance in the Afghan context of poverty and suffering. The twenty-four years of war in the country have certainly contributed to this, not least because of the huge collateral damage of the fighting. Surveys show that an estimated 22,000 villages were completely destroyed, 3,000 irrigation systems were blown apart and agricultural land has been rendered useless, given over to minefields, with an estimated ten million mines laid throughout the country. All of this has worked to the detriment of people's livelihoods. But war has merely interacted with other factors to render Afghans so vulnerable. The country was poor even before the war started. Then, during the conflict, control became associated with military rather than political or sovereign might; legitimacy was gained through military victory rather than through governance. Consequently there has been little investment in social infrastructure beyond family mechanisms. Government in Afghanistan has rarely been associated with social security and material provision. In addition, Afghanistan suffers from acute environmental fragility. This particularly showed in the devastating drought of 1999 to 2002, where, although numbers of famine-related deaths were relatively few, people stretched their economic coping mechanisms to a perilous extent in order to sustain their families (Global Movement for Children, 2001).

Studies that have looked at how Afghans have managed to sustain their livelihoods in the face of such overwhelming poverty consistently show that the labour of young people has become more and more of an important economic coping mechanism. Families have sent their children, especially boys, into the cash economy to work at everything from carpet weaving or mechanical labour to street selling. One survey showed there to be 28,000 children working on the streets of Kabul, not counting those working in sites hidden to the eye – for example, the estimated 36,000 working as carpet weavers (Terre des hommes, 2002). In Mazar-i-Sharif it was at one time calculated that the wages of young people accounted for 42 per cent of the total value of wage labour in the town. Young Afghan men from the age of fourteen upwards will often travel to find work, entering into the refugee economies of Pakistan, Iran and India (Global Movement for Children, 2001).

Such work takes young people into hazardous and often exploitative conditions, where they are at risk from physical harm. And, as much as young people value the responsibilities they have for providing for their families, they also worry about the dangers and threats they are thus exposed to. This fear and concern arises not only in the activities young people undertake to make monetary contributions but also in the domestic tasks – for example fetching water, collecting firewood – that are essential to the household economy. Part of the hazardous nature of the work young people engage in comes from the state of the physical environment. Damaged, dirty, ruined neighbourhoods expose adolescents to risk of injury if they are working on the street or going out and about to fulfil domestic tasks. At the same time working and providing for the family also undermine the time and commitment that they are able to devote to education, put pressure and strain on their family relationships and may increase emotional distress as they try to balance the many pressures upon and expectations of them with their own hopes and fears.

Thus although differentiated by age, gender, class and educational opportunity, it is possible to generalise that the experience of being an adolescent in Afghanistan is consistently one where obligation to family survival involves a heavy burden of responsibility. This leads to a lifestyle where, however much young people seek to protect themselves, it is often necessary for them to compromise their personal safety and protection in order to play a vital part in sustaining family life in times of great hardship.

The Challenges of Defining Interventions

As humanitarian workers approached the challenge of working with young people in Afghanistan, research and needs assessments consistently showed that identifying the responsibilities held by adolescents and alleviating the conditions in which they fulfilled them were going to be a key strategy. Strong recommendations were made, including a need for more information on the changing situation of young males, with proper analysis of the impact of conflict on family coping mechanisms and consequently on adolescents. It was also recommended that there needed to be greater understanding of the risks posed for these young people by their lifestyle and family involvement (Global Movement for Children, 2001).

Mines and UXOs

One very clear risk to young people as they went about their daily life and fulfilled their responsibilities was recognised as the danger of injury from landmines and unemploded ordinance (UXOs). In 2001 Afghanistan stood with Angola as the most heavily mined country in the world, with an estimated ten million mines still active in the ground. UXOs littered the country as well. Research showed that 5 per cent of all mine accidents and 85 per cent of UXO accidents were experienced by young people under the age of eighteen in the course of herding or agricultural activities. Of all of these 40 per cent were fatalities and 22 per cent resulted in serious disability (GMC, 2001). Clearly young people's domestic activities and waged labour took them onto paths and into places were they were at risk of landmine accidents. It was imperative therefore to seek protective measures against the dangers of mine accidents.

Even during the Taliban regime humanitarian agencies had provided landmine education – teaching young people to recognise danger spots for mines, to identify mines in the ground and how to take preventive and protective action when in a minefield.

Save the Children USA, for example, had developed a comprehensive mine education package and when, in 2001, the opportunity came to scale up the programme the agency undertook measures to have the material adopted into mainstream education. And yet it was clear that, although mine risk education could equip young people with the knowledge to protect themselves against mine accidents, there seemed to be no discernible impact of this knowledge on behaviour; improved knowledge of the danger of mines didn't stop them going into minefields or having accidents. With increasing concern for the limited influence of the mine education programme, Save the Children therefore decided to investigate more fully the risks of mines in the context of young people's everyday life and actions.

Save the Children conducted a short research project in one village in the Shomali valley north of Kabul. This valley had been a front line between Taliban and Northern Alliance forces for five years up to 2001 and was therefore heavily mined. Shomali was consequently the scene of heavy Coalition bombing, thus also becoming littered with cluster bombs during the war in October 2001. Yet, with the fall of the Taliban, by early 2002 hundreds of families who had been displaced from Shomali into Kabul were beginning to return to rebuild their homes and lives and were therefore at great risk from these mines and UXOs. The aim of the action research project was to establish how mines and UXOs figured in the lives of young people in a village of Shomali. Researchers conducted focus group discussions with boys and girls in a village, located just to the side of a large minefield, which, although marked by demining agencies, had yet to have any mines cleared from it. While red stones had been placed to mark the presence of mines, the minefield itself was completely open. Quick observation showed a daily traffic of young people walking through the mined area. Indeed, the research was startling for what it revealed of the extent to which landmines had become part of everyday life for Afghan adolescents (Save the Children, 2002).

For a start most of the young people in the village would walk casually through the minefield at least once a day. They followed tank tracks, which they said were proved to be safe by frequent passage over a long period. When the researchers asked why they walked through the minefield they gave reasons connected with fulfilling domestic tasks such as taking livestock for grazing or fetching water and firewood. But they also gave reasons such as walking to visit their relatives who lived in the village the other side of the minefield, going to market in the next village and because the path was a short cut to that next village rather than walking on the road. Interestingly young people said that they actually felt it was more dangerous to walk on the main road because of the heavy traffic there and because of the proximity of mines near the side of the road; the danger of having an accident on the road might be compounded by then veering off into a minefield. Compared with this, they said that the tracks through the minefield felt safer. For many reasons and through their own choices and perceptions of relative safety, young people in Shomali were going against one of the key warning messages of mine risk education – never go into a minefield.

But adolescents also encountered mines outside the marked minefield. All the families who had returned to Shomali were engaged in rebuilding their homes and gardens, where mines were strewn about. Young people talked about finding live mines in the rubble of their houses and in the overgrown beds of their former gardens. They also said that they actively took measures to remove the mines themselves, picking them up with shovels and often throwing them over their neighbour's wall, rather than following standard mine education advice which was to leave well alone and call in the professionals.

Again young people's domestic tasks took them into unmarked but heavily mined areas. In the village the irrigation ditches were full of mines, which had been washed down from areas higher up on the sides of the valley. Fearful of washing these mines into their gardens the villagers had closed off the irrigation ditches with the adverse effect of stopping the water necessary for agricultural production. This meant that adolescents were involved in the constant task of fetching water not only for use in the household but also for small gardens. To get this water they had to walk up to more remote areas where they were less likely to be sure of the location of mines. The same held for collecting wood – given that the Taliban had burnt down most trees in the area, wood was scarce and young people had to go daily to collect wood from hillsides full of mines. Once again, it was clear that they put the imperative of basic survival needs – such as fetching wood and water – over the risk of mine accidents. Whilst wood and water remained a necessity and the chance of a mine accident only a possibility, young people continued to take daily risks with mines. The same rationale was given for herding; adolescent boys said that they placed more importance on keeping their goats and sheep alive and healthy – a responsibility to which they attached great importance – by finding good grazing than they did on taking precautions to avoid mines. In addition many boys in the village went hunting for small animals that would supplement the family diet, and this activity took them to remote, wild and mined hillsides.

Even more than this, some young people went out of their way to dig out mines and explosives. They did this, first, as a money-making strategy. Boys, from as young as six years old, were heavily involved in an informal scrap metal and gunpowder market. They would scrape the gunpowder out of old bullets and explosives to sell, and collect metal from destroyed vehicles that had been blown up on a mined road. They then sold on the metal and gunpowder to traders, who came to buy it from nearby Kabul. In this way they supplemented the income of themselves and their families. Yet the risks were high – of the four mine- and UXO-related accidents in the month prior to the research, three had been caused by young people opening up bullets for gunpowder and losing fingers in small explosions. Secondly, young people also used mines in recreational activities. Adolescent boys talked about playing competitive games to see who could defuse the most mines, of building small fires over UXOs to make them explode and making homemade fireworks out of the gunpowder from bullets.

Clearly mines are part of everyday life for adolescents in the villages of Shomali. The imperatives of daily life and the responsibilities young people hold mean that all they can do is to take calculated chances about going into mined areas. But, more than this, the very risky aspect of mines and UXOs provides adolescents with income and fun. Young informants also said that they came into contact with mines at home, since each family hoarded a supply of their own for defence purposes. And those with personal disputes often had recourse to mines – people would throw the mines they found into the gardens of people they didn't like in the village. What this research showed, then, was that coming across mines was not an isolated occurrence for young people which it might take a mere modification of their behaviour to avoid. Instead the presence of mines was infused deeply into every part of life; young people came into contact with them not due to a lack of knowledge or ignorance but because of the complex actions of responsibility, leisure and social relations of which they were part. And, as a result of the interplay of these daily routines in which mines featured large, adolescents possessed an attitude to mines that saw them not as a danger to be avoided at all costs but as sometimes a nuisance, often just a fact of life that one might be lucky enough to avoid, and many times a magnet in themselves and a weapon in their own economic and social protection. In this kind of context, programming interventions were needed that went beyond prescriptive mine education messages and looked instead at how to encourage and allow young people to fulfill their responsibilities, economic opportunities and social relations with less risky behaviour and self-protection strategies that minimised risk.

Fighting

An equally complex picture emerged when looking at the issue of adolescent boys who were fighting as soldiers. The prevalence of child soldiers in Afghanistan has never been considered as great as in other conflicts. The profile of child soldiers in Afghanistan is different from, for example, many African conflicts where much younger boys fight (Global Movement for Children, 2001). Nevertheless there were underage fighters in both Taliban and Northern Alliance troops and a key post-11 September protection strategy was to demobilise and reintegrate them. Being an underage fighter was another very clear risk to the well-being of young men; fighting put them in physical danger of injury and death and vulnerable to other threats such as sexual abuse – research showed that the sexual abuse of boys was widespread in the armed militia (CFA, 2002).

Yet there were powerful motivations for adolescent males to take up arms and fight. As one report put it:

> Young people of 14–18 years are regarded as young adults and are often expected to fulfill the same obligations as older adults to protect home, community, and honor. Following decades of war in which large numbers of children have participated and in which the society became militarised at village level, violence and use of guns have been normalised. Several generations of young people have had extensive opportunities to learn patterns of soldiering and violent conflict resolution (CCF/CFA, 2002).

In 2002 the agency Christian Children's Fund (CCF) conducted research on the phenomenon of young fighters in the north-east of the country around Kunduz and Takhar (CCF/CFA). This research showed that young males joined militia groups out of the desire to defend their villages and families. They felt that they had a responsibility to fall in line with local commanders in order to position themselves and their families strategically with regard to local political dynamics. If they were protected by a powerful commander, then their life and that of their family would be qualitatively different from if they were opposed to the commander – for commanders often controlled the distribution of resources and the allocation of assets in village life. Young men also took up arms and fought for direct economic benefit. Some recruits spoke of joining a commander because they offered regular food and clothing and by absenting themselves from home they were one less mouth for their parents to feed. Others explained that what had taken them into the armed forces was their own accumulation of gambling debts. Instead of making their parents liable for the debt, which would have involved selling family assets, the boys took themselves off to the militia to earn the necessary money. But some young men clearly had no choice in the matter: forced recruitment was rife amongst the Northern Alliance structures, particularly as the offensive against the Taliban escalated in October 2001. Dictates would issue from the front line commanders to procure more fresh recruits and each village behind the lines would be expected to provide a quota of young men. Whilst richer families could buy off the commanders or even pay a poorer family to fill their son's place, less influential families had little choice but to submit their sons to fight.

Here then was a picture of male youth facing all the risks associated with fighting and carrying arms but being placed in that position by a series of complex social relations, including feelings of family honour and protection, seeking economic advantages, even as a result of their gambling. They were influenced to fight by responsibilities they had for their family, communities and commanders and by power dynamics in which, despite a move to centralised government, local military power was still the greatest source of political and community authority. Withdrawing young men from the risk of fighting would have to address this wider context, which was about social relations, responsibility, economic security, family coping strategies and political influence.

This complex situation came to light when aid agencies began to think about the demobilisation of child soldiers in Afghanistan. Following the fall of the Taliban regime and the establishment of a new government, demobilisation was seen as a key imperative for the stabilisation of the country. A large disarmament, demobilisation and reintegration (DDR) programme was proposed, with special measures for young fighters. The programme aimed to formally register a young man's exit from the armed forces, to take away their arms, to give them medical and psychosocial attention and then to provide some alternative form of livelihood through skills and vocational training. CCF, working in the north, went further and proposed that young men would get involved in community reconstruction projects working together in teams composed of former fighters and civilians and that they would take on community leadership. This was a scheme that aimed to fill the gulf of relationships and influence that young men might lose when coming out of the armed forces and was based on a fuller understanding of what took adolescents to fight and how these factors might be redirected in peaceful ways. Yet when the programme was implemented, the challenge remained of persuading the intended beneficiaries to leave the fighting profession. The spread of central government has been slow in Afghanistan and much of the country is still controlled by local warlords who hold all influence and power – both economic and political – over communities. In this context a young man and his family will receive political protection and economic benefit from remaining a member of a local militia. Loss of such protection and benefit proved a significant disincentive to participation in the programmes set up by aid agencies.

The Challenge of Defining Interventions

The example of landmines and that of fighting in armed forces speak of the challenge of defining interventions for adolescents in Afghanistan. Both clearly pose considerable threats to the protection and rights of young people sufficient to merit resource allocation and dedicated projects on the part of humanitarian agencies. And yet research shows how both these issues are embedded in a complex set of relations and circumstances. In the case of landmines, for instance, it was clear that they were an integral part of the fabric of life in an Afghan village where youth would encounter and negotiate them daily. The attitude to risk-taking with mines in the village was due to circumstances that didn't give the luxury of avoiding danger but were such that danger was part of daily life. In such a context intervention that comprised landmine education without addressing the reality of the context and the factors that took young people into contact with mines was going to be woefully inadequate. Likewise interventions for the demobilisation of young soldiers would be incomplete if they focused only on getting underage males out of the armed forces without accompanying measures addressing the factors that took boys to fight in the first place and offering compensation for the benefits forgone.

Obviously, in the social context of Afghanistan, where being an adolescent is associated with responsibility to family and social relations and where, due to the political history, the impact of warfare had made those responsibilities imperative, interventions that looked at merely addressing the risk per se and did not focus on social and economic responsibilities and political involvement were going to be inadequate.

The Challenges of Implementation

As the international aid community prepared for programme implementation in 2002, there was recognition of the high level of responsibility that defined the lives of young people. One response was to pursue implementation in collaboration with youth organisations and their members. Indeed, across the country in 2002 there was a flurry of partnerships created between international agencies and Afghan youth groups, and contracts were drawn up for these groups to implement everything from mine education programmes to small loan projects for demobilised soldiers. Such a strategy seemed ideal: it would accord Afghan youth official recognition of the high degree of participation they already had in daily life and it would mean that adolescents were responsible for the programmes that would benefit their peers.

Even during the Taliban era, Afghan youth groups had existed in regional capitals such as Kabul and Mazar-i-Sharif. Some of these groups had been established as the youth component of international organisations. In Mazar-i-Sharif, for example, the agency UN Habitat had established a youth wing whilst Save the Children UK had supported the establishment of another group. Other groups had been created under the auspices of local political leaders as the youth wing of nascent military organisations. With the fall of the Taliban and the return to power of regional warlords, these youth wings had flourished. Still other groups were created by young Afghans doing a number of self-help activities in their local communities. They ran extra schooling classes, religious teaching and, an activity possible only after the fall of the Taliban, computer classes. They also conducted charitable activities, including caring for street working children.

Youth groups were a ready infrastructure for international agencies to utilise. Their members had energy and enthusiasm, and they were seen as committed to the task of developing their country. Often the members were conversant with the language of development and especially that of rights and citizenship. They themselves advocated investment in their organisations as the Afghan 'leaders of tomorrow'. This democratic vocabulary resonated strongly with Western international agencies that expressed belief that support of citizenship amongst young people might help the germination of democratic principles that would flourish in Afghanistan in years to come. Agencies also saw that Afghan youth groups offered them a link to the common populace. Furthermore, working with youth groups fitted perfectly with the emerging discourse within humanitarian and development practice regarding the participation of beneficiaries. In short, it seemed practically, conceptually and ideologically appropriate for international agencies to fund Afghan youth groups.

Yet these partnerships soon proved incredibly troublesome. What international agencies appeared to ignore was that, although many of these youth groups were equipped with offices and sometimes full-time staff, they lacked any formal constitutional basis, acting as voluntary organisations without registration under Afghan law. Indeed, the Afghan government soon picked up on this anomaly and demanded that, if they were receiving funds, all Afghan youth organisations should be officially registered as NGOs. But this move became a mere formality, masking the reality that few of the Afghan youth groups had proper arrangements in place to clarify lines of control and accountability within the organisation. On top of this, few of the organisations had well defined accounting procedures. In the spirit of high hopes, new opportunities and raised expectations of post-11 September, programming in Afghanistan, practical questions of capacity and readiness for the roles being assigned were not asked of youth organisations. As one senior NGO manager put it:

> As soon as we hear the words 'youth organisation' we assume a spirit of enthusiastic and unblemished voluntarism and spirit within them; we see the opportunity to work with grassroots community organisations which seem to speak for a sector of the population we are only too delighted to work with. And in all this enthusiasm we ignore that these are young and inexperienced groups. By not recognising this, by buying into the idealism expressed by a 'youth' by not applying the same standards of accountability that we'd ask of adult partner organisations we are actually setting them up for gross corruption (Personal communication).

Indeed, the internal weakness in management and capacity of Afghan youth groups and the sudden high level of expectations put upon them soon led to serious fractures in both their internal and external relationships. For a start, the youth organisations showed signs of acute competitiveness towards each other. This was manifest quite blatantly, with youth organisations writing memos to potential international aid agency partners citing the weaknesses of other youth organisations, undermining the case for anyone but themselves to receive funds. This was particularly worrying given that youth groups were composed along ethnic lines and on a micro level their competitiveness for resources was mirroring the fractured state of Afghan politics as a whole. Such competition was a serious bar to any coordination and joint working amongst the various youth organisations.

Internally it became common for the youth groups to undergo splits and divide into breakaway organisations. These splits consistently happened due to internal disagreement about resource allocation. The youth groups were often founded and headed by one charismatic individual, it was he who would court partnerships with international agencies and convince them of his group's ability to implement the work. But, once resources were allocated, members of the youth group would often complain that this individual had too much sway over the money and the direction the group was going in and would break away in protest, always to found a new youth group of their own. And the stakes of these disagreements could be very high indeed. For example one youth group in Mazar-i-Sharif received a large grant from a UN agency to organise and host a youth conference. Soon afterwards, members of the same organisation came to other international agencies to complain that a large proportion of this grant was missing and could not be accounted for. They believed that their leader had appropriated the funds and had come to say that they would be forming a new youth organisation. At the same time they were petitioning international agencies not to fund the original group any further given the corruption. Word of this rebellion reached the leader of the original youth group and in reaction he called upon his father's support. This young man's father was a local warlord and political commander and in response to his son's request he sent troops to surround the organisation's premises and to intimidate the members into withdrawing their complaint and giving up their idea for a breakaway organisation. The siege was only lifted with the assistance of the local police.

Youth in Afghanistan not only carry responsibilities that in other settings would be associated with full adult status, but they are also political players. Indeed, political involvement is a strategy of male youth survival in Afghanistan. Anyone who is alive and in the country today has survived because they have managed to weave in and out of political and military alliances at the local and national level. Young men know how to command power and to influence situations and how to rely on military force if need be. Sometimes family responsibility and political engagement are the same thing – as is clear in the case of young men who fight with militia and secure family protection by aligning themselves with commanders.

Being a member of a youth group is not divorced from this reality. Indeed, youth group leaders are often in such a position precisely because they know how to situate themselves and their groups in the wider political relations. That astuteness relates to politics in their local communities but also to negotiating with international actors such as aid agencies. Aid agencies, with their resources and gateways to a wider world of funding and ideas, are merely one more part of the political scene to be negotiated and made relevant by youth leaders and their groups. The important thing is not the implementation of projects per se but the resources and access attached to that partnership. International agencies have been compelled by experience to wake up to the fact that they do not engage with young people in a political vacuum.

A further challenge in implementing projects through youth groups was their lack of representation of the lives of many young people in the country. The groups were certainly unrepresentative when it came to gender. Adolescent women were always in the minority in the youth groups. It was male youth who headed the groups, formed their alliances and set the agendas. If young women did take on leadership roles they were likely to be under the watchful eye of a brother and be very much in danger of having their reputation tarnished by getting involved in public work. This meant that the issues the groups were concerned with were often those more commonly faced by males – such as landmines and demobilisation – rather than issues faced by women – such as domestic burdens and disputes.

In addition to this, the groups were formed from a certain section of society, often university students in their late teens and early twenties. They had the time to reflect on 'youth' issues. Many of their peers, however, were living abroad in Karachi or Tehran sending back remittances for their families, or were away herding sheep in the hills, pushing carts around Kabul or taking in other people's washing as a way to earn a minimum income. These young people, who were not members of organised groups, had to grow up fast and did not have the time to implement other people's projects. Members of youth groups were uniformly confined to the middle and educated classes of Afghan urban society. Taking them as representative of all young people in Afghanistan was clearly a naive assumption on the part of aid agencies.

Improving Youth-focused Programming in Afghanistan

This chapter has reviewed how, subsequent to 2001, many agencies experienced tensions as they attempted to implement new programmes focused on Afghan youth. As a result of these difficulties, agencies were able to identify a series of important lessons about how to improve the quality of their work with youth in Afghanistan. This final section summarises those lessons and some of the subsequent changes that have been made to the design of programmes. It is too early to tell whether there have been improved outcomes as a result of these modifications. In one sense this chapter only partly documents an ongoing cycle of programme design and improvement. There is still need for constant vigilance and thorough evaluation of the changes integrated into youth-focused work in Afghanistan.

The first important shift that was introduced into the adolescent programming was a move away from single-issue-based work to a more holistic approach. The international child protection sector tends to be dominated by work on individual protection issues such as landmines, child labour, sexual exploitation, etc. Projects are defined by focusing on one of these protection threats or looking at special categories of vulnerable young people. Landmine education is a clear example of this: it assumes that giving young people the knowledge and information about the dangers of mines will be an automatic path to their enhanced self-protection. And yet, as the research discussed in this chapter so clearly shows, young people encounter mines and UXOs as a result of their everyday work and social activities. Even if they have knowledge about the dangers of mines, it is difficult to apply this in reality. At the same time, living with mines and UXOs as such an integral part of their daily life affects young people's attitude so that they do not necessarily see mines and UXOs as a serious danger, nor do they take all precautions against them. Indeed, sometimes they deliberately put themselves at risk.

In 2002 all demining agencies working in Afghanistan agreed on a significant shift in their mines education programmes. The new emphasis was on community-based definition and resolution of mine- and UXO-related problems (termed 'community-based mine risk education'). This shift came from recognition of the need to have a local understanding of the specific mine and UXO risks in any one area and to work with those affected most directly to work out relevant action plans to mediate these risks. Community facilitators were trained in action research techniques, to help local communities express and pinpoint specific mine threats, whether it was the build-up of mines in an irrigation ditch, the local trade in scrap metal collection placing their children in danger or the local Eid celebrations and home-made fireworks, which saw many young people losing fingers. These same community facilitators then supported local people to draw up action plans for addressing the threats and followed through in implementing these plans. For example, local communities might decide that in the interim before a minefield could be cleared, it needed better marking; or would call in a demining agency and clear a specific priority problem area. Young people were integral to forming and implementing these action plans.

Such an approach started to address the reality of the context in which young people were facing mine and UXO dangers. Likewise innovative demobilisation projects were established. These contended that it was not enough for young men merely to be demobilised from the forces: they then needed to be part of programmes that would assist them in developing an alternative livelihood.

Secondly, there was a move to strengthen the meaningful participation of young people in the projects. In 2002, Save the Children, for example, worked with youth councils in Kabul. Christian Children's Fund did the same in Kunduz and Takhar. Less structured than youth groups, youth councils acted as local forums where young people could discuss their concerns. Youth councils were closely tied to community councils so that, when young people identified a point of risk or concern and when they made plans to resolve this, they could take their ideas to the community council, made up of community members and school and religious leaders. Together the community council would work out how to support the young people to take the action they desired. NGOs made funds available for the councils to implement their action plans.

NGOs had to adapt their own procedures and management structures to accommodate this new way of working with groups of young people. It required the agencies to offer flexible funding to the youth councils and to be prepared to fund whatever ideas young people came up with. This is different from most funding approaches, where budgets are broken down into a number of discrete 'deliverables' well in advance of the money being allocated and spent. Similarly, the new style of youth-led programming required a flexible monitoring and evaluation system. One of the debates amongst youth-focused agencies in Afghanistan in 2002 was over the indicators that could be set in advance of youth-led projects to measure outputs that were not yet known or had yet to be determined by young people. In response, agencies recognised that they had to acknowledge the positive impact of the participation process as much as the concrete achievements of the project. This led to the development of process indicators such as 'number of ideas from young people that have been acted upon', and advocacy around the notion that assessment of the quality and methodology of the project was as valid as any quantifiable achievements. A high percentage of young people's ideas that were fulfilled would be taken as a measurement of success, even if this indicator did not specify what those ideas were. Such approaches were not easy to arrive at and took considerable discussion and experimentation amongst aid agencies. Likewise it took lobbying with donors to convince them that undesignated funding should be secured for implementing young people's ideas, through provision of a community fund, and this would be as accountable a way of allocating money as determining what concrete deliverables might be.

A recognition that responsibility for project implementation and resource management needs to be backed up with capacity building was a third important shift in the practice of NGOs. Due to the very conspicuous instances of corruption amongst youth groups who were awarded grant funding, there was growing recognition that extra care needed to be taken in building management capacity amongst these groups. For groups that were already established and had partnership agreements with aid agencies, there was a move towards management training alongside project and issue training. Save the Children, for example, learned that one of the youth groups whom they had a partnership agreement with had no financial procedures in place whatsoever. This agency then started a series of monthly training workshops led by their own financial staff on basic good practice, such as keeping a cash book and making a budget. To encourage a rigorous process of financial bookkeeping, they demanded monthly financial reports from the youth group. This minimised the margin for corruption and also transferred skills in management procedures.

At the same time, aid agencies decided upon a trend of working with loose forums of young people such as youth councils, rather than having these formalised as new youth groups. They learnt that, in the process of becoming formalised, youth groups became removed from the concerns of local development and became tied up with their own constitutional process and reputation and local power. Keeping youth forums as places of discussion and action, rather than places of bureaucracy and power play seemed to mitigate some of the challenges outlined earlier in this chapter.

Finally agencies recognised that they had to take issues of representation very seriously indeed. Although working with young groups built upon recognition of the high levels of responsibility accorded to young people in the country, youth groups seemed to provide a channel for only a minority of better-off male youth to get involved in development work. The other danger was that youth groups became used as the only mouthpiece for young Afghans. Youth group members could speak of their own experiences and concerns but did not canvass or lobby for the concerns of their less educated and privileged peers. A member of a youth group in Mazar, for example, was unlikely to have any contact with a young man in a rural nomadic family, to know of his life or to be able or willing to advocate on his behalf. To improve this, agencies began two things. First, as has already been mentioned, they began to work with looser forums of young people made up at a local neighbourhood level, where there were fewer barriers to membership and an acceptance that all people had the right to get involved in local issues. Secondly, they began to work with youth groups through training that explored questions of leadership and representation; what was it to be a youth leader in Afghanistan, who did they speak for, who should they speak for and how could this be achieved? Yet challenges remain, particularly when it comes to the involvement of girls. Girls still remain under-represented in youth councils and youth initiatives. The predominance of examples that are based on the experience of boys in this chapter merely reflects the fact that, as yet, far less is known about the lives of girls in Afghanistan and that access to them in their secluded and protected lives is extremely difficult. More work is required and flexible approaches must be developed to ensure that the issues faced by girls are better known and that girls, too, are given the opportunity to take an active part in their own and societal development.

Conclusion

Youth-focused programming in Afghanistan has come a long way since September 2001. After 11 September 2001 the huge demand for more intervention in the country led international aid agencies into a series of rapid programme relationships with youth, many of which were hastily and naively implemented. The emerging challenges and the strategies to address them show just what a demanding level of good-quality development work is required when working with young people. This chapter illustrates that, when designing and implementing programmes with war-affected adolescents in Afghanistan, it was not enough merely to extend existing projects such as the landmine education without better analysis of the risks, and the causes and consequences of those risks. Projects can be informed by a thorough analysis of the lives of the young. When this is done, programme design may fit more closely with real needs and be influential and motivating for young people's development. This chapter has also illustrated the level of political involvement that adolescents take on in conflict, whether it is because they are active in armed forces or, like the youth groups, they represent vested interests. This political knowledge will influence the place of adolescents in programmes implemented by aid agencies and must be taken into account. Likewise the evidence of this chapter points to the need for continual monitoring of the profile of participants. There is no room for complacency in assessing who can participate in projects and what the barriers are for others to get involved.

This chapter ends at the point at which I ceased to be involved with youth programming in Afghanistan, a stage where much had been learned and programmes had been adapted. The chapter illustrates what had been agreed at that stage, in 2003: that successful assistance for youth cannot be based on a series of assumptions about their needs and lives. Programmes based on external assessment proved inadequate in the Afghan context and there was a move to base interventions on thorough investigation and understanding. The impact of the newly developed programmes still needs to be assessed. Evaluation of the benefits and disadvantages arising from these new approaches is important to the continued evolution of well-defined and appropriate programmes. Yet a general lesson emerges from the project documentation of this chapter: the particular nature of protection and support that is required in any conflict will be specific to time and place. Each conflict should be understood for how adolescents are affected and all efforts at assistance should be based upon what they define as their greatest needs and priorities.

References

CCF/CFA 2002 *After the Taliban: a Child-Focused Assessment in the Northern Afghan Provinces of Kunduz, Takhar and Badakshan.* Richmond, VA: Christian Children's Fund International/Child Fund Afghanistan.

de Berry, J., Fazili, A., Farhad, S., Nasiry. F., Hashemi, S. and Hakimi, M. 2003 *Children of Kabul: Discussions with Afghan Famlies.* Westport, CT: Save the Children and UNICEF, Save the Children Federation.

Dupree, L. 1973 *Afghanistan.* Princeton, NJ: Princeton University Press.

Global Movement for Children, Afghanistan Working Group 2001 *Lost Chances: The Changing Situation of Children in Afghanistan.* Kabul: UNICEF.

Save the Children 2002 *Children and Youth's Risky Behaviour in a Mine-affected Village in Shomali, Afghanistan.* Kabul: Save the Children Afghanistan.

Terre des hommes 2002 *Needs Assessment of Children Working in Streets of Kabul.* Kabul: ASCHIANA Streetchildren Project/Central Statistics Office of Afghanistan.

10

Adolescence and Armed Conflict in Colombia: 'Resilience' as a Construction Emerging within Psychosocial Work

Diana Isabel Alvis Palma

We just want for Colombia to be a place where everyone, black, white, women, men, boys, girls to be one in equality, and we are willing to work towards this. We, young people, are creating a concrete task that wants to aid the construction of a new Colombia ... To the adults helping peace who are listening to us, we want to thank for understanding our call, thank so much for joining our message, this solidarity will make us stronger and more humane, it will help us build our lost happiness, to forget the days of this war, which is ours, and we are losing (Coalition Against the Involvement of Boys, Girls and Youth in the Armed Conflict in Colombia, 2003a).

The involvement of young people in armed conflict is a subject of global concern. In the effort to understand the specific situation of adolescents, experience from Colombia may be especially valuable. In this chapter I describe the political, sociocultural and psychological situation of adolescents in my country, their involvement in the armed conflict, and the efforts currently being made to support them. I particularly wish to reflect upon the approach to psychosocial assistance, highlighting resilience as a core practice. As I shall explain, I understand 'resilience' as a construction that emerges when people affected by socio-political violence, the organisations that seek to support them and the wider society engage together in a process of meaning-making where fresh resources and agency are constructed, and accounts of hope and of the future unfold. The promotion of 'resilience' is also inseparable from the pursuit of conflict resolution, reparation and the restitution of human and civil rights.

Context

Colombia has a population of 45,600,000 inhabitants, of which roughly three-quarters live in urban areas and the remainder are rural dwelling (UN, 2005). Around 20 per cent of Colombians are between the ages of ten and nineteen (which I take here to denote 'adolescence'). Over more than half a century of conflict,[1] youngsters in this age group have been involved with the various political-military groupings – 'state armed forces', 'paramilitary' and 'guerrilla'. The country has a huge geographical, ethnic and cultural diversity, as well as sharp differences in economic and social development that have left some areas in deep poverty and isolation. Indigenous peoples, Afro-Colombians and the poorest internal migrants predominate in these areas.

The UNDP Human Development Report (2003) identifies the armed conflict as the leading impediment to the country's social and economic development. In Colombia there is an armed political confrontation between guerrillas on the one hand and paramilitaries and the state army on the other. Drug trafficking has played a major role in maintaining the finances of the armed groups and has directly exacerbated the violence. With the election of Uribe as president in August 2002, the violence escalated considerably. The introduction by his government of the Democratic Security Policy has given rise to an increased militarisation of Colombian society. Civilians have become involved in peasant militias and as civilian collaborators and informants (International Crisis Group, 2003). Human rights abuses have increased and the rule of law has been undermined (Colombian Commission of Jurists, 2003). Those responsible for atrocities have operated in an atmosphere of impunity.

The armed conflict developed principally in the rural areas and in recent years has moved to the big cities. Within rural communities, illegal armed groups – paramilitary and guerrilla – exercise authority, severely hindering democratic governance and freedom of expression. People who support armed groups or are controlled by them through threats commonly infiltrate local and national institutions of government, such as the DAS (the government's Administrative Department for Security), the office of the mayor, local councils and committees that oversee the running of basic services. All armed actors compel the civilian population to support them, threatening, abusing and killing when they suspect individuals of supporting the enemy. Members of non-governmental organisations, community leaders and human rights defenders are common targets.

Numerous attempts at peace dialogues have failed. Meanwhile, the government routinely denies the socio-political factors that underlie the armed confrontation – reframing armed opposition as a terrorist threat. In consequence, most of the public investment goes to support war and arms while indicators of health and social welfare record a steady decline. According to UNICEF, 21.5 per cent (three million) of under-eighteens are excluded from the education system; 41 per cent live in poverty and 15.3 per cent live in abject poverty These figures suggest that many of our adolescents (whether directly linked to the conflict or not) are living in precarious economic and social conditions. Meanwhile, attacks on the civil population continue: disappearances, torture, forced migration, kidnapping for political and/or economic aims, and so on.

Adolescence

In this chapter, I refer to adolescents as boys and girls from ten to nineteen years old. However, there is no single understanding of 'adolescence' in Colombia. It is a social category constructed in relation to factors of race/ ethnicity, social class, cultural background and location (urban or rural). For the elites and the middle classes, particularly those living in urban areas, adolescence is understood as a period of the life cycle through which young people pass on their way to achieving adult status, and with that independence, autonomy and the full responsibilities and entitlements associated with adulthood. Parental economic support, engagement in formal education and the enjoyment of leisure pursuits are common characteristics of 'adolescence' in privileged urban Colombia.

Most of the poorest young people and those living in rural areas do not have access to education, health or social services and cannot rely on family support. Boys and girls frequently start working from an early age, doing farm work or domestic labour. They do not experience 'adolescence' in the sense described above: they are more like small adults, negotiating violence, poverty and social deprivation. These young people are frequently labelled as dangerous minors, as aggressive, as 'at risk' and as potential combatants and assassins. Thus institutional policies and practices have been addressed to control them.

At the level of national discourse, 'adolescents' are portrayed as citizens whose participation in society is to be promoted and whose voices as positive social actors are to be encouraged. This construction is supported by the Convention on the Rights of the Child, and the discourses of development and humanitarian organisations. Policies and programmes that seek to address 'adolescents' in accordance with this vision are taking shape in Colombia through the actions of NGOs and governmental authorities.

Adolescents' Involvement in Armed Conflict

'M', thirteen years old, lived with his family in a rural area controlled by an armed group. Members of that group lived on the land of M's family. He grew up in close contact with armed fighters and was socialized by them. To get free from the abuses committed by this group – including the rape of M's mother – the family moved. The armed group wanted M to join them, so they followed and threatened the family. As a result they had to move again but the threats continued. Eventually, the family sought asylum abroad in order to protect M and themselves.

Although most adolescents in Colombia are affected by the socio-political conflict – not least in terms of diversion of government funds from social provision to military spending – some of them experience the situation in a far more direct manner than their peers.[2] The armed conflict is complex and dynamic. Thus, the impact upon adolescents has changed over time, in both nature and scope. The process by which this age group (ten to nineteen) are affected is always shaped by social, cultural, economic and familial conditions that limit their choices and opportunities within society.

Recruitment

Estimates of the number of child combatants in Colombia vary from 6,000 to 14,000 (Human Rights Watch, 2003; Coalition to Stop the Use of Child Soldiers, 2004). Adolescents who join armed groups tend to come from areas where these groups have a strong presence, or from families in which members have been victims of a particular armed group; an estimated 90 per cent of the underage combatants are from rural areas.

When adolescents live in areas controlled by armed actors, they are socialised by them since childhood, as in the example of 'M' above. This shapes the development of their personality and outlook. Living in conflict areas, they have to face danger and threats as part of daily life. In such a situation, an armed group can hold out the promise of strength and protection.

According to the Human Rights Watch Report *You'll Learn Not to Cry*, which is based on 112 interviews of former child combatants, at least one out of every four irregular combatants in Colombia's civil war is under eighteen years old, with a typical age at recruitment between eleven and thirteen (Human Rights Watch, 2003). Children start to fight as young as eight. By the age of thirteen, most are trained in the use of automatic weapons, grenades, mortars and explosives, and participate in many of the atrocities of the Colombian conflict: 'watching captives being tortured, shooting captives as a test of valor, participating in assassinations of political figures and in "social cleansing", killings of drug abusers and petty thieves, and executing comrades – even friends, captured while trying to run away' (ibid.: 6).

All the illegal armed groups are known to recruit both boys and girls, who are engaged to a similar extent in fighting and killing. Girls, however, face gender-related violations of their rights such as rape, sexual harassment and forced use of the intrauterine device. Factors that propel recruitment in nearly all of the children's accounts include poverty, deprivation, underemployment, truncated schooling and lack of affection and family support. For example, one boy remarked:

> Both of my parents used to beat me. My father drank a lot and when he was drunk he'd beat me with a stick. I was very small and was paid only 4,000 pesos [US$1.50] a day on the coffee farm, but it was enough to live on. The FARC-EP[3] used to come by the farm sometimes. I had a friend who joined them. Then he helped me join. I was sick of working at the farm (Human Rights Watch, 2003: 36).

Children are also induced to join by promises of money (usually broken in the case of the guerrillas), thoughts of an easier life, a thirst for adventure, the desire to carry a gun and wear a uniform and simple curiosity. For example, another youth (seventeen years old) spoke about the guerrillas as follows:

> They move all around the countryside, and you see them in good spirits these people, with their guns and their uniforms. You get infected with the same spirit. That's what happened to me. I had some friends among the guerrillas who invited me to join. I didn't have a lot of contact with them, but they told me that the life was good, that there was plenty of food, clothing was provided, you wanted for nothing, so I got excited and off I went. It was my decision (ibid.: 37).

Human Rights Watch indicates that the high rate of underage recruitment is directly related to lack of opportunities. The war in Colombia is fought by the poor: 'children fight against other children whose background is very similar to their own, and whose economic situation and future prospects are equally bleak. With much in common in civilian life, children become the bitterest of enemies in war' (ibid.: 4).

The support for demobilised adolescent combatants has been developed in recent years. They are treated as 'children' in special circumstances and not as law offenders; and benefit from the assistance of national organisations such as the Colombian Institute of Family Welfare, and international organisations such as Save the Children and the International Organization for Migration. The approach is one of social insertion, which means assuring access to education and health services, working to reconstruct family ties, and helping demobilised young people to acquire the tools and resources to participate actively in society and generate income.

Internal Displacement

Displacement is another national tragedy linked to the armed conflict. Over the last fifteen years 700,000 children were displaced by the armed conflict. The displaced are predominantly rural dwellers who flee to urban areas in search of safety. It is frequently the case that adolescents witness horror before displacement (murders, tortures, massacres) and many personally experience harm and pain. Forced displacement almost always leads to severe deterioration in the quality of life of an adolescent's family. However, there are no coherent programmes to respond effectively to the needs of displaced families. The government has made some funds available for IDP assistance but the majority of this is for emergency aid in the first three months after registration and only 43 per cent of IDPs receive any help at all (UNHCR, 2003). The government's policy has been largely one of return, despite the continuing insecurity. The UN Resident Coordinator and UNHCR created the Thematic Group on Displacement (GTD) in 1999. The GTD provided coordinated inter-agency action to prevent displacement and to improve aid for those already displaced.[4] However, the effectiveness of these efforts in strengthening organisations and providing protection and services to the IDPs has been limited by a lack of funds and political will (IDMC, 2007). Consequently, conditions in the municipal areas, including Bogota where the greatest concentration of IDPs is found, are poor (ibid.). In addition, adolescents have lost relatives, family ties are broken, and they have to live in situations of overcrowding.

Fear and hate arise from the violent experiences that lead to displacement. In addition, adolescent males may have to negotiate family and societal pressure to take revenge for the death of a close relative. In receptor communities, which are the poorest ones, adolescents and their families face isolation and discrimination, and might become the targets of military clean-up operations.

Additional Challenges in Light of the Democratic Security Policy

The Democratic Security Policy (DSP) introduced by President Uribe, which legitimates the military solution to the conflict, has added to the risks to adolescents in several ways. First, when they are recruited to the government's network of collaborators and informants,[5] they run the risk of being murdered by the illegal armed groups. The use of young people in this way is difficult to prove (or disprove) because informants are not uniformed and work undercover (Human Rights Watch, 2003). However, suspicion of such involvement puts them at risk of punishment or execution to an extent potentially as great as if they were regular combatants. Secondly, measures taken by the authorities limit mobilisation and changes of residency. As a result, adolescents cannot run away, leaving them vulnerable to recruitment by the armed groups. Finally, occupation by military forces impedes the running of education and health services.

At the same time, the militarisation of society in light of the DSP is also evident in the media. Here, soldiers are depicted as national heroes and as role models with whom adolescents are encouraged to identify.

Forms of Violence

Young people face violent reprisals, the destruction of their homes and kidnapping. From 1996 to 2001, 1,258 under-eighteen-year-olds were kid-napped, twenty-six of whom died in captivity. In Colombia's cities, stray bullets from guerrilla–paramilitary street wars and military clean-up operations take the lives of many. In socio-economic terms, it is hard to know the extent to which adolescents have become marginalised and excluded due to the armed conflict. In cities, adolescents are often the main target, subjected to multiple forms of violence – political, criminal, domestic and structural – which intersect with and reinforce one another; in rural areas, whole communities may face additional hardships as a result of isolation by armed groups that deny them access to food, transport or medical care.

In Colombia the interrelatedness between family, political and social violence is palpable. Family violence and sexual abuse are both causes and consequences of the involvement of many young people in the conflict: two million children are maltreated each year in Colombia (UNICEF, 2002). In the Human Rights Watch report most respondents stated that family violence or sexual abuse was the main reason to join the armed groups. A high rate of family violence has, in turn, been commonly noted amongst displaced families.

> S, whose father died when she was two years old, told me why she joined an illegal armed group: 'Because I hate my mother, and I wanted to take revenge and make her suffer.' S comes from a poor rural area. At the age of six, her mother moved to a nearby town to work, leaving her three children (six, eleven and twelve years old) alone. She believed S's older brothers would take care of S, while she tried to earn a living. The mother engaged in a new relationship, distancing herself from the children. After three years of living in this situation, a neighbour took S back to her mother's house because she was suffering from malnutrition. The mother kept mistreating S for many years until she joined the armed group at the age of twelve. Once there, she started a sexual relationship with a man twenty years older.
>
> What is surprising is that only when she joined the armed group did S become visible for everybody: her mother rescued her from the armed group

and spoke with a family member to protect and take care of S in a different city. This was the first loving behaviour she had displayed for years. Furthermore, institutions began to give S psychosocial support. Far from her mother, S engaged with her new loving family and joined school.

From my point of view, there is a great need to understand better the connection between different kinds of violence as they manifest in the lives of adolescents. We have tended to consider them in isolation, or to understand the causal relationship between them in singular and simplistic terms. In contrast, we need to explore questions such us: What is the relationship between the abuse of power in public and private spaces? What kinds of conceptual links do adolescents make between, for example, discrimination and military mobilisation? Why do some adolescents who have experienced abuse in the family join armed groups while others do not? These kinds of questions have important implications for the development of interventions. For example, it would seem that in order to deal with children's enlistment it might be necessary to address not only domestic abuse and neglect but also the wider militarisation of society as manifest in media imagery and changing values.

The socio-political and economic conditions in most parts of Colombian society exercise strong constraints on the choices that adolescents can make. However, I am not saying that adolescents are passive or lack agency. They move from one context to another trying to make sense of their lives: for example, they join an armed group to avoid or escape family violence and sexual abuse, or in order to support their families; adolescent women try to escape domestic abuse through early pregnancy. Unfortunately, those solutions are part of new problems and lead to new abuses. They also lend currency to the labelling of young people as aggressive, sick or dangerous. Our challenge within organisations working to support adolescents is twofold: first, to comprehend the contexts in which their patterns of behaviour develop and, secondly, to engage in the transformation of the political, social and economic conditions that constrain their lives. Thus, psychosocial work is not a neutral practice when it involves standing up for the rights of adolescents violated by the state and military groups (Summerfield, 2002).

Psychosocial Impact of the Armed Conflict on Adolescents

In Colombia, there has been an increasing recognition of the psychosocial impact of war and the importance of psychosocial intervention for victims. This work has mainly been undertaken by NGOs. Corporación AVRE[6] has been a pioneer amongst these. Started in Bogota in 1992, the organisation also pays visits to seriously affected areas and has been taking part in regional, national and international networks.

Corporación AVRE understands that socio-political violence has psychosocial consequences at the individual, familial, community and group levels. The effects at these levels also interact (Buitrago, 2004). For example, socio-political violence damages the social fabric by generating intimidation, fear and distrust leaving people isolated and emotionally vulnerable (Martin, 1998). Furthermore, individual suffering profoundly affects one's family and community.

In common with the experience of others, we have seen that most people affected by socio-political violence will experience emotional suffering following violent events but only a minority will develop extreme symptoms of psychopathology, often determined by a previous mental disorder or disposition (Buitrago, 2004). We also believe that there is no universal response to violence. Psychosocial attention to adolescents affected by armed conflict must attend to cultural/social/political contexts, and not solely to biological and psychological understandings, according to which, for example, there is an automatic and universal relationship between exposure to specific events and traumatic sequelae.

Although established by psychiatrists, the work of AVRE does not only include direct therapy. It was recognised that activities are also required to repair the social fabric, to overcome impunity, to understand the social context in which violence occurs, and to identify, utilise and develop the resources existing within communities (ibid.: 239). To achieve these ends, three types of activity (named 'modalities', ibid.: 230) are used in ways that interrelate and reinforce one another.

1. Procedures and actions for strengthening organisations. AVRE seeks to participate in networks and coordinate activities with other organisations so that its work can be extended. This coordination takes place at the local, regional, national and international levels. AVRE provides psychosocial workshops for organisations involved with those affected by socio-political violence, and institutional development training for these organisations. Coordination is also achieved by participation in inter-institutional and inter-disciplinary programs. For example, AVRE has undertaken a project to strengthen democratic practices and civil resistance in the southwest of the country. Social and human rights organisations are taught to recognise the impact of socio-political violence upon the organisation and on their leaders. Then, together, they develop strategies, share resources and undertake projects that enhance their work, strengthen their internal workings and promote personal well being.

2. Clinical therapy. AVRE's psychiatrists and psychologists provide individual, family or group therapeutic sessions to aid emotional recovery

following socio-political violence. However, this modality is not seen as the sole answer to people's mental health problems: clinical work is performed in conjunction with the other two modalities and with other organisations. This clinical model is seen as especially important for the minority who have serious psychopathological sequelae.

3. Training. The aim of this modality is to build capacity among communities and expand the mental health, psychosocial and human rights work of AVRE. Specialised organisations are not currently able to cover all the needs for psychosocial intervention in Colombia (ibid.: 238). Consequently, AVRE trains members of communities affected by socio-political violence and organisations who already work with victims of socio-political violence. Trainees learn to analyse the social context of violence, recognise the emotional consequences of violent events, perform crisis interventions with individuals and groups, and mobilise the external resources necessary for a particular intervention. Some trainees, known as Popular Therapists, are trained to conduct individual and group interventions as well as fear and bereavement interviews. Others, known as Multipliers of Psychosocial Action, Mental Health and Human Rights are expected to work with their communities to spread knowledge and understanding of these matters and encourage civic participation.

These three modalities are intended to interact in a way that brings together a focus on human rights, the engendering of a democratic culture the strengthening of civic participation and giving voice to victims through claims for reparation and the restitution of rights. This goes beyond more traditional clinical interventions and is intended to contribute to the recovery of the entire community. There are not many organisations that approach psychosocial work with this degree of complexity. This may be due to a wish to maintain political neutrality and/or a narrow focus on technical issues. It can also be due to security concerns.

Resilience

For a long time the focus of psychosocial work has been upon pathology, damage and trauma and the ways that these may be prevented and overcome. Research into probabilistic models has explored the association between different variables ('risk factors') and psychopathology. In contrast, 'resilience' suggests a focus upon capacity and strength. Instead of enquiry into risk factors – such as the experience of violence, abandonment, displacement – the quest is to discover those factors and resources that contribute to protection and well-being. These may include dimensions of socio-economic status, age, gender and individual temperament, as well as the quality of parenting, educational provision, social networks and involvement in organised religion (Loughry and Eyber, 2003).

In this chapter I argue for an approach that is centred upon resilience. However, in my own experience it is important to consider resilience in a manner that takes it beyond the concern for protective factors – whether internal to the person or present within their environment. Furthermore, I am committed to processes that aim to promote resilience through encouraging a reformulation of the relationship between the individual and her/his environment. This is partly a matter of meaning – exploring new ways to jointly consider past events or current situations. It is also about finding new paths of action and future construction. My account of resilience is based on a systemic (Oliver, 1996) and social constructionist paradigm (Shotter and Gergen, 1994). This shift to understanding resilience as a process has invited a more complex and relational understanding of the person–environment relationship, breaking with an overly deterministic view and avoiding heroic accounts of resilience that may stigmatise the apparently 'non-resilient'.

The following is an example of how this process may unfold:

> When L's father was killed by an armed group, he, a sixteen-year-old boy, felt he must avenge his death, so he wanted to join an armed group. L expressed his feelings in a therapeutic session, which I noted as a normal response to an abnormal experience. Then I asked L how he understood what happened. In his account, he blamed himself for not staying with his father when he was taken. As homework, I invited L to do some enquiry amongst his family and the community members he felt closest to (after judging who would be keen and ready to do so), exploring different views of what happened. In the following session, we drew a kind of map with all the different meanings. There was no mention of the human rights violations and responsibilities that armed actors and state had in the situation, so I offered him this understanding to put on the map. We explored each of these understandings and the actions, and meanings linked to them: If you understand things in this way, what do you feel compelled to do next? Which of these views would help you most to become the kind of man/son that you would like to become? Who do you feel loyal to when you understand things in this way? What would your mates say about you if you decided to claim restitution instead of revenge? L reflected on how his experience was connected to that of other youngsters in the country. He cried when imagining killing somebody. We decided that our next step would be to invite to the next session another adolescent who had facing a similar situation. This, jointly with other conversations, helped L to interweave stories of hope and agency; new actions were legitimate for him. The last time I saw L he was working with an uncle; the family were getting support from non-governmental organizations to initiate an investigation to identify and bring to justice the people who killed his father.

Above all, I want to stress that resilience is resistance and construction. Resilience is the ability to resist the destructive effects of difficult circumstances and maintain physical, biological and psychological integrity. It is also the ability to construct a new positive life and self-identity, to create a meaningful tale out of distressing events. Interventions that aim to strengthen resilience cannot be dispassionate and neutral but need, instead, to be suffused with human warmth and the concern to help young people make sense of their lives (Cyrulnik, 2001). There is a shift from focusing on the internal mind of the individual in isolation to the relationships where we create meanings and actions (Cronen and Lang, 1995). The therapist is not an outsider to the process but actively engages in 'joint actions' with the adolescent in conversation (Shotter, 1993).

Informed by social constructionist ideas, Cronen and Lang (1995) claim that language does not describe reality, language creates reality; language is not about the action but it is the action itself. When we talk to each other we create a frame of reference for experience and for the emotions associated with that experience. From this perspective we can see the significance of the ways in which we label situations. The language of 'trauma' carries with it a set of implications quite different from the language of 'resilience'. In my professional practice, I find the focus on resilience leads to the discovery of choices and opportunities for action in contexts that might otherwise seem hopeless.

In summary, I highlight some key observations that have emerged from my own efforts to pursue an approach focused on resilience:

- Resilience emerges within contexts. There are no resilient individuals: they become resilient in particular situations.
- Resilience is both the result of an interactive process between individuals and their environment, and the construction that emerges from different relationships and contexts.
- Resilience is a prospective and a linguistic construction that involves the making of meaning specific to the cultural context.
- The meaning of experience is not an internal and private matter; it is shaped by social interaction and the social discourses in which we are enmeshed.
- Resilience can be promoted by various practices, which include the practices of institutions and social organisations, aid provision and psychotherapeutic styles. The emergence of resilience is constrained by practices that promote dependency, victimisation, stigmatisation, repression or political manipulation (co-optación).
- Resilience is an account or a story that emerges in the social interaction where people make sense of their experience of violence. The aim is to integrate the experience into a coherent narrative that spans public and private domains, where hope, agency and future emerge.

'Resilience' in Working with Adolescents

Focusing on resilience is particularly important with adolescents. From the conventional perspective of developmental psychology, adolescence is a stage where certain psychological developments occur, a stage that, according to common assumptions, is shaped by 'crisis'. This assumption may be particularly strong for adolescence in settings that are themselves seen as 'crisis', such as that of Colombia. I fear that such a view is self-fulfilling: the language of crisis creates only crisis itself.

I wish to promote the understanding of adolescence as a period of crisis and opportunity. Regardless of the problems and pain of early childhood, young people in the age group ten to nineteen are able to channel emerging capacities, independence and knowledge into transformation, rebuilding and reconnection. I encourage conversations – such as that with 'L' above – in which abilities and resources emerge in addressing experiences of violence. At the same time I also make room for the expression of suffering. I stress the active role of the adolescent as subject engaged in a dynamic process of meaning-making about experience that has important consequences in terms of resilience.

How adolescents express suffering will depend on the culture they belong to, family rules, education, the security situation, the nature of their involvement in the armed conflict, etc. Within everyday life this suffering can find expression in isolation, feelings of helplessness, aggression, promiscuity, alcohol or drug abuse; it can also emerge in creativity, solidarity and altruism. By understanding the context and language in which suffering makes sense it can be transformed. Thus, the promotion of resilience in adolescents affected by armed conflict represents a challenge to traditional ways to carry out psychosocial work. Adolescents are actively seeking meanings for their lives and we as helpers must enable them to discover a positive and productive sense of purpose, even when they have to face painful experiences of violence. In the following example of a therapeutic conversation, I show how to give meanings to different experiences and feelings in order to unfold resilience:

> M, a sixteen-year-old boy, spoke about his feelings of isolation and depression after his family was displaced. His father was a political and community leader threatened by government armed forces, so the family had had to displace. In the telling of his story, M spoke of feelings of shyness and loneliness when he was thirteen. I became very interested in exploring how these feelings were overcome. It was through playing music with a local group of young people, supported by the church. In the conversation we understood his feelings as a way of looking after his family, that is to say, by feeling isolated and depressed he was preventing himself from joining the local community again and thereby putting at risk the family security. M said that he must keep his family safe

because he was the only son/male in the family and expressed his sadness for losing his friends. Finally, we agreed that he already had skills to overcome isolation and that we would work out how to use them in the new family situation. In addition, we could explore family security issues in a meeting with the family to identify some supportive organizations.[7]

In our conversations, some questions were very useful to summon resources, hope and connectedness (to family, organizations, community): If your sadness had words, what would it say to your father? What would it say to us? To the armed actors? What needs to happen for you to look after your family and to use your skills to overcome your isolation? Who do you become closer to when you are isolated? Who else is involved in the family security? If your former friends were looking at you, what would they admire most about the way you are handling this situation? What advice would they give you to keep being a youngster? The last time I saw M his family had to move to a different neighbourhood because threats against his father continued; in M there was a sense of not being isolated, but his frustration as normally expected was back again.[8]

I mentioned above that when we talk to each other our social worlds are constructed. In different contexts adolescents engage in conversation in which they negotiate duties, rights and responsibilities. These conversations shape and are shaped by our different world views organised in discourses, narratives or stories. For example, parents might criticise their son for his school absences when acting within a social discourse in which education is a value and parents are constructed as responsible for getting their sons/daughters to school. However, this conversation would never take place between parents and sons when they are acting within a social discourse in which adolescents learn by joining with their parents in different labours.

When adolescents face an experience of violence there is a crash of meaning systems that opens up new contexts for conversations; by engaging in these conversations adolescents make sense of the experience at the same time as transforming it. These conversations might take place simultaneously in institutional, social or private spaces. The wished result is the construction of a coherent narrative to respond to traditional adolescent questions – who am I? Where do I belong? On whom do I rely? – within relationships that have been renegotiated with new rights, duties and responsibilities. I show this in the following example:

A social organization referred D, a thirty-year-old woman, to therapy. They were worried by her behaviour, which they judged was putting her life at risk. Her mother had 'disappeared' and D was participating in a judgment against the group responsible for it; she had already been threatened by that group, so she had to take careful security measures to protect herself and her family. D was the oldest daughter of three; her father was not living with the family since the parents' separation nine years earlier. During the first session, D expressed her concerns for the youngest sister, L (sixteen years old), who was having problems at school; it was clear that D had taken a mother's role in the family. I invited all the sisters to the sessions but only D and L came; P (the middle sister was working).

The therapeutic process unfolded multiple conversations between D, L and I: feelings about their mother's disappearance and their uncertainty about whether she was alive or dead; the judgment and its meaning to move into the future; the security and the sharing of information and decision-making processes within the family; the relationship between the sisters; and L's resources to cope in a new culture (she moved from a rural to an urban area). Although P did not come to the session I invited her to participate through doing joint homework with her sisters that they then brought back to the session.

The sisters decided that, for the time being, the best way to think about their mother was to imagine her presence as a candlelight; and we reflected at what times the candlelight became stronger, and at what time weaker. L was pleased to be involved and informed of the judgment and security situation; it positioned her as more equal and autonomous and not just a little girl to look after. We also reflected on the times when it would be more useful to relate as mother–daughter; and on the times when it would be more useful to relate as sisters in order to help L to complete her development. This gave D the confidence to surrender her role as overprotective mother, enabling her to continue with her own personal and emotional life. Meanwhile the court case was going on. When I finished my contact with L she was enjoying school, making new friends and getting on with life (at that point, they still did not have information about their mother).

Traditionally, psychotherapeutic spaces have been constructed as legitimate settings within which to have conversations that promote healing and recovery; and professionals have been trained to have particular kinds of conversation to support their clients through bereavement, debriefing, crisis intervention, etc. When defined in this way, the voice that is privileged is the professional one; which is claimed as legitimate, by virtue of the therapist's assumed objectivity (evidence-based practice). While this might be a useful construction at some times, at others it can constrain the multiplicity and richness of accounts.

In this approach to resilience, we are not looking for feelings, emotions, behaviours from within the person that accord with a universal picture that we – as observers and experts – have in our head in order to offer 'diagnosis'. Instead, we are deeply engaged in conversations where local understanding emerges, useful meanings and actions are coordinated, and new realities (emotional, cognitive, relational, political and social) are constructed in social networks and social worlds. Understanding resilience as a process means that we should attend to how hope, agency and choice are interwoven in the diverse public and private conversations and contexts in which we participate (not only traditional talk therapies).

The Collective Dimension

As the following example illustrates, it is also in collective practices that agency, hope and resources can be constructed:

> Medellín is one of the most important cities in Colombia, with the highest rate of violence. The Juvenile Networks of Medellin is a community-based organization that gathers young people from different juvenile groups who are committed to non-violence. The leaders of the network noticed fear, risk behaviours, disengagement and peer conflict. The psychosocial support that AVRE Corporation gave to the network helped youngsters to understand these feelings and behaviours as part of a collective experience connected to violence (not just as a subjective, personal or intimate experience). Then, the youngsters decided to work on strengthening the network by reconstructing the group's cultural memory at the same time that they obtained psychosocial tools to deal with the impact of violence. In the whole process the youngsters' voices were privileged, with adults stepping away from the position of 'experts' in order to construct along with the youngsters, taking into account their contexts and realities.[9] Afterwards, the group continued with its political work and enhancing democratic practices in the country.

The family should play an important role in supporting adolescents. However, for various reasons the conflict in Colombia has weakened the capacity of many families to play this role. Displacement and the socio-economic and psychological challenges associated with this impede the effective functioning of family units. In some cases, they are reluctant to reintegrate children who have been involved with armed groups. Adolescents themselves may choose not to return to families where abuse motivated them to enrol in the first place. Even in reasonably well-functioning families relatively little attention may be paid to adolescents in comparison to younger children. In some parts of Colombian society there is little appreciation for the specific situation of older children. For girls in particular the emphasis is placed upon their responsibilities (including care for younger siblings) with little attention to their needs. On the other hand, adolescents are frequently able to adapt better and more quickly to new social and cultural conditions, helping other family members to move on. In this example I seek to illustrate how stories of agency, belonging and care can emerge as a seed for transforming relationships and creating choices in a family seriously affected by domestic and political violence.

> L was a fifty-year-old, black woman and community leader who was forcibly displaced from one of the poorest rural areas in the country. She moved after N, her daughter, was first raped and then decapitated in front of her four children. N had also been sexually abused by her stepfather in childhood. L herself had a history of abandonment and rape as a child. At the start of

therapy, L blamed N for the sexual abuse ('she seduced him, he is not guilty'). During one of the sessions, I used the metaphor of the phoenix to create meanings around L's ability to 'rise from the ashes' and transform death into life. This emerging account helped L to create more choices and start transforming the relationship with her granddaughter, as L said:

> In the past session taking the role of each of my daughters helped me to connect with their feelings of sadness and fear when they faced the sexual abuse by their stepfather. I changed the blaming and anger towards her. In addition, when you show me how I have been able to transform death into life, I started wondering how I could help my granddaughter (K, fifteen years old and L's daughter) to move on in life. I now realize her suffering and pain. As our communication was broken many years ago, I wrote a letter to her: 'I want to let you know that I love you so much, and I wonder if you still need to be cared for by anybody, and if you want me to care for you'. K was very moved and responded affirmatively. They decided to invest some savings in a shop in order to increase the family income and pay for K's education as she wanted.

This action created a basis for K to engage in long-term therapeutic work to make sense of the brutal violence she had witnessed and speak about the suffering that was behind her drug abuse.[10]

Conversations that invoke the state, raising questions about responsibilities, the restitution of human rights and the need for reparation, are crucial. Intimidating political leaders who challenge systematic abuse has been one of the most important war strategies in the country. In this context, the psychosocial work should reconstruct political values that have been threatened by violence, as is shown in this example:

> B is a woman (thirty-three years old) who lived through child sexual abuse and severe family violence. As an adolescent, she escaped this family situation by joining a man that she did not love. She wanted to be saved. Her new family grew wealthy in a region controlled by an armed group. However, she again experienced abuse in this new relationship. Due to her activities as a community worker and human rights activist she was threatened and she had to move with her two boys (one adolescent, one child).
> As B told it, she was guilty because she had witnessed in silence many atrocities committed by armed actors; she felt she could have done something to stop these. She also felt guilty because her children were living in poverty in Bogotá, when they had had a comfortable life on the farm. In a session in which she brought up the story of the sexual abuse we explored how she had survived that experience; then I noted positively how in the actual situation she was able to move on from the abuse; she said it was when she started to work with human rights. Then I asked: 'Working in human rights: what does it tell you about yourself?' 'That I am no longer the silent child who was sexually abused and that I am helping other children to laugh'. 'If you look two years

ahead, what difference will your actions have made for your two boys?' 'I will have prevented them from becoming armed actors or being killed, I really will'. We also explored the obligations and entitlements connected to the story of 'helping other children to laugh', and how to carry it on in her new situation.

In a session with the two boys and the mother, I asked the adolescent boy: 'What is it about your mother that you are most proud of?' 'Her courage, she is a warrior, she defends rights for the good of people'. 'Have you taken the courage of your mother as your own?' 'It is difficult to say ... but I prefer to stay with my mother because my father was very harsh with us and difficult to love ... I have had the courage to leave my father and start a new life here, but it is difficult and painful'. Then I explored the pain, alongside other feelings, associated with the separation from his father; an emerging story of responsibilities led us to a reflection about the political–military situation that constrained family life in the farm. The last time I saw B, she was still struggling with her mood changes, but coping. She decided to adjust her political activities to the new situation, I noticed; she did it with a new sense of entitlement and responsibility in which more choices were available for her and her children.

Few young people actively choose to seek help in a conventional psychotherapeutic setting. Psychosocial reconstruction with adolescents should begin with collective actions that promote adolescents' self-organisation, participation, creativity and peer healing. We have noticed that adolescents are willing to be supported by adults when they challenge institutional practices and facilitate conversations within alternative community spaces (rap groups, sports clubs, youth clubs) where more egalitarian relationships are constructed and the peer group is privileged. Within such spaces, adolescents are more likely to seek support in directly addressing pain and suffering:

> Barrancabermeja is the main oil port in Colombia, with a tradition of social and trade union movements and a large number of displaced people. Defence of Children International runs the Girasoles en Barranca ('Sunflowers in Barranca'), a psychosocial programme for youngsters from the poorest communities. There is a community house organized by the young people themselves, where they can play music and sports, gather together and receive legal and psychological support. The members have created their own rules of coexistence that promote cooperation, communication, respect and participation. A psychologist has become the 'house mother' who supports the youngsters when they feel able to speak about sexual abuse, torture, abandonment, etc. This programme has enabled adolescents to reconstruct themselves – to see themselves as part of new groups, to make different choices, and to live according to new sets of values. Girasoles en Barranca has been cost-effective and its methodology has been promoted by governmental organizations.[11]

Having said that, we also have to remember that there are some adolescents who need specialised attention given by a psychiatrist. However, in Colombia, most adolescents have little hope of accessing such specialised services due to very limited support for mental health services in the country.

Preventing recruitment is the best way to avoid the awful experience of war. We have noticed that strengthening the youngsters' skills to solve conflict and take decisions, giving psychosocial tools to prevent recruitment, introducing adolescents to juvenile and social networks, and opening spaces for cultural, political and community participation are all building resources to resist engaging in the war.[12] In Colombia, these strategies are mainly adopted by national and international NGOs (for example, the Coalition against the Involvement of Boys, Girls and Youngsters in the Armed Conflict); governmental organisations promote the youths' participation in the Juvenile Local Committees. These are starting to develop but are not yet part of a proper policy for youth.

It is important to note that focusing on resilience not only yields significant benefits for adolescents. It also empowers us as helpers. Working with clients to construct new meanings, values and identities enables us to develop our own resources and helps in overcoming feelings of helplessness in the face of mass violence. 'Resilience' is not about conformism or resignation to an unjust status quo. Rather, the consistent focus within our conversations on the responsibility of perpetrators and the importance of accountability for the multiple human rights violations strengthens the conviction of all of us – 'therapists' and 'clients' alike – that personal well-being will always require reparation and the restitution of human rights.

Final Thoughts

I have argued that resilience is a prospective construction. Adolescents, in interaction with society, make sense of their lives and experiences and draw upon previously untapped resources in order to find new pathways for their lives. This conception of resilience invites us to move from causes and impacts to construction of meanings and positive action. Focusing on resilience creates hopes and promotes agency. The second decade of life is an important time to pursue this, a time when individuals are able and often very motivated to engage in constructing lives for themselves.

All of us have a responsibility to overcome the inequity and culture of impunity in Colombian society and politics. This is essential if we are to break the cycles of violence – domestic, political, criminal – that have dominated for so many years. By working with adolescents to find new ways to think and act, and by ensuring that they have the opportunity for meaningful, non-violent participation in society, we can open the way for a future far brighter than all of our pasts.

Notes

The author wishes to express her appreciation to Jason Hart and Marcela Salazar Posada for reading and commenting on the chapter, to Gloria Amparo Camilo, Jorge Torres, Dora Lucia Lancheros, team members of AVRE Corporation; and to Fernando Sabogal, Director of Defence for Children International in Colombia, for information provided for this chapter. Many of the ideas expressed in the chapter derive from the author's experience while working as a consultant for Corporación AVRE. They do not reflect an institutional position except where this is explicitly noted.

1. The assassination of the radical liberal politician, Jorge-Eliecer Gaitan (9 April 1948), was the starting-point for Colombia's constant cycle of violence and displacement, starting with the seventeen-year period called *La Violencia*. Revolutionary groups began to appear in 1953.
2. In the period 1992–2004, 9 per cent of central government expenditure was allocated to health, 20 per cent to education and 13 per cent to defence (UNICEF, n.d.).
3. Revolutionary Armed Forces of Colombia–People's Army (in Spanish *Fuerzas Armadas Revolucionarias de Colombia–Ejército del Pueblo*).
4. The GTD is composed of the International Organization for Migration (IOM), The World Bank, Food and Agriculture Organization (FAO), United Nations Population Fund (UNFPA), United Nations Office of the High Commissioner for Human Rights (UNOHCHR), Pan American Health Organization – World Health Organization (OPS-WHO), World Food Programme (WFP), United Nations Development Programme (UNDP), United Nations Children's Fund (UNICEF) and the UNDCP (UN Drug Control Programme). See Global Internal Displacement Monitoring Centre (n.d.).
5. According to the International Crisis Group (2003), Uribe recruited more than a million Colombians to act as collaborators and informants.
6. *Apoyo a Víctimas de violencia sociopolítica pro Recuperación Emocional/*Support to Victims of Sociopolitical Violence for Emotional Recovery.
7. I invite the reader to understand these meanings as ones among the many that could have emerged from that conversation. This way to understand the emotional situation made sense for both of us (M and I), and helped us (M, his family, the supportive organisations and myself) to move on. Some helpers might privilege the unfolding of meanings of loss and pain.
8. In my practice, it is the fact that experiences of violence happen over and over again that creates the main impediment for adolescents to overcome them. It is not about a retraumatisation, but about the political, economic and social situations that maintain war, poverty and inequity.
9. Information given by Jorge Torres, team member of Corporación AVRE.
10. Although there was in this family four children looked after by L, they were not getting any kind of support from any governmental programme (either education, health or social services). L and his son had to struggle every day to make a living for them.
11. Information given by Fernando Sabogal, Director of Defense for Children International.

12. For example, the national campaign 'We Boys and Girls Don't Want to Be in The War'. (See Coalition Against the Involvement of Boys, Girls and Youth in the Armed Conflict in Colombia, 2003b.)

References

Buitrago, J. 2004 'Internally Displaced Colombians: the Recovery of Victims of Violence Within a Psychosocial Framework', in K.E. Miller and L.M. Rasco (eds) *The Mental Health of Refugges. Ecological Approaches to Healing and Adaptation.* London: Lawrence Erlbaum Associates.
Coalition Against the Involvement of Boys, Girls and Youth in the Armed Conflict in Colombia 2003a 'Breaking with Silence and Fear', in *Bulletin Putchipu* Number 6 –English, Bogota: Coalición contra la vinculación de niños, niñas y jóvenes al conflicto armado en Colombia.
—— 2003b *Bulletin Putchipu*, Number 7 – English, Bogota: Coalición contra la vinculación de niños, niñas y jóvenes al conflicto armado en Colombia.
Coalition to Stop the Use of Child Soldiers 2004 *Global Report.* London: Coalition to Stop the Use of Child Soldiers www.child-soldiers.org accessed 22/09/05.
Colombian Commission of Jurists 2003 *Human Rights and Humanitarian Law – Colombia.* http://www.icj.org/world_pays.php3?id_mot=20 accessed 15/08/07.
Cronen, V. and Lang, P. 1995 'Language and Action: Wittgenstein and Dewey in the Practice of Therapy and Consultation'. *Human Systems: the Journal of Systemic Consultation and Management* 5: 5–43.
Cyrulnik, B. 2001 *La Maravilla del Dolor. El Sentido de la Resiliencia.* Mexico City: Ediciones Granica.
Human Rights Watch 2003 *You'll Learn Not to Cry.* New York: Human Rights Watch http://hrw.org/reports/2003/colombia0903 accessed 22 September 2005.
International Crisis Group 2003 *Colombia: President Uribe's Democratic Security Policy* available at http://www.crisisgroup.org/library/documents/latin_america/06_colombia__uribe_dem__security.pdf accessed 15 August 2007.
Internal Displacement Monitoring Centre 2007 *Colombia: Resisting Displacement by Combatants and Developers: Humanitarian Zones in North-west Colombia.* Geneva: IDMC www.internal-displacement.org/8025708F004CE90B/(httpCountries)/CB6FF99A94F70AED802570A7004CEC41?opendocument&count=10000 accessed 12 January 2008.
Loughry, M. and Eyber, C. 2003 *Psychosocial Concepts in Humanitarian Work with Children. A Review of the Concepts and Related Literature.* National Research Council Program on Forced Migration and Health. Washington DC: The National Academies Press.
Martin, E. 1998 *Violencia Sociopolítica y Trabajo Psychosocial.* Bogotá, Colombia: Corporación AVRE.
Oliver, C. 1996 'Systemic Eloquence', *Human Systems: the Journal of Systemic Consultation and Management* 7: 247–64.
Shotter, J. 1993 *Conversational Realities.* London: Sage.
Shotter, J. and Gergen, K. 1994 'Social Construction: Knowledge, Self, Others and

Continuing the Conversation', in S.A. Deetz (ed), *Communication Yearbook 17.* Thousand Oaks, CA: Sage.

Summerfield, D. 2002 'Effects of War: Moral Knowledge, Revenge, Reconciliation, and Medicalised Concepts of "Recovery"', *British Medical Journal* 325: 1105–7.

United Nations 2005 *World Population Prospects.* Department of Economic and Social Affairs http://esa.un.org/unpp.

United Nations Development Programme 2003 l *Conflicto Callejón con Salida Informe Nacional de Desarrollo Humano.* Colombia, http://www.pnud.org.co/indh2003. accessed 15/08/07.

United Nations High Commissioner for Refugees 2003 *Evaluation of UNHCR's programme for internally displaced people in Colombia.* www.unhcr.ch/cgibin/texis/vtx/research/opendoc.pdf?tbl=RESEARCH&id=3ebf5fef4 accessed 22/09/05.

UNICEF n.d. *Columbia Country Information,* available at http://www.unicef.org/infobycountry/colombia_statistics.html accessed 22 September 2005.

UNICEF 2002 *Letters from the New Government.* Bogota: UNICEF.

US Central Bureau of Statistics 2007 http://www.census.gov/cgi-bin/ipc/idbagg retrieved 15 August 2007.

PART V

RESEARCHING WITH ADOLESCENTS

11

Participatory Research with War-affected Adolescents and Youth: Lessons Learnt from Fieldwork with Youth Gangs in Ayacucho, Peru

Cordula Strocka

Introduction

> We may not have higher education or a superior leadership, like Shining Path had. But we do have capacities, we do have greatness; yet maybe because of our economic situation we can't show it. Gang members can be more capable than even a university student. Sometimes the university student doesn't know what's happening in society; that is why here in Ayacucho sometimes they tell students to write their thesis about us, so that they get to know our society. And these students get surprised once they become familiar with us, once the gang members explain to them about the lives they live in society. What we tell them takes them completely by surprise, and some of them even want to live with us for a while (Martín,[1] member of the youth gang 'Los Sangrientos').

In this chapter, I shall discuss the challenges, pitfalls and possible benefits involved in doing participatory research with adolescents and youths in the context of armed conflict and political violence. I shall present some of the lessons learnt during long-term field research with youth gangs in Ayacucho, a region situated in the central-southern part of the Peruvian Andes. The research was carried out in Huamanga, the capital of Ayacucho, with the participation of about a hundred, predominantly male, members of six local youth gangs.

The assertive statement cited above is taken from an interview with Martín, a 24-year-old youth gang member who worked as my research assistant for about seven months. In this interview, which was conducted towards the end of my field research, Martín looks back at the joint research process and makes a personal evaluation of his experience as co-researcher and the implications of the research for his fellow gang members. I chose this quote because it exemplifies the complex and ambivalent nature of so-called participatory research.

On the one hand, a comparison of this interview with earlier ones shows that active involvement in the research process enhanced Martín's self-esteem. It helped him discover that he and other youth gang members possessed positive qualities and capacities, despite their low socio-economic status and the dominant negative stereotype of youth gangs in the wider society. On the other hand, Martín's narrative about the university students' surprise also provokes some critical reflections about who, in the end and in the long run, benefits from participatory research, the research participants or the researcher. These and related thoughts about the meaning and impact of young people's participation in research, particularly in the context of armed conflict, will be addressed in this chapter.

First, I shall give a brief overview of the history of the armed conflict in Ayacucho and summarise some general characteristics of youth gangs in Huamanga. This will be followed by an outline of the thematic and methodological approach of my field research. Then, I shall describe the difficult balancing act of gaining gang members' trust, which was the necessary precondition for adopting a participatory approach. I shall further critically analyse some implicit assumptions of the participation paradigm in research and development, by discussing some of the challenges and difficulties that arose in the course of my fieldwork. In particular, I shall explore the nature of power relations, both between the researcher and research participants and among the latter, and their impact on the research process. Moreover, I shall argue that course and outcomes of participatory research are strongly influenced by the setting in which the participatory activities are carried out, and by the particular choice of methods and tools. Examples from my fieldwork with the youth gangs will be presented to illustrate these points. Finally, I shall address the question whether, and in what sense, my research contributed to the empowerment of youth gang members in Huamanga.

Ayacucho in the Aftermath of the Peruvian Civil War

Between 1980 and 2000, Peru was engulfed in a savage civil war, during which approximately 69,000 Peruvians were killed and 600,000 displaced (CVR, 2003). The majority of the victims came from indigenous communities of the Andean and Amazonian regions (ibid.). The internal war was triggered by the violent insurgency of the Maoist guerrilla group Sendero Luminoso (Shining Path), and the subsequent military reprisals by the Peruvian armed forces. In the course of the prolonged armed conflict, other actors joined in, such as the Túpac Amaru Revolutionary Movement (MRTA), paramilitary groups and peasant self-defence committees.[2]

The department of Ayacucho, situated in the central-southern part of the Peruvian Andes, was the birthplace of Sendero Luminoso[3] and the epicentre of the civil war.[4] Historically one of the poorest and most marginalised regions of Peru, Ayacucho was most severely affected by the prolonged armed conflict. Since the arrest of the Shining Path top leaders in 1992, the number of guerrilla attacks has plummeted. However, a small faction of Shining Path militants remains active in remote jungle areas of Ayacucho, funding itself with money from the drug trade (Burt, 2005). According to the final report of the Peruvian Truth and Reconciliation Commission (CVR), more than 40 per cent of the victims reported to be killed or disappeared during the war were from Ayacucho (CVR, 2003), which also produced the largest number of internally displaced persons (PAR, 2002). Huamanga, the capital of Ayacucho, alone has accommodated 30 per cent of all Peru's displaced persons (UNHCR, 1995). While at the beginning of the conflict, Huamanga had 69,533 inhabitants (Huber, 2003: 16), by 2004 the population had more than doubled, reaching an estimated 144,735 (ODEI, 2004). Most of the rural migrants who have permanently settled down on the outskirts of Huamanga live in conditions of chronic poverty (ODEI, 2003: 204) and receive no, or only very limited, assistance from the state or international agencies.

Nearly two decades of internal armed conflict have also had a profound impact on the social fabric of Ayacuchan society (González Carré et al., 1994; Reynaga Farfán, 1996; Theidon, 2004). Behind the semblance of normality that characterises daily life in Huamanga, there still lurks a general atmosphere of fear, mistrust and cynicism. People no longer believe in the state's ability to guarantee law and order, and acts of violent mob justice are therefore on the increase. Towards the mid-1990s, the initial relief over the demise of Sendero gave way to feelings of fear and insecurity, as the inhabitants of Huamanga and other urban centres of the region saw themselves confronted with rising rates of common crime and violence. In particular, new youth groups appeared in different parts of Huamanga and began to engage in violent street battles and petty crime (PAR, 2001). In the following years, these so-called *pandillas juveniles* (youth gangs) or *manchas*[5] became a matter of growing concern, for their numbers were perceived to be increasing dramatically. While in 1996 nineteen *manchas* were reported to be operating in the city, by 1998 there were thirty-six and by 2001 the number was estimated to be eighty-three, with a total of approximately 3,000 members (PAR, 2001). Other studies assumed an even higher number of up to 5,000 youths involved in over one hundred *manchas* (Ortega Matute, 2001).

Youth Gangs in Huamanga

The emergence of *manchas* in Huamanga can be traced back to the late 1980s, when the activity of the Shining Path in the region was on the increase (PAR, 2001). The first *manchas* soon became a target of Sendero's attacks, which considered them as groups of antisocial youngsters who lacked political consciousness and revolutionary ideology. In 1989, the persecution of *mancheros* (youth gang members) reached its climax with the killing of nine youths in a suburb of Huamanga. This bloodshed acted as a deterrent, putting a halt to the further proliferation of youth gangs for approximately three years. With the gradual decline of the political violence in the region after the capture of the Shining Path leadership in 1992, new *manchas* emerged in different parts of the city. Since then, their number is said to be increasing (PAR, 2001; Prado, 2003). In recent years, youth gang activity has expanded to other provincial towns and rural areas of the department of Ayacucho. This has raised fear among the population, which has come to perceive youth gangs as the 'new insurgents', simply because a large proportion of Shining Path militants in Ayacucho had been youth.[6]

Consequently, Huamanga's youth gangs have attracted a lot of attention in national and international media. Since the decline of the armed conflict, youth violence has been one of the major preoccupations of the media in Ayacucho. The number of *manchas* and the violent crimes purportedly committed by young people are often highly exaggerated, not only in sensationalist articles and TV documentaries (see, for example, Klingenberger, 1999), but also in publications by respected academics (e.g. Piqueras, 2003) and the government (PAR, 2001). Among the people of Huamanga, there is a general consensus about the dramatic increase of youth gang activity and youth violence since the mid-1990s. However, reliable statistics that could corroborate this claim do not exist. Exploiting the general feeling of insecurity among the population, the Regional Government of Ayacucho and the Municipality of Huamanga have been implementing a range of suppressive measures aimed at cracking down on youth violence. Yet these measures have largely failed to restore not only law and order, but also people's confidence in political authorities.

According to my own field research, the current numbers of active youth gangs and criminal offences committed by young people in Huamanga are far smaller than generally assumed. In 2003–4, at the time I carried out my fieldwork in Huamanga, there were approximately thirty-five active youth gangs in the city.[7] The number of members per gang varied between twenty and 150. Roughly speaking, about 1,000 young people were part of a youth gang, that is, approximately 3.5 per cent of the fifteen- to twenty-four-year-olds and 0.7 per cent of the total population of Huamanga. Thus, only a small minority of youths in Huamanga participated in *manchas*. The age of gang members ranged from eight to thirty years, the majority being fifteen to twenty years old. The vast majority of youth gang members I met were male. Female members – usually the male members' girlfriends – were mostly only loosely attached to the group. At the time of my fieldwork, there seemed to be no all-female gangs.[8]

Most gang members lived in peripheral suburbs of Huamanga, but there were also a number of *manchas* in central areas of the city. Youth gangs' territories were usually confined to a specific neighbourhood but some of the older gangs operated in and recruited their members from different parts of the city. Huamanga's youth gangs differed considerably from each other in terms of age and gender composition, size, residence of the members, etc. Rivalries were strongest between *manchas* with adjacent territories and between the oldest and most prestigious gangs. In street fights, youth gang members mostly threw stones, or used knives and other stabbing weapons. Only very few possessed firearms. Most *manchas* engaged in pickpocketing, mugging and burglary, but only on an occasional basis. Youth gangs in Huamanga were not systematically involved in drug trafficking, but individual members occasionally worked in the production of coca and *pasta básica* (raw cocaine).

The majority of *mancha* youths were children of rural migrants and therefore spoke Quechua[9] and Spanish. Many families of gang members had migrated to Huamanga as a consequence of the internal armed conflict, which particularly affected the rural areas of the Ayacucho region. A considerable number of gang members' families, however, had settled down in the city before the conflict erupted. Most of Huamanga's current *mancheros* were infants or young children when the internal war reached its climax, and therefore did not actively take part in the conflict.[10]

There is a tendency in Ayacucho to present any current social problem as a product of the civil war. Youth gangs are no exception to this rule. At least during my stay in Ayacucho in 2003–4, local NGOs and governmental institutions tended to portray gang members as war orphans, who were traumatised and brutalised by their direct exposure to the internal armed conflict.

Research Themes and Methodological Approach

When I started my field research in Huamanga in September 2003, one of my major objectives was to investigate whether there really existed a causal link between political violence and youth violence, as it has been commonly assumed and taken for granted in public discourse. My aim was to critically examine the conventional assumption that youth gangs and youth violence in Ayacucho were direct consequences of the internal armed conflict. Furthermore, I wanted to analyse how the social categories 'youth gang' and 'youth gang member' were constructed, both in public discourse and by gang members themselves.

The bulk of research on the impact of political violence on adolescents and youth has focused on individual psychopathology, particularly post-traumatic stress disorder (PTSD). However, as critics of this dominant trend have pointed out (e.g. Bracken et al., 1995; Summerfield, 1995, 2000; Bracken and Petty, 1998; Barber et al., 2006), using PTSD or other measures of individual pathology as sole or predominant indicators of psychosocial functioning, fails to capture the breadth and complexity of human experience in the face of armed conflict (Barber et al., 2006).

A further aim of my research was therefore to explore young people's experiences of political violence and its aftermath more holistically. Rather than focusing exclusively on the negative impact of exposure to armed conflict on individual youths, I also wanted to look at young people's positive coping strategies and adaptive behaviour, at both the individual and the group level. In particular, I was interested in exploring the positive functions youth gangs fulfil for their members. In other words, rather than regarding the formation of youth gangs as a criminal or pathological phenomenon, I wanted to find out if, and in what way, it represented a positive coping strategy for young people. As a consequence, I was interested in young people's social networks, the group dynamics and hierarchies within youth gangs, as well as the relations between rival gangs.

Participant observation seemed to me the most appropriate method for finding out about intra- and inter-gang relations. While most ethnographic work on youth gangs focuses on one single gang, I decided to study a sample of several *manchas* from different parts of Huamanga and chose a number of different methods, both quantitative and qualitative, because this would allow me to cross-validate my findings and draw more general conclusions.

Over the course of my graduate studies in psychology, I had become increasingly critical of the traditional 'extractive' approach of social scientific investigation, which treats research participants as objects to be counted and measured in order to generate disciplinary expert knowledge. When I was planning my field research in Ayacucho, I therefore decided to abandon this traditional mode of enquiry and adopt a participatory approach instead.

The principle of participatory research is that people become agents rather than objects of research (Nelson and Wright, 1995b: 51). Participatory approaches aim at a partnership based on more equal power relations between the researcher and research participants, which allows the latter to contribute actively to the research process. In short, the purpose of participatory research is to increase participants' understanding of their situation and their ability to act upon that knowledge in order to create positive change for themselves. Over the past two decades, participatory approaches have grown so rapidly in popularity, particularly in the field of international development and aid, as to nearly become a 'new orthodoxy' (Henkel and Stirrat, 2001), or, in the view of critics, the 'new tyranny' (Cooke and Kothari, 2001).

Most influential in the development and dissemination of participatory approaches to development has been the work of Robert Chambers, the father of 'participatory rural appraisal' (PRA) (e.g. Chambers, 1992, 1994b,c). In the PRA tradition, a vast array of different participatory tools and techniques has been developed and implemented in research projects and development programmes. Initially, participatory research and programming only included adults. In recent years, however, participatory methods have increasingly been employed by social scientists and practitioners working with children and adolescents, in both developing and industrialised countries (Hart and UNICEF, 1992; Boyden and Ennew, 1997; Johnson, 1998; Alderson, 2000; de la Cruz et al., 2002; Hart, 2002; Lowicki, 2002).

There are, however, different levels and understandings of participation in research. Participatory approaches differ in their understanding of participation as a means as opposed to participation as an end. Most contemporary participatory research tends to use participation as a means to, for example, enhance the effectiveness of a project, or improve the validity of the data collected (Nelson and Wright, 1995a: 17). Yet there exist also more radical approaches, such as participatory action-research (Fals-Borda and Rahman, 1991; Fals-Borda, 1998), which regard participation as an end, that is, as a fundamental human right, whose protection and promotion should be the primary goal of social scientific research. What all participatory approaches, regardless of their ideological background, seem to have in common is that they claim to contribute, in some way and to some extent, to the 'empowerment' of their research participants.

'Empowerment' is a term often used but rarely defined (Rowlands, 1995). Like 'participation' and 'community', 'empowerment' has an implicit positive connotation (Nelson and Wright, 1995a), but there is little consensus as to what it actually means. Some of the disagreement arises because the root concept, 'power', is itself highly disputed. In fact, one's understanding of empowerment depends on one's interpretation of power, and there are profound differences in the ways power can be understood and experienced.

For the purpose of my research, I adopted the following interpretation of empowerment, which draws on the definition by McWirther (1991, quoted in Rowlands, 1995: 103): 'Empowerment is a process by which young people (a) become aware of the power dynamics at work in their life context, (b) develop the skills and capacity for gaining some reasonable control over their lives, (c) exercise this control without infringing upon the rights of others and (d) encourage and support the same process in other young people'. To sum up, my understanding of participatory research implied the expectation that the active involvement of youth gang members in the research process would be an empowering experience for them, in the sense of the above definition.

In the final part of the chapter, I shall self-critically analyse whether this expectation was met. Prior to that, however, I shall describe the challenges and difficulties that arose over the course of my field research in relation to the use of participatory techniques. The next section deals with the first, and perhaps most challenging, step of my research, namely the process of gaining gang members' trust.

Trust: the Fragile Basis of Participatory Research

Participatory research requires a certain degree of mutual trust between the researcher and the research participants. Thus, getting access to Huamanga's *manchas* and gaining their trust was the first and certainly one of the biggest challenges of my fieldwork. There were a couple of institutions and organisations in Huamanga that worked with 'at risk' youth, but none of them specifically targeted young people involved in *manchas*. My individual attempts to establish contact with youth gangs were largely unsuccessful until I was finally introduced to Daniel, a former *mancha* leader. He became my first research assistant and a key intermediary in the process of establishing rapport with the local *manchas*. As the ex-leader of one of the biggest and most famous youth gangs in the city, Daniel was still widely respected among the *manchas*, and not regarded as an enemy because he had retired from gang activities a couple of years ago. So, when he put me in touch with several gang leaders, most of them permitted me to visit them in their neighbourhoods and introduce myself to their groups. However, my first meetings with the *manchas* were quite subdued and sobering occasions. *Mancheros* were usually very reserved, if not openly hostile. They denied belonging to any gang and were very suspicious about who I 'really' was and what my 'real' motives might be. As I later found out, many gang members had previously had negative experiences not only with the police, but also with journalists, researchers and representatives of NGOs and public institutions. They had often been physically and psychologically maltreated by police and military personnel, deceived by researchers and utilised in sensational documentaries and political campaigns. In the face of these past experiences, it was not surprising that *mancheros* took me for just another journalist or foreign researcher who would make false promises to get information from them, and later let them down and disappear. Gang members' mistrust was further confirmed by the fact that I intended to work with several rival *manchas* at the same time.

In my effort to gain their trust and shake off their suspicion, adherence to two principles turned out to be absolutely crucial: transparency and confidentiality. From the beginning of my fieldwork, I was very frank with the gang members about the purpose of my research. I made sure not to make any promises to them I knew I would not be able to keep, and always promised to treat everything they told me as confidential. In particular, I was very careful not to pass any information I got from one *mancha* on to another. This would have been considered as a severe breach of confidence and would have definitely led to my exclusion from the gangs, as happened in the case of another researcher the year before.

Building rapport with the *manchas* turned out to be a very slow and unpredictable process with frequent ups and downs. I realised that trust was difficult to gain but very easy to lose. Although over time I developed a generally positive relationship with the core members of six different *manchas*, and made good friends with a number of them, these bonds were fragile, and minor incidents were sufficient to loosen or destroy them. For example, shortly after a camping expedition with members of four rival gangs, during which we jointly produced a short video about the camp activities, I travelled to Lima for a couple of days. On my return, I was received with open hostility by the *mancheros*. It turned out that, in my absence, rumours had spread that the purpose of my trip to the capital was to sell the video to a national TV channel. As Mats Utas (2004: 211) rightly points out, 'Researchers tend to see inclusion as a permanent state – once you are inside, it is forever – whilst in a turbulent field such as that of conflict or post-conflict the promise of inclusion is permanently threatened'.

Participation and Power: Reflections on a Complex Relationship

Fluid Power Relations

In participatory development discourse, a number of dichotomies or opposi-
tions, such as 'uppers and lowers', 'North and South' or 'indigenous versus expert knowledge' (see Chambers, 1995, 1997), have become popular slogans. These oppositions are associated with notions of the 'morally good' and the 'morally bad', and to reverse them has become the main objective of participatory approaches (Kothari, 2001: 140). Accordingly, the aim of participatory research to create an equal partnership between researcher and research participants is based on the assumption that there exists a dichotomy 'powerful researcher versus powerless research subjects', which needs to be dissolved by 'empowering' the powerless.

In the course of my field research I came to realise that this binary concept of power as a 'thing' that people either 'have' or 'do not have' was far too simplistic. I became aware of the fact that the power difference between me and my research participants was neither clear-cut nor stable. In fact, especially in the beginning of my fieldwork, the power relations were often reversed. It was the *manchas*, and especially their leaders, who had the power to grant or deny me access to their groups, and who determined the conditions under which the gang was willing to collaborate with the research. Moreover, the roles of researcher and researched were also frequently reversed. In situations where I aimed to take on the role of a participant observer or a neutral facilitator, I often became, instead, the target of the *mancheros'* observation, who also curiously enquired into my private life.

Throughout the research process and in interaction with the youth gang members, my role and the roles of my research participants were constantly redefined and renegotiated. The ways *mancha* youths presented themselves and interacted with me varied strikingly according to the way they perceived me as a representative of a certain social category, such as 'wealthy foreigner', 'researcher', 'woman' or 'youth'. For example, particularly in the beginning of my fieldwork, *mancheros* thought I was doing my research on behalf of an international NGO. In recent years, Ayacucho has been visited by an increasing number of international aid agencies with an interest in supporting the 'victims of the political violence'. This has raised high expectations among the locals, who, as a consequence, tend to emphasise their 'victim' status in the hope of material assistance. Accordingly, in my initial interactions with youth gang members, many of them portrayed themselves as helpless 'victims', emphasising in their narratives the multiple discriminations and maltreatments they suffered. The same *mancheros*, however, when under the influence of alcohol, presented themselves as strong, powerful and invincible, and treated me as the 'weak woman' who needed their protection.

My perceptions of the youth gangs equally changed over the course of my fieldwork. I had to revise my initial view of them as a homogeneous group. Not only did the six *manchas* I worked with differ considerably from each other, but so did the members within each of the groups, individual gang members also held multiple social roles and identities apart from their *mancha* membership. And these social identities entailed different degrees and ways of exercising power. In situations where their gang identity was salient, for example, at meetings with fellow *mancheros* or during confrontations with rival gangs, the young people usually presented themselves as powerful, 'tough' and independent. In other social contexts, however, for example, at home or at school, it was apparent that youth gang members were still considerably accountable to adult authority figures, such as parents and teachers. Most youth gang members still lived with their parents or relatives and depended on them economically, one reason why many youth concealed their gang membership from their family.

In general, being a 'youth' in Ayacucho, means belonging to an intermediate social category of young people who are no longer regarded as a children, but have not yet made the transition to fully adult status, which is generally achieved through gaining economic independence from the parents, starting a family and establishing a household. Although many of the *mancheros* I worked with had children, and some were married or lived with their partners, none of them had managed to establish a household because of the lack of a stable job and regular income. When I asked young people in Ayacucho about their motives for entering a *mancha*, the majority replied that they wanted to 'make themselves respected' in their neighbourhood. For these youths, joining a gang and taking control over a territory represented a strategy to enhance their social status and exercise some kind of power.

In sum, over the course of my research, I came to realise that youth gang members were embedded and participated in a complex and constantly changing network of power relations. In fact, the relationship between me and the gang members was much more intricate and fluid than the simple idea of a static power hierarchy (with the researcher on the top and the researched on the bottom), which then needed to be reversed through 'participation' and 'empowerment'.

Group Dynamics

The *manchas'* internal power relations also strongly influenced the course and the results of my participatory research. For instance, the authoritarian style of leadership exercised by gang leaders and senior gang members tended to impede the active participation of less powerful members in research activities. This was even more the case if members of different *manchas* took part in the same activity. At the beginning of group activities, I usually asked participants to jointly draw up rules of conduct, which should help guarantee mutual respect and equal opportunities for participation. However, *mancheros* perceived these rules as binding only as long as their leaders abided by them. 'Handing over the stick' to the participants often meant handing it over to the gang leader or the most senior gang members, who then frequently ended up dominating the discussion.

Furthermore, youth gang members tended to interpret my attempts to act as a facilitator rather than an instructor, that is, to let them choose the research themes and the ways they wanted to deal with them, as weakness and indecision. When I encouraged a group of *mancheros* to decide about what kind of research activity they wanted to carry out, my suggestion was often just ignored, and even those gang members who were generally very interested in participating in the research tended not to take any initiative, unless I adopted a more leading and authoritarian role. This was, however, incompatible with my idea of participatory research.

I therefore resorted to the strategy of assigning the *mancha* leaders the role of group facilitators. I explained to them that this role required a lot of responsibility and implied monitoring the group activity and making sure that everybody had the opportunity to participate and was listened to with respect. This strategy worked well with gang leaders with whom I had developed a close personal relationship and who were willing to collaborate with the research. In situations where the *mancha* leader was absent or uncooperative, however, it became much more difficult and sometimes impossible to initiate a process of participatory research.

In short, participatory research activities carried out with members of one or several different youth gangs tended to replicate the power hierarchies within and between the groups. Although, of course, these group dynamics were an interesting object of study in itself, they nevertheless biased participatory research outcomes by privileging some voices above others.

The Role of the Setting in Participatory Research

In the tradition of PRA (see Chambers, 1994a,b,c), research activities are usually carried out in central public spaces, such as the main square of a village or a community hall. These locations are regarded as most convenient because they are easily accessible and familiar to the research participants. It is implicitly assumed that the public space in which PRA exercises are carried out is neutral and has no considerable influence on the outcomes of these exercises.

Yet in the case of my research, the setting played a major role in determining the process and the results of participatory activities. First of all, public places in the youth gangs' neighbourhoods proved to be inappropriate for participatory research activities. The *manchas* usually met after sunset at street corners or in bars or discos. However, insufficient illumination, noise, alcohol consumption and the observation or interruption by people not involved in the research, made it impossible to carry out participatory activities in those places. Furthermore, attempts to gather gang members in the daytime failed, because some of them worked, and the rest shunned the daylight, fearing to be identified as *mancheros*, both by the neighbourhood and by the police.

I therefore adopted the strategy of taking the gang members out of their usual social context, by inviting them for hikes and camping expeditions to the countryside, usually at the weekend. The *mancha* youths greatly enjoyed these excursions, which provided excellent opportunities for participatory research activities. In the rural environment, gang members became much more open and relaxed. Moreover, the spatial distance from their neighbourhood helped them to critically reflect upon their situation. The *mancheros* realised, often to their own surprise, that they felt and behaved differently when outside their neighbourhood, and that they were able to enjoy themselves without alcohol, drugs and the thrill of violence. This insight often prompted very deep and self-critical conversations among the gang members. These discussions were very different from the informal conversations *mancheros* had when hanging out at their regular meeting places in the neighbourhood. The chats there tended to centre on clashes with the police and fights with rival gangs, which were generally perceived as an essential and inevitable ingredient of gang life. Outside the neighbourhood context, however, identification with a particular *mancha* was of less importance. Consequently, during the excursions to the countryside, gang members tended to categorise themselves more generally as migrant lower-class youth and focused in their conversations more on the characteristics they shared with rival *manchas* (i.e. similar ethnic background and socio-economic conditions) than on the conflicts that divided them. Thus, as these examples show, the choice of a rural setting had not only facilitated the process of my participatory research but also clearly influenced the nature of the findings.

Participatory Methods: Limits and Potentials

Within the different strands of participatory research, a variety of different research instruments and methods have been developed. The majority of these methods, particularly those used in PRA, consist of the communal construction of visual representations of reality, for example in the form of maps, diagrams, matrices, timelines and calendars. These techniques of visual representation are supposed to be universally applicable and to generally facilitate 'participation' and 'empowerment' of local people. However, by setting the frame of what kinds of visualisations are acceptable, participatory approaches actually shape and confine the way in which research participants may have chosen to represent themselves and their reality. There is the risk of making people's lives and their social interactions linear and sterile as they fit into charts, diagrams and tables (Kothari, 2001: 147, 149). Moreover, participatory methods often heavily rely on linguistic representation of knowledge, thereby neglecting the fact that most knowledge is tacit and generated in practice (Mohan, 2001: 161). Thus, by using supposedly neutral visual techniques, participatory approaches may, in fact, encourage a particular Western way of seeing, understanding and representing the world (Henkel and Stirrat, 2001: 182).

During my research in Huamanga, I was frequently confronted with these limits of participatory methodology. For example, most *mancheros* refused to take part in research activities that involved writing and drawing such as mapping exercises or timelines because they said it reminded them of school. The vast majority of youth gang members I worked with had dropped out or been excluded from school because of truancy or antisocial behaviour, and, consequently, perceived themselves as inferior to their peers who had successfully finished their studies. The very act of writing or drawing maps and tables in a group setting therefore evoked negative memories of school failure in many of my research participants. Moreover, the structured nature of these kinds of written exercises also influenced the power relations between me and the *mancheros*, making them become much more hierarchical. Whenever I introduced a pen-and-paper exercise, the gang members immediately started treating me as a teacher and regarded the activity as a 'lesson' I was giving to them, and this considerably impeded their active participation.

I therefore increasingly came to use methods that were less structured and reliant on literacy or analytical reasoning, but allowed for alternative forms of expression. For instance, I conducted a number of focus group discussions and group interviews, in which the participants interviewed each other, making use of a tape recorder with a microphone – a method the majority of them enjoyed a lot.[11] Dynamic exercises that involved body movement and physical skills were also very popular among my research participants. I therefore adapted some of the mapping exercises in a way that the gang members could visualise ranking orders and relations through lining up and using their bodies as part of the visual representation, instead of drawing or writing it on a piece of paper. The youth gangs' favourite participatory techniques, however, were socio-drama and role play. The young people turned out to be born actors and created complex and realistic stories about their daily life without needing further help and instructions. Their performances not only provided me with qualitative data but also prompted a participatory process of reflection and debate among the youth gang members themselves. In order to foster this process, I therefore increasingly focused on the adaptation of dramatic techniques as research methods, drawing on elements of psychodrama therapy (Moreno, 1977; Holmes et al., 1994) and Augusto Boal's *Theatre of the Oppressed* (1979). These techniques proved to be very useful tools for participatory research, since they encouraged *mancheros* not only to critically reflect upon their situation and behaviour, but also to try out alternatives and jointly search for ways to improve their living conditions.

Participation and Empowerment

Overall, through the participatory tools and techniques I used over the course of my field research, I gathered rich qualitative data on various aspects of *mancha* life in Ayacucho, despite the described limitations and difficulties. Thus, from a perspective that regards participation primarily as a means to collect valid data, my research had been successful. However, as explained earlier, my understanding of participation is linked to the concept of empowerment. Accordingly, truly participatory research not only implies actively involving participants in research activities, but also promoting their participation in decision-making processes outside the research context.

In this section, I shall evaluate the impact of my field research on the participating *mancha* youths. In particular, I shall examine if, and how, active involvement in the research process was empowering for the young people.

Admittedly, participation in the research had negative side effects for some *mancheros*. Ayacucho is a relatively small town, and therefore local authorities, institutions and the media soon got wind of my research on the city's *manchas*. My activities with the youth gang members were being monitored suspiciously, and rumours spread that I was a supporter of the guerrillas, trying to indoctrinate and mobilise young criminals under the disguise of participatory research. Fortunately, I was never hindered in my work, nor did any of the participating *mancheros* get arrested or beaten up by the police for taking part in the research. However, the fear that this might happen was tangible among many of the youths I worked with, and this often hindered their active participation in the research. Furthermore, copies of taped interviews, photos and videos of the research activities, which I had given to the research participants, were not always treated by them confidentially, but shown and lent to friends and neighbours. Consequently, parents who had been ignorant of the gang membership of their children got alarmed, and in some cases reacted by severely punishing their offspring. There was also the case of a headmaster who forbade one of his pupils from taking part in a school excursion when he heard about the alleged existence of a videotape showing the boy being interviewed by other young people about his *mancha* membership.

Yet participation in the research process also triggered a number of unforeseen positive developments among the *mancheros*. Those who regularly took part in the research activities increasingly engaged in critical reflections upon their lives and developed strategies to improve their situation. For example, one of the participating *manchas*, in an attempt to counter the dominant negative stereotype of youth gangs, produced a written history of their group, based on interviews they conducted with each other. Furthermore, towards the end of the research process, four of the six participating *manchas* took part in a joint camping expedition. This camp was a unique experience for the gang members, since it brought members of rival gangs together under non-violent and cooperative conditions. The joint venture resulted in a significant reduction of negative attitudes, emotions and overt conflict between the rival gang members (Strocka, 2008). As a consequence of the camp experience, two of the participating *manchas* begun transforming themselves into non-violent youth organisations, and started carrying out activities for the benefit of children and youths in their neighbourhood. For instance, one *mancha* constituted itself as a formal youth organisation and changed its name from 'The Bloodthirsty Ones' to 'Association of Youth in Solidarity'. With the collaboration of local authorities and organisations, the association set up a small youth centre, where meetings and workshops for young people from the neighbourhood were held.

Another *mancha* that had participated in the camp started a similar process of redefining their gang identity. They set themselves the goal of forming a registered football team and improving the football pitch in their neighbourhood. As a first step, they organised a cleaning-up operation in order to clear their quarter of rubbish and scree. Neighbours and authorities were invited, and a number of them joined in the clean-up. They were positively surprised to see the youth gang members cleaning up the streets. Even the mayor of the district turned up and lent a helping hand.

My two research assistants Daniel and Martín were the driving force behind these activities. For both of them, as I observed over the course of several months, active involvement in the research process was an empowering experience in the sense that they acquired a critical consciousness of their situation in society and acted upon that situation analysis in order to create positive change for themselves and their peers. As ex-*mancha* leaders, Daniel and Martín possessed excellent leadership skills and managed to mobilise and motivate a large group of their fellow *mancheros* to take part in the research activities. As a consequence, however, the progress and success of the activities depended almost entirely upon the initiative of the two leaders. As soon as Daniel and Martín dropped out of the process – one found a job and the other was erroneously accused of murder and imprisoned for several months – the newly formed youth organisations disintegrated.

This was also partly due to lack of support by the neighbourhood and local authorities and institutions. Their reaction to the research project and the resulting youth-led activities was a mixture of surprise, suspicion and rejection. Apparently, the fact that youth gang members reorganised themselves as a formal youth association and organised activities for the benefit of their neighbourhood clashed both with the dominant image of *mancheros* as criminals and prevailing beliefs about 'legitimate' forms of youth participation. The widespread fear of youth gangs and a general suspicion about youth organisations in Ayacucho are, at least partly, a consequence of the mass recruitment of youths by Sendero Luminoso. The majority of Shining Path militants in Ayacucho were young people and, consequently, organised youth in general became increasingly associated with violent insurgency. This was particularly the case during the dictatorial government of Alberto Fujimori, who treated any kind of informal youth organisation as a suspected terrorist group. Although under the Toledo government there has been a certain revival of youth organisations as a result of campaigns to promote civic participation, participation of young people in Ayacucho remains largely restricted to adult-led activities within schools, churches, sports clubs and the populist party APRA (American Popular Revolutionary Alliance). Youth activities outside these institutional boundaries and initiated by young people themselves tend to be regarded as 'subversive'.

In sum, at least among some of the participating *mancheros*, active involvement in the research prompted developments that can be interpreted as first steps of an empowerment process. Yet these promising developments were not sustainable for at least two major reasons. First of all, most of the participating gang members did not fully identify with the research activities, but rather followed the charismatic leadership of Daniel and Martín. Once those two leaders dropped out of the project, the bulk of gang members also lost interest. And, secondly, the activities that were initiated by *mancheros* as a result of their joint reflection during the research process lacked the necessary social and material support by the wider society, because they conflicted with dominant understandings of youth participation.

Conclusions

In this chapter, I have discussed some of the challenges, limitations and possible benefits of participatory research, drawing on my research experience with Peruvian *manchas*. Traditionally, research on children and adolescents affected by armed conflict and forced migration has portrayed them as vulnerable and passive victims. In recent years, however, participatory approaches have called for the recognition of young people's agency and their active participation in research. However, participatory approaches tend to be based on a simplistic concept of power and neglect the implication of power relations for the production and representation of knowledge. A paradox of participatory research is that it recognises and at the same time denies young people's agency. Participatory approaches construct children as active 'agents' of research. But, at the same time, they tend to define their research participants as 'powerless' and therefore in need of being 'empowered' through processes of participation, initiated by 'powerful' experts. In order to resolve this paradox, researchers and development practitioners need to be more aware of the complex and fluid nature of power relations, not only between the researcher and the research participants, but also within the group of the latter.

My field research with Huamanga's *manchas* also made me aware of the limitations of participatory methodology. In fact, no research method is automatically participatory. What makes it participatory is the way it is used. Participatory research with children and adolescents is often misunderstood as simply making young people engage in activities that, the *researcher* believes, are 'fun' and appropriate to their age and developmental stage. In many so-called 'participatory' studies, girls and boys are not given the chance to choose among different methods those they find most appropriate, nor are they allowed to give their own interpretation of the visual products of research activities, such as drawings or maps. Moreover, even if research participants are given the choice between several methods, the nature of the methods itself may pose limits on meaningful participation. Maps, matrices, tables, timelines and all the other different techniques applied in participatory research are not neutral tools that can be used everywhere and with any group of participants. Researchers need to be aware that so-called participatory techniques may be as much 'Western' as traditional research methods, and therefore need to be adapted to the specific sociocultural context in which they are intended to be used. Research, in order to be truly participatory, needs to allow research participants, be they children, adolescents or adults, 'to generate their own categories, concepts, and criteria for understanding and changing their lives' (Mohan, 2001: 181). It needs also to be taken into account that research outcomes are not only shaped by the methods used, but also by the particular setting in which participatory activities are carried out.

Furthermore, participatory research is not automatically 'more ethical' than traditional scientific enquiry. In fact, due to the public nature of participatory research activities, ethical issues, such as confidentiality, need to be considered carefully, especially when the research involves young people and is conducted in the context of armed conflict (see Boyden and Ennew, 1997; Boyden and de Berry, 2004). War-affected adolescents and youths are exposed to particular risks because of their intermediate position in society: they are no longer regarded as 'innocent', 'vulnerable' children, but not yet recognised as 'mature' and 'responsible' adults. Adolescents are more likely than younger children to be recruited into military service and to attend school in far fewer numbers, and they are particularly vulnerable to economic exploitation and sexual abuse (Lowicki, 2000: 4–5). In situations of armed conflict, adolescents frequently have to assume adult responsibilities, and yet their strengths and capacities as constructive contributors to their societies go largely unrecognised. Moreover, because young people are often actively involved in the armed conflict, they tend to be seen by the wider society as a 'lost generation' of brutalised, unscrupulous youth.

Participatory research with adolescents and youth affected by armed conflict and forced migration must take into account local understandings of participation and the specific position of adolescents and youth in their respective societies. Research that deals with young people in isolation from their social environment and promotes a Western view of participation that conflicts with local understandings of youth participation will not be 'empowering', but rather will weaken the position of young people and create, or increase, tensions between the adult and adolescent generations. Researchers who wish to contribute to the empowerment of young people need to adopt the role of a learner rather than that of an expert or initiator of change. Truly participatory research is a mutual learning process, in which both researcher and participants change as a result of their joint experience. As Martín puts it: 'Working with us is like becoming a youth gang member yourself. It's putting yourself in our shoes'.

However, perhaps the biggest challenge of participatory research with young people in situations of armed conflict and post-conflict is to ensure that their active involvement in the research process does not put them at risk, and that, in the long run, both researcher and participants benefit from the knowledge and experience gained.

Notes

1. All names of individuals are pseudonyms.
2. According to the final report of the Truth and Reconciliation Commission (CVR), Sendero Luminoso is responsible for 54 per cent of the recorded casualties, the MRTA for 1.5 per cent. The responsibility for all other casualties lies with the government armed forces and – proportionally less – with paramilitary groups and peasant self-defence committees (CVR, 2003).
3. Sendero Luminoso was created in Ayacucho in 1968 as a radical Maoist faction of the Peruvian Communist Party. Its founder and principal ideologue was the philosophy professor Abimael Guzmán Reinoso, known by his followers as Presidente Gonzalo. Shining Path proclaimed a 'people's war' (*guerra popular*), which was aimed at the complete destruction of the Peruvian state (Starn, 1995), considered to be necessary for the building of a new classless society.
4. For an overview of the history of the conflict, see, for example, Poole and Rénique (1992), Stern (1998) or Gorriti (1999).
5. The terms *pandilla* (youth gang) and *pandillero* (youth gang member) have strongly negative connotations. Gang members in Huamanga therefore generally prefer calling themselves *mancheros* and refer to their group as *mancha*, which means 'group' or crowd'. I have adopted their usage of terms.
6. Shining Path leader Abimael Guzmán, a professor at the University of Huamanga, initially recruited the cadres among university students.
7. This estimate is based on a mapping of youth gang territories, carried out in the course of my fieldwork.
8. According to the reports of ex-*mancheros*, in 1999/2000 a number of all-female youth gangs emerged, which soon built up a reputation as being as violent as the male gangs. However, the all-female *manchas* quickly disintegrated as a consequence of repressive measures and their leaders falling pregnant.

9. Quechua, the ancient language of the Incas, is even today the most widely spoken indigenous language in the Andean highlands.
10. I do not know of any youth gang members who were Shining Path militants. A small number of the older *mancheros*, however, had joined the armed forces and taken part in fights against remaining splinter groups of the Shining Path in the subtropical area of Ayacucho.
11. See Hecht (1998) for the use of this method with street children in Brazil.

References

Alderson, P. 2000 'Children as Researchers. The Effect of Participation Rights on Research Methodology', in P.M. Christensen and A. James (eds) *Research with Children: Perspectives and Practices.* London: Falmer, pp. 241–57.

Barber, B.K., Schluterman, J.M. and Denny, E.S. 2006 'Adolescents and Political Violence', in M. Fitzduff and C.E. Stout (eds) *The Psychology of Resolving Global Conflicts: from War to Peace*, Vol. 2. Westport, CN: Praeger, pp. 171–90.

Boal, A. 1979 *Theatre of the Oppressed.* London: Pluto.

Boyden, J. and de Berry, J. 2004 *Children and Youth on the Front Line: Ethnography, Armed Conflict and Displacement.* Studies in Forced Migration. Oxford: Berghahn.

Boyden, J. and Ennew, J. 1997 *Children in Focus: a Manual for Participatory Research with Children.* Stockholm: Rädda Barnen.

Bracken, P.J. and Petty, C. (eds) 1998 *Rethinking the Trauma of War.* London: Free Association.

Bracken, P.J., Giller, J.E. and Summerfield, D.E. 1995 'Psychological Responses to War and Atrocity: the Limitations of Current Concepts', *Social Science and Medicine* 40: 1073–82.

Burt, J.-M. 2005 'Plotting Fear: The Uses of Terror in Peru', *NACLA Report on the Americas* 38 (6): 32–36.

Chambers, R. 1992 Rural Appraisal: Rapid, Relaxed and Participatory. Discussion paper 311. Brighton: Institute of Development Studies, University of Sussex.

—— 1994a 'The Origins and Practice of Participatory Rural Appraisal', *World Development* 22: 953–69.

—— 1994b 'Participatory Rural Appraisal (PRA): Analysis and Experience', *World Development* 22: 1253–68.

—— 1994c 'Participatory Rural Appraisal (PRA): Challenges, Potentials and Paradigm', *World Development* 22: 1437–54.

—— 1995 'Paradigm Shifts and the Practice of Participatory Research and Development', in N. Nelson and S. Wright (eds) *Power and Participatory Development: Theory and Practice.* London: Intermediate Technology Publications, pp. 30–42.

—— 1997 *Whose Reality Counts? Putting the First Last.* London: ITDG.

Cooke, B. and Kothari, U. 2001 *Participation: the New Tyranny?* London: Zed Books.

CVR 2003 *Informe Final.* Lima: Comisión de la Verdad y Reconciliación (CVR).

de la Cruz, M.T., Protacio-de Castro, E., Balanon, F.G., Yacat, J.A. and Francisco, C.T. 2002 *Small Steps, Great Strides: Doing Participatory Action Research with Children.* [Quezon City, Philippines]: Psychosocial Trauma and Human Rights Program UP

Center for Integrative and Development Studies, Arci Cultura e Sviluppo (ARCS), UNICEF.

Fals-Borda, O. 1998 *People's Participation: Challenges Ahead.* New York, London: Apex Press, Intermediate Technology Publications.

Fals-Borda, O. and Rahman, M.A. 1991 *Action and Knowledge: Breaking the Monopoly with Participatory Action Research.* New York, London: Apex, Intermediate Technology Publications.

González Carré, E., Reynaga Farfán, G., Valverde Baltazar, V., Rivera Cea, P., Gónzalez Carrasco, N. and Alarcón Guerrero, M. 1994 *Wakchaschay. Los huérfanos pajarillos: Situación social, económica y cultural de los menores refugiados en la ciudad de Ayacucho después de 1980.* Lima: Chirapaq.

Gorriti, G. 1999 *The Shining Path: a History of the Millenarian War in Peru.* Chapel Hill and London: University of North Carolina Press.

Hart, J. 2002 'Children's Clubs: New Ways of Working with Conflict-displaced Children in Sri Lanka', *Forced Migration Review* 15: 36–39.

Hart, R.A. and UNICEF 1992 *Children's Participation: from Tokenism to Citizenship.* Innocenti Essays, no. 4. Florence: UNICEF International Child Development Centre.

Hecht, T. 1998 *At Home in the Street: Street Children of Northeast Brazil.* Cambridge: Cambridge University Press.

Henkel, H. and Stirrat, R.L. 2001 'Participation as Spiritual Duty; Empowerment as Secular Subjection', in B. Cooke and U. Kothari (eds) *Participation: the New Tyranny?* London: Zed Books, pp. 168–84.

Holmes, P., Karp, M. and Watson, M. 1994 *Psychodrama since Moreno: Innovations in Theory and Practice.* London: Routledge.

Huber, L. 2003 *Ayacucho: centralismo y descentralización.* Lima: Instituto de Estudios Peruanos.

Johnson, V. 1998 *Stepping Forward: Children and Young People's Participation in the Development Process.* London: Intermediate Technology.

Klingenberger, V. 1999 'Pandillaje andino. Revelador documental sobre la nueva oleada juvenil en Ayacucho', Caretas. Ilustración Peruana. http://www.caretas.com.pe/1999/1563/pandillas/pandillas.htm.

Kothari, U. 2001 'Power, Knowledge and Social Control in Participatory Development', in B. Cooke and U. Kothari (eds) *Participation: the New Tyranny?* London: Zed Books, pp. 139–52.

Lowicki, J. 2000 *Untapped Potential: Adolescents Affected by Armed Conflict. A Review of Programs and Policies.* New York: Women's Commission for Refugee Women and Children.

—— 2002 'Beyond Consultation: in Support of more Meaningful Adolescent Participation', *Forced Migration Review* 15: 33–35.

Mohan, G. 2001 'Beyond Participation: Strategies for Deeper Empowerment', in B. Cooke and U. Kothari (eds) *Participation: the New Tyranny?* London: Zed Books, pp. 153–67.

Moreno, J.L. 1977 *Psychodrama*, Vol. 1, 2nd edn. New York: Beacon House.

Nelson, N. and Wright, S. 1995a 'Introduction: Participation and Power', in N. Nelson and S. Wright (eds) *Power and Participatory Development: Theory and Practice.* London: ITDG Publishing, pp. 1–18.

—— 1995b *Power and Participatory Development: Theory and Practice.* London: Intermediate Technology Publications.

ODEI. 2003 *Almanaque Estadístico de Ayacucho 2003.* Ayacucho: Instituto Nacional de Estadística e Informática (INEI), Oficina Departamental de Estadística e Informática Ayacucho (ODEI).

—— 2004 *Ayacucho: Compendio Estadístico 2003.* Ayacucho: Oficina Departamental de Estadística e Informática Ayacucho (ODEI), Instituto Nacional de Estadística e Informática (INEI).

Ortega Matute, J.M. 2001 'Pandillas juveniles en la ciudad de Ayacucho'. Unpublished thesis, Universidad Nacional San Cristóbal de Huamanga, Ayacucho, Peru.

PAR 2001 *Pandillas Juveniles en Huamanga.* Lima: Ministerio de Promoción de la Mujer y del Desarrollo Humano (PROMUDEH).

—— 2002 *Censo por la Paz. Comunidades campesinas y nativas afectadas por la violencia política 1980–2000.* Lima: Ministerio de la Mujer y Desarrollo Social (MIMDES).

Piqueras, M. 2003 *Solidaridad frente a homicidio. Ensayos sobre la violencia militante en el siglo veintiuno.* Lima: Instituto de Defensa Legal (IDL).

Poole, D. and Rénique, G. 1992 *Peru: Time of Fear.* London: Latin American Bureau.

Prado, G. 2003 'Ayacucho: pandillas juveniles en el escenario de la posguerra', *Ideele* 156: 72–77.

Reynaga Farfán, G. 1996 *Cambios en las relaciones familiares campesinas a partir de la violencia política y el nuevo rol de la mujer.* Lima: Instituto de Estudios Peruanos (IEP).

Rowlands, J. 1995 'Empowerment Examined', *Development in Practice* 5: 101–7.

Starn, O. 1995 'Maoism in the Andes: the Communist Party of Peru-Shining Path and the Refusal of History', *Journal of Latin American Studies* 27: 399–421.

Stern, S.J. (ed) 1998 *Shining and Other Paths: War and Society in Peru, 1980–1995. Latin America Otherwise.* Durham and London: Duke University Press.

Strocka, C. 2008 'Piloting Experimental Methods in Youth-gang Research: a Camping Expedition with Rival Gangs in Ayacucho, Peru', in G. Jones and D. Rogers (eds) *Youth Violence in Latin America: Gangs and Juvenile Justice in Perspective.* London: Palgrave Macmillan.

Summerfield, D.E. 1995 'Addressing Human Response to War and Atrocity. Major Challenges in Research and Practices and the Limitations of Western Psychiatric Models', in R.J. Kleber, C.R. Figley and B.P.R. Gersons (eds) *Beyond Trauma: Cultural and Societal Dynamics.* New York: Plenum Press, pp. 17–29.

—— 2000 'Childhood, War, Refugeedom and "Trauma": three Core Questions for Mental Health Professionals', *Transcultural Psychology* 37: 417–33.

Theidon, K. 2004 *Entre prójimos. El conflicto armado interno y la política de la reconciliación en el Perú.* Lima: Instituto de Estudios Peruanos (IEP).

UNHCR 1995 *Core Document Forming Part of the Reports of States Parties: Peru.* Geneva: United Nations Commission on Human Rights HRI/CORE/1/Add.43/Rev.1.

Utas, M. 2004 'Fluid Research Fields: Studying Excombatant Youth in the Aftermath of the Liberian Civil War', in J. Boyden and J. de Berry (eds) *Children and Youth on the Frontline: Ethnography, Armed Conflict and Displacement.* London: Berghahn Books, pp. 209–36.

12

The Place to Be? Making Media
with Young Refugees

Liesbeth de Block

There are two dominant discourses running through discussions about young refugees in the U.K. The first situates them as unwelcome residents. They are portrayed in the media as potentially criminal, on the edge of society, as excluded and excludable, needing to be socialised and required to cut their ties with their places of origin and become fully British. The priority is to educate them into the British way of life and values. The second discourse situates them as for ever only partially resident. They are victims of circumstance, troubled by past experiences and unchangingly belonging to that place of disruption and trauma. Work in schools with young refugees often focuses on the past, the country and culture of origin, and tends to treat the young person almost as a representative of a particular refugee experience and of the place from which they have travelled. It is a way of encouraging other children to empathise and to understand but can also become a process of 'exoticising' and distancing.

Both discourses rely on notions of nationhood, culture, belonging and identity that prefer to ignore or devalue transnational connections and interdependencies. With technological advances, media (as one of the cultural resources that young refugees draw upon) form an increasingly important part of most children's and young people's lives and are also changing the experience of migration and settlement. Satellite television, email and MSN,[1] the Internet, digital, still and moving-image cameras and mobile phones have opened up new worlds of communication locally and globally. This has offered opportunities for young people to keep in contact with friends and family but also ways in which they can participate more directly and independently in the wider public sphere. Media use, talk, production and communication are important areas of activity, independent of adults, through which many young people negotiate identity, friendships, family life and world events (Livingstone, 1998; Buckingham, 2000). For young refugees this is significant both for building social relations in new countries of residence and for maintaining some continuity with their places and cultures of origin (de Block, 2002). It can be an important resource for sharing and examining their experiences and rebuilding social connections.

The consideration of the relationship between children's uses of media, the developments of new media and the role that media play in the experience of migration raised several interesting questions for me. How might child-focused research help to inform a more complex, less static or essentialist understanding of refugee children? How might a focus on media be a useful way to undertake such research? As well as focusing on their consumption and uses of media, what might be particularly valuable about enabling refugee children to engage in media production? I began to explore these questions in two research projects.

First, in a small-scale research project based in a primary school in London I examined the ways in which a small group of refugee children (between the ages of eight and eleven) and their friends and families used talk about television (local and global) to facilitate building new social relationships as well as maintaining contact with their places of origin and diasporic family connections. This TV talk took both verbal and non-verbal forms. It crossed genres, language and generation. It was integrated into and inspired playground games. It became the basis of banter and repartee between the children, finding outlets ranging from small gestures and single words and phrases to long-running role plays. It was part of dinner-time conversations and central to family relations. For the children in the study, television and TV talk became a shared space in which inter-cultural communication was possible, especially when there was little else that they shared. As part of this research I began to make videos with the children, mainly as an additional research tool, allowing greater entry into their lives and thinking. But it also became a way in which the children themselves began to share some of their experiences with each other. This led me to thinking about using new media communications to facilitate a greater sharing of experience.

The second project arising from this was funded by the European Commission (Framework 5: Improving the Human Research Potential and Socio-economic Knowledge Base). Children in Communication about Migration (CHICAM) moved from researching uses of media to exploring how media production and exchange might allow refugee and migrant children to represent and to share their experiences of migration. A significant new element in CHICAM was the use of the Internet to facilitate a greater sharing of the young people's productions, both between the young people involved in the project aged between ten and fourteen and (eventually) among a wider audience. This reflected our awareness that many of these children were increasingly active users of global communications through family email connections, satellite television, chat rooms and so on (CHICAM, 2002, 2004a). The more overtly political objective was to explore how the content and processes of such communication could inform policy initiatives in the areas of migration and childhood, by making children's voices heard in the wider public arena. Indeed, three of the specific research themes were closely connected to relevant social policy areas: friendship and peer relations, school/work and family. The fourth theme was concerned with the media themselves. How do children use the 'languages' of digital media, both to create their own audio-visual 'statements' and to communicate with each other and with adults across cultural boundaries? This theme was particularly important considering the number of different languages represented in the project – both the European languages of the partnership but also the languages of origin for the children (which together amounted to more than twenty).

The practical media work was based in six 'clubs', one each in Germany, Italy, Greece, the U.K., the Netherlands and Sweden. These were mostly after-school clubs based in schools and community centres (in Greece, for example, the club met in the offices of the Council for Refugees) and all met weekly. The children attending the clubs were recently arrived refugees or migrants between the ages of ten and fourteen years. In some cases the children already knew each other, while in others it was the first time they had met. They came from a wide range of countries. The club in the U.K., for example, comprised children from Angola, Kenya, Somalia, Sierra Leone/Guinea, Sri Lanka, Pakistan, Lithuania, Russia and Colombia. The children therefore all had very different experiences of migration and motivations for migrating (Brah, 1996).

Each club was organised by a researcher and a media educator, although in several cases a community worker or teacher who knew many of the children outside the club also participated. The clubs used exclusively digital technology for filming, editing and disseminating material. Although there were some still images, most of the material produced was in the form of short videotapes, often only a couple of minutes in length. The projects were linked through a project website (www.chicam.net), which was designed on three levels. A public site held the project details and finished research papers, as well as compilations of the media productions from the clubs, organised on thematic lines. A second level, entered by password, was for the children in the clubs to view the productions from the clubs and to post and exchange comments about them. There was also a general bulletin board for topics not directly related to the media work. A third level was for the researchers, and provided a space to discuss research concerns and ideas as they arose and to enter brief weekly notes on the fieldwork.

So, while the first project focused on the children's uses of television in the style of a more orthodox audience research project, CHICAM was designed to concentrate on (digital) media production processes and Internet exchange. This reflected a desire to increase the level of participation and to explore how these adolescents could use digital media production to make their lives visible to other children and adults both locally and internationally. In this way we aimed not only to improve their active participation in the research but also to explore ways in which their visual representations could be used to influence and inform policy in the areas of research themes. The discussion in this chapter draws on the experience of both these projects.

Television as a Shared Space

We do not need to be in the same room at the same time watching the same television set to be able to enjoy particular programmes with our friends. Talking about it afterwards, or 'TV talk', still allows us to share our pleasures and criticisms and to relate screen events to our lived everyday experiences. This becomes part of the currency of our social relations. TV talk takes many forms: recalling, retelling and arguing about particular storylines, re-enacting a funny scene, discussing a news item, sharing the gestures or intonation of a favourite character, singing the theme tune of a popular soap or sitcom (Buckingham, 1993, 1996). TV talk requires that you watch the same programmes, even if at different times and in different places, and that there is a shared repertoire of references to draw on, thus creating a shared space for social interaction. Through global television, migrant and refugee children will have encountered many of the same programmes as their peers even if these were heard in different languages and viewed in different countries. They will also have media experiences that are particular to their circumstances and origin. These will include national, transnational and global broadcasts. Depending on where they have come from, they will have encountered programmes catering for particular migrant niche markets. Turkish youth in Western Europe, for example, have a range of programming that targets them specifically (Milikowski, 2000). Others will have to rely on programming at one remove from their origins. Refugees from the Democratic Republic of the Congo or from Somalia, for example, tend to tune into French or Italian satellite channels as the closest they can achieve to their places of origin. This breadth of media experience and the possibility to pick and mix in this way allows the creation of different 'shared spaces', which often mirror the different aspects of their transnational lives and facilitate the development of multiple identities and allegiances (Morley and

Robins, 1995; Morley, 2000). Below I set out a few examples of the ways in which young people use television to form continuities in disrupted lives, facilitate playground friendships, challenge family norms in relation to countries of origin and reception and assist in language and cultural maintenance. Television can become the focus of inter-cultural discussions and allow children to explore and sometimes come to terms with their own personal circumstances through identification with particular programmes and media characters.

Children arriving in the U.K. from many different parts of the world are generally familiar with certain U.S.-originating global products. They might have watched The Simpsons in several different countries. For one child (ten) I have worked with, it became an important point of continuity in his journeys from Somalia to Kenya to the U.K. It was an instant point of contact with the children he was trying to play with in his new primary school. Another boy from Kosovo (eleven) was included in a game because he was able to act Homer Simpson to perfection, despite the fact that he spoke hardly any English. In a similar way, satellite television allows children and adults to maintain links both with the programmes they used to watch before migration and with their languages and countries/regions of origin. A Kosovan family in Sweden loved to watch an Albanian soap opera they had known before they left Kosovo and that now raised important issues about inter-generational and gender relationships (CHICAM, 2004a). One point of recurring discussion both in the programme and within this family was how much freedom outside the home young women should be allowed. The programme was dealing with changing norms in Albania, and was then fuelling discussion for the family in relation to what was allowed in Sweden. Studies among Turkish youth in Europe watching Turkish television relate similar findings (Aksoy and Robins, 2000; Milikowski, 2000).

Other global media products are also important. Hindi films/videos, for example, also form an important part of family life and cultural continuity (Banaji, 2004). However, these are not restricted to Hindi-speakers. Bengali-, Urdu- and Somali-speaking families are all ardent viewers, although generally in my research it appeared to be the girls who were more dedicated viewers, while the boys appeared more reluctant. Participation was seen as a family duty and, although the boys did often enjoy the films, they were keen to state that they would rather be out with their friends and that the films were really made for women rather than men. It appeared to be a question of claiming an adult male stance and distancing themselves from the demands of the home and from their childhood pleasures. Some girls saw the watching of these films as a statement of cultural identity (Gillespie, 1995). Not only had watching these films been part of family life before migration but the films themselves, they claimed, felt culturally closer to, and more acceptable than, the Hollywood blockbusters they might enjoy and talk about with their other friends. Their Hindi film viewing was not so openly part of the young people's social talk and was kept more private for fear that this would be considered less acceptable by children from other cultures.

For many families, watching the news is a family or community ritual. Several of the Turkish/Kurdish families I have worked with would gather to watch Turkish news items, especially at times of crisis, such as the Turkish earthquakes or the capture of Abdullah Ocalan, the Kurdish political leader in 1999. Many of the children were very knowledgeable about the news, and international issues formed an important part of the school dinner-time interaction. As part of my fieldwork I often spent time in the dinner hall, sometimes sitting with the children and at others simply observing. There were often quite heated arguments about past as well as current international events that affected the countries the children came from. For example, topics covered included the 1990 Gulf war, the then current Kosovo war and conflicts in Somalia and Ethiopia. The general view appeared to be that national news broadcasts did not offer enough international news, and CNN and Al Jazeera were often mentioned as preferred options.

Both the television broadcasts and the discussion mediated their experiences. For example, during one dinner-time conversation at the time of the Kosovan war there was an exchange about the bombing that had started the previous day. A recently arrived Kosovan boy (eleven) was struggling to speak about his fear that his grandfather's house had been bombed and he was blaming the Russians and the Yugoslavs. Another child from Ethiopia (eleven) joined in and started talking about Russian connections with the conflict between Eritrea and Ethiopia, which at that time was threatening to erupt again. The Kosovan boy was clearly surprised that others in the school might have had or be experiencing similar fears to his. He was subsequently more able and willing to discuss his situation and his fears with me and, he said, with other children. The exchange appeared to allow him to see his situation in a different context and to feel slightly less isolated. Interestingly, these discussions were very rarely part of their formal education in the school classrooms.

At the same time, many of the children had mixed feelings about watching the news. On one hand, it was understood to be an important activity in their homes. Furthermore, the acquisition of knowledge and the consequent ability to participate in discussions were appropriate to their particular experience of other places and important to their claims on social maturity. On the other hand, some found it boring while others would refuse to engage in conversations about world events and would often prefer not to identify themselves as 'foreign' or 'refugee' in that way.

Individual children use television in more personal ways that can also relate to their status as refugees or asylum seekers and to their experiences of conflict and upheaval. One Ethiopian boy (ten) stated that he watched *Fresh*

Prince of Belair and *The Simpsons* because they taught him about family life. He was living alone with his father (whom he likened to Homer Simpson) and had no connections with his extended family back in Addis Ababa. They had been appealing their failed asylum application for several years and had been rehoused three times, and the father was suffering from depression. The boy said that these programmes offered him a view of family life that he himself did not have while also offering solutions to some problems he was experiencing in the home. He also stated that he had made himself an expert on television because he realised that it would make him popular with his peers. The most telling aspect of his television life, however, was the fact that he deflected any enquiry by others into his circumstances and family by playing the television expert and joker. He used TV talk to avoid questions and to create the private space that he felt necessary in order to cope with his situation.

Representing themselves and their lives through TV talk was thus an important part of these young refugees' process of adaptation and settlement and of maintaining continuity. Other research (Thorne, 1993) has confirmed the role that media talk plays in young people's identity negotiations as they move into adulthood, demonstrating the importance of understanding the specificities as well as the commonalities of these processes. However, there is also undoubtedly a danger of taking too celebratory an approach and I would like to add three notes of caution. While television and other media activities can form the shared spaces outlined above, they can also become excluding spaces. As I have already hinted, some more Western programmes tend to be readily 'acceptable' and dominant and there is a fear that admitting a love of different culturally 'marked' choices will set you apart as 'other' and thus risk social exclusion. Particularly at this age, this is a risk many are not prepared to run in public. Aspects of children's lives and cultures therefore become hidden unless there are opportunities created for more diverse forms of exchange and greater understanding of a range of media expression and enjoyment. Secondly, some languages, cultures and countries are simply not represented in the global mediascapes (Appadurai, 1996) that exist at present since they do not have their own media industries. And, finally, some young refugees, through economic factors, will not have as much access to the media hardware required as many of their peers. In both research projects there were families who could not afford to replace a television set once broken, who did not have computers and the Internet at home and whose access to cable or satellite television was intermittent depending on their economic circumstances. So while young people can use television to assist in negotiating social inclusion and facilitating active self-representations and the maintenance of multiple connections, media can also mitigate against cultural diversity and social exchange.

Moving on to Media Productions

In my discussions with refugee children, it is very clear that many are extremely knowledgeable about how programmes are made and that this also forms part of their TV talk. Viewers of Hindi films, for example, are often very conscious of the conventions of the genre, of how shots are set up and how illusions can be created (Banaji, 2004). For young people this applies especially to animations, one of the preferred genres for this age group. They watched programmes about the making of *The Simpsons* and *South Park*, amongst others. However, few of these children had had the opportunity to put their knowledge into practice. With digital technologies making it easy for children to make their own media productions, I began to explore ways of incorporating this into the research process. My initial set of questions revolved around how the children would draw on the varied but often culturally specific media and narrative forms in order to build a visual narrative. Would they only select those images and stories that were part of mainstream Western television or would they (and in what ways would they) pick and mix in their productions as they did in their talk? Would they relate some experiences such as those in the past in markedly different styles from those in the present? How would learning to edit affect how they created stories? How would they conceptualise the audience of their work?

These questions relate essentially to how their media production practices might reflect and/or grow from the ways in which they 'consume' media. Connected to this is the question of whether and in what ways the processes of making media (as well as the finished products) can form part of the research process itself. The assumption here is that the ways in which children make media are related to how they use media and that this would add new insights into their lives and new dimensions to the research process. Would making their own media representations offer the children a greater participatory role in the research and in what way would it alter the balance of power between researcher and researched? Would making media allow sufficient distance for them to be able to talk about difficult experiences (past and present) that in an interview situation would be too painful? Would using media offer the research another layer both in the gathering and analysis of data and in future discussions and dissemination?

As part of the data collection in the first study (de Block, 2002), I decided to experiment and to involve the children in making videos about their lives. The children filmed in their local area, at home and at school, and made cutout animations of their journeys to the U.K. This participatory use of media is increasingly popular in research with children, particularly within media and cultural studies (Gauntlett, 1996; Bloustein, 1998; Goldman-Segal, 1998). This approach offered a different means of accessing the children's experiences and studying their relationships both in and out of school. It took the focus off myself as researcher and allowed me to observe them through their own observations. What they chose to film and the talk that took place during the production process both confirmed and put under question some of my other data, creating a new set of enquiries. The videos formed an important part of my discussions with their families and facilitated the sharing of information I would not otherwise have gathered. Preparing the animations allowed the children to share information with each other (and with me) about their countries of origin, their families and the journeys they had made. It raised questions for them about how and what they represented about their lives and what they wished to share or keep private.

After the videos were completed I showed them (with permission) to other children in the school as a way of discussing different children's experiences of migration and/or getting to understand the experiences of their peers. Although each child's experience is particular, there were important ways in which these children could relate to and talk about each other's stories. Having these stories visually depicted allowed personal stories to be presented at a distance and allowed the viewer to discuss them sometimes more easily in relation to their own experiences. For the producers of the videos, the process of narration was an important way of making contact beyond their immediate group, of building shared histories among themselves and actively negotiating identities and a sense of belonging. For the research, this activity acted as an invaluable form of triangulation, enabling me to re-examine other data and ask new questions. The finished videos have also been an important platform through which the children's voices have continued to be heard directly when I have discussed the project with wider audiences.

This initial exploration also raised new questions, this time more in relation to research and how to analyse and interpret these visual data, how and when to maintain anonymity and how to present visual research data when the dominant accepted mode in research is still, despite technological advances, the written form. Finally, and related to all these, for research addressing policy issues, is the audience able and willing to include such presentations in their deliberations, especially when these representations might disrupt their established perceptions and existing policy and practice discourses? The second project sought to address some of these questions and to explore further the role of media productions by refugee children in research.

The CHICAM project produced more than fifty videos, which are on the website. They cover a wide range of topics and genres. Below I shall discuss two groups of videos that highlight the different roles that video production can play in young refugees' processes of settlement and inclusion. The first I have labelled 'Self-representation'. The second I have headed 'Communication through Youth Culture'. What became very clear early on in the project was that the ways in which 'audience' was or was not conceived or visualised by the young people were central to the ways in which they approached their video productions. In the two sections below I explore the implication of this. In the first project, described above, the audience was always seen as local and immediate: family, friends or in some cases the internal school community. In the CHICAM project the assumption of a wider audience was integral. This had important implications for the media production work and for the research process.

Self-representation

The first group of videos are all concerned directly with the experience of forced migration. On the whole they were group productions, and spoke more to the immediate club situation than to a wider audience. They often involved a lot of preparatory group discussion and negotiation that all yielded rich data for the research themes. The completed videos also provided a focus for further interviews and group discussions within the club as well as responses from other clubs through the intranet. These were often initiated and led by the researchers and media educators.

Several of the early videos made in the U.K. and the Dutch clubs were based on family photos and pictures of favourite objects. These ranged from a toy doll brought from Russia (via Israel) to the U.K., to a treasured family photo of a Somali girl's father who was no longer alive. The images were of past people, objects and places that carried with them emotions of loss and parting but that also formed an important continuity in their lives. The pictures were assembled and a voice-over was made in the format of an interview with another group member. The process of group production provoked much talk about family and memory. In one case a photo of a family home in Pakistan that was still lived in by the extended family prompted another member of the group to reflect on the fact that her family had had to move so often she felt she had no home. This led to a more general group discussion about the meaning of home. The children who made these videos were very pleased with the results but they regarded them more as personal essays for themselves and their families. They wanted to take copies of the videos home but did not see the point of putting them on the project intranet.

Another production, this time from the Greek club, was prompted by a documentary about war several of the club had seen on television. In this case the children quite spontaneously began to make a video on this theme. The end result is by no means a 'finished' production. It contains a slightly confusing mix of brief accounts spoken to camera of their experiences, drawings and discussions of professional photos of war. Again the processes of group discussion and production were more valuable than the final product or showing to a wider audience.

Drawings were often important means of talking about the past. In the U.K. club several members drew schools that they had attended and then filmed the drawings, focusing in on different parts of their drawings as they spoke. In this way they were able to reflect on their experiences of school and comment on their present schools, an important part of one of the research themes (CHICAM, 2004b). In the Netherlands two of the children (ten) had shared the experience of living in a reception centre. They did drawings of the units they had lived in and talked with the researcher and each other about their time there. Their emotions were mixed. They looked back at that time with a mixture of nostalgia and horror. They had made good friends there and had felt part of a community. On the other hand, they vividly related stories of traumatic events at the centre, a death and a deportation. They maintained that this shared experience was the basis for their very close friendship. However, in the final production that was placed on the intranet the drawings are shown with a very bare spoken account that does not include the emotional memories (www.chicam.net). These were reserved for the private talk within the group.

These productions were directly about the painful experiences of being a young refugee. The work in the clubs allowed such experiences to be shared with others and the use of visuals often facilitated the expressions of emotion that would otherwise have been difficult to share. However, towards the end of the year in which the clubs ran, more unusual productions started to appear in which the young people became playful and humorous in their visual images and narratives. This was partly because they were more familiar and confident with the technology but this does not entirely account for the shift. In Greece two boys filmed themselves play-acting Saddam Hussein and Osama Bin Laden, jostling and shoving each other with guns and playing 'mad' people to the camera. Another video plays with the idea of magic and transformation, reversing the flow of water and the movement of the actor.

Some of the researchers involved in the project were anxious that these productions were moving away from telling 'refugee' stories in the mode that fitted with the discourses set out at the beginning of this chapter. There was a tendency to expect the videos only to address issues of displacement, pain and loss. This was partly because there was a pressure to produce videos that would directly address the research themes in ways that would be easily acceptable within the policy discourses of the EU, and these videos were harder to categorise – were they made by refugees or were they examples of more general adolescent play? How could they be used as part of the research process and how did they address policy? But there was also another element to this that was harder to address. There was within the project, and among the researchers, that same tendency to exoticise, to over-empathise with the pain of the refugee experience and to dwell on it, not allowing the children to be both refugees and playful, successful adolescents – to be able to inhabit more than one identity. In short these videos moved away from the adult expectations of what a refugee child should produce – what in many respects the researchers, media educators in the project and the project design itself had anticipated would be the outcome of producing media with refugee children.

The broader question raised by these new productions was how we should interpret them and how they related to our other data. As well as observing the making of each video through all its stages, we discussed the work with the children before, during and post-production. In approaching these videos it became much more important to have a well-rounded picture of their lives, interests, media experiences and family and migration stories as well as their present lives. In this way we were able to analyse each video not so much as an expression of 'refugeedom' but as a depiction of that young person's life, passions, humour and particular experience of migration. By taking an ethnographic approach to the research we were able to particularise the experiences of migration (Brah, 1996) while also trying to seek commonalities and crossovers in the data. Images that had appeared to be unrelated to migration and being a refugee then became significant in relation to their everyday real lives rather than the stereotypes.

For example, a video entitled 'Magic' that at first we had seen simply as a fun exercise in developing editing skills could then be understood differently. The producer's favourite television programme when he was in Sierra Leone was a French magic show. In explaining what was important about it he talked at length about how he always used to watch this show and how he missed it now. He also said it was important because in making the video he had been working with his class tutor and he felt he had built a better relationship with him as a result and this would help him in school, where he was having trouble fitting in.

In another production a Lithuanian girl (thirteen) had filmed a series of apparently random objects and drawings intercut with shots of coloured surfaces. It was a very 'art house'-style production that was quite puzzling in the context of the research. In discussion with her and by referring to previous observations and interviews with her and her mother it was possible to gain a feeling for its significance. The objects were all connected in some way to memories of her grandparents and the family's separation from home. The coloured surfaces were in reaction to the feeling she had that everything in this country was grey. By putting these two elements together the video became a powerful and creative depiction of her emotional response to her situation.

They are both, in very different ways, playful pieces that incorporate past experiences into their present interests and concerns. The videos could be enjoyed and read at different levels depending on the audience. But for us, as researchers, the videos needed to be analysed as part of a wider set of data. Bringing each video together with interviews, long-term observations and other visual representations made in the clubs allowed us to cross-reference, to interpret and to allow different sets of data to inform and be elucidated by others. Individual videos often formed the basis of project discussions during which different interpretive routes such as discourse analysis or semiotics would be brought to bear. Above all, by spending a long time (over a year) with the children the researchers were able to draw on in-depth knowledge of the child, family and social context.

Although offering the children new ways of representing their experiences and also processing them, the first videos discussed above were not made for a wider audience. They are easily accessible, and they tell powerful stories. Yet they are also expected stories in the sense that they are clearly about being displaced. The experiences they depict are not generally applicable to adolescents but only to displaced adolescents. As videos that the project might want to show to a policy audience they act as useful illustration, confirming well-known narratives, perceptions and understandings and they support other data and research findings. Yet the young people maintained that these videos were private and they were often reluctant for them to be seen by a wide audience. The later, more playful, videos that the children were often keen to show their friends outside the club are harder to categorise as being made by refugees. In fact, in many cases, they appear to have nothing to do with being a refugee and more about making local connections through humour and play, about being adolescent. Indeed, that is just the point. The producers of these videos were not concerned with telling the story of their pasts, with portraying their troubles and difficulties, but rather with exploring the current resources at their disposal in order to make local connections through humour and play. They were interested in being young people, not in being refugees, or maybe more pertinently they were not subscribing to being refugees in the ways in which they are conceived in current discourses in public debate. In several of the interviews across the clubs this was the view they also expressed quite directly. This then brought into question one of the underlying assumptions of the project: that these young people would be interested in communicating with refugees in the other media clubs and in sharing their experiences of being refugees through their video productions.

Communicating through Youth Cultures

The early exchanges between the clubs took the form of a series of 'hello' videos introducing each club and its location. These were not designed to be personal stories but to let the other clubs know that they were there and a little bit about themselves. However, they were contacting strangers and many of them were quite nervous about how to present themselves. They focused – often in a rather formal way – on where they came from, using a map, rather than giving any details about their present environment. There was a tendency to detail the stereotypes of their locations. In the U.K. club they insisted on a red letter box (which was fairly hard to find) and a red double-decker bus. In Rome the video was located by the Coliseum (a significance lost on the other clubs).

Initial reactions to these productions were mixed. The children noticed details about each other: age differences, who was good-looking, who they thought they might like to be friends with. For some clubs, the videos did present important challenges to stereotypes. The Swedish club remarked on the dark skin of one of the U.K. girls. In Italy, the children thought that the German film came from Morocco because some of the girls were wearing the *hijab* (headscarf) – although in the U.K., this only raised suspicion about whether the video was indeed from Germany at all. The Dutch club asked where the mountains and snow were in the Swedish film (it was filmed in a seaside town in the south of the country). Comments about locations were also important. The children compared the fabric of their respective school buildings, the Swedish and U.K. schools comparing favourably with the Greek and Italian.

There was then some rather polite exchange of questions and answers between the clubs, checking ages, who had done what in making the films, and so on. A level of competition also began to emerge here – about which production looked more professional, which had used the best music, which children were better-looking. At least in the U.K. club, the children appeared to be judging the other children in order to assess whether they were 'cool' enough to consider at all. Members of several clubs were clearly impressed by the style and looks of particular children. Interestingly, the children in clubs in more 'stylish' countries such as Italy were deemed more 'attractive', fulfilling another form of national stereotyping. How these stereotypes had developed for the young people was a question we unfortunately did not pursue. What was clear from these exchanges was that the focus was on who they were now, and where they were living now, not where they had come from or what constituted their pasts (de Block and Sefton Green, 2004).

These 'hello' videos also reflected the ways in which the clubs had been set up. The work was influenced by the school setting and was treated in many ways as an extension to school. Their parents and guardians had mostly given permission for them to participate on the basis that it would support their learning. The project research themes were educational and worthy and by that point we had spent a lot of time in the clubs teaching technical skills and engaging in group-building activities. The clubs themselves were organised by adults and the young people had little sense of ownership.

The Italian production used a track by Eminem that marked it out from the rest. It was recognised by most of the other children and the video became an instant hit, with the children joining in the soundtrack and moving with the rhythm. This video also assisted in the opinion that the Italian club members were somehow more worthy of attention. Hip hop and rap are predominantly forms that carry an anti-establishment message. There was surprise that it could be included in one of the club videos. The music served as a powerful symbol of an international youth culture and rebellion that the club members almost universally responded to. It appeared to give them permission to experiment and to draw on different aspects of their interests and cultural references.

David, a boy of Angolan origin who had come to the U.K. as an unaccompanied minor composed a rap entitled 'The Place to Be'. In the group discussion about school he had been in opposition to the others in voicing his support for the school and blaming the students for bad behaviour. This was not the voice he generally used. He was often highly critical of things that happened and in fact was in a lot of trouble himself. When I suggested he do a rap about school he was keen and directed and edited the piece himself with only a little help. David's hero was the US rapper Tupac Shakur,[2] he wrote poetry at home and saw himself as an aspiring rapper.

The production is interesting in several ways. It uses a popular form (the rap) that still has a high youth status to send a message that challenges the perceived anti-establishment norms of youth culture. At the time there was a trend for young U.K. black artists (such as Ms Dynamite) to move against the gun culture and misogynist messages of mainstream U.S. rappers. He is tapping into this. His message is that school and getting an education is important, that you need to be strong and independent and resist gangs and drugs – the text of his rap is below. He said that he needed to look forward to his future and not back to his past and he resisted talking about the past at all. He wanted to disassociate himself from Angola and said he needed to adjust and belong to the U.K., to get an education and do well. His aspirations are strongly those of the migrant trying to make a better life, seeing education as the route to such a life. Yet in his experience of life in the U.K. and at his school this was hard to achieve. The video can be read in different ways. When I spoke to him about the video after it was completed he said that its message was aimed at all young people. He also stated clearly that he was a Londoner and did not want to be thinking about where he came from but rather to look to his future. The video is very clear. The words represent his personal demand that his aspirations be recognised. His command of the form demands that he be accepted as an integral part of global youth culture and as a Londoner, since he saw London as a centre of that culture. The words speak of the difficulties that young people face in his area of East

London on a daily basis. He also represents himself as an integral part of black London youth. What he is stating is relevant beyond his refugee status but it also speaks of it. He is part of both realities – being a refugee and a young black London youth.

THE PLACE TO BE
School fantastic the teachers are cool
I am a teen but don't take me as a fool
My mission is to study hard, be brave
Never fall apart
And dress smart
I came here to learn
Always look at where I'm gonna turn
Listen to the teacher if u wanna have a future
Try not to be an abuser
Cos if you're not qualified u a loser
Try to keep your head up
Never give up
Cos in the future u gonna pay your own bill
Starting tomorrow realise that school is for real
Cos if u turn into a gang dealing
Look at the pain u might feel
School school the place to be school
Be a man
I am tryin to help u my friend
We all go through hard times
So let me hold your hand
I won't say this again

Everyone in the club was really impressed and several of his friends came in to see it. He had been particularly pleased by his ability to play with the images in the edit. Soon after completing the video he decided to leave the club. The style of his message demonstrates that he is adjusting and taking on the forms and cultures of his new place of residence. The way in which he has mixed the form with his beliefs and experience makes this a powerful narrative of migration.

The video also generated several positive responses from the other clubs; 'Your video is more than beautiful, because it's still rap and I like rap very much' (from the Italian club). Boys in the Dutch and Swedish clubs quickly went on to make their own rap videos in response. Mohammed, an Albanian boy in the Swedish club, begins his rap with a pastiche of the American star 50 Cent, but then moves on, satirically employing the researcher's car as a 'limo', and concluding with an improvisation displaying influences from both Arabic and Albanian culture, thus adapting and transforming the genre. New media technologies assisted this production in two ways: first to film it and place it on the intranet but in addition Mohamed used his friend's mobile phone to provide the music for the last section of the rap.

However, while David was pleased with the flattering responses, he was quite offended by the other clubs' attempts at being cool and enthusiastic, and refused to reply to most of them. In effect, the other clubs had failed the test. They had latched onto the form but ignored the message of his video, which was actually about the importance of schooling – rather than the more subversive intention that seemed to have been read into it by some members of his audience (both the adults and the youth). When David did reply to the Dutch rap, he was careful to retain his expert status, and to make the most of the subcultural capital he had demonstrated: he gave them faint praise ('5 marks out of 10'), complaining that the rap was too fast and the movements were wrong. His friend also chimed in with criticisms of the rap, and, as a level of competition entered the exchange, communication effectively ceased.

But not all the contact focused on this more obvious 'Western' global culture. One of the boys in the Greek club was a very accomplished musician accustomed to singing to raise money for the political party he and his family were affiliated to. '*Tragoudi*' was produced by Elcin, a Turkish Kurdish boy, and is a rendering of a Turkish poem in Greek. The poem is by Nazim Hikmet, a poet who has been adopted by the Kurdish liberation movement in Turkey. Elcin plays a traditional musical instrument, the *saz*, and sings, while Rengin speaks the poem. The performance was filmed by Elcin. He set the camera up and then performed for the audience getting up at the end to come to the camera and switch it off. The show he has created draws on his ability to incorporate past and present references, languages and forms. The film met with a very positive response, particularly by children from Turkish and Turkish/Kurdish backgrounds; '*mehaba sesgin ve boran nasilsiniz sesiniz cok begendim ikinizdeharika soyluyorsunu ben de kurdum ama sizing dilinizi anlamiyorum ikinizide cok tatli buldum hayatinizda basarilar dilerim kendinize iyi bakin harkese selam optum gulegule. Ben meral*.[3] Even though the poem itself was sung in Greek, the video created a shared platform for these children to communicate in their common language, Turkish, and take some control of the communication. Although the children could not understand the language, the direct emotional appeal of the voice and of the music was clearly very significant.

Both 'The Place to Be' and '*Tragoudi*' quite specifically address an audience that will be familiar with their chosen genre since they are both active fans of the genres they employ in these videos. They anticipate their audiences in a way not possible with the first group of videos. They therefore know who they are addressing and can utilise the form to express aspects of their own lives and beliefs. Until quite recently, it has been rare for young people's media productions, whether they derive from schools or from more informal settings, to find a wider audience (Harvey et al., 2002). In this case the club intranet made this possible and this had an important impact on the process of production itself. The participants made the videos both for themselves and their friends and for other members of the clubs. This was an audience of peers. In addition, the work in the clubs gave them an opportunity to represent different aspects of their lives in a way that they had not had the opportunity to do before. They were able to move away from being school pupils and were encouraged to be active producers of their own media productions through all the stages of idea, planning, production and edit. As a result, it seemed to me, they were enabled to demonstrate their agency. They wanted to represent their capabilities to their peer audience and not be seen as victims. While most participants were able to talk about their pasts and some were very aware of the ways in which their experiences were different from those of many of their peers, they did not see themselves as victims or as caught in their difficult pasts but as active, creative individuals focused on their present living contexts and their futures, and this is what they wanted others to see. Having an audience to show this to made a difference.

Conclusion

I began this chapter by setting up two rather stereotypical perceptions of young refugees that fuel public debate in the U.K. and elsewhere. Underlying both is the question of whether refugees really ever want to 'belong' and be accepted as active participants in our society. I raised questions about the role of media consumption in young refugees' lives and pointed to the ways in which they use particular television programmes to negotiate their new lives and in building peer, family and community relationships and continuities. Particular programmes, channels and genres all play different roles in their lives, often crossing national and regional cultural boundaries.

I went on to ask what insights refugee children's media productions could offer both as a means of young people representing themselves and their experiences to a wider audience and also as a research tool. The work of the research projects demonstrated that media production can be a powerful means of developing personal representations of migration, offering children the opportunity to draw on their very different cultural resources and to share their experiences. There was a clear connection between their media consumption and their own productions. Yet while the genres were familiar they were able to adapt them to incorporate different popular forms. They played with shared youth cultures and references in powerful expressions of belonging or desired belonging rather than disconnection. Many of the productions I have described challenge stereotypes. They are not portraying images of victims but rather of competent adolescents able to draw on their pasts and yet focused more on present processes of settlement and the struggle for social inclusion.

The question then is who is the audience for these productions? The audience provided by the project intranet was very limited. The young people were addressing a particular selection of their peers, and the knowledge that what they shared were both the multiple experiences of being a refugee and the experience of trying to be included could well have influenced the productions. They were not addressing peers who might have a very different experience, or adults who might be unfamiliar with the cultures they were drawing on, or indeed others from their own original place and culture of origin, and we do not know how this might have influenced their representations or what significance this might have. All this still needs to be explored in future research.

There is also an issue as to how to use these representations as more than illustration. For research purposes the video production process was a tool to gather data. The final products form one aspect of an overall package and were interpreted in combination with other data and not on their own. The videos are used to support written documents (as here) and do not stand as independent statements, although some certainly could if policy and academic audience were more prepared and receptive. As societies become increasingly visually oriented, there is a greater need to address these anomalies. The experiences discussed here point again to the need to explore further how visual representations can be central both to the research and also to its dissemination.

The work of these research projects points to the fact that use of digital media can allow young people to develop and express their experiences and opinions on issues that directly affect their lives and that there is potential for this to be a useful way of addressing policy concerns. During the making of the videos, the children discussed many issues in relation to their experiences of schooling, living in their neighbourhoods and making friends, which have formed part of the policy recommendations arising from the CHICAM project. Both the children and their teachers said that they had grown in confidence through the project. Some of the children would have liked the work to continue and to become part of the mainstream activity of the school and not a separate activity for refugees alone, and this has formed part of the recommendations for both schools and community work. Yet it is important to remember that, while the young people were aware of the project audience and did participate in the exchanges, it was mainly the production process that they enjoyed. They were primarily interested in exploring their own lives and friendships within their new home environments and this should be the starting point for future projects.

Notes

1. Microsoft Network
2. Tupac Shakur was an important black American rapper. He was shot in 1996 but there is a myth that he is in fact still alive. There are lots of websites dedicated to him and his work and CDs are still being produced.
3. 'Hallo Elcin and Boran. How are you? I liked your voices a lot. You both sing very well. I am Kurdish too but I don't understand your language. I think you're both really cute. Wish you a lot of success in life. Take care. Love to everyone. Kisses. Bye. I am Meral'.

References

Aksoy, A. and Robins, K. 2000 'Thinking Across Spaces: Transnational Television from Turkey', *European Journal of Cultural Studies* 3 (3): 343–65.

Appadurai, A. 1996 *Modernity at Large: Cultural Dimensions of Globalization.* Minneapolis: University of Minnesota Press.

Banaji, S. 2004 'A Qualitative Analysis of Young Hindi Film Viewers' Readings of Gender, Sexuality and Politics On- and Off-screen'. Unpublished Ph.D. dissertation, University of London: Institute of Education.

Bloustein, G. 1998 '"It's Different to a Mirror 'cos it Talks to You": Teenage Girls, Video Cameras and Identity', in S. Howard (ed) *Wired-Up: Young People and the Electronic Media.* London: UCL Press.

de Block, L. 2002 'Television as a Shared Space in the Intercultural Lives of Primary Aged Children'. Ph.D. thesis, Institute of Education, University of London.

de Block, L. and Sefton Green, J. 2004 'Refugee Children in a Virtual World: Intercultural Online Communication and Community', in A. Brown and N. Davis (eds) *World Yearbook of Education Digital Technology, Communities and Education.* London: Routledge.

Brah, A. 1996 *Cartographies of Diaspora: Contesting Identities.* London: Routledge.

Buckingham, D. 1993 *Children Talking Television: The Making of Television Literacy.* London: Falmer Press.

—— 1996 *Moving Images: Understanding Children's Emotional Responses to Television.* Manchester: Manchester University Press.

—— 2000 *After the Death of Childhood: Growing Up in the Age of Electronic Media.* Cambridge: Polity Press.

CHICAM 2002 *Global Kids, Global Media: A Review of Research Relating to Children, Media and Migration in Europe.* Report to the European Commission, www.chicam.net.

—— 2004a *Visions across Cultures: Migrant Children using Visual Images to Communicate.* Report to the European Commission, www.chicam.net.

—— 2004b *School as an Arena for Education, Integration and Socialization.* Report to the European Commission, www.chicam.net.

Gauntlett, D. 1996 *Video Critical: Children, the Environment and Media Power.* Luton: John Libbey.

Gillespie, M. 1995 *Television, Ethnicity and Cultural Change.* London: Routledge.

Goldman-Segal, R. 1998 *Points of Viewing Children's Thinking: a Digital Ethnographer's Journey.* Mahwah, NJ: Lawrence Erlbaum Associates.

Harvey, I., Skinner, M. and Parker, D. 2002 *Being Seen, Being Heard. Young People and Moving Image Production in Informal Education: Findings from the 'Camera Action' Survey.* London: BFI.

Livingstone, S. 1998 *Making Sense of Television: the Psychology of Audience Interpretation*, 2nd edn. London: Routledge.

Milikowski, M. 2000 'Exploring a Model of De-ethnicization: the Case of Turkish Television in the Netherlands', *European Journal of Communication* 15 (4): 443–68.

Morley, D. 2000 *Home Territories: Media, Mobility and Identity.* London and New York: Routledge.

Morley, D. and Robins, K. 1995 *Spaces of Identity: Global Media, Electronic Landscapes and Cultural Boundaries.* London and New York: Routledge.

Thorne, B. 1993 *Gender Play: Girls and Boys in School.* Buckingham: Open University Press.

Notes on Contributors

Diana Isabel Alvis Palma is a psychiatrist and a systemic family therapist and supervisor. She worked as a consultant for the Corporación AVRE in her native Colombia from 2000 to 2005. Currently, she is a consultant family therapist in the Birmingham Children's Hospital – Child and Adolescent Mental Health Service. She is also an international consultant for the development of psychosocial and mental health programmes in Colombia, the Middle East and Africa.

Hanne Beirens works as a consultant for GHK Consulting Ltd, specialising in EU policies related to asylum and migration, youth, social affairs and employment. Prior to that she was a research fellow at the Institute for Applied Social Studies (University of Birmingham, U.K.) working on research projects regarding preventive services for children and young people, governance of local public services and engagement of citizens and users. She holds a master's degree in race and ethnic relations and a Ph.D. in sociology and ethnic relations (University of Warwick, U.K.). During her doctoral research on the participation of under-eighteens in armed conflict, Hanne worked as an intern for the Office of the United Nations High Commissioner for Refugees.

Jo Boyden is director of the Young Lives Project, a longitudinal study of childhood poverty in Vietnam, India, Ethiopia and Peru, housed within the Department of International Development, University of Oxford. Trained as a social anthropologist, for many years she was a social development consultant to a broad range of development and humanitarian relief agencies. From 1999–2005, she conducted research at the Refugee Studies Centre on children's and adolescents' experiences of armed conflict and forced migration. The focus of this research was the development of theory and empirical evidence on risk, resilience and coping in childhood, young people's economic, political and social roles and responsibilities, and social and cultural constructions of childhood and youth.

Andrew Dawes is a child psychologist and currently holds the post of research director in the Child, Youth and Family Development (CYFD) research programme at the Human Sciences Research Council in South Africa. He is an emeritus professor at the University of Cape Town and an associate fellow in the Department of Social Policy and Social Work at the University of Oxford. For many years the focus of his work has been on the impact of abuse, poverty and violence on the development of South African children, and the policy and programme interventions needed to address these problems.

Joanna de Berry is a social development specialist at the World Bank, currently working on projects in Eastern Europe and Central Asia. She has a background in anthropology and her Ph.D. considered post-conflict recovery in eastern Uganda, with a special focus on youth. She has worked with a range of agencies including UNICEF, NGOs and local government in the U.K., to implement community-based programmes with and for young people. She was the child protection adviser for Save the Children, U.S.A., Afghanistan, between 2001 and 2003. She is the co-editor of *Children and Youth on the Front Line: Ethnography, Conflict and Displacement*, published by Berghahn Books.

Liesbeth de Block is a lecturer in media, culture and communications at the Institute of Education, University of London, U.K., and a research officer in the Centre for the Study of Children, Youth and Media (www.childrenyouthandmediacentre.co.uk). Her research focuses on the relationship between media and young people and in particular the role that media play in children's experiences of migration. Previously she worked in London schools, supporting refugee children.

Jason Hart is a social anthropologist by training. His doctoral fieldwork focused on the construction of ideas of homeland and return amongst children living in a Palestinian refugee camp in Jordan. In addition, he has undertaken research in Sri Lanka, Bhutan, Nepal, India, Uganda and the Occupied Palestinian Territories, focusing on issues of participation, gender, humanitarianism, child rights and adolescence. He has worked as a consultant for organisations that include UNICEF, CARE International, Plan, and Save the Children. Since 2002 he has been working as a lecturer and researcher at the Refugee Studies Centre, University of Oxford, where he teaches on the M.Sc. in forced migration and conducts research into young people's experiences of armed conflict and displacement.

Homa Hoodfar has conducted field research on development and social change issues in Egypt and Iran, with an emphasis on gender, households, work and international migration in the Middle East. Further key research areas are women and Islam, and codification of Muslim family laws in the Middle East, Muslim dress code in the diaspora, and the impact of long-term forced migration on family structure and gender relations among Afghan refugees in Iran and Pakistan. She has authored, edited and co-edited a series of books: *Between Marriage and the Market: Intimate Politics and Survival in Cairo*; *The Muslim Veil in North America: Issues and Debates* (co-edited with Sajida Alvi and Sheila McDonough); *Building Civil Societies: A Guide for Social and Political Participation* (with Nelofer Pazira).

Madhur Kulkarni is a graduate student in clinical psychology at the University of Michigan, Ann Arbor. She studies the relationship between emotional regulation and traumatic stress in survivors of war-related violence, intimate partner violence and child abuse. Additionally, she is interested in the development and evaluation of community-based intervention programmes for individuals suffering from post-traumatic stress responses.

Hallie Kushner is a graduate student in the Department of Comparative Human Development at the University of Chicago. She has continued to pursue the intersection of mental health with broader social and cultural issues. Her current research is on the assessment and cultural understanding of suicide.

Gillian Mann has a background in education and anthropology. She has worked for over a decade in the field of policy and programmes for children in adversity, as a practitioner, researcher and policymaker. Recently, her work has focused on the experiences and perspectives of separated boys and girls in particular, including those children who live without their parents as a result of war, HIV/AIDS or both. Her latest research project explores social suffering among Congolese refugee children who are living illegally in Dar es Salaam.

Zoë Martell earned her MS in clinical psychology in 2003 at San Francisco State University (SFSU). She currently works as a lecturer in psychology at SFSU, teaching clinical psychology, abnormal psychology, theories of personality and community psychology. She plans to begin work on a Ph.D. in human sexuality in the autumn of 2008. Her current research interests focus on the effects of severe trauma and chronic illness on the formation of intimate relationships. Zoe is also a gallery-represented abstract painter, and is fascinated by the creative process as a means of expressing unconscious material. She suffers from a chronic illness (late-stage Lyme disease) and this has informed both her academic and her artistic work.

Jill McCall was a member of Kenneth Miller's 'Children of Refugees' lab in the San Francisco State University Psychology Department. This involved interviewing young people who had come from, or whose parents had come from, war-torn countries in the 1970s and 1980s. The stories she heard were rich, complex and deeply moving. From this research, Jill produced her master's thesis on the experiences of Iranian refugees in particular. Jill now lives and has a private psychotherapy practice in San Francisco.

Kenneth E. Miller is associate professor of psychology at Pomona College. He has conducted research on the mental health needs of war-affected populations in several countries, and consults regularly with community organisations doing mental health and psychosocial interventions in conflict and post-conflict settings. Together with Lisa Rasco, he co-edited the book *The Mental Health of Refugees: Ecological Approaches to Healing and Adaptation*, published by Lawrence Erlbaum in 2004. He is currently at work on a documentary film examining the impact of civil war on a village in eastern Sri Lanka.

Cordula Strocka is a psychologist by training and was educated at the Universities of Freiburg and Jena, Germany. She holds a Ph.D. in development studies from the University of Oxford. Dr Strocka has lived for several years in Bolivia and Peru, researching youth gangs, youth organisations, street children and child labour. She also conducted a participatory study for UNICEF on the situation of youth in post-conflict areas of Papua New Guinea and the Solomon Islands. In 2007, she worked as an international consultant for the German Development Service (DED) with ANFASEP, an organisation of widows and orphans, survivors of the political violence in Ayacucho, Peru.

Hirut Tefferi trained first in general psychology and later in educational measurement and evaluation. She has long experience of working with Save the Children Sweden in Ethiopia as programme officer and later as a programme manager in Kenya, managing the organisation's refugee projects in Kenya and a cross-border programme in southern Sudan. Later on, Hirut served as a regional coordinator for Children in Armed Conflict and Displacement (CACD) programme, being responsible for programmes in Eastern and Central Africa regions. She is currently the coordinator of a consultancy firm Child and Family Support Services (CAFSS) based in Ethiopia and engaged in consulting with agencies such as Save the Children and UNICEF in child protection, programme evaluation and child rights.

Mats Utas holds a Ph.D. in cultural anthropology from the University of Uppsala. He has worked as a lecturer in social and cultural anthropology at the University of Liberia and the University of Uppsala, as well as being a senior lecturer in sociology at Fourah Bay College (University of Sierra Leone). Utas has written extensively on child and youth combatants, media, refugees and gender in conflict and war zones. He has conducted fieldwork in Liberia, Sierra Leone and the Ivory Coast. His current research is on street-corner youth in urban Sierra Leone.

Index

www.ingramcontent.com/pod-product-compliance
Lightning Source LLC
Chambersburg PA
CBHW072059040426
42334CB00041B/1457